DEVIANCE AND MARGINALITY IN EARLY MODERN SCOTLAND

St Andrews Studies in Scottish History

Series Editor
Professor Emeritus Roger Mason (Institute of Scottish Historical Research, University of St Andrews)

Editorial Board
Professor Dauvit Broun (University of Glasgow)
Professor Michael Brown (Institute of Scottish Historical Research, University of St Andrews)
Dr David Ditchburn (Trinity College, Dublin)
Professor Emerita Elizabeth Ewan (University of Guelph)
Professor Clare Jackson (Trinity Hall Cambridge)
Dr Catriona MacDonald (University of Glasgow)
Dr Malcolm Petrie (Institute of Scottish Historical Research, University of St Andrews)

Sponsored by the Institute of Scottish Historical Research at the University of St Andrews, St Andrews Studies in Scottish History provides an important forum for the publication of research on any aspect of Scottish history, from the early middle ages to the present day, focusing on the historical experience of Scots at home and abroad, and Scotland's place in wider British, European and global contexts. Both monographs and essay collections are welcomed.

Proposal forms can be obtained from the Institute of Scottish Historical Research website: http://www.st-andrews.ac.uk/ishr/studies.htm. They should be sent in the first instance to the chair of the editorial board at the address below.

Professor Emeritus Roger Mason
Institute of Scottish Historical Research
St Andrews University
St Andrews
Fife KY16 9AL
UK
Email: ram@st-andrews.ac.uk.

Previous volumes in the series are listed at the back of this book.

DEVIANCE AND MARGINALITY IN EARLY MODERN SCOTLAND

Edited by
Allan Kennedy

THE BOYDELL PRESS

© Contributors 2025

All Rights Reserved. Except as permitted under current legislation
no part of this work may be photocopied, stored in a retrieval system,
published, performed in public, adapted, broadcast,
transmitted, recorded or reproduced in any form or by any means,
without the prior permission of the copyright owner

First published 2025

The Boydell Press, Woodbridge

ISBN 978 1 83765 022 4

The Boydell Press is an imprint of Boydell & Brewer Ltd
PO Box 9, Woodbridge, Suffolk IP12 3DF, UK
and of Boydell & Brewer Inc.
668 Mt Hope Avenue, Rochester, NY 14620-2731, USA
website: www.boydellandbrewer.com
A catalogue record for this book is available
from the British Library

The publisher has no responsibility for the continued existence or
accuracy of URLs for external or third-party internet websites referred to in
this book, and does not guarantee that any content on such websites is, or
will remain, accurate or appropriate

Contents

List of Contributors	vii
Acknowledgements	ix
List of Abbreviations	x
Introduction: The Deviant Margins ALLAN KENNEDY	1

Part I: Conceptualising Deviance

1	Conceptualising Deviant Sex in Seventeenth-Century Scotland ALLAN KENNEDY	15
2	Assault in the Margins: Gendered Violence in Seventeenth-Century Bute ASHLYN CUDNEY	30
3	Disorderly, Deviant, Dangerous: Defining Words as Witchcraft in Early Modern Scottish Communities SIERRA DYE	45
4	'Believing na evill nor injury': Space, Place, and Crime in Sixteenth-Century Scottish Burghs J. R. D. FALCONER	61

Part II: Performing Deviance

5	Piracy, the State, and the Burghs of South-West Scotland, 1560–1603 SCOTT CARBALLO	79
6	'Ane legall man quhairof we are glad': Male Violence, Female Agency, and the Quest for Legitimacy in the Story of Seumas an Tuim GRAHAM WATSON	94

CONTENTS

7 Covenanting Women in Scotland: Nonconformity, Marginality,
   and Community, *c*.1660–1690   109
   SCOTT EATON

8 Life at the Margins of Law and Order: James Macpherson –
   The Scottish Robin Hood   124
   ANNE-MARIE KILDAY

Part III: Testing the Boundaries

9 The Common Musician and Deviance in Early Modern Scotland   141
   AARON MCGREGOR

10 Marginally Speaking: Insults and Concepts of Marginality in
   Sixteenth-Century Scottish Towns   157
   ELIZABETH EWAN

11 Ejected Academics: Marginalised Scottish University Professors
   between the Reformation and Revolution   172
   SALVATORE CIPRIANO

12 Partial Conformity in Restoration Scotland, 1662–1669   191
   JAMIE MCDOUGALL

Afterword   207
Index   212

Contributors

Scott Carballo completed his PhD in 2024 on piracy and the western burghs of Scotland during the period 1560–1625 at the University of Stirling. He is currently a Postdoctoral Research Associate in the School of Innovation and Technology at Glasgow School of Art. He works primarily on the Unpath'd Waters project, an AHRC-funded consortium which aims to unite the UK's maritime heritage collections and disseminate them through the use of novel technologies.

Salvatore Cipriano is Associate Director of Career Coaching and Education at Stanford University, where he supports the career development of PhD students and postdoctoral scholars. He received his PhD in History from Fordham University in New York City in 2018. His research focuses on the history of higher education in early modern Scotland, Ireland, and North America, and his scholarship has appeared in *Scottish Historical Review* and *Journal of British Studies*.

Ashlyn Cudney is a PhD candidate at the University of Edinburgh, specialising in early modern Scottish history. Her dissertation examines ecclesiastical and secular bias on the island of Bute in the seventeenth century. She is interested in deviance, social control, concepts of marginality and peripherality, gender, and cultural transmission.

Sierra Dye is Assistant Professor of Gender History at Cape Breton University. She is a graduate and former Postdoctoral Fellow of the University of Guelph, and her contribution to this volume arose from her doctoral research. Her dissertation is being prepared for publication as a monograph provisionally entitled *Devilish Words: Speech, Gender and Evidence in Scotland's Witch Trials*. She is the co-editor of volumes 4 and 5 of the Guelph Series of Scottish Studies, *Gender and Mobility in Scotland and Abroad* (2018) and *Networks and Networking in Scottish Studies: Essays in Honour of Elizabeth Ewan* (forthcoming).

Scott Eaton is a social and cultural historian of the early modern British Isles. His research interests include the history of witchcraft, print culture, puritanism, and Scottish covenanting women. He is an independent researcher, and an Interpretation Planner at Tandem Design, Belfast.

CONTRIBUTORS

Elizabeth Ewan is University Professor Emerita, History and Scottish Studies, University of Guelph, Canada, and researches gender and crime in Scotland c.1450–1600. Publications include the co-edited *The New Biographical Dictionary of Scottish Women* (2018), *Nine Centuries of Man* (2017), and *Children and Youth in Pre-Modern Scotland* (2015).

J. R. D. Falconer is Associate Professor in the Humanities Department at Grant MacEwan University in Edmonton, Alberta, Canada. His research and publications deal with urban history and family history, petty crime, and social networks in early modern Scotland. He is the author of *Crime and Community in Reformation Scotland: Negotiating Power in a Burgh Society* (2013) and the editor of *The General Account Book of John Clerk of Penicuik, 1663–1674* (2022). He is currently working on a monograph-length study of the merchant turned laird, John Clerk of Penicuik (d. 1674).

Allan Kennedy is Lecturer in Scottish History at the University of Dundee. He specialises in the political and social history of the early modern period, and he also serves as Consultant Editor of *History Scotland* magazine. His publications include *Governing Gaeldom: The Scottish Highlands and the Restoration State* (2014) and *Serious Crime in Late-Seventeenth-Century Scotland* (forthcoming).

Anne-Marie Kilday is Vice-Chancellor and Professor of Criminal History at the University of Northampton. She has published widely on the history of crime in Scotland, including *Women and Violent Crime in Enlightenment Scotland* (2007), *A History of Infanticide in Britain* (2013), and *The Violent North? Crime in Scotland 1660–1960* (2019).

Jamie McDougall researches covenanting at the local level in the 1640s and the Restoration. He completed his doctoral thesis at the University of Glasgow in 2018 and has since published a range of articles on covenanting and popular religious culture in the early modern period. He currently works as a history teacher in London.

Aaron McGregor is Lecturer in Music Performance at the University of Aberdeen. His research interests include the history of traditional and classical music in Scotland, as well as early dance music, and he has published a number of articles on these topics. As a freelance violinist, he has appeared with a number of ensembles, and his performances are often focused on seventeenth- and eighteenth-century Scottish fiddle music.

Graham Watson has worked as an archaeologist, a museum and heritage professional, and a senior manager in public leisure services. In 2015 he completed his PhD on early medieval Northumbria at St Andrews University. He is now undertaking independent research on the north-east Highlands in the seventeenth century.

Acknowledgements

The editor would like to thank Roger Mason and Caroline Palmer for their help, encouragement, and guidance throughout the preparation of this volume. Gratitude is also due to Graeme Morton and Alan MacDonald for their support, and to my family for putting up with my periodic absorption in the project. I would also like to thank all the contributors for their dedication and hard work in bringing the book to fruition.

Abbreviations

Aberdeen Rec.	Extracts from the Council Register of the Burgh of Aberdeen (4 vols, Aberdeen/Edinburgh, 1844–71)
ACA	Aberdeen City Archives, Aberdeen
AUL	Aberdeen University Library, Aberdeen
BUK	*The Booke of the Universall Kirk of Scotland* (3 vols, Edinburgh, 1839–45)
DCA	Dundee City Archives, Dundee
ECA	Edinburgh City Archives, Edinburgh
Edinburgh Rec.	M. Wood et al. (eds), *Extracts from the Records of the Burgh of Edinburgh* (9 vols, Edinburgh, 1927–67)
Elgin Rec.	W. Cramond (ed.), The Records of Elgin (2 vols, Aberdeen, 1908)
Glasgow Rec.	J. D. Marwick et al. (eds), Extracts from the Records of the Burgh of Glasgow (8 vols, Glasgow, 1876–1913)
GCA	Glasgow City Archives, Glasgow
GUL	Glasgow University Library, Glasgow
HAC	Highland Archive Centre, Inverness
IRSS	*International Review of Scottish Studies*
Inverness Rec.	W. Mackay and H. C. Boyd (eds), Records of Inverness (2 vols, Aberdeen, 1912)
NLS	National Library of Scotland, Edinburgh
NRS	National Records of Scotland, Edinburgh
ODNB	*Oxford Dictionary of National Biography*
RPCS, 1st Series	J. H. Burton and D. Masson (eds), *The Register of the Privy Council of Scotland, First Series* (14 vols, Edinburgh, 1877–1898)

ABBREVIATIONS

RPCS, 2nd Series	D. Masson and P. H. Brown (eds), *The Register of the Privy Council of Scotland, Second Series* (8 vols, Edinburgh, 1899–1908)
RPCS, 3rd Series	P. H. Brown et al. (eds), *The Register of the Privy Council of Scotland, Third Series* (16 vols, Edinburgh, 1908–70)
RPS	K. M. Brown et al. (eds), *The Records of the Parliaments of Scotland to 1707*, www.rps.ac.uk
SCA	Stirling Council Archives
SHR	*Scottish Historical Review*
SUL	St Andrews University Library
Stirling Rec.	R. Renwick (ed.), Extracts from the Records of the Royal Burgh of Stirling (2 vols, Glasgow, 1887–89)
TNA	The National Archives, Kew

Introduction:
The Deviant Margins
Allan Kennedy

First introduced by Émile Durkheim towards the end of the nineteenth century, *anomie* has proved one of the most enduringly influential concepts in both sociology and criminology. In its initial formulation, *anomie* referred to a posited state of chronic social instability resulting from friction between new and traditional forms of labour in the industrial world. Durkheim later developed the concept to describe an individual state of hopelessness rooted in the absence of adequate mechanisms of social regulation. In such circumstances, people can develop wildly unrealistic personal aspirations, with *anomie* resulting from the realisation that these goals are unattainable.[1] Although not initially intended as a way to explain deviance, *anomie* relatively quickly came to be applied to the study of crime. In this form, it means a suggested state of such extreme dislocation from, or disillusionment with, wider society that an individual or group loses all normal inhibition against committing deviant, transgressive, or criminal acts. *Anomie* thus results in a nihilistic but not necessarily irrational calculation that there is simply no longer any good reason to obey the rules.[2]

Debate around *anomie*, its meaning and validity, has been fierce, and this discussion continues. But the relationship between social disadvantage and deviant behaviour highlighted by *anomie* theory has, explicitly or otherwise, proved useful for scholars of the early modern period. In part, this is because the pressures associated with social marginalisation often brought with them a practical necessity to break laws or challenge behavioural norms in order to survive: poor people might be forced to steal, immigrants compelled to settle and work without licence, ethnic minorities pushed to break cultural taboos in order to sustain their identities, and religious nonconformists brought into unavoidable conflict with penal laws.[3] Perhaps more significantly, however,

---

[1] E. Durkheim, *The Division of Labour in Society*, trans. W. D. Halls (Basingstoke, 1984); E. Durkheim, *Suicide: A Study in Sociology*, trans. J. A. Spaulding and G. Simpson (London, 1952).

[2] B. DiCristina, 'Durkheim's Theory of *Anomie* and Crime: A Clarification and Elaboration', *Australian and New Zealand Journal of Criminology*, 49:3 (2015), 311–31; D. Downes, P. Rock and E. McLaughlin, *Understanding Deviance: A Guide to the Sociology of Crime and Rule-Breaking* (Oxford, 2016), chapter 5.

[3] On the causes of criminal deviance, including the contribution thereto of various forms of social marginality, see R. B. Shoemaker, *Prosecution and Punishment: Petty Crime and the Law in London and Rural Middlesex, c.1660–1725* (Cambridge, 1991), chapter 3; N. Garnham, *The Courts, Crime and the Criminal Law in Ireland 1692–1760* (Blackrock,

the very possession of a marginalised identity often brought with it an automatic reputation for deviance, or a tendency towards reconceptualising otherwise unproblematic behaviours as suspicious. This designation as a 'normative' threat was plainly experienced, for example, by the Romani, whose itinerant lifestyle and cultural distinctiveness tended to be defined as inherently transgressive, even in the absence of specific deviant acts, and it was often applied as well to the (vagrant) poor, increasingly cast as agents of disorder and vectors of criminality.[4] Understanding the contours of early modern societies, then, requires careful consideration of the multi-layered relationship between social exclusion and the practice, and conceptualisation, of deviance.

Marginality, Deviance, and Scotland

In a Scottish context, the extant literature on both deviance and social marginality is, on the surface, thin. Crime history, for example, is extremely patchy. Aside from Anne-Marie Kilday's *longue durée* survey (which in any case focuses more on the modern period), no attempt has been made to construct an overarching history of Scottish criminality in early modernity. Instead, historians have to content themselves with a hotchpotch of individual studies, generally focused on a discrete locality or a particular offence. Such work has greatly improved our understanding of the forms and nature of criminal deviance, but has only done so in a scattershot and unsystematic way, leaving very many gaps.[5] More low-level forms of deviance – 'immoral'

1996), chapters 9–10; P. Griffiths, *Lost Londons: Change, Crime and Control in the Capital City 1550–1650* (Cambridge, 2008), chapter 4; S. Howard, *Law and Disorder in Early Modern Wales: Crime and Authority in the Denbighshire Courts, c.1660–1730* (Cardiff, 2008), chapter 2; G. Walker, *Crime, Gender and Social Order in Early Modern England* (Cambridge, 2003).

4   D. Cressy, *Gypsies: An English History* (Oxford, 2018); A. L. Beier, *Masterless Men: The Vagrancy Problem in England, 1560–1640* (London, 1985); R. Jütte, *Poverty and Deviance in Early Modern Europe* (Cambridge, 1994), chapter 8; D. Hitchcock, *Vagrancy in English Culture and Society, 1650–1750* (London, 2016).

5   A.-M. Kilday, *Crime in Scotland 1660–1960: The Violent North?* (Abingdon, 2019); G. DesBrisay, '"Menacing their persons and exacting their purses": The Aberdeen Justice Court, 1657–1700', in D. Stevenson (ed.), *From Lairds to Louns: Country and Burgh Life in Aberdeen, 1600–1800* (Aberdeen, 1986), pp. 70–90; J. G. Harrison, 'Women and the Branks in Stirling, c.1600 to c.1700', *Scottish Economic and Social History*, 18:2 (1998), 114–31; F. Bigwood, 'The Courts of Argyll, 1664–1825', *Scottish Archives* 10 (2004), 27–38; J. G. Harrison, 'The Justices of the Peace for Stirlingshire 1660 to 1706', *Scottish Archives*, 12 (2006), 42–52; B. P. Levack, 'The Prosecution of Sexual Crimes in Early Eighteenth-Century Scotland', *SHR*, 89:2 (2010), 172–93; J. R. D. Falconer, *Crime and Community in Reformation Scotland: Negotiating Power in a Burgh Society* (London, 2013); W. W. J. Knox, 'Homicide in Eighteenth-Century Scotland: Numbers and Theories', *Journal of Scottish Historical Studies*, 94:1 (2015), 48–73; A. Kennedy, 'Crime and Punishment in Early Modern Scotland: The Secular Courts of Restoration Argyllshire, 1660–1688',

or 'prophane' behaviour, for example – have attracted some comment in passing,[6] but no in-depth analysis save in Margo Todd's magisterial survey of Protestant culture up to the mid-seventeenth century.[7] Social marginality is similarly under-developed as a research topic. No sustained interrogation of the concept of 'marginality', of the type offered, for example, by Jacob Selwood and David Hitchcock for England, currently exists, and very many key marginalised groups, such as migrants, ethnic minorities, or unlicensed and irregular workers, have not been adequately studied.[8] This paucity is not because Scottish historians consciously reject 'marginality' as an explanatory paradigm – as we will see below, it is implicit in a great deal of the extant scholarship – but rather reflects the more general sparsity of Scottish social history, the development of which since the publication of T. C. Smout's pathfinding *A History of the Scottish People* has tended to be fitful and uneven.[9]

A partial exception to this picture of historiographical weakness can be found around the topic of sex. Admittedly, 'ordinary' sexual behaviour in and of itself has not attracted much attention, but thanks largely to the voluminous survival of ecclesiastical court records (on which see below), a fair amount of work has been done on both sexual deviance and the marginalising impact of such behaviour. This body of research has made it clear that the boundaries of acceptable sexual behaviour were very narrow, but that people routinely transgressed them nonetheless, leading Scotland to develop an unusually energetic system of detection and punishment. Moreover, the routine deployment of shaming penalties in response to sexual misconduct, while largely intended as a mechanism of atonement and eventual readmission into the community of the godly, had the effect of temporarily pushing sexual deviants to the social periphery. This dynamic was even starker in cases of more extreme or sustained sexual misbehaviour, which were often punished through physical expulsion from the community or, in the worst cases, bodily destruction (burning the corpses of those executed for bestiality, for instance). Here, too, we see the centrality of marginalising impulses – a visceral desire to eject or expunge – as a response to sexual deviance.[10] Even for this comparatively well-served topic, though,

---

International Review of Scottish Studies, 41 (2016), 1–36; C. Falconer, *Justice and Society in the Highlands of Scotland: Strathspey and the Regality of Grant (c.1690–1748)* (Leiden, 2022); A. Kennedy, 'Deviance, Marginality, and the Highland Bandit in Seventeenth-Century Scotland', *Social History*, 47:3 (2022), pp. 239–64.

[6] See, as an example, C. R. Langley, *Cultures of Care: Domestic Welfare, Discipline and the Church of Scotland, c.1600–1689* (Leiden, 2019).

[7] M. Todd, *The Culture of Protestantism in Early Modern Scotland* (New Haven and London, 2002).

[8] J. Selwood, *Diversity and Difference in Early Modern London* (Farnham, 2010); Hitchcock, *Vagrancy in English Culture and Society.*

[9] T. C. Smout, *A History of the Scottish People, 1560–1830* (London, 1969).

[10] H. Cornell, 'Gender, Sex and Social Control: East Lothian, 1610–1640' (Unpublished PhD thesis (University of Edinburgh, 2012); A. Glaze, 'Women and Kirk Discipline: Prosecution, Negotiation, and the Limits of Control', *Journal of Scottish Historical Studies,*

historiographical gaps remain, the most glaring probably being that virtually nothing is known about same-sex desire. With sexual transgression, as with so many other aspects of deviance and marginality, historians of early modern Scotland are faced with a very incomplete picture.

On one level, scholars' comparative reticence in tackling these issues head-on is rather puzzling. Paucity of sources is the historian's evergreen lament, but in a Scottish context, the source-base for researching both marginality and social deviance is comparatively rich. Judicial records often form the spine of such investigation, and the voluminous records of Scotland's central jurisdiction, the justiciary court (later the high court of justiciary), provide plenty of densely detailed documentation with which to work. When combined with the patchier but still substantial corpus of records surviving from lower and private jurisdictions, this adds up to an enormous weight of potentially very useful material, particularly for the period after around 1660. Judicial records can be supplemented by a range of other source-types, including administrative, financial, and literary, all of which potentially have a great deal to say about deviance and social marginality – in particular, Helen Dingwall's exhaustive mining of the financial and taxation records of 1690s Edinburgh, demonstrating *inter alia* that a substantial proportion of the population (perhaps up to a quarter) faced some degree of social exclusion on account of poverty, shows how such material might be fed into the discussion.[11]

What really makes Scotland stand out, however, is its stock of ecclesiastical sources. The myriad church courts integral to Scotland's Presbyterian Kirk structure spent a great deal of their time rooting out and punishing various forms of social and religious deviance, especially sexual, and they therefore offer scholars huge scope for assessing how far such misbehaviour was associated with social disadvantage. All of these source-types are problematic, of course, not least because they are all external to the individuals deemed 'marginal' or 'deviant'; in using them, we can only ever see such people through a thick shroud of official and mainstream prejudice. This, however, is equally true for other early modern societies, and it therefore remains the case that scholars ambitious to explore deviance, marginality, and the link between them have

---

36:2 (2016), 125–42; M. F. Graham, *The Uses of Reform: 'Godly Discipline' and Popular Behavior in Scotland and Beyond, 1560–1610* (Leiden, 1996); L. Leneman and R. Mitchison, *Sin in the City: Sexuality and Social Control in Urban Scotland 1660–1780* (Edinburgh, 1998); L. Leneman and R. Mitchison, *Girls in Trouble: Sexuality and Social Control in Rural Scotland 1660–1780* (Edinburgh, 1998); B. P. Levack, 'The Prosecution of Sexual Crimes in Early Eighteenth-Century Scotland', *SHR*, 89:2 (2010), 172–93; P. G. Maxwell-Stuart, 'Wilde, filthie, execrabill, detestabill and unnatural sin: Bestiality in Early Modern Scotland', in T. Betteridge (ed.), *Sodomy in Early Modern Europe* (Manchester, 2002), 82–93; Todd, *Culture of Protestantism*, 291–7; D. Stevenson, 'Recording the Unspeakable: Masturbation in the Diary of William Drummond, 1657–1659', *Journal of the History of Sexuality*, 9:3 (2000), 223–39.

[11] H. M. Dingwall, *Late 17th-Century Edinburgh: A Demographic Study* (Aldershot, 1994), especially chapter 8.

in Scotland a very rich body of source material that also remains surprisingly under-utilised.

Yet while historians of Scotland have generally been slow in tackling either deviance or social marginality as distinct or explicit themes, the link between the two is nonetheless implicit in a great deal of recent social history. Take, for example, the post-1980s burgeoning of women's history. This has emerged as probably the strongest corpus of scholarship dedicated to a marginalised or under-privileged group in early modernity, and we now have a far clearer picture than in the past of women as social, religious, political, and economic actors.[12] Contained within this literature is a substantial body of work dedicated to female deviance, especially infanticide, sexual misadventure, and the use of violence, and much of that, in turn, is shaped

---

[12] For early surveys, see: M. H. B. Sanderson, *A Kindly Place? Living in Sixteenth-Century Scotland* (East Linton, 2002); chapter 8; R. A. Houston, 'Women in the Society and Economy of Scotland, 1500–1800', in R. A. Houston and I. D. Whyte (eds), *Scottish Society 1500–1800* (Cambridge, 1989), pp. 118–47; E. Ewan and M. M. Meikle (eds), *Women in Scotland c.1100–c.1750* (East Linton, 1999). On social issues, see: K. Barclay, 'Negotiating Patriarchy: The Marriage of Anna Potts and Sir Archibald Grant of Monymusk, 1731–1744', *Journal of Scottish Historical Studies*, 28:2 (2008), 83–101; K. Barclay, *Love, Intimacy and Power: Marriage and Patriarchy in Scotland, 1650–1850* (Manchester, 2011); J. Stevenson, 'Reading, Writing and Gender in Early Modern Scotland', *The Seventeenth Century*, 27:3 (2012), 335–74; D. Simonton and K. Barclay (eds), *Women in Eighteenth-Century Scotland: Intimate, Intellectual and Public Lives* (London, 2013); D. L. Simonton, '"To Merit the Countenance of the Magistrates": Gender and Civic Identity in Eighteenth-Century Aberdeen', in K. Cowman, N. J. Koefoed, and Å. K. Sjögren (eds), *Gender in Urban Europe: Sites of Political Activity and Citizenship, 1750–1900* (London, 2014), pp. 17–32; J. R. Baxter, 'Elizabeth Melville, Lady Culross: New Light from Fife', *Innes Review*, 68:1 (2017), 38–77; R. Mason, 'Women, Marital Status, and Law: The Marital Spectrum in Seventeenth-Century Glasgow', *Journal of British Studies*, 58:4 (2019), 787–804; R. Mason, 'Coercion or Consent? Women, Property and Legal Authority in Early Modern Scotland', *SHR*, 102:2 (2023), 232–53; C. Spence, '"By her own mouth speaking": Women's Authoritative Voices in Early Modern Wills and Testaments', *SHR*, 102:2 (2023), 273–89. On religion, see: A. Raffe, 'Female Authority and Lay Activism in Scottish Presbyterianism, 1660–1740', in H. Smith and S. Apetrei (eds), *Religion and Women in Britain, c.1660–1760* (London, 2014), pp. 61–78; L. Doak, 'Rediscovering the Voices of "fanatick wives": The Cultural Authority of Covenanting Women in Restoration Scotland', *SHR*, 102:2 (2023), 254–72. On politics, see: K. P. Walton, *Catholic Queen, Protestant Patriarchy: Mary, Queen of Scots, and the Politics of Gender and Religion* (London, 2007); D. Barret-Graves, 'Mermaids, Sirens, and Mary Queen of Scots: Icons of Wantonness and Pride', in D. Barret-Graves (ed.), *The Emblematic Queen: Extra-Literary Representations of Early Modern Queenship* (London, 2013), pp. 69–100; N. Cowmeadow, '"Your Politick, self designing sister": The Role of Katherine, first Duchess of Atholl in the Scottish Parliamentary Elections of 1702', *Parliaments, Estates and Representation*, 33:1 (2013), 1–19; N. Cowmeadow, 'Simply a Jacobite Heroine? The Life Experience of Margaret, Lady Nairne (1673–1747)', in A. I. Macinnes and D. J. Hamilton (eds), *Jacobitism, Enlightenment and Empire, 1680–1820* (London, 2014), pp. 29–42. On work and the economy, see: E. C. Sanderson, *Women and Work in Eighteenth-Century Edinburgh* (London, 1996); C. Spence, *Women, Credit, and Debt in Early Modern Scotland* (Manchester, 2016).

by an awareness of gender dynamics.[13] The killing of newborn babies, for example – probably the most gendered of all criminal offences – has typically been interpreted as a mechanism for escaping the serious practical and reputational challenges facing unmarried mothers, or as an attempt to deal with the consequences of the coercion and power imbalances often associated with sexual intercourse.[14] The result of gender-sensitive approaches like this is that women's deviance is generally understood, in part at least, as a way of negotiating the disadvantaged position to which early modern society confined them. While the language of 'marginality' might not always be deployed, therefore, research into women's deviance is often very strongly geared towards exploring the link between the two concepts.

The deviance/marginality connection is also implicit in much of the extant scholarship around poverty and poor relief. Rosalind Mitchison's pioneering work throughout the later twentieth century established an orthodox understanding of poverty that emphasised the weakness of Scotland's Old Poor Law, and thus the difficulty faced by Scots of limited means in sustaining a significant or stable position in the society around them.[15] More recent work – most of it in conscious reaction to Mitchison's model – has sought to nuance the picture and, to some extent, rehabilitate Scottish poor relief mechanisms, formal and informal.[16] As part of that revision, the role of illicit activities – petty theft, begging, unregulated

---

[13] Y. G. Brown and R. Ferguson (eds), *Twisted Sisters: Women, Crime and Deviance in Scotland since 1400* (East Linton, 2002); E. Ewan, 'Impatient Griseldas: Women and the Perpetration of Violence in Sixteenth-Century Glasgow', *Florilegium*, 28 (2011), 149–68; J. R. D. Falconer, '"Mony Utheris Divars Odious Crymes": Women, Petty Crime and Power in Later Sixteenth Century Aberdeen', *Crime and Misdemeanours* 4:1 (2010), 7–36; Harrison, 'Women and the Branks'; C. Hartlen, 'Catching Fire: Arson, Rough Justice and Gender in Scotland, 1493–1542', in S. Butler and K. J. Kesselring (eds), *Crossing Borders: Boundaries and Margins in Medieval and Early Modern Britain* (Leiden, 2018), pp. 153–73; A.-M. Kilday, '"Monsters Of the Vilest Kind": Infanticidal Women and Attitudes to their Criminality in Eighteenth-Century Scotland', *Family and Community History*, 11:2 (2008), 100–16; A.-M. Kilday, *Women and Violent Crime in Enlightenment Scotland* (Woodbridge, 2007).

[14] A.-M. Kilday, *A History of Infanticide in Britain c.1600 to Present* (Basingstoke, 2013).

[15] For the fullest expression of Mitchison's ideas, see R. Mitchison, *The Old Poor Law in Scotland: The Experience of Poverty, 1574–1845* (Edinburgh, 2000).

[16] R. E. Tyson, 'Poverty and Poor Relief in Aberdeen, 1680–1705', *Scottish Archives*, 8 (2002), 33–42; K. Wilbraham and C. Lodge, 'Responses to Poverty in Ayrshire, 1574–1845', *Scottish Archives*, 8 (2002), 57–70; L. Stewart, 'Poor Relief in Edinburgh and the Famine in 1621–24', *International Review of Scottish Studies*, 30 (2007), 5–41; K. Cullen, *Famine in Scotland: The 'Ill Years' of the 1690s* (Edinburgh, 2010); J. McCallum, 'Charity Doesn't Begin at Home: Ecclesiastical Poor Relief beyond the Parish, 1560–1650', *Journal of Scottish Historical Studies*, 32:2 (2012), 107–26; J. McCallum, 'Charity and Conflict: Poor Relief in Mid-Seventeenth-Century Dundee', *SHR*, 95:1 (2016), 30–56; J. McCallum, '"Fatheris and Provisioners of the Puir": Kirk Sessions and Poor Relief in Post-Reformation Scotland', in J. McCallum (ed.), *Scotland's Long Reformation: New Perspectives on Scottish Religion, c.1500–c.1650* (Leiden, 2016), 69–86; J. McCallum, *Poor Relief and the Church in Scotland, 1560–1650* (Edinburgh, 2018); K. Barclay, *Caritas: Neighbourly Love and the Early Modern Self* (Oxford, 2021).

work, irregular charity, and so on – in ameliorating want, and consequently in mitigating the social disadvantages attendant upon poverty, has been increasingly emphasised.[17] Most of the existing research around this topic approaches it through the prism of poor relief, and the actual experience of poverty, its marginalising effect and its relationship to deviant behaviour, remains largely unexplored. But even with this limitation, it is clear that scholars of the early modern poor have derived valuable insights from reflecting on the deviance/marginality dyad.

Rather different forms of both marginality and deviance are prominent in our picture of religious nonconformity. Intolerance was hard-wired into the Church of Scotland following the Reformation of the 1560s, and successive monarchs were similarly convinced that a monolithic Kirk, preferably under their control, was vital for national stability. As a consequence, dissenting religious belief tended to be viewed as illegitimate, even seditious, and those adhering to such movements laboured under severe social and legal disadvantages. Sustaining religious tradition in these circumstances necessitated 'deviant' behaviour, whether in the form of withdrawing from Church of Scotland services, attending illicit ceremonies and prayer meetings, harbouring 'rebel' clergy, or even partaking in armed insurrection, all of which had the effect of entrenching marginality still further. Much of the extant research focuses on Roman Catholics and, especially, dissenting Protestants, but some work, uncovering broadly similar dynamics, has also been done on smaller sects like the Baptists and Quakers.[18] In all of this,

---

[17] See in particular, A. Glaze, 'Sanctioned and Illicit Support Networks at the Margins of a Scottish Town in the Early Seventeenth Century', *Social History*, 45:1 (2020), 26–51; C. R. Langley, *Cultures of Care: Domestic Welfare, Discipline and the Church of Scotland, c.1600–1689* (Leiden, 2019).

[18] I. B. Cowan, *The Scottish Covenanters 1660–88* (London, 1976); J. Buckroyd, *Church and State in Scotland 1660–1681* (Edinburgh, 1980); E. H. Hyman, 'A Church Militant: Scotland, 1661–1690', *Sixteenth Century Journal*, 26:1 (1995), 49–74; R. S. Spurlock, '"Anie Gospell Way": Religious Diversity in Interregnum Scotland', *Records of the Scottish Church History Society*, 37 (2007), 89–119; R. S. Spurlock, *Cromwell and Scotland: Conquest and Religion 1650–1660* (Edinburgh, 2007); R. S. Spurlock, '"I do disclaim both ecclesiasticke and politick popery": Lay Catholic Identity in Early Modern Scotland', *Records of the Scottish Church History Society*, 38 (2008), 5–22; R. S. Spurlock, 'The Politics of Eschatology', *Baptist Quarterly*, 43:6 (2010), 324–46; A. Raffe, *The Culture of Controversy: Religious Arguments in Scotland, 1660–1714* (Woodbridge, 2012); J. Stephen, *Defending the Revolution: The Church of Scotland 1689–1716* (Farnham, 2013); T. Mcinally, 'Support Networks for the Catholic Mission in Scotland', *Innes Review*, 65:1 (2014), 33–51; A. T. N. Muirhead, *Reformation, Dissent and Diversity: The Story of Scotland's Churches, 1560–1960* (London, 2015); R. S. Spurlock, 'The Tradition of Intolerance in the Church of Scotland', in H. J. Selderhuis and J. M. J. L. van Ravenswaay (eds), *Reformed Majorities in Early Modern Europe* (Leipzig, 2015), pp. 215–312; C. McMillan, '"Scho refuseit altogiffer to heir his voce": Women and Catholic Recusancy in North East Scotland', *Records of the Scottish Church History Society*, 45 (2016), 36–48; A. Raffe, 'Archibald Pitcairn and Scottish Heterodoxy, c.1688–1713', *Historical Journal*, 60:3 (2017), 633–57; N. McIntyre, 'Conventicles: Organising Dissent in Restoration Scotland', *SHR*, 99:supplement (2020), 429–53.

the self-reinforcing link between marginality and deviance is very much centre-stage.

As noted above, race remains strikingly under-discussed in Scottish social history. This has, however, begun to change recently with the emergence of new work focused on discrete ethnic groups, especially Gaels, but also Romani people and people of colour. While much of this corpus remains embryonic, it has nonetheless begun to underline, yet again, the intimate relationship between marginality and deviance. Hostility and denigration towards these groups, sometimes, though not always, codified in discriminatory statutes, served to curtail the scope available to them for engaging with wider society, increasingly either confining them to particular roles or locales, pressuring them to leave, or stimulating an impulse towards assimilation. The response – whether it be enslaved Africans seeking freedom, Gaels resisting the confiscation of customarily-held land, or something else entirely – was often conceptualised as 'deviant' and criminal. Even more perniciously, 'deviance' was often detected in the basic forms of ethnic minority lifestyles, so that, for example, the very itineracy of the Romani could be cast as sinister, barbarous, and disordering, even in the absence of specific further misbehaviour.[19] For ethnic and cultural minorities, then, social marginality was often a fundamental fact of life, as was the persistent charge of being incorrigibly deviant.

In the themes outlined above – women, poverty, religious nonconformity, and race – the link between deviance and marginality is typically left implicit rather than actively interrogated. A more overt marrying of the two concepts, however, marks the by now very substantial body of research into Scottish witch-hunting. Christina Larner, who largely pioneered the field in the 1980s, was relatively coy, conceptualising the witch-hunt as fundamentally a religious phenomenon whose aim was to protect orthodox belief and structures. While it did so in such a way as to impact much more heavily

---

[19] S. Daiches, 'The Jew in Scotland', *Records of the Scottish Church History Society*, 3:3 (1929), 196–209; C. W. J. Withers, *Gaelic Scotland: The Transformation of a Culture Region* (London, 1988); A. I. Macinnes, *Clanship, Commerce, and the House of Stuart, 1603–1788* (East Linton, 1996); R. Clyde, *From Rebel to Hero: The Image of the Highlander 1745–1830* (East Linton, 1998); D. Broun and M. MacGregor (eds), *Mìorun Mòr nan Gall, 'The Great Ill-Will of the Lowlanders'? Lowland Perceptions of the Highlands, Medieval and Modern* (Chippenham and Eastbourne, 2009); M. Newton, *Warriors of the Word: The World of the Scottish Highlanders* (Edinburgh, 2009); D. MacKinnon, 'Slave Children: Scotland's Children as Chattels at Home and Abroad in the Eighteenth Century', in J. Nugent and E. Ewan (eds), *Children and Youth in Premodern Scotland* (Woodbridge, 2015), pp. 120–35; A. MacCoinnich, *Plantation and Civility in the North Atlantic World: The Case of the Northern Hebrides, 1570–1639* (Leiden, 2015); J. Turnbull, 'Venetian Glassmakers in the Prestonpans Area in the Seventeenth Century', *Scottish Archives*, 23 (2017), 103–13; S. P. Newman, 'Freedom-Seeking Slaves in England and Scotland, 1700–1780', *English Historical Review*, 134:570 (2019), 1136–68; D. Cressy, *Gypsies: An English History* (Oxford, 2020), chapter 1; D. Alston, *Slaves and Highlanders: Silenced Histories of Scotland and the Caribbean* (Edinburgh, 2021), chapters 7–8; S. Mullen, *The Glasgow Sugar Aristocracy: Scotland and Caribbean Slavery, 1775–1838* (London, 2022).

on women than men – and Larner was very clear that gender assumptions played a vital role here – this was more akin to a side-effect than an intended feature.[20] It was left to Julian Goodare, in an influential intervention in 1998, to set out a more strident case. Whatever the initial intentions, the witch-hunt, he argued, very clearly developed into an attack on women as women, by which he meant that its primary impact was to police female behaviour in the belief that femininity, as the ultimate source of evil in the world, required vigilant monitoring.[21] Since Goodare's essay, a slew of further contributions (including more from Goodare himself) exploring the connection between witchcraft and women's speech, sexuality, social relations, economic roles, and domestic activities have left little room to doubt that both the concept of 'witchcraft' and the mechanisms of witch-hunting served, in large part, as a way to buttress (and sometimes, for 'witches' themselves, to contest) contemporary ideals of femininity: ideals that worked, of course, to restrict women to a secondary position.[22] In exposing this feedback loop – transgressive activity conceptualised largely as a rejection of suffocating social constraint, and responded to in such a way as to reinforce that subordination – historians have established witchcraft as perhaps the clearest contemporary example of the urgent, intimate relationship between deviance and marginality.

New Horizons

Building on these foundations, but also seeking to extend the conversation in fresh directions, the essays in this volume all try to unpack the linkages between transgressive behaviour and social disadvantage in early modern Scotland, with a particular (though by no means exclusive) focus on the seventeenth century. The opening part, entitled 'Conceptualising Deviance', seeks to tease out the precise relationship between the book's two organising concepts of 'deviance' and 'marginality', both generally and with reference to specific cases. Allan Kennedy begins by exploring sexual deviance. Reconstructing the narrow range of 'acceptable' sexual activities, Kennedy shows that this strict attitude was rooted in a diverse array of dangers – spiritual and material, personal and collective – that were assumed to flow from unrestrained sexuality, and which in turn required the marginalisation of those practising such sexual looseness. By means of a 'deep dive' into seventeenth-century Bute, Ashlyn Cudney then exposes the web of class and gender biases that

[20] C. Larner, *Enemies of Gods: The Witch-Hunt in Scotland* (London, 1981); C. Larner, *Witchcraft and Religion: The Politics of Popular Belief* (Oxford, 1984).
[21] J. Goodare, 'Women and the Witch-Hunt in Scotland', *Social History*, 23:3 (1998), 288–308.
[22] Much of the most important work is collected in: J. Goodare (ed.) *The Scottish Witch-Hunt in Context* (Manchester, 2002); J. Goodare, L. Martin and J. Miller (eds), *Witchcraft and Belief in Early Modern Scotland* (Basingstoke, 2008); and J. Goodare (ed.), *Scottish Witches and Witch-Hunters* (Basingstoke, 2013).

surrounded early modern understandings of violence, showing in turn how the legal system worked to reinforce ideals of femininity and restrict women to a subordinate social role – while also, on occasion, providing them with a platform to exercise an unexpected degree of autonomy.

Chapter 3 sees Sierra Dye look into perhaps the most notorious marginalised groups of the early modern period – 'witches'. In particular, Dye explores the connection between witchcraft accusations and 'disorderly' speech, demonstrating that a 'witch' was typically someone who used curses, insults, or threats to disrupt the proper workings of society. This pattern, Dye contends, reflected the power of speech to define conformity and acceptability, and conversely, the marginalising power of ill-chosen words. Bringing the opening part to a close, J. R. D. Falconer's analysis of the relationship between space and petty crime in sixteenth-century burghs offers something of a counterpoint. Transgression, in his analysis, was not the exclusive preserve of the disadvantaged; rather, it was part of the standard toolkit deployed by 'mainstream' Scots to negotiate community relationships. Deviance, in Falconer's telling, did not always go hand in glove with marginality.

Mindful of Falconer's caveat, the next four essays are collected together under the title 'Performing Deviance', and they explore the range of deviant behaviours that might emerge from, or overlap with, marginality. Scott Carballo focuses on piracy, assessing in particular how both central government and local communities along the south-western coastline responded to its challenge not only by compensating victims, but also by trying to curtail the legal and physical space within which pirates could operate – in other words, by pushing these very distinctive deviant groups ever further to the margins. Graham Watson then turns our attention to the consequences of outlawry. Reflecting in-depth on the notorious bandit James Grant of Carron, sometimes known as 'Seamas an Tuim', Watson uncovers a range of strategies for both mitigating social vulnerability and mapping a path back to the mainstream – as well as some mechanisms permitting women to exercise agency.

Scott Eaton tackles a rather more complex intersection of marginalising forces in his exploration of covenanting women in the later seventeenth century. Through careful mining of key items of spiritual writing, he shows how gender and religion conspired comprehensively to isolate these women from the social mainstream – a situation to which they often responded by establishing new, clandestine social networks among the godly. Part two closes with Anne-Marie Kilday's revisiting of the infamous case of James Macpherson, a reputed Gypsy executed at Banff in 1700. Kilday uses this incident to explore the persistent marginalisation of Gypsies in the early modern period, as well as to demonstrate how this narrative both reflected Gypsies' alleged *penchant* for deviance and drove them towards just such a lifestyle.

The book's final part is all about 'Testing the Boundaries', with its focus being on how the distinction between 'acceptable' and 'deviant', or between 'mainstream' and 'marginal', could be negotiated. Aaron McGregor focuses on 'common' and itinerant musicians, showing how long-standing suspicion of their role in fomenting deviant behaviour was nonetheless leavened by recognition of their value in moulding the early modern soundscape (especially in towns). The vernacular music revival of the eighteenth century further underlined this tension between disapproval and appreciation. Elizabeth Ewan then shifts focus to the realm of verbal violence, exploring how insults could be used to damage their intended victims by associating them with undesirable marginalised groups or behaviours, while also working to shore up the speaker's own position through an implicit claim that they themselves enjoyed the authority of the 'mainstream'.

The final two chapters offer much tighter case studies. Salvatore Cipriano looks at the phenomenon of academics' ejection from Scottish universities between 1560 and 1690, finding that such expulsions generally flowed not from concerns over ability or orthodoxy, but from the espousal of 'deviant' political positions. Importantly, however, the meaning of 'deviant' shifted across the period, defined largely by external political forces, so that teaching at Scottish universities not infrequently involved delicately balancing academic inquiry with political flexibility. Jamie McDougall then closes the volume by discussing the under-explored phenomenon of 'partial conformity' during the Restoration, a mechanism by which individual Scots, both clerical and lay, could express disaffection with the era's Episcopalian ecclesiastical structures without suffering the adverse consequences necessarily attendant upon explicit nonconformity – a strategy, in effect, for testing how deeply 'deviant' one could be without suffering marginalisation.

Collectively and individually, these studies significantly expand our understanding of the connection between deviance and marginality in early modern Scotland, providing new insights into both the role of transgressive behaviour in causing or shaping social disadvantage, and the reliance on deviance as a response to ostracisation. At the same time, the scope for breaking, challenging, or nuancing this link is a recurring theme of the book. This is not, of course, the last word on the topic, not least because the essays do not deal significantly with eighteenth-century evidence, and bringing this into the discussion would allow for deeper reflection on *longue durée* patterns and changes over time. Instead, the authors hope that the new vistas opened up in this volume will stimulate further research, allowing scholars to mine the deviance/marginality relationship still more fully with a view to enhancing our understanding of how early modern Scotland conceived of itself, and how it was organised.

PART I

CONCEPTUALISING DEVIANCE

1

Conceptualising Deviant Sex in Seventeenth-Century Scotland

Allan Kennedy

Writing in his *History of My Own Time*, first published posthumously in the 1720s, the Anglo-Scottish churchman and bishop of Salisbury, Gilbert Burnet, commented on the 'severe discipline' with which seventeenth-century ministers in Scotland supervised their flocks. Of particular note, he suggested, was their treatment of those who had committed sins of a sexual nature:

> For fornication they were not only reproved before these [i.e. ministers], but there was a high place in the church, called the stool or pillar of repentance, where they sat at the time of worship for three Lord's days, receiving admonitions, and making professions of repentance on all these days; which some did with many tears, and serious exhortations to all the rest, to take warning by their fall. For adultery they were to sit six months in that place, covered with sackcloth.[1]

Modern historians have tended to follow Burnet, and others, in emphasising the seriousness with which sexual deviance of all kinds was treated in early modern Scotland. Modern research into ecclesiastical discipline has shown that it amounted to a system of intensive control over how people used their bodies, one that individuals actively engaged with as a means of negotiating the boundaries of acceptable sexuality.[2] The criminal justice system stepped in for more serious sexual offences, particularly those, like incest, sodomy, and bestiality, that were regarded as breaching natural law. Secular prosecution of such transgressions was generally more rigorous and frequent in Scotland than in many other European countries, especially England, although even

---

[1] Gilbert Burnet, *Burnet's History of My Own Time*, ed. O. Airy (2 vols, Oxford, 1897), vol. 1, pp. 272–3.

[2] M. F. Graham, *The Uses of Reform: 'Godly Discipline' and Popular Behaviour in Scotland and Beyond, 1560–1610* (Leiden, 1996); L. Leneman and R. Mitchison, *Sin in the City: Sexuality and Social Control in Urban Scotland 1660–1780* (Edinburgh, 1998); L. Leneman and R. Mitchison, *Girls in Trouble: Sexuality and Social Control in Rural Scotland 1660–1780* (Edinburgh, 1998); M. Todd, *The Culture of Protestantism in Early Modern Scotland* (New Haven, 2002); A. Glaze, 'Women and Kirk Discipline: Prosecution, Negotiation, and the Limits of Control', *Journal of Scottish Historical Studies*, 36:2 (2016), 125–42.

here there was still room for accused individuals to defend their positions and test the boundaries of acceptability.[3]

This expansive, albeit sometimes surprisingly fluid regulatory framework ensured that sexual deviance and social marginality went hand in hand. Committing an act of disorderly sex (or, perhaps more accurately, getting caught doing so) automatically placed one outside accepted norms, and rendered one deserving of scorn; as the general assembly put it in 1699, 'Let all Uncleanness be abhorred: Pollute not the Temples of the Holy Ghost, which your Bodies are, Consecrated to him in Christian Baptism; but let every one possess his Vessel in Sanctification and Honour'.[4] The marginality of the sexual deviant was expressed in the penalties typically used against them. Shaming punishments, like those described by Burnet, placed the sinner, metaphorically and physically, on the edge of their communities; the habitual banishment of sex workers offered a visceral demonstration of their untouchability; and the almost-invariable execution of those engaged in the most serious sex crimes, often followed by the destruction of their bodies through fire, likewise underlined that there was no place for sinners of such a stamp.[5] This approach to deviant sex was rooted in well-developed ideas about the wider harms it might invite, and the deeper flaws – personal and corporate – it was thought to reflect. This chapter seeks to explore that conceptualisation with particular reference to seventeenth-century evidence. It will begin by establishing the boundaries of acceptable sexuality in the early modern period, before moving on to explore, firstly, the assumed relationship between deviant sex and the self, and, secondly, the significance 'unnatural' sexual behaviour was thought to have for the community more widely. In so doing, the chapter will seek to explain why sexual deviance retained such marginalising power, and what this meant for both individual Scots and the wider society around them.

---

[3] P. G. Maxwell-Stuart, '"Wilde, filthie, execrabill, detestabill and unnatural sin": Bestiality in Early Modern Scotland', in T. Betteridge (ed.), *Sodomy in Early Modern Europe* (Manchester, 2002), pp. 82–93; B. P. Levack, 'The Prosecution of Sexual Crimes in Early Eighteenth-Century Scotland', *SHR*, 89:2 (2010), 172–93; A. Kennedy, 'Crime and Punishment in Early Modern Scotland: The Secular Courts of Restoration Argyllshire, 1660–1688', *IRSS*, 41 (2016), 1–36; H. Cornell, 'Gender, Sex and Social Control: East Lothian, 1610–1640' (Unpublished PhD thesis, University of Edinburgh, 2012).

[4] *A letter from the Commission of the General Assembly of the Church of Scotland, met at Glasgow, July 21, 1699 to the Honourable Council, and inhabitants of the Scots colony of Caledonia, in America* (Edinburgh, 1699), p. 9.

[5] Cornell, 'Gender, Sex and Social Control', chapter 3; Glaze, 'Women and Kirk Discipline'; Maxwell-Stuart, 'Bestiality in Early Modern Scotland'.

The Boundaries of Sex

The boundaries of acceptable sexual behaviour in early modern Scotland were, of course, narrow. The basic position was laid out by Hugh Binning, minister of Govan, for whom all temptations of the flesh were fundamentally dangerous:

> You see then how much power the flesh hath in man, so that it is no wonder that every natural man hath this denomination, one after the flesh, one carnal, from the predomining [sic] part, though the worst part. Every man by nature, till a higher birth come, maybe called all flesh, all fashioned and composed of the flesh, and after the flesh, even his spirit and mind fleshly and earthly, sunk into the flesh, and transformed into a bruitish quality or nature. Now the great purpose of the Gospel is, to bring alongs a deliverer unto your spirits, for the releasing and unsetteling of them from the chains of fleshly lusts.[6]

Sex, in this reading, was one of the many temptations that could draw the faithful away from a godly life. Unrestrained sex could also, as a corollary, be a marker of spiritual degeneracy; John Napier, for example, pointed to sexual libertinism, and in particular 'whordome and vile Sodomie', as proof of the corruption of the Roman Catholic Church, numerous of whose popes, he averred, had been adulterers, sodomites, fornicators, and other stamps of sexual deviant.[7] Sex, of course, had the power to do all this because it was enjoyable. In the rather coy phrase of the man-midwife James McMath, 'coition' produced 'a most pleasureful Tickle and Delight', but crucially, this was a mechanism of conception, because, he claimed, 'no Woman could ever Conceive' unless both parties achieved orgasm.[8] Sex, then, was necessary for procreation, but also very dangerous, and therefore to be treated with the utmost care. For John Makluire, writing from a medical perspective, the pleasures of sex should never be sought for anything other than procreative purposes, since doing otherwise abused the bodies God had provided for mankind. Sex should, moreover, be performed carefully and sparingly, because 'the immoderate vse of this naturall exercise doth weaken the body, and hinder all generation'.[9] Others went further still. It was not enough, claimed George Monro, to have sex for procreation; one also had to be procreating for the right reasons. People should be having children, he suggested, not to

---

[6]   Hugh Binning, *The Sinners Sanctuary; Or, A discovery made, of those glorious priviledges offered unto the penitent and faithful under the Gospel* (Edinburgh, 1670), pp. 230–1.

[7]   John Napier, *A Plaine Discouery of the whole Reuelation of Saint John: set downe in two treatises: The one searching and prouing the true interpretation thereof: The other applying the same paraphrastically and Historically to the text* (Edinburgh, 1593), p. 45.

[8]   James McMath, *The Expert Mid-Wife: A Treatise of the Diseased of Women with Child, and in Child-Bed* (Edinburgh, 1694), p. 10.

[9]   John Makluire, *The Bvckler of Bodilie Health, Whereby Health may bee defended, and sicknesse repelled* (Edinburgh, 1630), p. 72.

carry on the family name or to inherit lands and possessions, but to create 'Creatures like themselves to joyn with them in Praises and Services, and to partake with them in the Felicities of GOD'. Sex, from this perspective, had to be treated essentially as an act of worship.[10]

Vital to containing the temptations and dangers associated with sex was the institution of marriage – supposedly a divine creation, instituted before the Fall, which human laws were unable fundamentally to alter.[11] James VI (r.1567–1625) reflected at some length on marriage, and on its relationship to sexual activity, in his kingship manual of 1599, *Basilikon Doron*. Marriage, he wrote, was a divine mechanism 'for staying of lust, for procreation of children, and that man should by his Wife get a helper like himself'.[12] It was, consequently, important to get married, to do so at a relatively young age, and to marry a suitable person capable of bearing children. It was also vital to confine one's sexual activities within marriage. Pre-marital sex was inherently corrupting, and men should seek to keep their bodies 'cleane and vnpolluted, till ye giue it to your wife; whome-to onlie it belongeth'. Adultery, meanwhile, represented a breach of the 'solemne promise' given to God upon marriage, and was likely to invite ruin because 'God is euer a seueare avenger of all perjuries'.[13] James was, of course, thinking through these issues from the perspective of a king, but his underlying assumptions – that marriage was the only safe, appropriate setting for sexual activity, and that sex outside marriage was both immoral and dangerous – closely tracked the wider values of the age.

While all non-procreative, extra-marital sex was taboo, there was nonetheless a broadly-recognised hierarchy of offences. At the bottom, generally causing the least concern, was fornication, or sex between unmarried people. Although made a statutory offence in 1567, fornication was almost never treated as a criminal matter, and instead tended to be dealt with by kirk sessions as a purely disciplinary affair.[14] Adultery also fell into this category on occasion, but only if it was a single, self-contained lapse. If it was 'notorious', generally meaning open, repeated, or resulting in children, then it was regarded as a very serious affront to divine authority.[15] Fornication and adultery were the two most commonly-prosecuted sexual offences in early modern Scotland, but also known were the three 'extraordinar' crimes grouped together by George Mackenzie of Rosehaugh, the Restoration-era lord advocate, in his treatise *Laws and Customes of Scotland in Matters Criminal* (1678). These were incest, bestiality, and sodomy, all of which were invariably capital offences, and which were set apart from both fornication

---

[10] George Monro, *The Just Measures of the Pious Institution of Youth Represented according to the Maxims of the Gospel. In Several Essayes* (Edinburgh, 1700), p. 38.

[11] James Dalrymple, *The Institutions of the Law of Scotland* (Edinburgh, 1681), p. 28.

[12] James VI, *Basilikon Doron*, 2nd edn (Edinburgh, 1603), pp. 76, 81.

[13] *Ibid.*, pp. 73, 81.

[14] *RPS*, A1567/12/13.

[15] *Ibid.*, A1563/6/10; George Mackenzie, *The Laws and Customes of Scotland, in Matters Criminal* (Edinburgh, 1678), pp. 169–84.

and adultery (at least in its 'single' form) by their extreme irregularity, as well as by being (in the words of James Guthrie in a 1661 report to parliament) 'contrairie to the light and law of nature'.[16] Of these three, it is worth noting that the last – sodomy – was almost never prosecuted in Scottish courts, not because it did not happen (we can probably assume that same-sex sexual encounters did in fact take place), but presumably because of the difficulties involved in discovering and proving an offence about which all interested parties had a strong motive for remaining silent.

Arguably in a category of its own was rape, which, uniquely among sexual crimes, had the distinction of being one of the 'four pleas' (along with murder, robbery, and wilful fire-raising) reserved to the jurisdiction of the crown. The actual incidence of rape in early modern Scotland is impossible to assess, largely because an underdeveloped understanding of 'consent', combined with a preference for avoiding criminal proceedings except in the most egregious cases, ensured that rape was typically reconceptualised in contemporary sources as mere fornication.[17] The crime was defined as the 'violent carrying away [of] a woman from one place, to another, for satisfying the Ravishers lust'.[18] This definition ultimately allowed for the emergence of two distinct, but often overlapping concepts of rape. One of these was non-consensual sex, whether or not abduction was involved. This was the understanding used in 1681 when James Sinclair was charged with raping Janet Bruce in her own home.[19] The other form of rape was abduction of a woman with a view to forcing her into marriage, generally so as to secure control over her property. Rape of this kind might involve non-consensual sex, but equally it might not. In 1616, indeed, Sir Patrick Chirnesyde was charged with rape for allegedly abducting a male victim, Adam Frenche of Thornydykis, and marrying him to his daughter, with no suggestion at all that there had been a sexual assault of any kind.[20] Crucially, however, both forms of rape, unlike most sexual offences, overlapped with other criminal behaviours: non-consensual sex was a form of violent physical assault, while abduction and forced marriage was tantamount to property theft. Rape, therefore, was not a purely sexual offence, and this perhaps explains its unusual position as one of the 'four pleas'.[21]

All of these sexual standards were, of course, heavily gendered. The policing of sexual behaviour certainly fell more heavily upon women than men, although there is some debate about whether this was by design or simply because pregnancy made it less possible for women to escape the consequences of illicit sex.[22] It is clear, however, that female sexuality in

---

[16] *Ibid.*, p. 4, p. 9; *RPS*, A1661/1/72.
[17] Glaze, 'Women and Kirk Discipline', at pp. 177–9.
[18] Mackenzie, *Laws and Customes*, p. 163.
[19] NRS, JC2/15, High Court Books of Adjournal, 1678–82, fols 380r–382r.
[20] R. Pitcairn (ed.), *Ancient Criminal Trials in Scotland* (3 vols, Edinburgh, 1833), vol. 3, pp. 402–15.
[21] Levack, 'Prosecution of Sexual Crimes', at pp. 178–80.
[22] M. Graham, 'Women and the Church Courts in Reformation-Era Scotland', in E. Ewan and M. M. Meikle (eds), *Women in Scotland c.1100–c.1750* (East Linton, 1999),

the abstract was regarded as more dangerous than its male counterpart. Women were thought to be generally more lustful than men, making them more likely to engage in disorderly or deviant sex.[23] But since they needed a partner in order to do so, men were well advised to be on their guard against wanton women ready to tempt them into sin. Equally, women, it was feared, could use the promise of sex to gain advantage over men. One English ballad, reprinted in Edinburgh in 1685, fused both these ideas together to sketch out a comically nightmarish scenario:

> Her Curls, like Streamers waving, seem to court
> Each spritely Combatant to storm the Fort;
> Whilst naked panting Breasts too plainly shew
> Th' insatiate Thirst that she endures below.
> And though in Single Life she oft be naught,
> Yet when at length some doating Fop sh' hath caught
> And into wretched Noose of Wedlock brought,
> By Midwife-Rules she boldly goes to Bed,
> And on the Novice pawns a Maiden-head:
> Who starts next Morn to see her in his Arms;
> She's perfect Hag, when stript of Arts gay Charms
> The painted Roses of her Cheeks are dropt,
> Hunch-back's discover'd, with Pads underpropt;
> He's forc'd with strong Perfumes to guard his Nose
> From poys'nous Whiffs of Breath, Arm-pits, and Toes.[24]

Female sexuality, then, was a snare for weak, unwary men, tempting them into either sin or ruin, and perhaps both. All this, of course, linked back to the biblical story of Eve, the arch-temptress responsible, through her ensnarement of Adam, for allowing evil into the world. Consequently, while stepping outside the boundaries of acceptable sexuality was dangerous for both men and women, there were additional factors that made the sexual deviance of women particularly concerning.

Deviant Sex and the Self

The narrow boundaries of acceptable sexuality were dictated, in part, by concern about what unrestrained sexual activity might do to the individual. On one level, this was about fears of divine punishment, which is what James

---

pp. 187–98; G. DesBrisay, 'Twisted By Definition: Women Under Godly Discipline in Seventeenth-Century Scottish Towns', in Y. Brown and R. Ferguson (eds), *Twisted Sisters: Women, Crime and Deviance in Scotland Since 1400* (East Linton, 2002), pp. 137–55.

[23] S. Dye, 'To Converse with the Devil? Speech, Sexuality, and Witchcraft in Early Modern Scotland', *IRSS*, 37 (2012), 9–40.

[24] Anonymous, *Fore-warn'd, Fore-arm'd: Or, A Caveat to Bachelors, in the Character of a Bad Woman* (Edinburgh, 1685).

VI had in mind when he brought up the unhappy fate of his notoriously promiscuous grandfather, James V (r.1513–42). The 'double cursse' of leaving behind only an infant girl as a successor was 'the reward of his incontinencie', while James VI, with his 'greater continency', had been allowed to retain two healthy sons as 'the frutes following ther-upon' (perhaps a somewhat ironic boast given contemporary suspicions about James' possible sexual relationships with his male favourites).[25] The negative material consequences of sexual deviance might also be rather more manmade – this was certainly the experience of Andrew Lothian, whose fornication with one Elspet Shaw in the 1640s saw him lose his position as minister of Falkland, while also making it difficult to acquire the testimonial of good character that would have allowed him to secure another parish.[26] Even when it did not result in tangible loss, the sense of shame attached to sexual deviance should not be underestimated. Appearing before the presbytery of Cupar in 1647, Jonet Jethseman claimed to be 'wounditt in soule, greived in spirit, and sore pressed vnder the burden of ane adulterie committed by her nyne yeirs agoe'. Such were her feelings of guilt about this affair that she asked the presbytery to assign penance 'as the onlie meane to heale her woundes and calme her spirit', and two individuals, Mrs Walter Greig and William Row, were assigned to offer spiritual comfort while the brethren considered how to proceed.[27] The acuteness of Jethseman's shame may well have been unusual, but it nevertheless serves to underline how breaching the tight sexual codes of the seventeenth century could provoke very uncomfortable feelings of guilt, even in the absence of any material penalty.

The shamefulness of sexual deviance ties into the concept of befoulment. Associating sin with dirtiness was not, of course, unique to sex; Elizabeth Melville, in her 1603 poem *Ane Godlie Dreame*, instead conceptualised all sins as a type of filth in which 'sensles saules ar drownit'.[28] But the language of dirtiness was especially common for sexual offences, with the tone being set by parliament and privy council, both of which deployed it routinely.[29] Adultery was 'abominabill and filthy'; fornication was a 'fylthie vice'; incest was 'vile and fylthie'; buggery was a 'filthie and vyild cryme'; and rape was rooted in 'filthie humour'.[30] Anyone engaging in such unclean acts unavoidably

---

[25] James VI, *Basilikon Doron*, p. 75.
[26] J. Kinloch (ed.), *Ecclesiastical Records: Selections from the Minutes of the Presbyteries of St Andrews and Cupar (1641–1698)* (Edinburgh, 1837), p. 135.
[27] *Selections from the Minutes of the Presbyteries of St Andrews and Cupar*, M.DC.XLI-M. DC.XCVIII (Edinburgh, 1837), pp. 117–18.
[28] Elizabeth Melville, *Ane Godlie Dreame* (Edinburgh, 1603), unpaginated.
[29] 'Uncleanness' as a concept also applied to masturbation, but this, unlike the offences discussed here, was never prosecuted, and indeed rarely even mentioned, in early modern Scotland. D. Stevenson, 'Recording the Unspeakable: Masturbation in the Diary of William Drummond, 1657–1659', *Journal of the History of Sexuality*, 9:3 (2000), 223–39.
[30] *RPS*, A1563/6/10, A1567/12/14, A1567/12/13, 1645/11/28; *RPCS*, 1st Series, vol. 10, p. 267.

stained their soul, but also their body, as one piece of advice literature from 1693 made clear when discussing the 'hated sin of Uncleanness':

> In your very heart entertain no thought that has any prospect to that Sin: for albeit ye should forbear the grosser Acts of Uncleanness, yet if you do with any delight entertain such sinful Thoughts and Fancies: It is to be feared, your forbearance flows not from a principle of the fear of God, or love to Him; and that your lodging such filthy Suggestions, will bring you under great danger of being guilty of the gross Acts of Uncleanness, which are utterly destructive to Man, even in relation to his temporal Beeing; Curses following that Sin, being plain from Scripture.[31]

The suggestion in this text that even contemplating the possibility of fornication, let alone engaging in it, could tend towards the irreparable besmirching of both body and soul underlines how deeply ingrained was the association between deviant sex and metaphorical befoulment.

If sexual deviance could cause spiritual dirtiness, it could also act as an advertisement of an already befouled soul. The famous case of Major Thomas Weir is instructive here.[32] He was executed in 1670 for a bewildering array of sex crimes, including incest, adultery, and bestiality, stretching back fifty years. In his criminal indictment, however, these offences were very much positioned as symptoms, rather than causes, of inner wickedness:

> It is no small agrivatione (if any can be) of so great wickednes and inpietie that being guiltie and conscious to himself of so great and hyneous abominationes and being altogider voyd of religione and fear of god he hade the confidence or rader impudence to pretend to fear god In a singular and eminent way and did mak professione of stricknes pietie and puritie beyond vthers.[33]

Weir, then, was a man without religion or scruple, and this inner darkness was the ultimate root of his grossly licentious lifestyle. The situation was not always this dire, however, and a rather more benign form of spiritual weakness was hinted at by Robert Leslie, found in 1663 to have committed adultery with Barbara Lennox in Wick. He pleaded in mitigation that 'his familie is at a distance in Orkney and his wyfe is extreme sick', perhaps implying that his relationship with Lennox had been a form of escape from an otherwise lonely personal life.[34] His situation provoked a sympathetic response, and as such it hints at a general understanding of human frailty. People were imperfect, and if sexual deviance might reveal deep wickedness, it could also be a simple, and forgivable, reflection of the fundamental fallibility of postlapsarian mankind.

---

[31] Anonymous, *A fathers advice to his son at the university: wherein is hinted some general directions, which may be usefully read by persons of any age or sex* (Edinburgh, 1693), p. 33.

[32] D. Stevenson, *King or Covenant? Voices from Civil War* (East Linton, 1996), chapter 5.

[33] NRS, JC2/13, High Court Books of Adjournal, 1669–73, fols 8v–12v.

[34] NRS, CH2/47/1, Presbytery of Caithness, 1654–88, pp. 75–7.

Beyond befoulment, deviant sex was often also connected with an erosion of basic humanity. Of course, given contemporary ideas about the ungodly temptations of sex, performing acts of sexual deviance was habitually understood in terms of surrendering to base or unworthy impulses. This, certainly, was the narrative offered by William Hamilton in 1656 to explain his adulterous activities in Lesmahagow; he had, he claimed, been the subject of repeated 'tysing' by his paramour, Jonet Hamilton, who had done everything from getting him drunk to climbing into bed beside him, and eventually he had succumbed to these accumulated provocations.[35] Hamilton's weakness was thoroughly ordinary, but in more extreme cases, the capitulation to base impulse might be regarded as so complete or shocking as to call into question the deviant's place in the civilized world. Such was the fate of the Fife schoolmaster George Sinclair, who was convicted in 1628 of multiple counts of adultery and fornication, and of sexually abusing several of the young girls attending his school. He was described as a 'vyle and filthie liever and abuser of his body' whose crimes were 'nocht worthie to be hard be ony chast christiane eir'.[36] A sense of being less than fully human could easily become a charge of animality. Bestiality, for obvious reasons, had particular power in this regard, something made explicit in the case of James Fiddes, who was convicted in 1650 of copulating with a cow and whose actions were condemned not just as 'filthie' and 'unnatural', but also as 'beistlie'.[37] A sense of animalism emerged rather more obliquely from the deposition of one witness, Robert Law, in the 1691 bestiality trial of Thomas Wisheart:

> He saw the pannells [accused's] hands about the mears hinder pairts holding about her burdine banes And working too and frae upon her with his bodie as a stoned horse uses to doe to a mear And when he wes within a penniestone cast The pannell looked over his shoulder and seeing the deponent he came off and pairted [...] And he saw her casting up her taill and casting out behind as mears doe when a ston'd horse pairts from them.[38]

In drawing so close a parallel between Wisheart and a 'stoned' – that is, non-castrated – horse, and moreover in suggesting that the mare involved responded to him accordingly, Law's testimony cast Wisheart as effectively an animal himself. But language of this kind was not restricted to bestiality: Johne Broune, for example, was described as being in a 'beastlie rage and furie' when he raped Katherene Rae in Edinburgh in 1605.[39] Sexual deviance, therefore, had the power to strip people of their higher faculties, to subordinate them to base impulses and drag people down to the level of beasts.

---

[35] J. Robertson, *Ecclesiastical Records: Selections from the Registers of the Presbytery of Lanark (1623–1709)* (Edinburgh, 1839), p. 99.
[36] S. A. Gillon and J. I. Smith (eds), *Selected Justiciary Cases, 1624–1650* (3 vols, Edinburgh, 1953–74), vol. 1, pp. 95–6.
[37] *Ibid.*, vol. 3, pp. 854–5.
[38] NRS, JC2/18, High Court Books of Adjournal, 1690–3, pp. 467–72.
[39] Pitcairn, *Ancient Criminal Trials*, vol. 3, p. 464.

If deviant sex tended to corrupt and diminish, it was also widely assumed that it acted as a kind of gateway offence; those giving in to sexual temptation were, it was thought, far more likely engage in other forms of misbehaviour. This argument was articulated by the town council of Edinburgh in 1699, when it banned women from serving in taverns. Female servers, the council suggested, often had a history of fornication, a practice they tended to perpetuate with their young, impressionable male patrons. This had 'yet a more dangerous tendency to the corrupting of Youth, and will in all probability occasion a greater grouth of Immorality'.[40] Women, of course, were especially vulnerable to this 'slippery slope' argument, both because of the greater shame associated with female promiscuity, and because of the danger of pregnancy. Sometimes the resulting transgressions were relatively minor: Margaret Thomesone was for example charged in 1646 with forging a testimonial so as to have her daughter, conceived in adultery with John Edmestoun, minister of Yell, baptised.[41] In other cases, desperation led to more serious law-breaking. Janet Fraser in Dingwall, suspected in 1685 of 'being big with child, and destroying therof', seemingly sought an abortion.[42] In the worst cases, women could be driven to infanticide. This was the fate of Renfrewshire's Isobell Gray, who was executed in 1678 for murdering her newborn child in order 'to conceall her wickednes and adulterie' with her paramour, John Steinson.[43]

It was not just in attempting to conceal the consequences of transgressive sex that further misbehaviour might emerge. The sensational prosecution of David Nicolson and Marion Maxwell in 1694 encapsulated the supposed capacity of sexual deviance to spur people towards more general criminality. Having engaged in the 'wicked practice of Adulterie', Nicolson and Maxwell, driven by their lust for one another, allegedly hatched a plot to murder Nicolson's wife, Jean Lands. When this failed, they instead decided to frame Lands and her sister Margaret (who had long hindered Nicolson and Maxwell in their relationship) for attempting to murder Nicolson, to which end an elaborate forgery was concocted, eventually sucking in both a local apothecary, John Eliot, and the lord advocate himself, Sir James Stewart of Goodtrees.[44] While few cases were as salacious as that of Nicolson and Maxwell, their story nonetheless spoke to the supposed power of sexual impropriety to drive people, no matter how virtuous they might previously have been, to further corruption. Once illicit sex had opened the door to sin and depravity, the temptation to walk boldly through could be irresistible.

---

[40] *Act anent women-servants in taverns, &c* (Edinburgh, 1699).

[41] Gillon and Smith, *Selected Justiciary Cases*, vol. 3, pp. 689–90.

[42] W. Mackay (ed.), *Records of the Presbyteries of Inverness and Dingwall, 1643–1688* (Edinburgh, 1896), p. 357.

[43] NRS, JC2/15, fols 16r–17r.

[44] NRS, JC2/19, High Court Books of Adjournal, 1693–9, fols 38r–74v.

CONCEPTUALISING DEVIANT SEX

Deviant Sex and the Community

While unbounded sexuality supposedly had the potential to cause serious damage to the individual, it was also regarded as a threat to the wider community. Perhaps most obviously, sexual misdemeanours often caused collateral damage. Sexual assault, of course, invariably resulted in very serious trauma for the victim. Jonet Boussie was only around ten years of age when Alexander Gylour attempted to rape her in 1640, and his attack resulted in the 'ryveing of hir secreat pairtis to the effusione of hir blood and danger of her lyffe'.[45] Harm similarly rippled out from cases of bestiality. Andro Love from Kintyre, who was convicted in 1662 of abusing ten separate cows and horses, not only victimised all of these animals, but in so doing damaged (and ultimately destroyed, given that animals involved in such cases were habitually slaughtered) the property of at least six different people.[46] Even at the least heinous end of the sexual misdemeanour spectrum, victims were often not hard to find. In 1649, for example, James Sandilands, 1ˢᵗ Lord Abercrombie was said to have suffered great 'greif and anger' upon learning of his wife's adulterous affair with Sir Mungo Murray.[47] Five years earlier, John Murray in Penstoun, East Lothian had found himself duped into accepting another man's child as his own on account of his wife's pre-marital fornication with John's own brother, William.[48] An overture submitted to the general assembly in 1644 raised the spectre of a slightly different danger. Upon attending college for the first time, it was claimed, many young men found themselves tempted into fornication with local women, who then used this to leverage promises of marriage, 'to the great grief' of the boys' parents 'and to the great appearance of the ruine and overthrow of their estate'.[49] Breaching the limits of acceptable sexuality, in short, had the potential to cause a range of direct, measurable harms to people well beyond the transgressors themselves.

Aside from the direct impacts of sexual deviance, there was a wider concern about its potentially disordering effect on the surrounding community. It might, for example, undermine social cohesion by promoting feelings of fear or insecurity, especially when uncontrolled sexual desire was coupled with other forms of disorder – this was certainly a point made following the rape of Katharine Rae, mentioned above, which had taken place on Edinburgh High Street 'quhilk sould be ane saiftie and place of refudge to all honest men and wemen'.[50] Also of concern was the possibility that sexual deviants might inspire others to similar misbehaviour, an idea we have already seen underpinning Edinburgh burgh council's ban on female tavern-servers in

[45] Gillon and Smith, *Selected Justiciary Cases*, vol. 2, pp. 518–20.
[46] NRS, JC2/10, High Court Books of Adjournal, 1661–6, fols 75v–76r.
[47] Kinloch, *St Andrews and Cupar*, (Edinburgh, 1837), p. 143.
[48] Gillon and Smith, *Selected Justiciary Cases*, vol. 3, p. 690.
[49] *Records of the Kirk of Scotland* (Edinburgh, 1838), pp. 405–6.
[50] Pitcairn, *Ancient Criminal Trials*, vol. 3, p. 464.

1699; women with a history of fornication were simply too great a 'Snare to the Youth', likely to divert them into 'Leudness and Debauchry'.[51] Disorderly sex, it was further felt, might threaten the institutions of marriage and family around which communities were constructed, which is why the notorious adultery of which Margaret Hamiltoune was accused in 1665 was described as 'breaking and violating the most sacred and strait bonds, religione and civil, and of natiour and humanity it self'.[52] More amorphously, there was widespread anxiety that sexual deviants, by their very presence, damaged the respectability and cohesion of their communities. This thinking was made explicit in the case of Thomas Squeyar, 'ane commoun harlot' and 'vicious fornicatour' (among other vices) who was exiled from the town of Inverness in 1608. After numerous attempts by the kirk session to rehabilitate him, the burgh court finally decided that Squeyar was 'ane vnvorthie member to have ony residence in ony cristian citie or commun vealthe', and gave him twenty-four hours to leave.[53] Ejection was also the standard punishment for sex workers – women like the thirty-two 'whoors' ordered to be transported overseas from Edinburgh in 1695 – whose trade was similarly regarded as a source of disorder.[54] The case of Margaret Reid is particularly striking from this perspective. She was banished from the parish of Canongate in 1624 for 'seducing Marion Crawfurd as ane comane baud in convoying the said Marioune to Leith and Edinburgh To comit huirdome and harlotrie wit the laird of Bochinvare'. Reid – who was presumably paid for her procurement services – was a 'bawd', in effect running a sex-trafficking business.[55] Such organised trade in vice underlined the potential of unrestrained sexual desire to both introduce and sustain disorderly conduct in seventeenth-century communities. This, in turn, underpinned a pervasive fear that the continued presence of promiscuous or sexually deviant individuals within a given locality was fundamentally harmful.

It was also feared that sexual deviants might damage their communities by challenging or undermining public authority, especially ecclesiastical. The synod of Argyll complained in 1640 that many women guilty of fornication and adultery refused to satisfy Church discipline, instead 'thrust[ing] themselves in the service of gentlemen [...] thinking thereby to be sheltered from the censure of the church'.[56] More particularly, the brethren of Caithness were vexed in 1663 by the case of John Macinnes and Cathrine nein Rob, who had been cohabiting adulterously for eighteen years, but constantly evaded ecclesiastical censure by 'vaging from place to place'.[57] A similar, though more drastic, response came from Margaret Fraser, who in 1673 was sentenced to excommunication by the

---

[51] *Act anent women-servants in taverns.*
[52] NRS, JC2/10, fols 248v–250v.
[53] *Inverness Rec.*, vol. 2, pp. 57–8.
[54] NRS, PC2/25, Privy Council Decreta, 1694–5, fol. 217r–v.
[55] NRS, CH2/122/1, Canongate Kirk Session, 1613–19, p. 206; Glaze, 'Women and Kirk Discipline', at pp. 132–3.
[56] D. C. MacTavish (ed.), *Minutes of the Synod of Argyll, 1639–1661* (2 vols, Edinburgh, 1943–4), vol. 1, p. 13.
[57] NRS, CH2/47/1, pp. 75–7.

session of Inverness for bearing an illegitimate child (conceived, she claimed, through rape), but evaded her fate by fleeing to London.[58]

As well as occasioning straightforward evasion of ecclesiastical authority, sexual deviance might also work to undermine specific parts of the Church's work, not least its regulation of marriage; it was largely to shore up ecclesiastical authority – and position – that irregular marriages, especially those predicated on sexual intercourse between the betrothed, were subject to such censure throughout the early modern period.[59] Similarly seeking to defend marriage from the dangers of sexual incontinence, the general assembly in 1600 mandated that people should not be permitted to marry somebody with whom they had committed adultery, because the ability to do this might drive them to have an affair in the first place, 'thinking therby to be separate from their awin lawfull halfe marrowes [i.e. spouse], to injoy the persons with quhom they have committit adulterie'.[60] The rite of baptism might be similarly threatened. In 1624, for example, Jaffray Irwing of Robgill discovered that his three sons, born in incest with his sister-in-law Agnes Cairletoun, could not legally be baptised in Scotland, so he circumvented the Church's authority by having them baptised in England instead.[61] Even the Church's responsibility for the registration of burial might be open to sexually motivated abuse. The writer John Fraser was accused in 1674 of trying to cover up his adultery by presenting 'ane false testificat' to the session of Edinburgh suggesting that his wife was dead, thereby allowing him to become engaged to his paramour, Helen Guthrie.[62]

Yet the danger posed by sexual deviance was potentially even wider still. In 1690, parliament reiterated all existing laws against profaneness, including 'fornicatione and uncleanness', with the observation that doing so 'concernes the honour and glory of God and peace, welfare and prosperity of the kingdome'.[63] The idea that national prosperity required moral behaviour was of course far from unique, and indeed underpinned the contemporaneous 'reformation of manners' movement in England.[64] In a Scottish context, the most commonly-expressed concern was that failing to tackle sexual immorality would call down the wrath of God, a possibility raised explicitly during the prosecution of Alexander Gourlay for incest in 1626:

> The abhominable and vyle syn of incest being sa detestable in the sicht of our omnipotent and almytie God [...] and zit nevertheles the said

---

[58] Mackay, *Inverness and Dingwall*, pp. 39, 41, 42, 46, 47, 57, 58, 61, 69.
[59] K. Barclay, *Love, Intimacy and Power: Marriage and Patriarchy in Scotland, 1650–1850* (Manchester, 2011), pp. 43–4.
[60] *Acts and Proceedings of the General Assemblies of the Kirk of Scotland* (Edinburgh, 1839–45), p. 953.
[61] Pitcairn, *Ancient Criminal Trials*, vol. 3, p. 576.
[62] NRS, JC2/14, High Court Books of Adjournal, 1673–8, fols 14v–17r.
[63] *RPS*, 1690/4/116.
[64] S. Hindle, *The State and Social Change in Early Modern England, 1550–1640* (Basingstoke, 2002), chapter 7.

detestabill vyce being so frequently practizet uithin this kingdome [...] that ze samyn eternall God in his just judgementis hes occasioun to plague the realme or natioun quhair that vyce is practizet in caice ordour be nocht tane for restraneing thairof.[65]

There was also a sense that sexual deviance might inhibit Scotland from realising its potential as a godly society. The Glasgow general assembly of 1638 gave particularly clear expression to this idea when it noted that failing to root out all forms of profanity, including sexual, would represent a fundamental breach of the nation's recently-renewed covenant with God, dooming its mission to remake the Church of Scotland according to the divine blueprint.[66] A different fear was articulated in 1628 by William Struther, who suggested that sexual immorality threatened the very fabric of society by undermining the institution of the family:

> Filthinesse, hath layed off the former vaile of shame, and is now impudent: Fornication, Adulteries & Incests, out-face the Light and multiplie out of number: And the couenant of God in marriage is lesse respected and keeped then light promises amongst men: Whereby thogh their were none other sinnes, a way is made to ouerthrow families, for God cannot blesse Inheritance in the hands of wrongous Heires.[67]

Whether through divine wrath, spiritual enervation, or social collapse, then, the persistence of deviant sex was understood as a threat to national stability, and its eradication, conversely, a potential means of national rebirth.

The pervasive sense that deviant sexuality was a source of general, and not just individual harm found its most elaborate expression in witch-belief. Across the seventeenth century, it came increasingly to be assumed, certainly in elite and learned understandings, that witches confirmed their submission to the devil by copulating with him, and historians have generally regarded this as a vicarious expression of deeper concerns about the disordering impact of deviant sex.[68] This can be traced particularly clearly in the proceedings against the Inverness witch Isobel Duff in 1662. Although Duff's submission to the devil was sealed in the normal way through copulation, the manner in which this was achieved was more unusual. She was allegedly tricked into sex by the devil taking the form of a local soldier, known only as 'Tailiour', with whom she had previously committed serial fornication. Duff's satanic

[65] Gillon and Smith, *Selected Justiciary Cases*, vol. 1, p. 53.
[66] *Records of the Kirk of Scotland*, p. 424.
[67] William Struther, *Scotlands warning, or a treatise of fasting containing a declaration of the causes of the solemne fast, indyted to bee kept in all the Churches of Scotland, the third and fourth sundayes of this instant moneth of May Anno 1628. & the weeke dayes betwixt them, as they may be goodly keeped in Townes. Together with a direction how to proceed in the religious obseruation of any soleme fast* (Edinburgh, 1628), pp. 19–20.
[68] J. Goodare, 'Women and the Witch-Hunt in Scotland', *Social History*, 23:3 (1998) 288–308; Dye, 'Converse with the Devil?'.

coupling, therefore, was directly facilitated by past sexual misbehaviour, and to underline the point, it was claimed that she had sex with both 'Tailiour' and the devil 'efter the maner of beastes at her back pairtes'. Although the precise meaning of this phrase is unclear, the implication of further sexual debauchery is unmistakable. The Duff case offers an unusually forthright articulation of the role played by disorderly female sexuality in witch-belief. It was promiscuity that had made Duff vulnerable to Satan, and thus it was her sexual deviance that had, in a very direct sense, allowed the forces of evil to take root.[69] Isobel Duff's trial, then, underscores the intimate connection between witch-belief and disorderly (female) sexuality. All that, in turn, demonstrates the acute danger sexual deviance was assumed to pose to the entirety of Scottish society.

Conclusion

Seventeenth-century Scotland was a place gripped by fear of deviant sex. An oppressive framework of Church discipline and civic law placed Scots' sexual behaviour under unprecedentedly minute scrutiny, the intention being to confine sex within the narrow bounds of acceptability defined by marriage and procreation. All of this was necessary because sex, quite simply, was dangerous. Those engaging in unrestrained sexual activity risked befoulment of both soul and body, which might well have immediate material consequences, but which also, and more importantly, could begin to strip away their higher sensibilities and, perhaps, lead them into further, more heinous sinning. At the same time, any society that allowed such behaviour to go unchecked was running a major risk, because sexual deviance, quite apart from any immediate harms it might cause, could potentially undermine community harmony, destabilise the structures of authority, call down the wrath of God, and ultimately provide a bridgehead for all manner of other evils. These multifarious hazards meant that disorderly sexual conduct could not be tolerated. Those engaging in it had to be placed on the margins of society and not allowed in from the cold, if at all, until they had undergone a rigorous process of correction. Of course, the reality was not quite as stark as the theory, and in day-to-day life people likely enjoyed far more latitude – and indulgence – than we might expect. Nonetheless, on a conceptual and rhetorical level, standards were strict in the extreme, and the basis for this conviction was not knee-jerk or unthinking prudishness. It was, rather, a widespread belief that doing anything else was simply too risky, both for the individuals concerned and for the wider community of which they were part.

---

[69] A. Kennedy, 'The Trial of Isobel Duff for Witchcraft, Inverness, 1662', *SHR*, 101:1 (2022), 109–22.

2

Assault in the Margins: Gendered Violence in Seventeenth-Century Bute

Ashlyn Cudney

Research over the last ten or fifteen years has indicated that the longstanding belief that abuse committed by women was overwhelmingly verbal, whilst male abuse was physical, is not wholly accurate; there is a more complex story to be told.[1] Not only were women, in fact, perfectly capable of deploying physical violence, but they could also be powerful adversaries in the ecclesiastical and secular courts through strategic litigation and acting as crucial witnesses. Despite this agency, the courts supported, maintained, and reinforced patriarchal ideals which disadvantaged women as both victims and perpetrators. In this chapter, I argue that women's violence is underrepresented in the secular court records due to gender and class biases which prevented them from accessing justice, and that women were disadvantaged inside the courtrooms due to being viewed as complicit in their own assaults.

This chapter uses seventeenth-century ecclesiastical and secular court records from the island of Bute to explore gendered differences in the perpetration, investigation, and disciplining of interpersonal violence. Bute is an ideal case study to understand interpersonal violence as detailed records for both the Rothesay burgh court and kirk sessions exist nearly uninterrupted for the latter half of the seventeenth century. Early modern Scotland's judicial system consisted of an expansive network of local and central courts, all supporting and negotiating their overlapping jurisdictions, personnel, and power. Because sin and crime were often indistinguishable for seventeenth-century Scots, it is necessary to look to both ecclesiastical and secular courts to understand the experience of overlapping social control at the lowest level. To this end, I employ an intersectional approach to demonstrate how layers of oppression affected gendered experience.

This chapter first analyses gendered differences surrounding the use of weapons, as they were solely associated with male offenders, establishing a distinct power dynamic. The role of masculinity, drunkenness, and

---

[1]   A.-M. Kilday, 'Angels with Dirty Faces? Violent Women in Early Modern Scotland', in R. Hillman and P. Ruberry-Blanc (eds), *Female Transgression in Early Modern Britain, Literary and Historical Explorations* (Farnham, 2014), pp. 141–62; E. Ewan, 'Disorderly Damsels? Women and Interpersonal Violence in Pre-Reformation Scotland', *SHR*, 89:2 (2010), 153–71; E. Ewan, 'Impatient Griseldas: Women and the Perpetration of Violence in Sixteenth-Century Glasgow', *Florilegium*, 28 (2011), 149–68.

socioeconomic status in the perpetration of violence forms a crucial part of this analysis. Moreover, I use cases of domestic violence to demonstrate that women were required to present with characteristics that emphasised their passivity and submission if they were to be accepted as innocent victims. This chapter also explores the role of vexatious prosecution among the quarrelsome and litigious elite, strategically utilising the courts for personal gain. This research illuminates the tendency of women victims to resort to the secular courts solely in cases of severe injury, highlighting the significant barriers they faced in accessing justice, such as higher standards of evidence, perceived bias, and financial outlay. As such, the chapter illustrates how both ideas about and responses to deviant violence helped confirm and shape the intersectional marginalisation of early modern women in Scotland.

Weapons and Alcohol

In seventeenth-century Bute, women were never cited for physical assaults using weapons. Potentially, this is evidence of scribal gender bias, as kirk sessions and burgh courts alike were more concerned with the harm inflicted than the means of assault.[2] Perhaps, because men were more likely to be armed with whingers [knives], dirks, or even swords, while women were generally expected to be unarmed, injuries inflicted by them were more severe, and the weapon therefore more likely to be noted. Elizabeth Ewan observes that, in early modern Glasgow, women were equally likely to use weapons, but they tended to use household items like keys, tongs, or pans which were conveniently on hand.[3] Likewise, Anne-Marie Kilday observes that Lowland Scotswomen used weapons in as many as 65 per cent of assault cases.[4] Such trends, however, were not in evidence in Bute. Indeed, only one Bute woman was cited for using a weapon of any sort in interpersonal assault. In May 1700, Elspeth Frissell was found guilty of assaulting her husband, James Hunter, by throwing 'firie turf' at him, dried peat sods used in domestic heating and cooking.[5] This assault – part of a broader pattern of domestic abuse between the couple which will be discussed later in this chapter – very much conformed to the expectation that women, typically having access only to their hands and feet, would be forced to improvise if they did use weaponry.

Men, particularly elite men, were therefore overwhelmingly more likely to be cited for using weapons in physical assaults. In July 1670, John Muir,

---

[2]   Ewan, 'Disorderly Damsels', p. 165.
[3]   Ewan, 'Impatient Griseldas', pp. 161–2.
[4]   A.-M. Kilday, *Women and Violent Crime in Enlightenment Scotland* (Woodbridge, 2007), p. 95.
[5]   H. Paton (ed.), *Kingarth Parish Records. The Session Book of Kingarth, 1641–1703* (Edinburgh, 1932), 211.

an officer of the Rothesay burgh court, accused Duncan M'Allester, also a burgh officer, of attacking him. Muir testified that M'Allester 'sett upone him to tak his lyff with a durk'.[6] Two witnesses affirmed that M'Allester did not merely seek to maim Muir with his weapon, as bad as that would have been, but intended to kill him. For his offence, the burgh court ordered M'Allester to find two cautioners (persons providing surety), both of whom were also officers and burgesses, and pay a 500 merk (£333) fine.[7]

The use of weapons was not limited to intra-gender assault; elite men also used weapons to increase their physical advantage over unarmed women. In July 1665, Marion N'Conochie accused burgh officer Matthew Muir of assault.[8] She asserted that Muir hit her over the head with a staff, a heavy, solid stick or pole sometimes augmented with spikes or a spearhead.[9] Curiously, Muir was not fined. Instead, he was imprisoned in the tolbooth until he was able to find a cautioner. Given the burgh officers' apparent willingness to act as cautioners for each other, it was likely not long until he was released. The reasons that M'Allester received a substantial fine whereas Muir was only temporarily imprisoned were not explained. Perhaps the intention behind the assaults was considered, reflecting M'Allester's alleged intent to murder. Most likely, however, the dispute between two burgh officers and burgesses was considered a more severe offence as it disrupted the communal peace to a greater degree. The gender dimension is impossible to ignore, however; Muir suffered no long-term consequences for his assault on a woman, despite the potentially lethal nature of the attack.

Drunkenness was sporadically mentioned as an exacerbating factor to physical assault. While men were officially expected to practise moderation, they were socially encouraged to participate in a lively drinking culture, and as a result did not face the same taboos around excessive drinking as women.[10] In a modern context, it has been observed that when men drink amongst other men, they are more likely to participate in sexist, racist, and homophobic discourse – behaviour that both affirms their individual masculinity and reinforces camaraderie.[11] This held true for the early modern period as well; Angela McShane demonstrates that alehouse joviality fostered male bonding and reduced inhibitions, leading men to participate in the singing of sexually explicit drinking songs that also encouraged overindulgence and glorified violence.[12] Perhaps this alcohol-induced misogyny contributed to

[6]   M. B. Johnston (ed.), *Rothesay Town Council Records, 1653–1766* (Edinburgh, 1935), p. 191.

[7]   *Ibid.*, p. 191.

[8]   *Ibid.*, p. 102.

[9]   J. Cooper, *Scottish Renaissance Armies 1513–1550* (Oxford, 2008), p. 30.

[10]   A. Shepard, 'Manhood, Credit and Patriarchy in Early Modern England c.1580–1640', *Past & Present*, 167 (May 2000), 75–106, at p. 103.

[11]   K. Mullen et al., 'Young men, Masculinity and Alcohol', *Drugs: Education, Prevention and Policy*, 14:2 (2007), 151–65, at p. 152.

[12]   A. McShane, 'Drink, Song and Politics in Early Modern England', *Popular Music*, 35:2 (2016), 166–90, at pp. 170–1.

several drunken attacks on Bute women.[13] In April 1658, Margaret N'Nicoll appeared before Rothesay burgh court with her face visibly 'mankit and blae' (mutilated and bruised) from a drunken assault.[14] In addition to the assault, N'Nicoll's attacker, Thomas M'Vrarthie, slandered her by calling her a witch and a witch's get [child], and publicly accused her and her mother of killing an entire family through witchcraft. M'Vrarthie was found guilty of both the slander and 'straicking and abuseing' M'Nicoll on the face. He was fined £50 and imprisoned until he found a cautioner.

Women were comparatively less apt to abuse alcohol publicly at all; only 18 per cent of all offenders on Bute cited for drunkenness were women.[15] In fact, only one woman in this study was characterised as being drunk during a physical assault.[16] Several historians have identified alcohol as an exacerbating factor for interpersonal violence, and pubs or alehouses were the most common locations for physical confrontations.[17] James Brown describes drinking houses in seventeenth-century Southampton as 'heavily gendered if not entirely gender-specific'.[18] He found that there were few socially-sanctioned reasons for women's presence at alehouses: acting as an alewife, participating in courting rituals, or visiting with family.[19] Regardless of their reason for being present, women in alehouses required strict male supervision, either from an employer, potential partner, or family member.[20] Given all this, as well as Bute's size and relatively sparse population distribution, drinking often took place domestically, and since the home was a space for women's sociability, this likely explains why all the cases of women's drunken verbal assault featured female victims.[21]

---

[13] Johnston, *Rothesay*, p. 18; H. Paton (ed.), *Rothesay Parish Records: The Session Book of Rothesay, 1658–1750* (Edinburgh, 1931), p. 80; Paton, *Kingarth*, pp. 53, 55; NRS, CH2/111/2, Dunoon Presbytery Minutes, 1639–1686, p. 77.

[14] Johnston, *Rothesay*, p. 18.

[15] Of the twenty-seven cases of drunkenness on Bute, only five featured female offenders.

[16] Paton, *Kingarth*, p. 85.

[17] A-M. Kilday, *Crime in Scotland 1660–1960: The Violent North?* (London, 2018), p. 130; D. D. Gray, *Crime Prosecution and Social Relations: The Summary Courts of the City of London in the Late Eighteenth Century* (New York, 2009), p. 97; C. A. Whatley, 'Order and Disorder', in E. Foyster and C. A. Whatley (eds), *A History of Everyday Life in Scotland, 1600–1800* (Edinburgh, 2010), pp. 191–216, at p. 206; B. A. Hanawalt, 'The Host, the Law, and the Ambiguous Space of Medieval London Taverns', in B. A. Hanawalt and D. Wallace (eds), *Medieval Crime and Social Control* (Minneapolis, 1998), pp. 204–23, at pp. 211–13.

[18] J. R. Brown, 'The Landscape of Drink: Inns, Taverns and Alehouses in Early Modern Southampton' (Unpublished PhD dissertation, University of Warwick, 2007), p. 192.

[19] *Ibid.*, pp. 188–93.

[20] Hanawalt, 'London Taverns', pp. 206–10; T. E. Brennan, *Public Drinking and Popular Culture in Eighteenth-Century Paris* (Princeton, 1988), pp. 147–8.

[21] Paton, *Kingarth*, p. 85.

'Good Victims' and 'Perceivable Perpetrators'

Bute kirk sessions perceived women's verbal abuse as a justification for physical violence; male offenders were still disciplined, but their female victims were also held accountable for provoking their own assault. In January 1651, a male offender named only as M'Lashen was summoned by Kingarth kirk session for assaulting More N'Ilrevie.[22] He initially denied the assault, arguing that, in the heat of an argument, he had raised his hand to intimidate N'Ilrevie, but did not strike her. N'Ilrevie countered that he had indeed hit her, prompting M'Lashen to confess. Despite both N'Ilrevie and M'Lashen confessing to arguing with each other, only N'Ilrevie was found guilty of flyting (arguing), while M'Lashen was convicted of assault. Crucially, however, they received the same sentence of performing public repentance over four successive Sundays. Clearly, the Kingarth elders held N'Ilrevie and M'Lashen equally culpable, judging N'Ilrevie's verbal attack comparable to M'Lashen's physical one. The all-male composition of the kirk session no doubt benefited M'Lashen in this case; there would have been little difficulty in believing that N'Ilrevie's verbal combativeness had forced his hand, literally and figuratively.

Men, also, engaged in harassment and slander that led to physical altercations. Men's words, however, were not seen as triggers for assault to the same extent as women's. In fact, men's slanderous name-calling was regarded as trivial in the face of physical attack. For example, in December 1671, Angus M'Ilhuy called Adam Kelburne a 'knaife', meaning a scoundrel, rogue, or rascal.[23] Kelburne responded by hitting M'Ilhuy, prompting the burgh court to intervene. Unlike More N'Ilrevie, M'Ilhuy was held only partially accountable; while Kelburne was fined £10, M'Ilhuy was only fined £5. Clearly, slanderous name-calling was seen as a lesser offence compared to Kelburne's assault. This pattern – M'Ilhuy's fine being half that of Kelburne's – was typical in male assault cases which also featured slander as a contributing factor, although sometimes the gulf was even greater. William Glass, who was assaulted by Alexander Jamiesoun after calling Jamiesoun a 'knave' and saying that he 'wold be hangit or killed as his brother was befoir him', for example received a £4 fine against the £20 imposed on Jamiesoun.[24] Clearly, men's words were perceived as less powerful than women's in provoking and inciting male violence. This, in turn, reflected a wider tendency – both in Bute and Scotland more generally – to regard female querulousness with deep impatience, as well as a desire to control the female voice.[25]

---

[22] *Ibid.*, pp. 28–9.
[23] Johnston, *Rothesay*, p. 215.
[24] *Ibid.*, p. 268.
[25] J. C. White, 'Women, Gender, and the Kirk Before the Covenant', *IRSS*, 45 (2020), 27–53, at p. 43; M. Todd, *The Culture of Protestantism in Early Modern Scotland* (New Haven, 2002), p. 259; S. Dye, 'To Converse with the Devil? Speech, Sexuality, and

Women's perceived complicity in their own assaults extended into the domestic sphere. In April 1664, James Frissel, the local schoolmaster, was called before Kingarth kirk session for hitting his wife on the sabbath.[26] He confessed that they had argued, but claimed he had not hit her. Instead, he shifted the blame. Frissel told the elders that he was unable to 'keip house with hir' anymore. The elders, presumably startled by his implicit threat of impending separation, called Frissel's wife to appear at the next session meeting. When she did, she was found guilty of scolding and flyting with her husband.[27] She was fined 1s and warned that, if she were found guilty again, she would be placed in the jougs (an iron collar fixed to a wall). Frissel was required to perform no such repentance for his role in their discord, or for his suspected abuse.

The concept of the 'good victim' is well established in legal theory.[28] The 'good victim' is one who embodies obedience and submission, even in the face of cruelty.[29] To be considered credible, the battered woman should demonstrate powerlessness, passivity, and weakness;[30] she should be 'deferential, submissive to authority, and compliant to the demands of others'.[31] Frissel's wife, by verbally fighting back, was no longer a believable victim. How the session perceived Frissel was just as important to their understanding of the abuse. The concept of the 'perceivable perpetrator' relates to an individual whose characteristics align with the courts' biases about how a typical abuser looks and acts.[32] The presence of these characteristics affects the courts' likelihood of believing an individual capable of physical abuse. Legal scholar Elizabeth MacDowell argues that, for a victim to successfully convince the courts of their abuse, they must both present as a 'good victim' and prove that their abuser is a 'perceivable perpetrator'.[33] Stereotypes about class, occupation, ethnicity, and gender manifest in powerful biases which may produce – or fail to produce – 'perceivable perpetrators'. As Frissel was the schoolmaster, and clearly respected in his community, he did not present as a believable perpetrator. His class, occupation, and reputation excluded him from the stereotype of the abuser.

Witchcraft in Early Modern Scotland', *IRSS*, 37 (2012), 9–40, at p. 20.

[26] *Ibid.*, p. 32.

[27] *Ibid.*, p. 33.

[28] K. Crenshaw, 'Mapping the Margins: Intersectionality, Identity Politics, and Violence against Women of Color', *Stanford Law Review*, 43:6 (1991), 1241–99, at p. 1270; L. Goodmark, 'When is a Battered Woman not a Battered Woman? When she Fights Back', *Yale Journal of Law & Feminism*, 20 (2008), 75–129, at pp. 82–3.

[29] E. Foyster, *Marital Violence: An English Family History, 1660–1875* (Cambridge, 2005), p. 86.

[30] L. S. Kohn, 'Barriers to Reliable Credibility Assessments: Domestic Violence Victim-Witnesses', *Journal of Gender, Social Policy & The Law*, 11:2 (2003), 732–48, at p. 741.

[31] Goodmark, 'Battered Woman', at p. 83.

[32] A. Durfee, 'The Use of Structural Intersectionality as a Method to Analyze How the Domestic Violence Civil Protective Order Process Replicates Inequality', *Violence Against Women*, 27:5 (2021), 639–55, at p. 649.

[33] MacDowell, 'Theorizing from Particularity', at p. 534.

Even when the abuser presented as a 'perceivable perpetrator', if the victim did not have the characteristics of a 'good victim', they were still vulnerable to blame. In May 1678, Patrick M'Pherson was suspected by the Kingarth kirk session of beating his wife, Geillis Stewart, on the sabbath. The Kingarth elders were already familiar with M'Pherson. He had been accused of fornication on several occasions, first in January 1666, then again in 1670 and 1672. While sexual mores were certainly more relaxed for men, repeated bastard-begetters were a strain on the community. Worse still, in February 1671, M'Pherson had been accused of rape and evading his kirk-ordered discipline. The elders, remarking that M'Pherson was 'a profligate, debauched, unruly, scandalous person, disobedient to discipline', referred him to the civil magistrate to bind him to obedience.[34] M'Pherson was clearly a 'perceivable perpetrator' to the elders, previously guilty of disobedience, assault, and sexual immorality.

M'Pherson's reputation did not protect Stewart from the ire of the court. Like M'Pherson, Stewart was not a stranger to the kirk session. She was first accused of fornication in June 1667, but later absolved. Only two years later, in January 1669, she was found guilty of fornication when she fell pregnant out of wedlock. Stewart first cited John Bane McKaw as the father of her baby. Both McKaw and Stewart were ordered to pay a £4 fine and complete three weeks of public repentance, but the kirk session was not convinced that he truly was the father of her baby. They suspected Stewart of also committing fornication with M'Pherson. He initially denied the accusation, but the elders had a 'strong presumption' that he was 'too familiar' with Stewart, and despite having no evidence of fornication, they ordered him to begin public repentance. Three weeks later, Stewart confessed to fornication with M'Pherson ten months earlier. Only then did M'Pherson confess, but he stopped short of admitting paternity; M'Pherson accused Stewart of committing fornication with several other men, although those accusations proved to be unfounded. Stewart and M'Pherson must have reconciled and married some time prior to their domestic violence incident in 1678. Perhaps it was this history of sexual indiscretion that excluded Stewart from being a 'good victim', but she was also known for being troublesome in other ways, having been accused of theft in January 1673. Stewart's grim reputation was confirmation to the elders that it was her 'cursing and swearing which provoked him to beat her'.[35] Despite M'Pherson's own bad name, Stewart was deemed to share responsibility for her own abuse. She was ordered to do public repentance alongside her husband.

---

[34] Paton, *Kingarth*, pp. 41, 59, 68, 69, 79, 113.
[35] *Ibid.*, pp. 51, 53, 57, 59, 60, 83, 114.

Women and Physical Violence

Despite the contemporary perception that physical violence was the preserve of men, women could deploy it. In January 1698, Kingarth kirk session reported that Elspeth Frissell – whom we met at the start of this chapter – 'contends with her husband quhen he crosses her and threatens her'. The session warned Frissell that she would incur a £10 fine if she were to continue challenging her husband. She did not heed the elders' warning; two years later, in May 1700, she and her husband, James Hunter, were accused of 'flyting, squabbling, fighting, and casting firie turfs at each other'.[36] Both Frissell and Hunter denied the accusation, but several witnesses came forward detailing serious abuse from both spouses. Patrick M'Cirdie said that he heard them striking, beating, and scolding each other. Several other witnesses testified that Frissell threw turf at Hunter, burning his skin. In retaliation, Hunter hit Frissell twice on the arms with tongs, the wounds being so great that she had to bind her arm afterwards.

The violence was so alarming that the couple's young daughter sought help. The young girl found a neighbour, Janet Jamieson, a domestic servant, and told her through tears that her father was going to 'murther [murder] her mother'. By the time Jamieson responded, however, the violence had dissipated.[37] Female neighbours, friends, servants, and family members could challenge abusive husbands and act as crucial witnesses in the courts to recount episodes of abuse and recurrent violence, likely due to the proximity within which women lived and interacted.[38] Men were seemingly less likely to intercede in violence against women unless they perceived it to be life-threatening.[39] While patriarchal ideals situated men as protectors,[40] women were, in effect, largely responsible for protecting each other from the violent hands of Bute men.

This was not an isolated instance of abuse for this couple. Their daughter explained that they 'did shamefully flyt and scold without bonet or kerchief and that [she] herself was so terrified that she could not sleep'.[41] In early

---

[36] *Ibid.*, pp. 193, 211.

[37] Paton, *Kingarth*, p. 212.

[38] L. Leneman, '"A tyrant and a tormentor": Violence Against Wives in Eighteenth- and Early Nineteenth-Century Scotland', *Continuity and Change*, 12:1 (1997), 31–54, at p. 43; J. McEwan, 'Attitudes towards Male Authority and Domestic Violence in Eighteenth-Century London Courts', in S. Broomhall and J. Van Gent (eds), *Governing Masculinities in the Early Modern Period: Regulating Selves and Others* (Farnham, 2011), pp. 247–62, at p. 257; Foyster, *Marital Violence*, p. 193.

[39] In March 1658, Janet Spence was brutally assaulted by two excisemen who were inquiring about her husband's excise debt. Several men attempted to intercede on her behalf, but only one man physically intervened. This is the only case where men intervened in violence against a woman on Bute. Johnston, *Rothesay*, pp. 270–1.

[40] B. Capp, *When Gossips Meet: Women, Family and Neighbourhood in Early Modern England* (Oxford, 2003), p. 235.

[41] Paton, *Kingarth*, p. 213.

modern Scotland, a woman's head covering was a sign of respectability; to be seen without one suggested immorality.[42] This account therefore implied to the elders that Frissell's aggression excluded her from the status of a 'good victim'. Hunter was also failing to adhere to societal norms by removing his bonnet. Not only were they both arguing shamefully, but they could not even wait to get dressed properly before doing so. This, in fact, was a marriage on the verge of breakdown; several witnesses noted that the couple '[had] no agreement' and that Hunter '[was] resolved to leav his wife becaus he could not heav peac with her'.[43] The session decided that Frissell and Hunter should be disciplined 'both in ther bodies and means'. They were ordered to stand in the jougs on the sabbath, with their offences written on their chest, and fined £10 each.

Outside of the family unit, interpersonal assault was most commonly prosecuted among elite men.[44] A surprising 53 per cent of assault cases in Bute communities featured elite offenders, with 51 per cent having elite victims.[45] This disproportionate representation of such individuals in assault prosecutions may indicate the existence of a particularly combative and vitriolic elite population. While the cases unfortunately do not illuminate the individual causes of violent altercations among the elite, the political climate of seventeenth-century Bute provides some important contextual clues. Flashpoints such as the covenanting revolution (several members of the Bute elite refused to sign the National Covenant, for example) and James VII's nomination of the town council of Rothesay in 1687 helped to break the local elite into factions, stirring up personal and political animosities that may have underpinned a culture of combativeness.[46] However, we cannot discount the possibility of vexatious prosecution. Martin Ingram's study of early modern Wiltshire utilises quarter session material and church court records to explore the community's relationship with both secular and religious authorities. He shows that having multiple legal institutions on hand facilitated vexatious prosecution as a form of covert aggression.[47] Something similar might have been happening in Bute, although if so, it has left little trace. More concretely, the Bute elite seem to have viewed assault as a financial opportunity; if they turned the other cheek, they would be entitled to more compensation when the case went to trial. In December 1671, John Galie, a burgess carpenter, was accused of assaulting three men: Adam Kerr, the brother of former burgh officer John Kerr; Patrick Kerr, a burgess; and

---

[42]   Ewan, 'Disorderly Damsels', at p. 169.

[43]   Paton, Kingarth, p. 212.

[44]   High socioeconomic status was determined by landowning, presence on the secular and ecclesiastical courts, burgess status, familial ties, and the number of servants employed.

[45]   Of the forty-three cases of interpersonal assault on Bute, twenty-three featured elite offenders and twenty-two had elite victims.

[46]   Johnston, Rothesay, pp. 424–37; Paton, Kingarth, p. 6.

[47]   M. Ingram, 'Communities and the Courts: Law and Disorder in Early Seventeenth-Century Wiltshire', in J. S. Cockburn (ed.), Crime in England: 1550–1800 (London, 1977), pp. 110–34, at p. 118.

Peter Gray. Patrick Kerr was severely wounded in several parts of this body 'to the great effusioune of his blude'. John Kerr and Gray were likewise 'bludit and woundit', with the majority of their injuries being sustained in their hands. Despite having the advantage of outnumbering their assailant, none of the three men were reported as fighting back against Galie's assault. Instead, they took their case to the burgh court for retribution, and they were awarded substantial compensation: Galie was required to pay Kerr £20, and Gray and Adam received £10 each.[48]

The middling sort and poor, however, tended to react to violence with violence, and thus incurred monetary fines under the burgh court's authority. This suggests socioeconomic differences in the conceptualisation of masculinity. Seventeenth-century Scotsmen carried whingers, dirks, and even swords as outward symbols of violent masculinity, as well as for practical purposes.[49] The symbolic power of wearing the weapon was key, and could be augmented by using ornate, detailed metalwork to demonstrate wealth and status, over and above the capacity to inflict lethal harm. For elite men, masculinity came to be perceived through self-restraint and participation in the 'litigating society' of seventeenth-century Scotland.[50] Poor men, however, were unable to participate meaningfully in either symbolic demonstrations of masculinity, or in the strategic deployment of litigation.[51] Modern sociological research has demonstrated that poorer men who are unable to attain power through wealth, education, or employment create a 'protest masculinity' which often encourages physical violence as a form of domination.[52] Something similar can perhaps be seen in seventeenth-century Bute. In February 1662, James Stewart and Robert M'Gilcheren were accused of 'breaking the kings peax' after their public physical assault. Stewart provoked the violence by assaulting M'Gilcheren first, causing M'Gilcheren to respond by striking Stewart in return. The burgh court found Stewart's guilt to be the greater, and fined him £5.[53] Because M'Gilcheren merely retaliated, he was also fined, but only in the amount of £3. Both men were then ordered to be imprisoned until they paid their fines. Whereas the elite countered violence with litigation – attacking their assailants' wallets rather

[48] Johnston, *Rothesay*, pp. 216–17.
[49] J. Eibach, 'Violence and Masculinity', in P. Knepper and A. Johansen (eds), *The Oxford Handbook of The History of Crime and Criminal Justice* (Oxford, 2016), pp. 229–49, at p. 239.
[50] A. M. Godfrey, *Civil Justice in Renaissance Scotland: The Origins of a Central* Court (Leiden, 2009), pp. 402–3. T. Reinke-Williams, 'Manhood and Masculinity in Early Modern England', *History Compass*, 12:9 (2014), 685–93, at pp. 488–90.
[51] H. Genn, *Paths to Justice: What People Do and Think About Going to Law* (Oxford, 1999), p. 260.
[52] R. W. Connell and J. W. Messerschmidt, 'Hegemonic Masculinity: Rethinking the Concept', *Gender & Society*, 19 (2005), 829–59, at pp. 847–8; P. England and S. Ronen, 'Sex and Relationships among Youth: An Intersectional Gender Lens', *Contemporary Sociology*, 42:4 (2013), 503–13, at p. 508; J. Miller, *Getting Played: African American Girls, Urban Inequality, and Gendered Violence* (New York, 2008), p. 110.
[53] Johnston, *Rothesay*, p. 72.

than their bodies – the middling sort and the poor were far readier to respond through equal violence.

Physical violence generally occurred within socioeconomic groups as opposed to between them. Attacks on public authorities, especially, occurred only among the elite.[54] For example, in December 1682, James Stewart, the son of a wealthy landowner of Largizean, repeatedly refused to appear before the kirk session on charges of fornication. When the kirk session sent an officer to retrieve James on the appointed date to ensure his compliance, James assaulted him, stating that he 'card not for the minister and Session'. Instead of reporting the offence to the burgh court, the kirk session gave James an ultimatum: either he appeared before the kirk session and complied with their orders, or they would turn him over to the burgh court.[55] This was a serious threat, as assaults on public officials were seen as attacks on the town, and therefore punished harshly.[56] James conceded, apologising to the elders, stating that he was 'young, foolish and ignorant', and promising to be a 'good bairne' in the future.[57] James' assault was perceived as merely a youthful indiscretion; after giving his oath, the session released James from all ecclesiastical discipline.

If social status fundamentally conditioned the way violence was deployed and responded to, the same could be said about gender. The burgh court's focus on blood as an indicator of the severity of an attack likely excluded and discouraged women from accessing justice. The legal phrase 'a great effusion of blood' was medieval and early modern shorthand used to describe the physical effects of violence, representing either the actual or estimated amount of blood that resulted from the assault, or an assumption based on the visible injuries of the victim.[58] All five of the female assault victims mentioned in the burgh court were severely harmed, with either visible facial wounds or other evidence of vicious assault.[59] It is clear from this that women only took assault cases to the burgh court if they were the victims of serious bodily harm and had undeniable evidence. Men's cases, however, were often void of detail or evidence. In 1656, Hector Bannatyne of Kames, a Rothesay kirk session elder, was found guilty of assaulting Alexander Wode, a former Rothesay burgh officer.[60] Hector was fined £5 for the assault, but nothing is recorded as to the cause, nature, or injuries sustained from the assault.

While scribal bias may partially explain the differing levels of detail recorded in these cases, women's more general under-representation was

---

[54] NRS, CH2/111/2, pp. 69–70; Johnston, *Rothesay*, pp. 14, 94.

[55] Paton, *Kingarth*, pp. 136, 140. The session minutes state that James was the brother Ninian Stewart of Largizean, but the baptism records list him as Ninian Stewart's son.

[56] Ewan, 'Disorderly Damsels', p. 164.

[57] Paton, *Kingarth*, p. 140.

[58] M. D. Meyerson, D. Thiery, and O. Falk, 'Introduction', in M. D. Meyerson et al. (eds), *'A Great Effusion of Blood?' Interpreting Medieval Violence* (Toronto, 2003), pp. 3–16, at pp. 3–4.

[59] Johnston, *Rothesay*, pp. 14, 18, 102, 270–1.

[60] *Ibid.*, p. 262.

more likely rooted in a perceived lack of credibility that prevented them from accessing the burgh court entirely. Michael Wasser and Louise Yeoman have found that the testimony of women was considered akin to that of children, perjurers, or thieves; to maintain the high standards of evidence, women were not deemed fit to testify. In cases which carried a financial penalty greater than 40s, women were excluded entirely.[61] If the testimony of women was required, this represented a necessary lowering of judicial standards in order to obtain a conviction. This is not to say, however, that women were entirely excluded from participating in the burgh court. Midwives were crucial authorities in the secular and ecclesiastical policing of women's bodies, relied upon to attest to the approximate age of newborn babies, inspect women's bodies for signs of pregnancy or childbirth, and interrogate women during labour in an effort to establish paternity in cases where it was doubtful.[62] 'Women of skill'[63] were also tasked with investigating the bodies of women suspected of infanticide or secret pregnancy to search for signs of recent or impending childbirth. These women were usually mothers, knowledgeable in the female realm of pregnancy, birth, and childrearing. While certainly women were disadvantaged on the whole, these finer gradations demonstrate that 'at its most local and intimate level, patriarchal order depended on the agency of women as well as men; but it also depended on the marking out of distinctions *between* women that granted authority to some and excluded others'.[64] Despite women having the capacity to act as crucial resources for the burgh court, they were never utilised; instead, these forms of female authority were solely invoked by the kirk sessions on Bute. Indeed, women were never used as witnesses in the burgh court for cases of assault. Instead, the burgh court was disproportionately utilised by elite Bute men and was likely perceived as inaccessible for most women – and lower-status men – because it skewed to the needs of this minority.

There were other possible reasons for the relative absence of women from the assault processes before the burgh court. Women's experience of assault, both as victims and as offenders, was generally taken less seriously than men's, since violence involving men was seen as a larger and more significant threat to the communal peace.[65] At the same time, the burgh court required victims to consign money to present their cases to the court. It is likely that few female victims had the capital to do so, given that they were paid half

---

[61] M. B. Wasser and L. A. Yeoman, 'The Trial of Geillis Johnstone for Witchcraft, 1614', *Miscellany of the Scottish History Society XIII* (Edinburgh, 2004), pp. 83–145, at p. 98.
[62] L. Gowing, *Common Bodies: Women, Touch and Power in Seventeenth Century England* (New Haven, 2003), p. 159; L. Leneman and R. Mitchison, 'Scottish Illegitimacy Ratios in the Early Modern Period', *The Economic History Review*, 40:1 (1987), 41–63, at p. 60; Capp, *When Gossips Meet*, pp. 302–6.
[63] In November 1687, the Rothesay kirk session sent several 'women of skill' to investigate the body of a woman suspected of infanticide. These women were all the wives of current or former burgh officers. Paton, *Rothesay*, p. 70.
[64] Gowing, 'Ordering the Body', p. 45.
[65] Ewan, 'Disorderly Damsels', p. 158.

of men's wages,[66] when the outcome of any pursuit would be unclear. As a result, although assault was a secular crime and should have been heard by the burgh or sheriff, women tended instead to turn to the kirk session, where they were victims in 50 per cent of the assault cases heard – a significantly higher percentage than for the burgh court, albeit from a very small sample of only eight cases overall.[67] While, as Michael Graham argues, women may well have 'found kirk sessions more approachable and responsive to their needs for justice, support and protection', sessions were also much more lenient for both men and women, ordering public repentance rather than substantial financial penalties, and this only benefited the offender; had it been at all attainable, victims might have preferred significant financial compensation to symbolic public satisfaction.[68] It seems probable, then, that women did not simply prefer the kirk session, but that the barriers to access presented by socioeconomic and gender bias led a disproportionate number of women to conclude that the Church represented their only real option for dealing with a grievance.

Socioeconomic and gender differences are especially clear in the handling of domestic violence. Only 14 per cent of couples accused of domestic violence were of high socioeconomic status.[69] While most seventeenth-century Scots lived on the margin of subsistence, the ubiquity of poverty would not have alleviated the stress it brought to individuals and families. In a modern context, there is considerable evidence to show that the most severe instances of marital violence occur disproportionately among low-income women.[70] Sociologists Jennifer Nixon and Cathy Humphries hypothesise that tensions around lack of money, and frustration with their inability to establish power in employment, increase perpetrators' likelihood of committing violence at home.[71] Moreover,

[66] In 1791, the average annual wage of a female domestic servant was £3 to £4, and men averaged £6 to £8 annually. These wages had recently been raised by 30 per cent, so the wages for domestic servants in seventeenth-century Bute were significantly less. A. J. S. Gibson and T. C. Smout observed that wages were stagnant throughout the latter half of the seventeenth century but increased by over 300 percent between 1760 and 1790. Given this data, we can reasonably assume that female domestic servants on Bute made as little as £1 annually throughout this period. A. J. S. Gibson and T. C. Smout, *Prices, Food and Wages in Scotland 1550–1780* (Cambridge, 1995), p. 289; *Old Statistical Account of Scotland*, vol. 1, p. 310.

[67] A. Kennedy, 'Crime and Punishment in Early-Modern Scotland: The Secular Courts of Restoration Argyllshire, 1660–1688', *IRSS*, 41 (2016), 1–36, at p. 21.

[68] M. F. Graham, 'Women and the Church Courts in Reformation-Era Scotland', in E. Ewan and M. M. Meikle (eds), *Women in Scotland c.1100–c.1750* (East Linton, 1999), pp. 187–98, at p. 187.

[69] Only two out of the fourteen couples accused of domestic violence were of high socioeconomic status. The individuals identified here were a burgess and a schoolmaster. Paton, *Rothesay*, p. 49; Paton, *Kingarth*, p. 32.

[70] A. Browne and A. S. Bassuk, 'Intimate Violence in the Lives of Homeless and Poor Housed Women: Prevalence and Patterns in an Ethnically Diverse Sample', *American Journal of Orthopsychiatry*, 6:2 (1997), 261–78, at pp. 263–4.

[71] J. Nixon and C. Humphreys, 'Marshalling the Evidence: Using Intersectionality in the Domestic Violence Frame', *Social Politics*, 17:2 (2010), 137–58, at p. 148.

poverty also leaves the victim dependent on the abuser for financial support. In relatively remote communities like Rothesay and Kingarth, economic dependence would have been compounded by physical isolation.[72] Early modern women had fewer opportunities to support themselves and their families independently, and less control over their individual finances to save money for fleeing abusive marriages[73] – an issue especially acute for poor women. Women could sometimes rely on their families for support while leaving an abusive spouse, since violence against a woman was perceived as an attack on her natal family as well, although it is unclear if such support networks were particularly strong in a specifically Scottish context.[74] Bute parents certainly supported their unmarried daughters, for example by attempting to conceal their offences from the kirk session and protecting them from the hardships of unwed motherhood.[75] However, there appears to have been reluctance to get involved in the domestic life of a married daughter. Certainly, women's natal families on Bute were never recorded as having intervened in domestic violence, perhaps indicating that families felt it was inappropriate to insert themselves into marital discord, even if it became violent. In fact, one Bute mother even refused to testify to the kirk session when she witnessed her daughter being abused.[76] Unless women had the financial support of the kirk session or their natal families, they would have had to discreetly save money without the knowledge of their husbands to afford the initial costs of separation, meaning that poor women were forced to stay in violent marriages longer.

The kirk session only enacted financial penalties for domestic violence offenders on two occasions, both of which we have already encountered. The first was a £10 fine for Patrick M'Pherson in 1671, a particularly troublesome, disobedient offender, and the second was in 1700, when they ordered a £10 fine for both James and Elspeth Frissel, repeat offenders.[77] The reason for this judicial reticence seems to have been twofold: first, those convicted of marital abuse were comparatively poor, and therefore they would likely have been unable to pay a fine; and second, the elders likely recognised that deepening perpetrators' poverty would only exacerbate the violence.

Conclusion

Analysing the secular and ecclesiastical courts of Bute unveils a complex system of gender and socioeconomic bias, shedding light on the pervasive nature of violence and the unequal treatment of female offenders and victims. This

---

[72] Nixon and Humphreys identified social isolation and physical entrapment as significant factors in fostering and prolonging domestic violence. *Ibid.*, p. 148.
[73] Kilday, *Crime in Scotland*, p. 130; Capp, *When Gossips Meet*, p. 78.
[74] Foyster, *Marital Violence*, p. 183; R. Mitchison, *Life in Scotland* (London, 1978), p. 14.
[75] Paton, *Kingarth*, p. 75; Paton, *Rothesay*, pp. 37–8.
[76] Paton, *Kingarth*, p. 202.
[77] *Ibid.*, pp. 114, 213.

chapter has demonstrated that the secular courts on Bute primarily benefited the needs of the elite, who were able to access the court and understood how to navigate the judicial process. The intricate interplay of alcohol, age, and reputation in the perpetration and prosecution of violence is underscored by the role of factors like gender and socioeconomic status in shaping patterns of aggression. Moreover, the obstacles faced by female victims, who were only able to seek recourse in the secular courts when subjected to severe injury, were daunting and tedious. Finally, we have seen that women could be formidable physical opponents, both inside and outside of their homes. Operating within the patriarchal society of seventeenth-century Scotland, the kirk sessions' and burgh court's investigation and disciplining of physical assault uniquely disadvantaged women, and poor women most of all.

3

Disorderly, Deviant, Dangerous: Defining Words as Witchcraft in Early Modern Scottish Communities

Sierra Dye

On 3 January 1602, the Ayrshire kirk session of Dundonald called on Margaret Forgushill to give evidence against her neighbour Agnes Lyon, whom she had earlier accused of witchcraft. Specifically, the session sought the names of witnesses who could attest that Lyon 'spak thay wordis' Forgushill had previously reported to the minister.[1] When Forgushill could not name anyone who could corroborate her story, Lyon was summoned and swore 'vpon hir aith' that she had said no such words, whereupon the session found Forgushill to be a 'lyar vpon the said Agnes'. Meanwhile, the session turned its attention to Forgushill's own manner of speaking: in particular, the suspicious report that she had begged Katherine McTeir to heal her cow and restore its milk. After inquiry into 'quhat wer the wordis that [Forgushill] spake', she eventually confessed that she had 'askit hir kyis milk' from Katherine 'for Goddis saik'.

Asking a person for healing or action 'for God's sake' was a well-known anti-bewitchment charm, intended to force a suspected witch to withdraw or reverse a curse with the talismanic power of God's name. Even in 1602 it was referred to as 'the custome of auld' and was considered, at best, superstitious ignorance, and at worst, blasphemy and consulting with witches.[2] These words significantly alarmed the session elders, who asked why Forgushill had asked in such a manner, and who had taught her to do so. Further investigation proceeded with additional witnesses called, including McTeir herself. Katherine admitted that she 'spak with [Forgushill] and reprovit hir of hir wordies bot denyit ony forther', but eventually confessed that Margaret had indeed asked her for the cow's health while on her knees and that she herself responded by saying 'God send hir hir kyis milk'. Astounded at this admission, the session inquired why Katherine had allowed such a petition, let alone answered in such a fashion, which in effect 'wes the taking of wichrie vpon hir self'. McTeir answered she was 'bot ane pure bodie' and

---

[1] The specific words were not recorded. H. Paton (ed.), *The Session Book of Dundonald, 1602–1731* (Edinburgh, 1936), p. 1.

[2] *Ibid.*, pp. 2, 5, 6.

could therefore not come to complain to the session herself, but would accept whatever repentance the session asked of her.

Unfortunately for several of the parties involved, this inquiry into the 'words that were spoken' initiated a cascading investigation into suspected slander, witchcraft, and more, which continued to preoccupy the Dundonald session for the next three years. Witnesses were called from across the parish to share what they knew of McTeir and to provide evidence of her suspected witchcraft, as well as the names of other suspected charmers and witches. Much of the testimony involved community disputes and quarrels between Katherine and her neighbours, followed by misfortune, which over time developed into a reputation for witchcraft; as one neighbour put it, 'ane ill voice [...] went of hir in the cuntrie'. Again and again, McTeir's words were reported, repeated, and scrutinised as potential evidence of witchcraft, such as when she said to one apparently healthy woman that she 'wald noth leif long', and 'that it fell out sa'.[3] While not all the evidence against McTeir was verbal, the session's close attention to what words had been spoken, to whom, and why, as well as what happened as a result, is highly indicative of the heightened interest that officials had in these speech acts. But why were some words interpreted as witchcraft, while others were viewed as slander, scolding, or the 'passionate speiches' of 'irratate and cholerik' old women?[4] Why, for example, was Agnes Lyon – the first person in this case to be accused of witchcraft – found innocent of all charges, while Margaret Forgushill, her accuser, was found guilty of slander and superstition, and yet Katherine McTeir and others were exposed as alleged magical practitioners? As will be shown, this was largely a question of evidence, particularly evidence of efficacious speech acts. But the attention paid to words in this case, and many others, shows a deeper anxiety over disorderly and deviant speech in early modern Scottish society.

This chapter will take a closer look at the initial investigations conducted by kirk sessions and local courts in their quest to uncover witchcraft and other verbal crimes in sixteenth- and seventeenth-century Scotland. In particular, it will seek to trace the different interpretations of utterances as evidence of either magical power or slanderous defamation. Both were forms of dangerous speech that harmed their targets, whether through malicious or maleficent means, and thus represented a threat to their communities. Spoken words also formed the main body of evidence used to define and prosecute these speech crimes, leading to heightened surveillance and scrutiny of *all* kinds of speech acts, especially those made by women.[5] This chapter will therefore focus on the questions asked and evidence collected by local officials as they investigated suspected witches

---

[3] Ibid., p. 11.
[4] S. A. Gillon and J. I. Smith (eds), *Selected Justiciary Cases, 1624–1650* (3 vols, Edinburgh, 1953–74), vol. 1, pp. 99, 100–1.
[5] See S. Dye, 'To Converse with the Devil? Speech, Sexuality, and Witchcraft in Early Modern Scotland', *IRSS*, 37 (2012), 9–40.

and slanderers. In labelling certain utterances as disorderly, and others as 'devilish' witchcraft, local authorities made a clear statement to the community as to whose words were marginal and deviant and whose were spoken with godly authority and conviction.

Investigating Witchcraft in Early Modern Scotland

Kirk sessions were an important cog in the wheel of witchcraft prosecution.[6] While kirk sessions and presbyteries did not have the legal authority to prosecute witches themselves, they played a key role in initiating the trial process and providing evidence crucial for later prosecution and conviction.[7] Once suspicions had been raised, or allegations of witchcraft made by a community member, then the kirk session would investigate. They would usually begin by calling the suspected witch to appear before the session, sometimes repeatedly, to respond to the allegations made against them. Depending on the severity of the charges, or the fervour of the community, the accused might be detained and imprisoned for a more formal interrogation by local officials, but usually the early stages of questioning took place publicly during regular session meetings. At this time, the session would also call on witnesses to come forward and report anything they knew as to the doings or reputation of the accused.

Reputations were important in early modern Scotland, and being 'brutit' or reputed as a witch could sometimes be enough on its own for the Kirk to initiate proceedings, and could even be listed in the indictment as one of the charges. These reputations often developed over long periods of time and frequently featured repeated community conflicts – particularly verbal conflicts – where words spoken or muttered in anger were followed by misfortune. For example, in Aberdeen, Isobel Strauchein was so well-known for her flyting and threatening behaviour that the entire parish was aware of her, and many prominent people testified 'that thei never hard ony guid taill tauld upone hir, bot all ewill, and mony haid gottin harme be hir', particularly to those she 'promisit ane ewill turne'.[8]

To promise someone an 'ill turn' or cause them to 'rue' their actions was commonly considered evidence of a curse, powered by a witch's malefice. For example, in 1639, Adam Blackwood testified before the Kirkcaldy session that James Kodie had told him and several others that Janet Durie had promised

---

[6] Burgh courts also played a role in early investigations and could hold trials by commission. For example, see A. Kennedy, 'The Trial of Isobel Duff for Witchcraft in Inverness, 1662', *SHR*, 101:1 (2022), 109–22.

[7] On the process of witch-hunting, see for example C. Larner, *Enemies of God: The Witch-Hunt in Scotland* (Edinburgh, 1981, 2000); S. Macdonald, *The Witches of Fife: Witch-Hunting in a Scottish Shire, 1560–1710* (East Linton, 2002); B. Levack, *Witch-Hunting in Scotland: Law, Politics, and Religion* (London, 2008).

[8] *The Miscellany of the Spalding Club, Volume One* (Aberdeen, 1841), p. 177.

she would 'caus him to rew it' when he had 'stickit hir swyne [stabbed her pig]', after which Kodie had fallen ill and died.[9] In 1661, Magdalen Watsone testified that Margaret Murray had got into a heated debate with Watsone's husband while drinking, and that Murray had said 'she should make him repent of his speiches'; later that night, he 'became almost speechless' and then died twelve days later.[10] These kinds of promises and threats between neighbours were common occurrences in the daily quarrels of community life, particularly among women for whom verbal retaliation was sometimes the only viable option.[11] In fact, many accused witches had a history of trouble with the kirk session, having previously been punished for slander, defamation, or cursing, or having themselves pursued a slander case against another.[12] But when ill-tempered words were followed by disease or harm of unexplained origin, this could be considered evidence of devilish sorcery, particularly when numerous witnesses could vouch for the efficacy of these utterances.

Prophetic speaking, too, could be interpreted as efficacious speech acts that revealed the witch's deviant nature and unholy knowledge and power, such as in 1623 when Isabell Haldane was accused of having predicted the sickness and death of a woman with the words: 'Make you ready for death, for before Faste[rnis] Even you shall be taken away', and 'as the said Isabell spake, so it happened'.[13] Other accusations against Haldane included mumbled words, spoken charms, and making potions and drinks for healing. Such powerful charms and healing prayers were widely considered indicative of witchcraft in popular imagination. For example, Jonet Anderson was repeatedly admonished by Stirling kirk session for charming, but she was referred to the presbytery in 1621 when she admitted to charming Patrick Mungwall's wife's sark by putting 'hir handis on it' and saying the following words: 'Three bitter thingis hes yow bittin, ill hairt, ill ee, ill toung all meast; uther three, may the beit, the Father, the Sone, and Holy Ghost'.[14] The presbytery expressed keen interest in these utterances and questioned her repeatedly over several days as to whether she 'usis ony uther wordis in hir charmis' and 'what she meinit be thais wordis' and others.[15] Further evidence was sought that attested to the efficacy of her charms, as well as her knowledge of the future, and many witnesses were asked to repeat any words they had heard spoken. Only on having it 'avowit in hir faice' did

[9] NRS, CH2/224/1, Presbytery of Kirkcaldy, 1630–53, p. 256.

[10] NRS, CH2/145/7, Elgin, St Giles Kirk Session, 1648–75, p. 259.

[11] L. Martin, 'The Devil and the Domestic: Witchcraft, Quarrels and Women's Work in Scotland', in J. Goodare (ed.), *The Scottish Witch-Hunt in Context* (Manchester, 2002), pp. 73–89; J. Goodare, 'Women and the Witch Hunt in Scotland', *Social History*, 23:3 (1998), 288–308; Dye, 'Converse with the Devil'.

[12] A. Cordey, 'Reputation and Witch-Hunting in Dalkeith', in J. Goodare (ed.), *Scottish Witches and Witch-Hunters* (London, 2013), pp. 103–20, at p. 104.

[13] J. Stuart (ed.), *Extracts from the Presbytery Book of Strathbogie, 1631–1654* (Aberdeen, 1843), p. xi.

[14] *RPCS, 2nd Series*, vol. 8, p. 345.

[15] *Ibid.*, pp. 346–7.

Anderson confess to various additional charms 'be saying of thir wordis'. The efforts of the presbytery to discover the words that were spoken clearly indicate just how important such utterances were in proving and prosecuting witchcraft.

The evidence-gathering stage in witchcraft prosecutions therefore focused heavily on harmful or healing speech, especially in cases where the most sought-after form of evidence – a confession to paction with the devil – was absent. In part, this was about conforming to local ideas as to how a witch should behave, but the association between words and witchcraft was not limited to popular belief; it also appeared in judicial definitions of witchcraft, where efficacious speech acts could be considered evidence of 'tacit paction' with the devil. In speaking any words with an intent to do harm, or heal, or in any way alter God's predestined plan, the witch had by implication agreed to serve the devil.[16] Proving such words had been spoken, and that an effect had followed, was thus key to the successful prosecution and conviction of witches, and much of the effort of kirk sessions and burgh courts focused on gathering just such verbal evidence of efficacious speech. This hyper-focus on the words spoken had significant impacts on the community, but also reflected a wider concern with monitoring early modern speech in Scotland.

Defiant and Disorderly Words: Defamation, Slander, Scolding

While words were certainly critical to the prosecution of witchcraft, not all deviant speaking was determined to be *maleficium* by the courts and kirk sessions. Some remarks were found to be merely insulting or defamatory; others were disorderly and disruptive to the peace of their communities. It is worth exploring, then, how these other verbal sins and crimes were proven and punished by Scottish kirk sessions and burgh courts. The following analysis reveals a shifting and sometimes porous boundary between slander and sorcery, shedding further light on early modern perceptions and preoccupation with speech.

Words of all kinds were of particular interest to kirk sessions. Certainly, monitoring and punishing illicit or injurious speech was a major part of the Church's crusade of public discipline and keeping of a godly society. Blasphemy, slander, scolding, defamation, flyting, banning, and swearing were all disciplined by the Kirk, although at times the lines of jurisdiction blurred, with burgh courts also being involved in punishing public offences.[17] The lines between the crimes themselves were also sometimes unclear; as Elizabeth Ewan notes, in late medieval Scotland, 'Scottish secular authorities

---

[16] Sir George Mackenzie, 'A Treatise on Witchcraft' (1678), reprinted in A. Gardner, *A History of the Witches of Renfrewshire* (Paisley, 1877), p. 16.

[17] E. Ewan, '"Divers Injurious Words": Defamation and Gender in Late Medieval Scotland', in R. A. McDonald (ed.), *History, Literature and Music in Medieval Scotland* (Toronto, 2002), pp. 163–86, at p. 165. See also J. R. D. Falconer, *Crime and Community in Reformation Scotland: Negotiating Power in a Burgh Society* (London, 2013).

made no firm distinction between the offences of scolding and defamation/ slander', while 'strublance' – a disturbance of the peace – seemed to walk the line between verbal and physical violence.[18] In the post-Reformation period, 'sclander' referred to both slander and scandal, and in both cases, the meaning seems to be harm done by words, rumour, or report. Usually, this harm was done to one's reputation, which represented a significant threat to the social order. Rumour and public insult both had the potential to undermine authority by attacking the integrity of the individual within the community.[19] For example, 'thief' was a common insult applied to both men and women that implied dishonour and dishonesty, while women's sexual reputations were often attacked with the common insult 'whore'; as Ewan puts it, 'in a society in which so many transactions were made on credit, public reputation was critically important to livelihood. If one's honesty, sexual or otherwise, was publicly called into question, credit might become difficult or impossible to obtain'.[20]

Slander and defamation were thus taken very seriously by both ecclesiastical and secular authorities. In 1587, for example, the Elgin kirk session passed a 'General Act anent sclander', setting out that a first offence was punishable by sitting on the stool of repentance with a paper on one's head, followed by begging forgiveness from both the offended party and the congregation. A second offence was to be met by a requirement to stand in the jougs (an iron collar fixed to a wall) on Sunday before noon, after which the offender would be banished. This act was immediately put into effect against Meddie Innes for her manifest slander upon Margaret Russell; nothing daunted, Innes continued her slandering and was punished again the following year, being admonished to 'kepe hir tounge clos from bakbytting, slanderinge and flytting aganis ony w[ith]in this toun'.[21] The session revisited the act and passed new ones against disruptive speech, such as on 17 May 1592, when they recorded the general act against 'filthie langage', and on 17 February 1598, when the session ordained that all elders of the burgh should carry a purse with a 'brazen mowthe' to collect penalties from those who banned [cursed] and blasphemed God's name.[22]

---

[18] Ewan, '"Diverse Injurious Words"', pp. 164, 178. E. Ewan, 'Impatient Griseldas: Women and the Perpetration of Violence', *Florilegium*, 28 (2011), 149–68, at p. 153.

[19] See for example, L. Gowing, *Domestic Dangers: Women, Words, and Sex in Early Modern London* (Oxford, 1996); S. Bardsley, *Venomous Tongues: Speech and Gender in Late Medieval England* (Philadelphia, 2006); T. Fenster and D. L. Small (eds), *Fama: The Politics of Talk and Reputation in Medieval Europe* (Ithaca, 2003); G. Walker, *Crime, Gender, and Social Order in Early Modern England* (Cambridge, 2003); C. Boswell, 'Divisive Speech in Divided Times? Women and the Politics of Slander, Sedition, and Informing during the English Revolution', in M. Weisner-Hanks (ed.), *Challenging Women's Agency in Early Modernity* (Amsterdam, 2016), pp. 119–40.

[20] Ewan, '"Diverse Injurious Words"', p. 172.

[21] *Elgin Rec.*, vol. 2, pp. 7–8.

[22] *Ibid.*, pp. 23, 63.

Indeed, kirk session records are littered with cases of slander, flyting, and swearing, which seem to have occupied a good portion of the elders' time and concern. In 1562 in Aberdeen, the elders ordered 'all common skolds, flyters, and bardis to be baneist the toun and nocht sufferit to remaine thairin, for na request'.[23] In Perth in 1581, it was ordained that 'every flyter convicted of flyting, shall pay half a mark to the poor, stand upon the Cross Head, and make public repentance for satisfaction of the kirk and party', while in 1617, 'an chair of stone' was ordered to be built 'for setting of flyters and slanderers therein'.[24] In 1622, Violet Gardner was charged with scolding in the church and 'profaning the Lord's Sanctuary in flyting with Janet White immediately after their private prayers'; she answered that the reason was that Janet had 'abused her with vile words'.[25] In 1631, Gilbert Henderson was convicted of calling the Perth session 'false lownes, false knaves, a turd for you all'. He was ordered to pay a fine of £100 to repair the vaults of the kirk, and to declare repentance on his knees.[26]

Publicly asking forgiveness of the offended party and the congregation was a typical punishment meant to restore the defamed person's reputation and reinstate the disobedient speaker in the community, but also to serve as an example, such as when Robert Acheson was ordered to ask forgiveness for his slander as 'an exempill to utheris'.[27] Often this apology was performed in front of the congregation, on one's knees, a practice common in both pre- and post-Reformation churches.[28] The public and performative nature of the repentance and forgiveness ceremony was meant to re-establish harmony and social order following the harm and disruption caused by the words spoken.[29] In some cases, the offender was also required to declare 'foul tongue, thou lied' as part of the ritual 'unsaying,' sometimes while also grasping the offending organ.[30] In 1571 in Inverness, Thomas Symsoun and his wife, Katte Hendrie, were both punished for physically and verbally attacking the bailie with many 'injurious words'.[31] Hendrie called the bailie a 'false commong auld theiff', while Symsoun's words were so foul the scribe refused to record them in detail. Thomas was ordered to be imprisoned and to attend the kirk session

---

[23] J. Stuart (ed.), *Selections from the Records of the Kirk Session, Presbytery, and Synod of Aberdeen* (Aberdeen, 1846), p. 9.

[24] *The Chronicle of Perth: A Register of Remarkable Occurrences Chiefly Connected to that City, From the Year 1210 to 1668* (Edinburgh, 1831), pp. 53, 76.

[25] J. Maidment (ed.), *The Spottiswoode Miscellany: A Collection of Original Papers and Tracts, Illustrative Chiefly of the Civil and Ecclesiastical History of Scotland, Vol. 2* (Edinburgh, 1845), p. 301.

[26] *Chronicle of Perth*, p. 96.

[27] G. Donaldson (ed.), *The Court Book of Shetland, 1602–1604* (Edinburgh, 1954), p. 3.

[28] Ewan, '"Diverse Injurious Words"', pp. 173–4. M. Todd, *The Culture of Protestantism in Early Modern Scotland* (New Haven and London, 2002), p. 157.

[29] *Ibid.*, pp. 156–7.

[30] E. Ewan, '"Tongue You Lied": The Role of the Tongue in Rituals of Public Penance in Late Medieval Scotland', in E. D. Craun (ed.), *The Hands of the Tongue: Essays on Deviant Speech* (Kalamazoo, 2007), pp. 115–36, at p. 116.

[31] *Inverness Rec.*, vol. 1, pp. 207–9.

and take his tongue in his hand and say 'toung you lied', while his wife was sentenced to be taken to the market cross and have the 'branks' – a form of iron muzzle – put upon her head.

The branks were another example of performative punishment for verbal disorder and disobedience. Appearing as early as 1546 in Scotland, they functioned as symbolic 'bridles' for deviant speakers, both male and female (but mostly female).[32] The branks were generally reserved for cases of slander and defamation, such as in 1570 when Christine Beowis was punished for 'wrangus rabutting sclandering and defamyng' of Jasper Dempster's wife, and was ordered to sit in the parish church with the branks on her head during the time of preaching before the whole congregation.[33] They could, however, also be used for punishment of other crimes, including sexual ones, but again these were mostly reserved for female transgressors. In Strathbogie in 1646, for example, a brother and sister confessed to incest and the brother was ordered to provide financial reparations and make repentance in sackcloth, while his sister was ordered 'to satisfie in brankis and joggs to the contentment of the parochin'.[34]

Interestingly, John Harrison has found that, in Stirling, women who were branked were often accused of the same kinds of curses and ill-wishes that witches were accused of; the main differentiating feature was the outcome. When no misfortune followed a curse, then the words were seen as simply malicious rather than malefice – yet such disorderly and disobedient words still required punishment and were targeted for control.[35] This certainly seems to be true in investigations of illicit speech elsewhere. For example, in Shetland in 1603, Maidlaine Williamsdochter was punished for saying to Gilbert Thomsone 'that the haile thing that he did and luikit on wald never thryfe'. Although the format of this statement is very similar to curses found in many witchcraft cases, the utterance here was instead adjudged to be slander. She was fined three merks to be paid to the king and three to Gilbert, whereas he was fined one merk for striking her in retaliation.[36] In 1597 in Elgin, Andro Dick was accused of having 'sclanderit [Robert Malleis] *with* witchcraft', a phrasing that clearly equated the two crimes. Dick confessed he had prayed his malice at Malleis for buying a cow that he himself had hoped to purchase, and 'for the speking of quhilk the eldaris juges him in the wrang'.[37] He was therefore ordered to ask for Malleis' mercy and promise never to do so again under pain of public repentance.

---

[32] D. M. Walker, A *Legal History of Scotland, volume* 3 (Edinburgh, 1995), p. 339; J. Harrison, 'Women and the Branks in Stirling', *Scottish Economic and Social History*, 18 (1998): 114–31; Ewan, '"Diverse Injurious Words"', at pp. 175–6.

[33] *Inverness Rec.*, vol. 1, p. 193.

[34] Stuart, *Presbytery Book of Strathbogie*, p. 64. For more on the relationship between women's sexual and verbal disobedience, see Dye, 'Converse with the Devil'.

[35] Harrison, 'Women and the Branks', p. 126.

[36] Donaldson, *Court Book of Shetland*, p. 103.

[37] *Elgin Rec.*, vol. 2, p. 56. Emphasis added.

Here we can clearly see the equivalence between slander and witchcraft – both were speech crimes that did harm to their victims, either through attacking reputation or by magical means. In this case, we can presume that no actual ill luck followed Andro Dick's prayer of malice, otherwise the case could easily have progressed further. Without evidence of a supernatural effect, the words could not be proven as witchcraft, but they could still be punished as slander since they had broken the bounds of godly conversation and acceptable speech, but more importantly due to their perceived intent to do harm.

Speech as Evidence: Finding Witnesses for Words

In cases of speech crime, it was critical to find 'honest' witnesses to attest that they had heard the words – whether disorderly or diabolical – uttered. In July 1602 in Shetland, Jhone Strand was accused of slander and evil speech, specifically for slandering the folk of the entire parish, saying 'that thair wes nocht ane honest man within the haill parochin except thrie'.[38] Evidence was given by four 'honest' witnesses who deponed 'all in ane voice that they hard the wordis spokin'; Strand was therefore fined three merks for every honest house and person slandered in the parish, a substantial sum. In 1605, the widow Margaret Robinson accused Katherine Kanyeaucht of slandering her as a witch, saying that Katherine had 'uncharitably' with a 'malicious mynd' complained before 'sundry honest nichtbouris' that Robinson had bewitched her and her house. Brought before the Aberdeen session, Kanyeaucht denied she had spoken such slanderous phrases, but several witnesses were brought forward to testify in her presence that 'they hard hir speik and affirme the wordis foresaidis', which Kanyeaucht could no longer deny. She was not only convicted of the slander, but was further censured for being 'a common sklanderer of hir nichtbouris and a common banner and swearer, blaspheming the name of God'.[39]

Defamatory and disruptive speech acts could draw the attention and ire of the kirk session, but could also be considered evidence of witchcraft, if there were enough witnesses. Margaret Watson, for example, was brought before the session of Sandness in 1708 for her 'continual cursing and imprecations', which led to her being accused of witchcraft.[40] When asked if she was a witch, she answered 'how could she be a witch and not know of it', but the session continued its investigation, calling witnesses and the heads of families who deponed that 'she was a great Cursor'. In the trial of Marion Inglis, a neighbour testified the suspected witch was known as a 'dubyous banning flytting woman', with others likewise testifying she was known to be

---

[38] Donaldson, *Court Book of Shetland*, p. 3.
[39] Stuart, *Synod of Aberdeen*, pp. 48–9.
[40] NRS, CH2/1071/1, Presbytery of Shetland/Presbytery of Lerwick, 1700–2016, p. 155.

prone to banning.[41] While slander, flyting, and banning were all much lesser crimes compared to witchcraft, it is clear that these kinds of disruptive and disorderly words were potentially relevant points of evidence for witchcraft prosecution, and thus remained of interest to the session.

Regularly slandering one's neighbours not only carried the risk of punishment, but could lead to further inquiries into other, more dangerous forms of speech. In 1623, the quarrelling and flyting between William Cock and his wife, Alison Dick, and their neighbours at length became so clamorous that the burgh court in Kirkcaldy was obliged to step in and require the contentious couple to promise:

> not to live sic a vitious and licencious lyff, be cursing, swearing, and abusing of the nychtboris of this burgh, in sic sort as they have done heirtofeir. Quhilk, if they doe, they bind and obleis them to be content to be banisht this burgh and liberties thairof, and iff ever thairafter they be fund to resort within the same, they are content to be scourgit throu the towne and banisht.[42]

Perhaps unsurprisingly, the loud arguments and numerous disputes of the couple led to their eventual trial and execution for witchcraft. Indeed, many of the key points of evidence brought against them involved curses and prophetic speeches uttered during their many public fights with each other and the community. For example, when Robert Whyte struck William Cock during a disagreement, Alison Dick allegedly told him 'Wherefoir have yee striken my husband I sall caus yow rew yat'; in response, Whyte said 'I sall give yow als much, away witch', to which Dick replied 'witches tak ye witt and the grace from yea'. That same night, Whyte became 'bereft of all his witts', which was affirmed to be true by a neighbour and Robert's daughter, Jonet, 'upon hir oath.' Jonet Whyte added she had later gone to Dick and reproved her and lay 'the wytt of hir father's sickness upo[n] hir'; Dick, seeing an opportunity, said 'lett him pay me then, & he wilbe ye better and if he pay me not he wilbe ye wors, for thair is none that does me wrong bot I goe to my god and pleans [u]pn them and within four and tuentie hours I will gett amends of them'. Added after this in a darker hand is 'quhilk she ansred upon hir oath', signifying the importance of this testimony as well as of the oath as evidence.[43]

Such inclusions and marginalia highlighting 'oaths' and even 'great oaths' appear at several points in this case. While oaths were judicially important in trials and investigations of all kinds, they are particularly notable in witchcraft cases where witnessed words were so fundamental to the case. Evidence given

---

[41] NRS, CH2/124/1, Corstorphine Kirk Session, 1646–85, pp. 40–2.

[42] L. MacBean, *The Kirkcaldy Burgh Records, with Annals of Kirkcaldy, The Town's Charter, Extracts from the Original Documents, and a Description of the Ancient Burgh* (Kirkcaldy, 1908), pp. 157–8.

[43] NRS, CH2/636/34, Old Kirkcaldy (St Bryce) Kirk Session, 1614–45, pp. 283–9.

against Isobell Ferguson in 1661 in Newbattle, for example, included several allegations of disputes and conflicts with her neighbours and even her own family.[44] Several witnesses testified 'upon their oath' to hearing words that later led to destruction, such as when Ferguson's daughter-in-law testified that she had said she would 'cause the Devill [to] put them assunder', and that their 'bairne would be poore before he was right'.[45] When questioned, Ferguson denied saying the words, but allowed it might have been the devil that put them asunder. In the face of such evidence, denial was insufficient; desperate to prove her innocence, she agreed to be tested by pricking and the notorious witch-finder John Kincaid was sent for.[46]

Proving a Negative: The Absence of Utterances

If evidence of words, particularly powerful words, was key to proving witchcraft, then what were the options for *disproving* it? In the central courts, advocates spent much of their time trying to show that either no words had been spoken, or that the words had had no supernatural effect, or that the effect did not match the words.[47] While these arguments were not always successful, the focus on powerful speech acts as potential evidence of witchcraft further illuminates how popular and judicial definitions agreed upon this common point. Ideally, however, it was in a person's best interest to avoid a formal trial altogether, so it is worth examining how people attempted to defend themselves in the early stages of investigation by showing they were *not*, in fact, a witch. But how did one prove a negative?

Taking an oath of innocence was one potential option here. This worked in the initial case discussed in this chapter, when Agnes Lyon swore 'vpon hir aith' that she had not spoken as Margaret Forgushill had reported. Since Forgushill could not provide further evidence beyond her own report, and considering that she herself was also under suspicion for superstitious behaviour, this may have been enough on its own to convince the session of Lyon's innocence. But the question of taking an oath from a suspected witch was one that troubled the authorities in general. This issue was brought up directly by the presbytery in Strathbogie on 25 September 1644:

> The said day, it vas enquyred by one of the brethren if it be lawfull, for alledgit sorcerie, to tak the suspect persons oath, quhilk vas alledgit to be

---

[44] NRS, CH2/276/4, Newbattle Kirk Session, 1653–73, pp. 49–51.

[45] *Ibid.*, p. 50.

[46] Ferguson later confessed to meeting the devil and the case was referred to the central courts. For more details, see NRS, JC26/27, High Court Processes, 1661, bundle 9.

[47] See S. Dye, '"Devilische Wordis": Speech as Evidence in Scotland's Witch Trials, 1563–1736' (Unpublished PhD thesis, University of Guelph, 2016), pp. 171–99.

the practise of some brethren vthin the province. The brethren thoght not such courses lawfull; referred the consideratioun heirof to the provinciall.[48]

As blasphemers and servants of Satan, the great deceiver himself, a suspected witch's word on its own could not be trusted. So additional evidence was sometimes needed to 'disprove' witchcraft.

Another option as a defence was to find witnesses who could attest to the good and 'honest' reputation of the accused. Honesty was a catch-all term to indicate not only honour and integrity in speech but in conduct and character as well. In 1589, the Perth session asked 'certain honest neighbours' whether or not it was true that Robert Watson's wife, Guddal, was a witch and what likelihood of evil they saw in her. Four men, 'being enquired severally as they would answer to God, what they kend', all agreed that she was 'but an honest poor woman, who wrought honestly for her living', without whose help her elderly husband would have been dead. Consequently, the session ordered that John Watson and his daughter Helen should both be punished for slandering her as a witch.[49]

Pursuing slander litigation against one's accuser was another option for defending oneself against suspicions of witchcraft. In 1604, Helen Gib filed a bill of slander against Helen Cassie, saying Cassie had 'maist schamefullie sclanderit' her upon the high street by calling her 'commoun witche', and alleging she had practised certain 'godles' charms. When questioned, Cassie denied calling Gib a witch, but 'openly affirmed, in presence of the whole session, that she spoke those words to the said Helen Gib', saying that a year earlier she had seen Gib take drops of water from the spout of the Nether Mylne, mix it with water from the kirkyard, and use it to cast a charm around her house while saying the words 'this is deid and quick tuyis or thryis'. When the session asked if she had any additional witnesses, Cassie answered she was the only one present as Gib's servant at the time. Since there were no other witnesses and Gib had already denied these events, Cassie was convicted 'of sclander vtterit and avowit be hir', for which the session ordered her to immediately beg forgiveness by sitting down upon her knees in the presence of the session and craving God's pardon 'for hir sclander forsaid vtterit be hir, and to crawe [Gib's] forgiwens in lykmanner for the same, and to grant scho knows nothing of hir bot that scho is ane honest woman', which she immediately satisfied. In doing so, Cassie made reparations by ritually and publicly restoring Gib's reputation as an 'honest woman'.[50]

---

[48] Stuart, *Presbytery of Strathbogie*, pp. 60–1.

[49] *Chronicle of Perth*, pp. 59–60.

[50] Stuart, *Synod of Aberdeen*, pp. 38–9. My thanks to Elizabeth Ewan for drawing my attention to this case. While Gib appears in the *Survey of Scottish Witchcraft* for a separate slander case in 1600, no formal accusation or trial for witchcraft is recorded: J. Goodare, L. Martin, J. Miller and L. Yeoman, *The Survey of Scottish Witchcraft*, https://witches. hca.ed.ac.uk/ [accessed 14 April 2024]; see also NRS, CH 2/146/1, Ellon Presbytery, 1597–1607, pp. 62–8.

Pursuing a slander case was therefore a viable avenue to restore one's reputation within the community, but this path carried its own dangers. After all, the kirk session was responsible for investigating both slander and witchcraft, and the charge of one sometimes led to an investigation for the other. For example, Christine Watson in 1622 in Falkirk attempted to protect herself by pursuing a bill of slander against John Dun, kirk officer, for allegedly spreading rumours that he had seen Watson cast some liquid into a vat of small drink while bidding the devil to go out altogether.[51] When the session questioned Dun, the officer at first defended his statements and offered additional details, but eventually admitted to lying about the events. He was punished for the lie and defamation by temporarily being relieved of his office, but unfortunately for Watson, the case sparked further enquiry into her actions and suspected witchcraft, leading to additional reports and witness statements against her. Several people, including Margaret Davidson, confessed to consulting with her as a witch by seeking their health from Watson 'for God's cause.' On being asked why she had done this, Davidson said that Watson had promised her 'a sarkful of sare bainis [shirt full of sore bones]', after which she had immediately become ill of 'ane great seikness'. Another witness, Janet Buchanan, deponed that she had sought her health from Watson when she fell ill after quarrelling with her over a debt; in response, Watson replied 'God send [her health] to her', and also prescribed a drink of hot wine and spices. Buchanan did not quite follow the advice, but instead drank a hot ale, after which she recovered.[52]

Both matters were put on hold for the next two months, but inquiries began again in January as the session sought more detail about the allegations. Watson attempted again to deflect attention back on her accusers, lodging bills of slander against both women. She particularly attacked Janet Buchanan's character and conversation, alleging 'the said Janet to be ane infamous, prophane, and ungodlie p'soune, quho hes bein brot up and hauntit among [associated with] witches as apeiris; as also that the said Margaret Davisoune was infamous and godles'. The case eventually ended up being passed through a series of courts until a large panel of witnesses all came forward to give collective testimony declaring 'all in ane voice that they knew nothing of [Christine Watson] bot honestie'. This overwhelming show of community support (ten witnesses are listed) was apparently enough to convince the session of Watson's innocence, and both Janet Buchanan and Margaret Davidson were punished as slanderers. As Buchanan had, by her own admission, sought to consult with Watson as a witch, she was also punished as a 'consultor of witches'. Since she presented no defence to the session, they ordered her to make repentance in sackcloth for the next six weeks, and on the last day to 'humblie confess and acknowledge hir filthie

---

[51] G. I. Murray, *Records of Falkirk Parish: A Review of the Kirk Session Records of Falkirk from 1617 to 1689, vol. I* (Falkirk, 1887), pp. 31–3.
[52] *Ibid.*, pp. 34–40.

and abominable falt, to the glorie of God and exempill of utheris to committ the lyk, and ther to confess and mak promeis of amendment of lyf'.[53]

Without the support of the community, Watson would likely have been formally charged and possibly executed for witchcraft. Her alleged threats certainly bore the hallmarks of magical malfeasance, but with enough witnesses prepared to attest to her honest reputation, she successfully avoided a trial. Others were not so lucky. In Brechin, Janet Couper came before the session in November 1649 to claim she had been 'scandalized' as a witch. Unfortunately for her, Scotland was in the midst of both civil war and a virulent witch-hunting frenzy, and the session chose instead to investigate Couper herself, calling ten witnesses who deponed that disputes with her had been followed by illness, miscarriage, or the spoiling of butter or ale; one woman even alleged she had seen Couper talking to a dog – taken to be Satan in disguise – on the bridge. The case quickly took on demonological characteristics when Couper was interrogated and confessed to meeting the devil and renouncing her baptism, as well as naming several other alleged witches in the community, who were likewise investigated and charged for witchcraft.[54]

In the same year, in Corstorphine, Beatrix Watson filed a complaint of slander against the schoolmaster, James Chalmer, for calling her a witch before the kirk session. However, once brought to the session's attention, the elders felt it necessary to conduct further inquiry into her reputation. They called for anyone with any knowledge of Watson's doings to come forward and testify against her, which several did. Many of the encounters described by the witnesses involved suspicious words and speech acts, including threats, prayers, or unintelligible mutterings. In one dispute, Watson allegedly said to the husband of a woman indebted to her 'if I gett not that silver from your good wyff [...] It shall be blak silver to hir'. The session inquired further into this, and 'being asked if she spake these wordis', Watson at first denied it, but upon being confronted by her accuser, she confessed to saying the words, but qualified that she had not done so out of malice. Another woman allegedly fell ill and lost her words and wits after flyting with Watson; when she was sent for to reverse the curse, Watson uttered 'some wordis' that were not overheard, but then she 'said thryce God send thee thy haill [...] and thy tongue both, for [...] I have bein praying all night for thee and I know thou will gaite thy haill'. After 'the speaking of these wordis', there was a loud noise and a dark rat-like shape leaped out of the bed and the bedstead shook; when the woman later awoke, her speech and health were restored to her. In one of the final charges against Watson, it was alleged she had said to her husband one morning, 'lye still a whil with me for this will be the last fryday that ye will ryse from my syde', which was viewed as a prophecy of her own conviction. Upon 'being asked if that was true or not', she at first denied

---

[53] Ibid., p. 38.
[54] NRS, CH2/40/1, Presbytery of Brechin, 1639–61, pp. 159–61.

saying these words, but when she was told that 'hir husband had spoken it to Robert Scott his brother', she answered 'it is true I said it'. The session asked that she be held in prison until her further trial could be arranged, but once left alone in her cell she hanged herself, a sad confirmation of her earlier prediction.[55]

Conclusion

Clearly, witchcraft was linked with words in both popular imagination and judicial definitions. The questions asked by kirk sessions repeatedly focused on the words that were spoken, how they were spoken, and the effects that followed. When properly witnessed, these verbal acts formed a core of evidence that could be used to prosecute and convict the suspected witch. Many of these cases came to light as a result of verbal quarrels, slander, and defamation, and at times slander litigation could even be used – albeit not always successfully – to protect against charges of witchcraft. The fact that women had long been associated with unruly and uncontrolled speech meant that they were much more likely to come to the attention of the kirk and burgh officials for acts of disruptive speaking.[56] While women could and sometimes did engage in acts of physical violence,[57] engaging in verbal violence was more usual.[58] Using their words – to protect themselves, to exact revenge, or to gain resources – was an act of agency and a viable, if dangerous, strategy to navigate patriarchal society. In some cases, it is possible that women may even have embraced their reputations for witchcraft and powerful words, either through genuine belief or for practical reasons.[59] Regardless, the common association between disorderly words and women meant that most witches would be found in their midst.

Perhaps the larger point to be made here is what this correlation reveals about early modern Scottish society. Words, like deeds, were powerful and could be used for good as well as evil. In post-Reformation Scotland, the Kirk's desire to foster religious conformity and a godly society required close attention to people's utterances, punishing those which were defined as disobedient, disorderly, and even deviant. Significantly, the word 'devilish' was widely used to define all sorts of acts, utterances, and practices, including those associated with witches. Use of this term in commissions and indictments served consciously to evoke and imply the influence of the devil, even where there was

---

[55] NRS, CH2/124/1, pp. 31–3.
[56] Dye, 'Converse with the Devil'; Goodare, 'Women and the Witch-Hunt'.
[57] Ewan, 'Impatient Griseldas'; E. Ewan, 'Disorderly Damsels? Women and Interpersonal Violence in Pre-Reformation Scotland', *SHR*, 89:2 (2010), 153–71.
[58] Ewan, '"Diverse Injurious Words"'; Martin, 'The Devil and the Domestic'.
[59] See, for example, E. Wilby, *The Visions of Isobel Gowdie: Magic, Witchcraft, and Dark Shamanism in Seventeenth-Century Scotland* (Eastbourne, 2010).

no evidential proof of his participation.[60] Yet 'devilish' was also applied well beyond the bounds of witchcraft allegations, and in the end simply associated one's behaviour – verbal or otherwise – with sin, blasphemy, and immorality. It signified a threat, a harm, to the community, and thus could only be countered with 'godliness', conformity, and honest conversation.

[60] Dye, "'Devilische Wordis'", pp. 221–32.

4

'Believing na evill nor injury':
Space, Place, and Crime in
Sixteenth-Century Scottish Burghs

J. R. D. Falconer

On 1 August 1582, around 'five hours efter noone', Margaret Cryst, Jonet Porteous, and Elizabeth Crawford violently assaulted Margaret Leggat in 'hir own dwelling hous' in Canongate.[1] After entering Leggat's home, the trio 'cast her downe upoun the floore', punched and kicked her 'in the wambe', grabbed her by the arms, pulled off her curche (cap), and proceeded to strike her repeatedly with a set of iron tongs. Afterward, the group departed the house, taking with them the iron tongs and a piece of linen broadcloth. At first glance, the account suggests that this was a simple case of theft with violence. However, the entire encounter needs to be set within a broader, ongoing dispute. The court records go on to state that after leaving the house, Cryst 'came at the samyn tyme upoun' Alison Leggat, Margaret's sister, and Alison's husband, Robert Bond. She began to verbally assault the couple, calling Alison a 'comon theif, biche huir, and the said Robert a comoun theif'. Cryst added that 'the said Alesoun wold do with the said robert as she did with hir first guid man and that all the bairnis quhilkis she buir was neuer ane of thame his bot uther mens'. But this was not the end of the matter. Later that evening, Cryst went to 'the duelling house of Duncan Garlaw' where Alison and Robert were at their supper 'in maist quiet manner'. In front of Garlaw, Cryst repeated the 'former iniurious wordis'.

None of the accounts explicitly identify what motivated Cryst to commit these acts. Yet, through each action Cryst sought to disturb the Leggat/ Bond household and violate the safe confines of the family's lived space. Importantly, the records make clear that Margaret and Alison Leggat were not entirely scatheless in the matter. According to the next account in the court records, Margaret Leggat had gone to Cryst's house a few hours before the events already discussed. Leggat confronted Cryst in the adjoining 'clois' and 'cruelly' assaulted her 'on divers partis of hir bodie'. The indictment continues with allegations that Alison Leggat had also gone to the same close, and there struck Cryst on the head with a baton and, 'intending to

---

[1] The following two paragraphs are based on cases found in ECA, Canongate Burgh Court Books, 1569–1666, GB236/SL150/1/4, pp. 289–90.

have slane the said Margaret', punched and kicked her 'upon her wambe'. In her testimony, Cryst emphasised that she had been in a 'most peaceable and quiet manner doing her lawsome business within her clois lande believing na evill truble nor skayth of na manner' when both assaults took place. For their actions, the court convicted Margaret Cryst and Margaret Leggat and ordered them to make amends; the court found Alison innocent of all charges, and chose not to prosecute Porteous or Crawford, indicating that their involvement came at Cryst's 'spetial causing and comanding'.

Like most cases of interpersonal violence brought before Scottish burgh courts in the latter half of the sixteenth century, Margaret Cryst's case sheds light on how burgh residents managed ongoing disputes. It also highlights how the location and time of day at which petty criminal offences occurred could transform how individuals experienced urban places. Throughout this period, Scots frequently resorted to committing a variety of petty offences to right perceived wrongs, to restore order after conflict disrupted the peace, and to achieve justice that they believed the courts had failed to provide.[2] Their actions were rooted in the belief that unresolved conflicts, like most social ills, posed a significant threat to more than just the immediate victims; like a disease, they threatened the social body.[3] When left untreated, they could become a dangerous contagion that weakened the community's social bonds. From the perspective of magistrates, offenders who committed crimes to resolve ongoing disputes posed a threat to the social body regardless of the seriousness of the offence. Thus, when Thomas Straquhen assaulted John Hay on a Dundee street in 1558, the court clerk noted that such actions were 'in gret contemption of the acts and statuts of this burgh and ane evill example to utheris'.[4]

Fear of the threat that any unresolved conflict posed explains, at least in part, how making amends became deeply 'embedded in the fabric of Scottish justice'.[5] Order was achieved through a negotiation of social power between individuals or individual households, each seeking to balance out the challenges they faced daily.[6] This essay argues that across the spectrum of early modern burgh society, petty offences were a form of social exchange

---

[2]   See for example J. R. D. Falconer, *Crime and Community in Reformation Scotland: Negotiating Power in a Burgh Society* (London, 2012); E. Ewan, 'Scottish Portias: Women in the Courts in Mediaeval Scottish Towns', *Journal of the Canadian Historical Association*, 3:1 (1992), 27–43.

[3]   In 1593, Aberdeen's town council concluded that a large number of the burgh population were, 'by reason of some unlawful cause and odious crimes [...] very contagious enemies to the common weill of this burgh'. ACA, Council, Bailie and Guild Court Registers (CA) 1/1/30/16–17.

[4]   DCA, Burgh and Head Court Book, 1558–1561, 29/07/1558.

[5]   J. Wormald, 'Bloodfeud, Kindred and Government in Early Modern Scotland', *Past & Present*, 87 (1980), 54–97, at p. 54; Falconer, *Crime and Community*.

[6]   J. R. D. Falconer, '"Mony utheris divars odious crymes": Women, Petty Crime and Power in Later Sixteenth Century Aberdeen', *Crimes & Misdemeanours*, 4:1 (2010), 7–36; Falconer, *Crime and Community*.

with the power to shape social relations and influence how individuals experienced urban places. Central to this form of social exchange was the fact that most offenders wanted an audience for their crime or at the very least were unconcerned about whether their actions remained concealed or hidden from view. Thus, as part of the process of re-setting social relations, most petty offences committed in Scottish burghs during this period took place out in the open or during a time of day when others were close by to witness or hear the exchange. In exploring these dynamics, the chapter will also complicate the link between 'deviance' and 'marginality' established in the rest of this volume by demonstrating that transgressive behaviour was not necessarily an expression or consequence of social isolation. Deviance, instead, could be firmly rooted within the social mainstream.

Using Urban Space

To some extent, the built environment of early modern Scottish burghs helped to facilitate this form of social exchange.[7] Burgage plots were often separated by ditches, walls, or fences, marking some separate living space between neighbours. However, such barriers tended to be poorly constructed and offered only a thin veil of privacy.[8] Court records reveal that having relatively easy access to most places within a burgh made the negotiation of what constituted acceptable social exchange a crucial aspect of urban life. They also guide us to the fact that the built places and social boundaries found in Scottish urban centres were much more than a simple backdrop to daily life.[9] Importantly, these sources highlight the fact that urban life was about place – the built environment or landscape, local social systems, and

[7] For an excellent introduction to Scottish towns, see E. P. Dennison, *The Evolution of Scotland's Towns: Creation, Growth and Fragmentation* (Edinburgh, 2018).

[8] Inquiries into early modern concepts of 'private' and 'public' suggest that the contemporary meanings of these words were 'varied' and 'unstable' to the point of being entirely elusive. What can be discerned from contemporary perspectives on private and public space is a contrast between the former as 'secretive and hidden' and the latter as 'shared and visible'. E. Longfellow, 'Public, Private, and the Household in Early Seventeenth-century England', *Journal of British Studies*, 45:2 (2006), 313–341, 314; See also L. Gowing, '"The Freedom of the Streets": Women and Social Space, 1560–1640', in P. Griffiths and M. Jenner (eds), *Londinopolis: A Social and Cultural History of Early Modern London, 1500–1750* (Manchester, 2000), pp. 130–51; J. Nugent, '"None Must Meddle Betueene Man and Wife": Assessing Family and the Fluidity of Public and Private in Early Modern Scotland', *Journal of Family History*, 35:3 (2010), 219–31.

[9] A. White, 'The Impact of the Reformation on a Burgh Community: The Case of Aberdeen', in M. Lynch (ed.) *The Early Modern Town in Scotland* (London, 1987), pp. 81–101; E. P. Dennison, A. Simpson and G. Simpson, 'The Growth of Two Towns', in E. P. Dennison, D. Ditchburn and M. Lynch (eds), *Aberdeen Before 1800* (East Linton, 2000), pp. 13–43; L. Stewart, *Urban Politics and The British Civil Wars* (Leiden, 2005); E. P. Dennison and M. Lynch, 'Crown, Capital, and Metropolis Edinburgh and Canongate: The Rise of a Capital and an Urban Court', *Journal of Urban History*, 32:1 (2005), 22–43.

the framework of social relations.[10] It was also about space, or a 'practiced place', where the actions of urban social actors transformed the built environment through their everyday use.[11] As some have suggested, 'space was the medium through which society was produced'.[12]

Burgh court records make clear that inhabitants had a keen awareness of their burgh's built environment and of the expected use of public or private urban spaces. Individuals navigated burgh streets, markets, taverns, closes, and shops; they met with their neighbours, discussed trade, conducted business, and witnessed and participated in a variety of social exchanges – all within a context framed by written regulations and customary rules. While intended to help maintain order and stability, such regulations were rooted in gendered notions of the appropriate behaviour that defined the proper 'use' of shared and individual spaces.[13] Crucially, these social practices produced 'space' and contributed to how individuals experienced urban life. Moreover, an internalised sense of these rules influenced the specific actions of perpetrators of interpersonal violence, theft, or acts of vandalism and how their victims responded to these acts. Victim testimonies highlight the physical and emotional harm suffered as a result of petty crimes. They also provide insight into the sites where individuals chose to commit their criminal activities and how perpetrators and victims experienced such places before, during, and, sometimes, after the crimes.

Occasionally, victim testimonies convey contemporary expectations of the proper use of urban space. Having suffered a violent attack, theft, or destruction of their property, victims understood the offence as a violation of what should have otherwise been a regulated, safe space. In many instances, the act of offending was predicated on such an awareness. Feelings of fear and apprehension, safety and assuredness, often informed by power and gender relations, imposed meaning on the urban landscape. Even when the court records fail to capture how individuals felt in particular locations within a burgh, it is clear that gender undoubtedly informed the 'symbolic connotations of space'.[14] There was also an element of negotiation at play. In cases where an ongoing dispute resulted in some form of interpersonal

---

[10] P. Withington, *The Politics of Commonwealth: Citizens and Freemen in Early Modern England* (Cambridge, 2005), p. 88.

[11] M. De Certeau, *The Practice of Everyday Life*, trans. S. Rendall (Berkeley and Los Angeles, 1998), p. 117.

[12] A. Flather, *Gender and Space in Early Modern England* (Woodbridge, 2007), p. 2; Certeau, *The Practice of Everyday Life*; H. Lefebvre and C. Levich, 'The Everyday and Everydayness', *Yale French Studies*, 73 (1987), 7–11.

[13] R. Houston, 'People, Space, and Law in Late Medieval and Early Modern Britain and Ireland', *Past & Present*, 230:1 (2016), 47–89, at p. 86; Gowing, '"The freedom of the streets"', at p. 132; G. Walker and J. Kermode, 'Introduction', in J. Kermode and G. Walker (eds), *Women, Crime and the Courts in Early Modern England* (Chapel Hill, 1994), p. 4.

[14] R. Pain, 'Crime, Social Control, and Spatial Constraint: A Study of Women's Fear of Sexual Violence' (Unpublished PhD thesis, University of Edinburgh, 1994), p. 417.

violence, the perpetrator's actions, despite being 'in contemption of the acts and statutes' of the burgh, were often motivated by an interest in maintaining or restoring, rather than undermining, order and stability to their lives. More importantly, these cases highlight that such crimes were committed not solely by marginal groups but by a cross-section of burgh inhabitants.

Although recent histories of crime place criminals in well-defined locations inhabited by marginal groups, a close examination of Scottish burgh court records for this period reveals that the individuals most likely to commit interpersonal violence, theft, vandalic crime, or statutory offences did not live a static existence on the margins; in terms of lifestyle, these were not individuals who only on occasion 'moved, worked, and lived in proper citizens' space'.[15] Most individuals convicted of committing petty offences in Scottish burghs were not career criminals. Their experience reflects Paul Griffiths' warning that "criminalities' are moral titles and any person might one day step outside the law'.[16] More importantly, cases found in the burgh court records show that social boundaries were at times quite permeable, that committing an offence did not immediately make an individual a criminal or exclude them (permanently) from belonging.[17] By most accounts, the act of making amends (either through the courts or through a coerced, extra-legal action) was meant to restore a wrongdoer to their place in burgh society. Court-imposed acts of making amends most often took the form of fines, donations, and public acts of repentance. Banishment from the burgh, either temporarily or permanently, was the harshest punishment magistrates could use to deal with petty offenders in early modern Scottish burghs.[18] This was often imposed as a last resort and was an indication that the courts and their officers saw no other remedy for the victim or one that would restore the offender or the town to proper order. Thus, in November 1561, Robert Jak, an Aberdonian tailor, was brought before the burgh court, labelled a 'common brigand' and 'nightwalker', and charged with robbing various persons within the burgh. For his crimes, the court banished Jak from the burgh permanently.[19]

---

[15] P. Burke, *The Historical Anthropology of Early Modern Italy* (Cambridge, 1987), pp. 3–7; P. Griffiths, 'Overlapping Circles: Imagining Criminal Communities in London, 1545–1645', in A. Shepard and P. Withington (eds), *Communities in Early Modern England: Networks, Place, and Rhetoric* (Manchester, 2000), pp. 115–33, at p. 129.

[16] *Ibid.*

[17] For a discussion of this, see Falconer, *Crime and Community*; C. Herrup, 'Law and Morality in Seventeenth-century England', *Past & Present*, 106 (1985), 102–23.

[18] On banishment as a punishment, see Falconer, *Crime and Community*, 35–43; E. Ewan, 'Crossing Borders and Boundaries: The Use of Banishment in Sixteenth-Century Scottish Towns', in S. Butler and K. J. Kesselring (eds), *Crossing Borders: Boundaries and Margins in Medieval and Early Modern Britain: Essays in Honour of Cynthia J. Neville* (Leiden, 2018), pp. 237–57.

[19] ACA, CA/1/1/24/300.

Sensing Space

Scholars should be cautious when analysing the language used in burgh court records. Often, it is difficult to know with certainty whether descriptions of the offences, motives, consequences, or impact originated with the court clerk who documented the events or with the individuals more directly involved. Regardless, the words and phrases convey a contemporary sentiment about how crime could alter an individual's sense of space. When William Cullen, a Canongate tailor, 'invaded' his neighbour John Kirkwood's 'dwelling house and buith' in the middle of the afternoon and struck Kirkwood's son on the forehead with a small sword, his actions undermined the family's expected sense of security and imposed on the space a hostility not naturally existing there.[20] On 6 June 1575, the Aberdeen burgh court convicted two burgh officers, Alexander and Thomas Rolland, of striking a bellman while he was 'executing his office' and for 'manessing of Patrick Menzies bailie'.[21] The Rollands were obviously unimpressed by these Aberdonian officeholders and their actions while serving the burgh. Their frustration became even more apparent two weeks later when the court convicted Thomas Rolland for the 'violent occupatione of the townhouse'.[22] From the perspective of the assize that heard Rolland's case, he deliberately set out to disrupt the space the burgh magistrates occupied daily. The clerks in Canongate and Aberdeen saw in Cullen's and Rolland's actions an attempt to dominate violently spaces that should have been left undisturbed.

Conversely, when Isobel Pratt went to John Bolly's workbooth to pick up a set of tongs that he had promised to have ready for her, she believed the space to be safe. According to testimony Pratt provided to the court, she entered Bolly's booth 'in most quiet and sober manner', and, awaiting Bolly, she stood at the 'duir of the said John's booth seekand na manner of injuries nor manner of evil to have been done'. At this point, Bolly 'moved by ire and malice concealed in his heart put violent hands on Isobel and struck with his faldit neif [fist] to hir head'.[23] Whether the words used to describe this exchange belong to Pratt or the clerk documenting the encounter, they emphasise the fact that Pratt was meeting an expectation that 'good' women were to conduct their 'public' activities 'quietly and unobtrusively'. Bolly's actions, however, draw attention to the permeable boundaries between perceived public and private spheres.[24] The exchange between Pratt and Bolly may have resulted from a business transaction gone wrong. Regardless, it is likely

---

[20] ECA, GB236/SL150/1/3, p. 43.
[21] ACA, CA/5/1 Bailie Court Books, 1st Series (6 June 1575).
[22] ACA, CA/5/1 (17 June 1575).
[23] ECA, GB236/SL150/2, p. 518.
[24] E. Ewan, 'Crime of Culture? Women and Daily Life in Late-Medieval Scotland', in Y. G. Brown and R. Ferguson (eds) *Twisted Sisters: Women, Crime, and Deviance in Scotland since 1400* (East Linton, 2002), pp. 117–36, at pp. 117–18.

that Bolly's actions were reinforced by a sense of confidence he felt from being in 'his' workbooth, a familiar space shaped by his daily experiences. As Amanda Flather has demonstrated, 'spaces can be gendered, even when they are shared by men or women, through perception, experience and use'.[25] Regardless of what was behind the conflict, Bolly may have also sensed Pratt's vulnerability, being alone and within his space, and sought to exploit that for his own gain.[26] Having 'home' advantage could prove a favourable condition for such actions.

This was abundantly clear to two Canongate officers tasked by the bailies with distraining goods from John Morrison's dwelling house on account of Morrison's outstanding debts. Upon entering the home in February 1583, the officers were met by Morrison and his wife, who began hurling insults at them. When one of the officers tried to carry off a set of pewter plates, the pair tore them out of his hands and knocked the cap off his head, causing it to land in a fire. The officer, who had been simply following the bailies' orders, stooped down to retrieve his hat, burned his fingers in the process, and then suffered further indignity when the couple drove him from the house at sword point. Given the proximity of their neighbours and the lively street life, numerous witnesses likely observed Morrison and his wife's violent defence of their house against an unwelcome (albeit legitimate) invasion.[27] Through their use of verbal and physical violence, the pair sought to preserve the integrity and dignity of their dwelling place and their control over that space. The court's decision to convict Morrison and his wife only for failure to repay the debt, acquitting them of any wrongful behaviour against the officers, could be taken as an indication that the bailies recognised that the couple's sense of place warranted their spirited defence.[28] As John Carter Wood has argued, 'violence [could be] employed to define and defend space'.[29]

In the cases examined so far, the individuals involved expressed spatial awareness. Moreover, they (or the clerk documenting their case) conveyed clear expectations of how members of the burgh community ought to experience urban places. Isobel Pratt, Alison Leggat, and Margaret Cryst all emphasised their belief that while in their house or yard, or while they were conducting business, they should have encountered 'na manner of injuries' and 'na evill truble nor skayth'. They also reflected on the fact that

---

[25] A. Flather, 'Early Modern Gender and Space: A Methodological Framework', *La(s) casa(s) en la Edad Moderna* (2017), 23–44, at p. 29.

[26] See for example Koskella, 'Gendered Exclusions'; Flather, *Gender and Space*; Gowing, '"The freedom of the streets"'.

[27] R. Laitinen, 'Nighttime Street Fighting and the Meaning of Place: A Homicide in a Seventeenth-century Swedish Provincial Town', *Journal of Urban History*, 33:4 (2007), 602–19, at p. 616; A. Korhonen, 'To See and to be Seen: Beauty in the Early Modern London Street', *Journal of Early Modern History*, 12:3–4 (2008), 335–60.

[28] ECA, GB236/SL150/1/5, p. 228.

[29] J. C. Wood, 'Locating Violence: The Spatial Production and Construction of Physical Aggression', in K. D. Watson (ed.), *Assaulting the Past: Violence and Civilization in Historical Context* (Newcastle, 2007), pp. 20–37, at pp. 22–3.

at the time they experienced a violent challenge from their neighbours, their minds were 'quiet and sober', and their own actions were 'lawsome' and 'peaceable'. Whether genuine or rhetorical, these sentiments reveal a contemporary set of beliefs. Crucially, a distinction emerges between how individuals experienced urban space as victims compared with how they experienced it as offenders. While the court clerks may have emphasised this distinction in their accounts, the specific nature of these offences suggest that the perpetrators purposely sought to equalise the relationship, restore a sense of security, or establish a sense of empowerment that had been previously compromised through an ongoing conflict.

A similar objective is apparent in the methods Andrew Low used to prosecute a dispute with Margaret Watson and her husband, Robert Stones. According to the testimony provided to the burgh court, Low, 'with malise and set purpois', chased Watson from her yard into her house, throwing stones at her back while calling her a common thief. Having followed Watson into the house, he began 'cast[ing] stones at the said Robert himself being sitting in tables with honest persons and molesting the said Robert and Margaret'. The assize also heard that one of Watson and Stones' neighbours, Margaret Henryson, had come to the door of the house, obviously curious about the commotion Low's intrusion caused. The clerk noted that Henryson, 'believing na evill nor injury as said', became Low's next victim when he 'cruelly' struck her on the mouth and nose with his 'faldit neifs'. Like so many of the cases heard in Scottish burgh courts during this period, this was not a simple case of one malcontent seeking to disrupt the peace, break the law, or violate his neighbours; the assize also heard that Stones and Watson had previously visited Low's house, assaulted his daughter Helen, and attacked Low by 'riving the hair out of his beard [...] besides [saying] divers injurious words and specially of the said Andrew that he is mensworne [perjured] theif and theif of his hands'.[30] By targeting Stones and Watson in their home, and with a greater audience present, Low defiled their lived space in a way comparable to what he had experienced in his own home when the couple assaulted him and his daughter. As was the case with Margaret Cryst and the Leggat family, Low's actions reflect an intent to restore and repair the damaged reputation and integrity of his household.

A dispute between Elizabeth Ferguson, Isobel Kinkaid, and their respective female servants resulted in several altercations across various Canongate locations, spanning twenty-two months from July 1573 to May 1675. Physical assaults took place at Ferguson's dwelling house, at the tavern run by Kinkaid's husband, William Carmichael, and at the house belonging to Ferguson's mother. Meanwhile, verbal violence occurred on the 'kingis calsay' and on the street outside the tavern. The testimonies provided describe the level of violence: fists and feet used to injure the body, insult and

---

[30] ECA, GB236/SL 150/1/4, p. 102.

accusation to bruise the reputation of each of the women involved, as well as the proprietor of the tavern. But this exchange also had the potential to harm more than just those immediately involved. Following the physical assault on Ferguson and her servant at Ferguson's home, the pair followed Kinkaid and her servant onto the bustling streets of Canongate. They declared that Kinkaid was a 'comon bordallar [keeper of brothels] sayand that she kept ane bordall [brothel]'.[31]

Impugning the respectability of the family's tavern was an effective way for Ferguson to attempt a rebalancing of the power dynamic that emerged from the assault she experienced outside her house.[32] Not only did her words have the power to diminish Kinkaid's household's ability to earn an income, but they also stained the establishment and any burgh inhabitant who chose to spend time in that space. Each site where violence erupted between the foursome was 'public' in the sense that others – Ferguson's immediate neighbours, the burgh's community members, and the tavern's patrons – held expectations of each space. In addition, this conflict did not play out in secret, veiled, or isolated locations that would obscure the violence from eyewitnesses. This was partly because these types of activities were part of daily life in the burgh; they were a form of social exchange that shaped and reshaped a burgh community's physical and social boundaries.

Assaults, thefts, and destructive behaviour could also have a more apparent corruptive impact on urban space. In 1574, using the 'depositione of famous witnesses', the Aberdeen burgh court convicted John Sanders of wilful disobedience and for disturbing the town by climbing up the north side of the tolbooth and 'brakin the top of the knok'.[33] Two decades earlier, David Spanky had denigrated Dundee's court by proclaiming publicly that 'yare wes na justice [to be found] in the tolbouthe'.[34] From Spanky's perspective, the people of Dundee could find no satisfaction in law at the central site in the burgh where residents were expected to seek justice. In his mind, the magistrates' previous decisions and actions had undermined the integrity of the tolbooth. Clearly, the magistrates did not see it the same way. To restore their reputation and that of the tolbooth, the court ordered Spanky to make amends by donating to the almshouse and publicly seeking the bailies' forgiveness. In response, Spanky sought 'remedy of the law' alleging that there was 'grievous harm done to him' by the court. Even though both sides of this dispute had different notions of whose actions had caused harm to the reputation of the tolbooth, both sought justice that would repair that damage.

---

[31] ECA, GB236/SL 150/1/1, 408–9; ECA, GB236/SL 150/2/, 169.
[32] Elizabeth Ewan has argued that 'alehouses were often associated in the popular mind with dubious and criminal activities [...] Working in an alehouse was not necessarily a good road to social respectability'. Ewan, 'Crime or Culture', p. 124.
[33] ACA, CA/1/1/28/227.
[34] DCA, Burgh and Head Court Book, 1550–1554, 29/7/1551.

On occasion, an individual might also pretend to be unaware of the space they occupied or less bothered by the impact their actions had on a particular place. Andrew Spicer has shown that divine worship and holy services *made* a church 'sacred space'.[35] Churches could also be 'theatres of conflict'.[36] In 1583, Aberdeen burgh court declared that because Patrick Leslie and George Troup had assaulted each other in St Nicholas kirk, 'being the house and place dedicat to God', their actions made their 'cryme more odious and haynous'.[37] This was also the case on New Year's Day 1552, when a conflict between Alexander Ferguson and John Downe became violent within St Nicholas kirk. For instigating the fight and for 'strubling the gud town and kirk and stopping of godly service', the court required Ferguson to set things right.[38] He was to 'appear at the time of high mass with two pounds of wax in his hands and ask God and the town forgiveness of his offence [...] and gif he does siklik in tym to cum to be banist of the town'.[39] Obviously unsatisfied with how the court had attempted to settle the matter, John Downe and Alexander Johnson reciprocated two weeks later by attacking Ferguson in the kirk 'in tym of goddis seruice'. The court ordered Johnson to appear before the congregation at Candlemas and replicate the acts of repentance the court had previously ordered Ferguson to discharge.[40] If performing specific acts and functions made a space sacred, then the opposite may also be true. Any sacrilegious appropriation, violation, or desecration of sacred places disturbed that space, necessitating positive actions to restore its sanctity.

It is difficult to conclude definitively that burgh residents were more likely to commit petty offences in high-traffic areas of the burghs. Still, the high streets, markets, and even the kirk(yard)s were common sites of interpersonal assaults. Whether jostling in the populated areas of the burgh or seeking a larger audience to bear witness, using such space to resolve conflict and address wrongdoing through extra-legal means could provide a deterrent to further wrongdoing and establish a legacy. It also mirrored the legitimate processes of regulating the community. Burgh councils, elected annually, worked with the provost, bailies, and deans of guilds to create wide-ranging statutes that regulated life in the towns. Collectively, the magistracy also established the guidelines for punishing crime. Elizabeth Ewan has suggested that the public nature of publishing these guidelines – often by open proclamation at the market cross – paralleled how officials punished the offender: publicly and at

---

[35] The emphasis is mine. A. Spicer, '"What kind of house a kirk is": Conventicles, Consecrations and the Concept of Sacred Space in post-Reformation Scotland', W. Coster and A. Spicer (ed.), *Sacred Space in Early Modern Europe* (Cambridge, 2011), pp. 81–103, at pp. 90–1; See also M. Graham, 'Conflict and Sacred Space in Reformation-Era Scotland', *Albion*, 33:3 (2001), 371–87.

[36] S. Carroll, *Enmity and Violence in Early Modern Europe* (Cambridge, 2023), p. 406.

[37] ACA, CA/1/1/31/325.

[38] ACA, CA/1/1/21/288.

[39] *Ibid.*

[40] ACA, CA/1/1/21/302.

a site where magistrates could expect a larger audience.[41] Thus, the market cross or the kirk were frequent sites of public punishment. For example, Thomas Durrant, William Forest, and Besse Allan were each placed in the govis (stocks) in Aberdeen 'thair to stand with crown of paper on thair heids fra nyne houris to twelf and thereafter to be present to the mercat croce to stand publickly schewand the caus of thair demerits wherefor they war convikit'.[42]

On occasion, the courts could require offenders to return to their crime scene to make their amends. Their actions helped cleanse the space while also engaging those living close to that location to participate in an act of restoration. For example, in 1585 Anabell Chalmer returned to William Mackourtnay's dwelling house to make her court-mandated amends after she had previously visited the home and attacked William's wife and daughter.[43] While restoring peace and order was the intended objective of public punishments, it also left an impression on the audience and formed associations with the space. According to witness testimony, when David Low struck Marion Kyntor on Aberdeen's high street he was not content to rely solely on physical violence to overpower his victim; Low also attacked Kyntor's reputation by making the public claim that her deceased husband, James Ewyn, had been 'leid to the gallowis, his hands were bound behind his bak'.[44] For his offence, the bailies ordered Low to appear within the tolbooth, publicly revoke the words spoken against Kyntor and her husband, and ask the injured party's forgiveness.

Secrecy and Observation

The location and type of offence influenced how people perceived urban spaces, as did the timing of these crimes. Most of the previously examined cases highlight the willingness of individuals to commit offences during daylight hours. But there should be little doubt that offences committed after nightfall, described in the records as 'under the silence of night', could add a heightened sense of terror and vulnerability for victims.[45] If a victim was

---

[41]   E. Ewan, '"Tongue You Lied": The Role of the Tongue in Rituals of Public Penance in Late Medieval Scotland', in E. Craun, (ed.) *The Hands of the Tongue: Essays on Deviant Speech* (Kalamazoo, 2007), pp. 115–36.

[42]   ACA, CA/1/1/27/174.

[43]   ACA, CA/5/1 (18 Feb 1585).

[44]   ACA, CA/5/1 (10 May 1595).

[45]   For example, of the 1,861 cases prosecuted in Aberdeen's burgh court between 1540 and 1590, less than 1 per cent (seven) of those cases involved activities that took place at night. Of course, we must be mindful of the 'dark figure of unrecorded crime', those incidents of wrongdoing that were never prosecuted and thus left no record behind. We also have to consider uneven recording from burgh to burgh. Based on surviving records, there was only a single case in Dundee and ten cases in Canongate during this same period. Nonetheless, the records suggest that the majority of petty criminal activities took place during the day.

found in their bed or roused from their sleep, disoriented and off-guard, by a noisy intruder, the crime could have an impact not only on the individual but also on the space that had previously been a sanctuary for its occupant. As others have argued, it could at once allow for a respite from the day's labours while creating an opportunity for some to exploit the possibilities that darkness provides.[46] Ordinances passed throughout this period suggest that Scottish magistrates, at least, were most concerned with the possibility of the latter, with individuals behaving improperly on burgh streets and being out of doors after sundown.[47] In Edinburgh, for example, the town council ordered that no persons remain on the streets 'after the ringing of the ten-hour bell at night'.[48] Many of the accounts convey the typical perception held by the magistracy that those inclined towards disobedience and towards being outside their dwelling house after dark were drunk and idle persons, usually masterless or without connection to the burgh, who spent their time lurking in dark corners, 'persewit the nychtbouris and inhabitantis of this burgh, bot committit divers robreis and utheris villannyis, unworthy to be hard of in a weele governit citie'.[49]

In 1594, Aberdeen's bailie court convicted a local minister, Thomas Bissett, of using weapons prohibited by law and for attacking Andrew Gray and James Walker on the burgh's street 'under silence of the night'.[50] Like the vast majority of individuals brought before the burgh courts on account of wrongdoing, Bissett was not a career criminal, nor what contemporaries would have considered a ne'er-do-well. Driving home the point that individuals believed that the burgh ought to be quiet after sundown, a dittay against James Anderson and Andrew Hay alleges that the pair had gone to the dwelling house belonging to Walter Strange and 'his wyf' on 31 July 'under silence of nyt at 10 hours at evin *be way of oppression*'. According to testimony provided, the alleged victims described the horrific incident by reference to the fact that they were 'at thair dwelling house [and] wes in quiet and sober manner to have passit to yair beddis'.[51] The contrast is clear: the appropriate use of their living space was, in the minds of the victims, altered by the actions of the alleged intruders.[52] Contemporaries were undoubtedly

---

[46] B. D. Palmer, *Culture of Darkness: Night Travels in the Histories of Transgression* (New York, 2000), pp. 17–18; A. R. Ekirch, *At Day's Close: Night in Times Past* (New York, 2006); C. Koslofsky, 'Princes of Darkness: The Night at Court, 1650–1750', *The Journal of Modern History*, 79:2 (2007), 235–73.

[47] For an example of this type of ordinance passed in Aberdeen, see NRS, CH2/448/1, St. Nicholas Kirk Session, p. 7.

[48] *Ibid.*

[49] *RPCS, First Series*, Vol. 9, p. 133.

[50] ACA, CA/5/1 (7 March 1594/5).

[51] ECA, GB236/SL150/1/2, pp. 236–7.

[52] As David Postles has argued, 'to perpetuate an abuse in its space was to abuse the dignity of the town'. D. Postles, 'The Marketplace as Space in Early Modern England', *Social History*, 29:1 (2004), 41–58, at p. 42.

worried about the shroud of secrecy that nighttime created. There was a common perception in this period that nighttime offered more opportunities for criminal activity, akin to dark alleys harbouring criminals during the day. As Roger Ekirch has argued, 'night gave birth to the rule of law', preventing victims from protecting themselves from harm while limiting neighbours from coming to aid those in need.[53]

Yet, it was not always the case that nighttime aided the culprit by providing a greater shroud of secrecy for their illicit activities. After Walter Cassy attacked Marion Sherar in her own house 'vnder silence of nycht', the bailies noted that it was the testimony of 'divers famous witnesses' that contributed to Cassy's conviction for the crime.[54] One evening in March 1577, Isobel Balzart and her daughter Elizabeth Jameson attacked Balzart's sister-in-law, Alison Watson, in her dwelling house 'under silence of the night'. According to the clerk, Watson escaped 'certain death' only through the aid of 'God and her neighbours'.[55] Despite curfews and the fear of night, neighbours were often close enough at hand to intervene and prevent an assault from becoming deadly. With 'sett purpose and provocation' and 'in most detestable and shameful manner under silence of night', John Murray and Richard Brewer, two close friends from Leith, broke 'gods and our sovereign lords peace' on the night of 25 November 1583.[56] It is unclear what sparked this conflict; the two frequently drank together in each other's 'dwelling houses' and attended the kirk together on a regular basis. According to the bailies, Murray 'would have slane him in his own house if not Richard better defended and the supply of gud and godly neighbours'. Whatever caused the two men to come to blows, their actions undoubtedly disturbed their houses and the entire neighbourhood. This was no minor scuffle. The magistrates convicted Murray and Brewster of using weapons, drawing blood, smashing doors, stealing goods, mutilating fingers, and invading each other's houses. For their violent crimes, the court demanded that the two men repair the damage to their relationship and the damage caused to Murray's door. In response, both men made 'faith they feared dred bodily harm'. Despite the magistrates' best intentions to restore the peace between the two men, the activities of 25 November had left a lasting impression on the two families, the familiar places they frequented, and their neighbours.

If the availability of 'gud and godly neighbours' could help aid individuals like Alison Watson and Richard Brewster, then their proximity, enabling them to observe, could also sometimes help offenders achieve their objectives. On 28 July 1584, at eight o'clock in the evening, 'and thairby under silence and cloud of night', a foursome of brothers, each a burgess

[53] Ekirch, *At Day's Close*, pp. 84–8.
[54] ACA, CA/1/1/28/493.
[55] ECA, GB236/SL150/1/3, p. 1125.
[56] The rest of this paragraph is based on information in ECA, GB236/SL150/1/4, pp. 358–60.

and a bonnet-maker, came to the dwelling house of William Symmer, also a bonnet-maker. According to the account, Symmer had been sitting quietly and soberly at his supper when the brothers began yelling at him from the street.[57] Although the Canongate burgh court clerk employed the formulaic 'expecting no evil or harm nor injury from no persons', he noted that Symmer 'especially' expected no harm from the individuals now invading his space.[58] The clerk emphasised that Symmer should have had no reason to fear his would-be assailants, implying familiarity with the group and a sense of safety among known associates. What followed then was particularly, and intentionally, distressing for Symmer. The clerk noted that the brothers taunted Symmer 'be thair braggis, boistis, dispitful talk openly in presens of the haill neighbours dwelland nairby'. One of the brothers, Robert Paterson, demanded that if Symmer wanted to avoid being hanged by the foursome, then he should come out of his house and publicly make amends for having previously assaulted another of the brothers, William Paterson. The brothers' call for Symmer to leave his house's more restricted space and engage them on the street suggests that they wanted their actions to have a wider impact.

An important aspect of this case is that the entire encounter involved the Paterson brothers' premeditated use of the street in front of Symmer's house as a public stage for their ritualised justice. In this regard, they attempted to appropriate the legitimate use of public space from the magistrates for punishing wrongdoers. The dittay suggests that Symmer had previously made his court-mandated amends for the offence he committed against William Paterson, but 'not being penitent enough', the Paterson brothers sought fuller reparation.[59] While it is true that the brothers had gone to Symmer's house at 'nighttime' to seek their 'justice', their actions suggest that they did not want a shroud of secrecy for their activities. The fact that burgh clerks often identified the period after seven o'clock in the evening, even in the summer when the days were longer, as being 'under the silence of the night' points to a social construction of safe time that paralleled the social construction of safe space. The Paterson brothers chose a time when Symmer was likely to be found in his dwelling house and when Symmer's neighbours would also be present to witness the exchange. Since Symmer's reputation and credit in the burgh were as much the intended targets as his body, the Patersons' activities required a larger audience.[60] In the end, the court acquitted the brothers of the charges of violence and uttering threats; however, they were

---

[57] ECA, GB236/SL150/1/5, pp. 118–20.
[58] *Ibid.*
[59] *Ibid.*
[60] E. Ewan, '"Many Injurious Words": Defamation and Gender in Late Medieval Scotland', in R. A. McDonald (ed.), *History, Literature, and Music in Scotland, 700–1560* (Toronto, 2002), pp. 163–86; L. Gowing, 'Language, Power and the Law: Women's Slander Litigation in Early Modern London', in J. Kermode and G. Walker (eds), *Women, Crime and the Courts in Early Modern England* (Chapel Hill, 1994), pp. 26–48.

each convicted of disturbing the town's, and their neighbours', peace.[61] According to the magistrates, the real danger the Paterson brothers posed was to the peace and tranquillity of the streets and to the magistrates' authority to police the use of urban space.

Conclusion

Individual experiences in Scottish burghs helped to create lasting impressions. These impressions shaped how individuals interacted with those locations moving forward, turning them into meaningful places.[62] Streets connected the different quarters or zones within early modern Scottish burghs, enabling social exchange and the exchange of goods, creating space for the exercise of both legitimate and illegitimate power. The locations where petty offences occurred, the time of day at which they took place, the nature of those offences, and how the courts punished offenders, reveal the often-negligible distinction between appropriate and appropriated uses of shared spaces such as markets, streets, churches, and public buildings. Illustrating this point, because of their dissatisfaction with how the magistrates had previously carried out the task of punishing Symmer, the Patersons attempted to force him to make further amends on the streets of Canongate.

Contemporary court records reveal that petty offences influenced how individuals thought about their built environment, how they responded to conflict, and how they conceptualised neighbourliness. They also reveal how sixteenth-century allusions to neighbourliness were illusory. While contemporary clerks and magistrates might overemphasise the danger of acts committed under silence of the night and threats posed by maintaining a shroud of secrecy, they rarely acknowledged that prescriptive ideals like neighbourliness were in many ways a veil cast over social relations, obscuring the inherent tensions within urban communities. For the most part, these tensions were kept in check by statutes, good governance, and community values. But, on occasion, they led to forms of social exchange that could be disruptive. Such exchange was not always intended to undermine burgh ideals and customs; often, individuals resorted to such behaviour to restore the order disturbed by their neighbours' actions. Ultimately, the records do not inform us as to whether the Paterson brothers and William Symmer restored their working relationship, or whether Murray and Brewster resumed their routine of drinking together nightly and attending the kirk on the sabbath as friends, or whether other damaged reputations were fully restored, and neighbourliness resumed. Petty offences, like other forms of social exchange, helped early modern Scots to develop expectations about particular places within their burgh. Through their social actions and social exchanges, individuals like

---

[61] ECA, GB236/SL150/1/5, pp. 118–20.
[62] Houston, 'People, Space, and Law', p. 85.

Margaret Cryst, Elizabeth Kinkaid, William Symmer, or Richard Brewster witnessed their lived places transformed by petty offences. While, therefore, the other essays in this book explore the intimate relationship between deviance and marginality, this chapter serves as a reminder that the two were not always mutually dependent. Illegal, transgressive, and deviant behaviour was also an important tool of social exchange for people firmly located within the mainstream, and to be 'deviant' was not necessarily a signal – or a cause – of marginality.

PART II

PERFORMING DEVIANCE

5

Piracy, the State, and the Burghs of South-West Scotland, 1560–1603

Scott Carballo

The burghs on the south-west coast of Scotland, from the Solway to the Clyde, have received limited academic scrutiny, certainly compared to the port towns in the east and north of the country. This may, perhaps, be a lasting legacy of conventional economic histories which viewed the western ports as inconsequential during the late sixteenth century.[1] It is not the objective of this essay to argue that the ports of the west coast saw the same level of trading activity as the larger burghs on the east coast; that would be folly. However, customs duties and exchequer rolls can only tell part of the story. On the west coast, maritime activity – though certainly less in volume than on the east coast – retained a wholly distinctive character; and international trade, channelled through the region's royal burghs, was conducted in a wholly different maritime theatre. In the Irish Sea region, the seafaring communities of England, Scotland, Wales, Ireland, and the Isle of Man jostled for position. This milieu was further complicated by ongoing friction between Gaelic communities and their Lowland neighbours in Scotland and Ireland. The Irish Sea connected these communities, who shared and competed within the same maritime space – often in harmony, but also in conflict.

Given that the Irish Sea and its adjoining waterways connected the three kingdoms of England, Scotland, and Ireland, how the mariners of the coastal communities – individuals who, in a geographical and geopolitical sense, thus occupied a profoundly marginal theatre – interacted is of great import. Piracy by subjects of one kingdom on those of another in shared maritime space inevitably created conflict. Throughout the late sixteenth century, governing institutions in England, Ireland, and Scotland all set about trying to curtail localised piracy. In England, maritime aggression was a problem for Elizabeth I (r.1558–1603) from the outset of her reign, not least because traditions of maritime depredation had been upheld and even encouraged by her father, Henry VIII (r.1509–47).[2] For Elizabeth, this activity damaged

---

[1] For an example of this perspective, see S. G. E Lythe, *The Economy of Scotland in its European Setting* (Edinburgh, 1960).

[2] J. C. Appleby, *Under the Bloody Flag: Pirates of the Tudor Age* (Stroud, 2009), pp. 81–7; N. A. M. Rodger, *The Safeguard of the Sea: A Naval History of Britain, 660–1649* (London, 1997), pp. 182–4.

diplomatic relations with other major European powers, most notably France and Spain. Scotland, too, had engaged in maritime depredation throughout the fifteenth and sixteenth centuries, and these traditions still persisted at the accession of James VI in 1567.[3]

It is against this precarious backdrop that mariners of the western burghs of Scotland operated. In their journeys south, they sailed close to theatres of war in Ireland, and sailed past English and Welsh towns where pirates were based. The route north was no less dangerous. These waterways were dominated by the Highland galleys, carrying Gaelic clansmen who were often unscrupulous in their attacks. Piracy, as the primary form of deviance among early modern seafaring peoples, was an omnipresent threat (and also an alluring opportunity) for many. This essay will assess the response to piracy as it affected the communities of south-west Scotland. It will incorporate both national and regional perspectives, showing how lack of resources and effective proactive measures at a national level were compounded by complicity on the part of officials and an appetite for cheap merchandise at a local level. Piracy persisted throughout the sixteenth century in the waters of the British and Irish archipelago, and the response by governments and local authorities focused heavily on recouping financial losses. In analysing the response to piracy, this essay will show how both central and, particularly, local authorities sought to position piracy as an illegitimate and deviant activity. Their responses to this challenge, while often aiming to minimise the harmful effects of pirate activity, also focused on ejecting or chasing away would-be pirates, underlining their determination to confine the pirate to a marginal position on the fringes of society.

Piracy and the South-West

Before assessing the reactions of state and local authorities to piracy in the late sixteenth century, it is first necessary to outline the problem of piracy as it affected the seafaring communities of south-west Scotland. It is also important to note that while this essay will show that many in the south-west fell victim to piracy during the period, many also took to piracy themselves, with varying degrees of success.[4] For example, a Dublin

---

[3] D. Ditchburn, 'Piracy and War at Sea in Late Medieval Scotland', in T. C. Smout (ed.), *Scotland and the Sea* (Edinburgh, 1992), pp. 35–58; S. Murdoch, *Terror of the Seas? Scottish Maritime Warfare 1513–1713* (Leiden, 2009), pp. 111–17.

[4] South-western Scots as aggressors in piracy is an important aspect of Scottish maritime history which requires further investigation, but cannot be discussed here. See S. Carballo, 'Piracy and the Southwest Burghs of Scotland in an Irish Sea Context, 1560–1625' (PhD Thesis, University of Stirling, 2023), chapters 1, 2 and 6. For general appraisals of Scots as pirates, see Murdoch, *Terror of the Seas?*, pp. 111–57; J. Macinnes, 'West Highland Sea Power in the Middle Ages', *Transactions of the Gaelic Society of Inverness*, 48 (1976), 518–56.

merchant named Thomas Capron was attacked twice in the north of Ireland by pirates operating out of Ayrshire. The first attack was at the hands of an Ayr burgess named Robert Jameson in April 1581, which saw Jameson spoil goods to the value of £200 sterling. Capron was attacked again a year later, in April 1582, this time by Adam Montgomery, laird of Braidstane. Braidstane had been provided information on Capron's whereabouts by the crews of four small boats of Glasgow, which had 'rode hard by' Copran in order to ascertain what he had on board as cargo.[5] The passing of information, and repeated attacks in the same area, speak to a piratical network in the south-west in the early 1580s.

Nonetheless, mariners setting out from the Scottish western burghs were very much at risk of piracy from the outset of their journeys, whether it was through the Irish Sea or North Channel. The two chief threats to shipping came from English and Welsh pirates, and from Scottish Highlanders and Islemen. These two communities represented the two different piratical traditions present in the waters around the British and Irish archipelago in the sixteenth century, which have been outlined by John Appleby and other scholars of piracy. Appleby distinguishes between the 'commercialised seaborne plunder' of Lowland communities in England, Wales, the English Pale in Ireland, and southern Scotland; and the 'subsistence sea raiding' practised by Gaelic communities in the Scottish Highlands and Islands and in the Gaelic regions of Ireland.[6] The characterisation of Gaelic piracy as 'subsistence sea raiding' perhaps requires some refinement, but there is certainly a distinction between piracy practised by Gaels and Lowlanders in the late sixteenth century.[7]

The Highlands, however, was not a homogenous zone, and not all seafaring kindreds can be associated with 'Gaelic piracy'. Several clans in the sixteenth century, though, had indeed acquired a reputation for piracy – most notably the MacNeills of Barra, the MacLeans of Duart, the MacLeods of Lewis, and the MacDonalds of Islay and Kintyre (Clan Donald South).[8] Many of those engaged in piracy were themselves displaced or were on the losing side of wider geopolitical conflicts in the Highlands. Piracy in the western Highlands and Islands was often a resort of the most marginalised seafarers, and was tied to wider developments in the region. Participation in the mercenary trade to Ireland, the gradual expropriation of clan lands by

---

[5]   British Library, Add MS 11405: Miscellaneous Papers of Sir Julius Cæsar, Judge of the Admiralty, 'Spoiles comitted upon the English by Scottish pirates since 1 Aprill 1571. and a vewe of Scottish iniustice', fols 102–5.

[6]   Appleby, *Under the Bloody Flag*, p. 22.

[7]   Domhnall Uilleam Stiubhart has discussed the nature of Gaelic piracy during this period in his study of the Macneills of Barra. D. U. Stiubhart, 'Three Archipelagos: Perspectives on Early Modern Barra', in P. Martin (ed.), *Castles and Galleys: A Reassessment of Historic Galley-Castles of the Norse-Gaelic Seaways* (Laxay, 2017), pp. 172–95.

[8]   Macinnes, 'West Highland Sea Power', p. 539; D. Gregory, *History of the Western Highlands and Isles of Scotland, from AD 1493 to AD 1625: With a Brief Introductory Sketch, from AD 80 to AD 1493* (Edinburgh, 1836, repr. Edinburgh, 2008), pp. 232–3.

the Scottish crown and other acquisitive clans, and the unstable political climate in the Highlands, all played a part in pushing individual clans into piracy.[9] Aonghas MacCoinnich has also drawn attention to the maritime clashes of Scottish Highlanders and Lowlanders on the west coast due to the Lowland burghs' fishing activities in the Western Isles.[10] The violence that often accompanied Highlanders' attacks made the Gaels fearsome seafarers, and this danger was well-known to the western burghs.

Pirate crews operating out of England and Wales also threatened the burghs of south-west Scotland. English and Welsh attacks on Scottish ships in the Irish Sea region even caused significant diplomatic strain between the Tudor and Stuart monarchies. English sea power far eclipsed that of Scotland during this period, and English predilections for maritime plunder meant that Scots were not exempt from attack, despite the official diplomatic status of mutual amity at this time. Attacks ranged from professional pirate operations to opportunistic plunder. Pirate crews operated particularly out of south Wales and the English west country. In the 1560s, English and Welsh pirate crews roved between England and Ireland, often coming north – sometimes to plunder, sometimes for shelter from English patrols, and sometimes to sell their stolen goods in Manx and Scottish ports.[11]

Historians of England have thoroughly assessed English and Welsh piracy, particularly during the reign of Elizabeth I, and have demonstrated the limitations of the English state apparatus on several fronts.[12] The conflict of interest between central and regional political authorities at the time prevented any cohesive assault on piracy throughout the kingdom, and was exacerbated by conflicts of jurisdiction between central and local admiralty courts.[13] The lack of a standing navy, and the small number of ships in crown service, resulted in an uneasy alliance between the Elizabethan admiralty and private mercantile interests for the maintenance of English sea power. This was not a dependable preventative measure against piracy, domestic or

---

[9]   Carballo, 'Piracy and the Southwest Burghs of Scotland', pp. 64–9, 129–37; A. Cathcart, 'A Spent Force? The Clan Donald in the Aftermath of 1493', in R. Oram (ed.), *The Lordship of the Isles* (Leiden, 2014), pp. 254–70, at pp. 256, 268–70; G. Hayes-McCoy, *Scots Mercenary Forces in Ireland*, pp. 8–37. For detailed perspectives on the internal politics of the Gaeldom, and wider military developments, see Gregory, *History of the Western Highlands and Islands*, pp. 151–301; R. Crawford, 'Warfare in the West Highlands and Isles of Scotland, c.1544–1615' (Unpublished PhD thesis, University of Glasgow, 2016).

[10]   A. MacCoinnich, *Plantation and Civility on the North Atlantic World: The Case of the Northern Hebrides, 1570–1639* (Leiden, 2015), pp. 95–6.

[11]   For examples of English and Welsh attacks on Scots in the Irish Sea region, see TNA, HCA 1/36, High Court of Admiralty: Oyer and Terminer Records, Examinations of Pirates and Other Criminals, 1560–1565, fols 12–14, 86–92, 93–100.

[12]   On the Elizabethan state's handling of piracy, see K. R. Andrews, *Elizabethan Privateering: English Privateering during the Spanish War, 1585–1603* (Cambridge, 1964); M. G. Hanna, *Pirate Nests and the Rise of the British Empire, 1570–1740* (Chapel Hill, 2015), pp. 21–57; Rodger, *Safeguard of the Sea*.

[13]   L. M. Hill, 'The Admiralty Circuit of 1591', *Historical Journal*, 14 (1971), 3–14.

international.[14] Furthermore, the almost constant state of undeclared war with Spain in the late sixteenth century, disrupted by periods of actual war (most notably from 1585), resulted in the deregulation of the privateering industry, which blurred the lines between legal and illegal plunder and caused a general increase in maritime violence.[15] The governmental shortcomings mentioned here were all underscored by the inescapable reality that enforcement of anti-piratical measures was dependent on officials who were willing to overlook piracy for personal financial gain, from lords admiral all the way to port authorities and local commissions.[16] Many of these features of the English experience, as we will see, mirrored the challenges faced by the Scottish state in tackling piracy.

Piracy and the Scottish State

In the early modern period, pirates were tried in the admiralty courts of whatever nation apprehended them. Unfortunately, the records of the Scottish admiralty courts have not survived for the period under investigation here. This is regrettable, and may explain the lack of scholarly assessment of piracy in Scotland, but it need not preclude investigation into how the Scottish state dealt with pirates, as other institutions also addressed the problem. Piracy, it is true, did not feature prominently in the business of parliament under Mary I (r.1542–67) or James VI (r.1567–1625), and when it was mentioned, it was usually in passing, as part of wider discussion about developments in trading practice and regulation.[17] This should not lead us to underestimate the level of concern successive governments in Scotland had for piracy, since tackling it did not necessarily require updated legislation; it had been viewed as a universal crime for centuries, and no legislation was likely to be effective in altering the criminal behaviour of Scots travelling at sea, or of the foreign mariners who attacked Scots.

However, other governing institutions in Scotland were more active in the suppression of piracy, most obviously the privy council. This was the main organ of day-to-day governance in the kingdom, and it directed policy towards piracy in the sixteenth century. Yet no comprehensive attempt to limit pirate activity can be traced before 1587, perhaps reflecting lack of capacity thanks to the political turmoil of Mary's personal rule, the ensuing

[14] Rodger, *Safeguard of the Sea*, pp. 343–6.
[15] N. A. M. Rodger, 'Queen Elizabeth and the Myth of Sea Power in English History', *Transactions of the Royal Historical Society*, 14 (2004), 153–74; D. M. Loades, *England's Maritime Empire: Seapower, Commerce, and Policy, 1490–1690* (Harlow, 2000), pp. 122–31.
[16] Andrews, *Elizabethan Privateering*, pp. 22–9; R. W. Kenny, *Elizabeth's Admiral: The Political Career of Charles Howard, Earl of Nottingham, 1536–1624* (London, 1970), pp. 42–5, 63–8.
[17] For examples of such legislation, see *RPS*, 1581/10/28, 1581/10/90, A1600/6/1.

Marian Civil War (1567–73), and James' long minority.[18] Once James had reached his majority, however, the privy council began turning its attention to the challenge of piracy. On 7 July 1587, orders were sent to the eastern and northern shires to arm themselves against pirates and be in readiness to suppress any attacks 'with munitioun, artaillerie and all other weirlike engines' due to the recent increase in piratical attacks near Scottish coastlines affecting not only Scots, but visitors bringing trade goods to the country.[19] This initiative omitted the south-western shires, since the privy council preferred to deal with the west separately through a 'Proclamation for suppressing broken men on the Borders and pirates', in which those of the southern shires were ordered to be in 'reddines to repair to sic pairtis be sey or land'. This proclamation evoked previous legislation enacted by James V (r.1513–42) in which wapenschaws were required in the shires to take stock of defensive capabilities and armoury stocks. This proclamation was a response to border raids and the 'trouble caused by the pirates' and 'utheris evill disponit personis'.[20] Piracy in the south-west, then, was being addressed alongside contemporaneous disorders in the Border regions, and was linked to other forms of deviance on land. This was the first time the privy council had instituted any initiative concerned with piracy since the 1540s. Before 1587, they had intervened in many piracy cases, but only on a case-by-case basis, and in a purely reactive manner.[21] The initiatives in 1587, however, proved to be a one-off. No other proactive measures were taken for the remainder of James' reign, and instead, the privy council returned to a reliance on reactive measures to deal with individual cases and problems as they arose. This was the type of response the council had used in in 1577, when it intervened in a case of piracy involving a band of burgesses from several towns around the Firth of Clyde. This group had plundered a visiting ship from Brittany while its sailors were on shore in Irvine. All those named as perpetrators of this attack were denounced as rebels and summoned to appear before the council in Edinburgh, reflecting the council's view that the attack represented a threat to the 'gude friendschip and amytie standing betuix the realmis of France and Scotland.'[22]

In addition to the privy council, the convention of royal burghs also took action in the late sixteenth century to offset the damage done by pirates. It is unsurprising that this institution sought to protect Scottish shipping; it was essentially an assembly of urban merchants, exactly the kind of people most likely to be the targets of piratical attack. By taking measures against

---

[18] J. E. A. Dawson, *Scotland Re-formed, 1488–1587* (Edinburgh, 2007), pp. 302–25; M. Lee, *Government by Pen: Scotland Under James VI and I* (London, 1980), pp. 4–5.

[19] *RPCS*, vol. 4, pp. 195–6.

[20] *Ibid.*, p. 196.

[21] See, for example, *RPCS*, vol. 1, pp. 39, 104, 336–7, 517–18; vol. 2, pp. 222–3, 405, 603–4, 636–8; vol. 3, pp. 255, 368–89.

[22] *RPCS*, vol. 2, pp. 653–4.

piracy, the burghs were protecting their own interests.[23] Analysis of the records of this body reveals that piracy was viewed as a serious problem, and it took various measures to tackle it. In 1574, for example, a ship and bark were commissioned by the convention to clear the east coast of Scotland of pirates, and to help secure goods travelling through English waters by means of a convoy system.[24] This was the standard reaction to increases in piratical attacks on specific coastlines. In the absence of any naval patrols (like those in England), the Scots relied on private vessels to secure their coastline.[25]

As well as these recognised tactics, some of the convention's actions against piracy were less orthodox. The convention engaged in its own brand of foreign diplomacy in 1575 in the hope of reducing piratical attacks on Scots by the inhabitants of the Dutch city of Vlissingen (known in English as Flushing). The convention wrote directly to William I, prince of Orange (r.1544–84), asking him to 'put sic ordour to his pepill as oure natioun be nocht trublitt be thame in tymes cuming'.[26] These complaints to the Dutch coincided with English representations in the same year, as part of which Elizabeth I demanded that William address the damage being done to English shipping.[27] There is no evidence of any action on the issue on the part of the crown, parliament, or privy council, and therefore it can only be concluded that the convention had stepped in to fill the void created by central government's lethargy.

The convention was also forced to act against piracy in 1580, when the problem was discussed at length over a six-day sitting. In this session, it was agreed that the most common danger to Scottish shipping was 'the pirats of the inglis natioun', and a petition was drawn up on behalf of the burghs to be sent to the king and privy council for action to be taken. The same day, the convention resolved to raise money for an expedition to the Highlands to destroy Highlanders' fishing equipment in the shire of Inverness.[28] The Lowland burghs' presence in the western Highlands increased in the late sixteenth century due to their mercantile interests in the fishing markets, particularly the herring trade. The burghs, with the support of James VI's government, fiercely defended their fishing rights, while local Highland elites saw the exploitation by Lowland fisheries as an imposition on their rights and a threat to their source of revenue.[29]

---

[23] T. Pagan, *The Convention of Royal Burghs of Scotland* (Glasgow, 1926), pp. 1–52; J. D. Mackie and G. S. Pryde, *The Estate of the Burgesses in the Scots Parliament and its relation to The Convention of Royal Burghs* (St Andrews, 1923); A. R. MacDonald, *The Burghs and Parliament in Scotland, c.1550–1651* (London, 2007), pp. 7–10, 57–66.
[24] J. D. Marwick (ed.), *Records of the Convention of Royal Burghs of Scotland* (8 vols, Edinburgh, 1866–80), vol. 1, p.p 27, 31.
[25] For a full discussion of this, see Murdoch, *Terror of the Seas?*, pp. 113–27.
[26] Marwick, *Royal Burghs*, vol. 1, p. 44.
[27] Appleby, *Under the Bloody Flag*, pp. 139–44.
[28] Marwick, *Royal Burghs*, vol. 1, pp. 101–2.
[29] A. MacCoinnich, 'The Maritime Dimension to Scotland's "Highland Problem", ca. 1540–1630', *Journal of the North Atlantic*, 12 (2019), 44–72.

It is clear that the convention acted to protect the interests of the merchant class during this period, sometimes overstepping its legal remit. In 1575, it enacted a statute which sought to make a 'generale law' that would offset the commercial damages to ships pillaged at sea.[30] This 'law' dictated that all safe goods and even whole ships were made liable in the event of an attack by pirates, in order to compensate the losses sustained when a ship was pillaged. It also empowered the magistrates of seaports to levy a tax on all personnel on board the ship to help compensate for these losses, granting them the power to arrest anyone who refused, and to confiscate a ship and the safe goods until compensation was made.[31] This was a thinly veiled attempt to protect the interests of the merchants against piracy at the expense of the wider maritime community. Evidently, it proved difficult to enforce, as the convention had to 'inviolably' reassert this act in 1580, but inserted a clause exempting clothes, sea chests, and goods taken on at a later port in an attempt to placate outraged sailors.[32] Ultimately, this did not have the desired effect, and a letter representing a united front of 'skippers, awneris, maisters, and mariners' was sent to the privy council in September 1580. The sailors argued, correctly, that the convention had acted without proper commission from the king (or his regent) to pass a national act. The maritime community continued by emphasising that 'in tymes bygane, quhen thair schippis and guidis were pilleit, thay offerit thamselffis ready to defend and withstand the pyrattis', and when they had asked for the assistance of the merchants, 'they alluterlie refusit'.[33]

The convention was operating on murky legal grounds here. It was not a legislative body and could not enforce national initiatives without ratification of the crown and parliament. However, as a conglomerate of individual burghs, each with considerable local autonomy, and administered by their own town councils, there was real potential for enforcing its orders *de facto*. Ultimately, the privy council sided with the coalition of discontented sailors. It was thought the convention's measure would cause 'great hurt of his Hienes croun and estate royall' should it be implemented without ratification of parliament. The council was also fearful of the precedent that could be set by allowing the convention to set the terms for a national taxation initiative, however small.[34] Regrettably, though, the matter was deemed outside of the remit of the privy council, and referred to the admiralty court, records of which have not survived. The ultimate outcome of this dispute, therefore, remains unknown.

Throughout the late sixteenth century, then, the convention of royal burghs of Scotland was increasingly concerned with piracy, and was willing to take independent action in the absence of sustained interventions from

[30] Marwick, *Royal Burghs*, vol. 1, pp. 44–5.
[31] *Ibid.*
[32] *Ibid.*, pp. 99–100.
[33] *RPCS*, vol. 3, p. 308.
[34] *Ibid.*, pp. 308–9.

crown, parliament, or privy council – even if its actions sometimes proved problematic. As an institution which straddled the divide between national and local politics, the convention was ideally placed to assess the causes of piracy, and the effects of pirates' activities on Scottish shipping. However, its attention was almost entirely focused on the interests of the merchant community, occasionally at the expense of those who took the journeys that were also threatened by piracy. For the wider maritime community, therefore, other solutions were required, and responsibility for developing these tended to devolve onto local communities themselves.

Local Efforts to Limit Piracy

Piracy in Scotland, as in England, was often viewed as a local or regional problem. A key difference, however, was that naval resources in Scotland were far fewer than in England. Standing navies were not yet established in either kingdom, but in England, the crown retained ships in its service to patrol the seas around its borders. As Steve Murdoch has shown, Scotland could not mimic its southern neighbour in this regard. Rather, the Scots depended on private interests to perform this task, and the response to piracy also largely depended on privateering forces.[35] Often, it was left to local towns or regional magnates to carry out this service in the crown's name, or even to protect their own interests.

On the western seaboard, reliance on powerful magnates to combat piracy was especially obvious. The earl of Argyll, for example, tended to take the lead in the waterways of Argyll and western Inverness-shire.[36] In the south-west, the situation was no different. When the burghs of the Solway region began attracting the attention of the privy council for interacting with pirates in the 1560s and 1570s, it was to the various wardens of the West March that the council looked. Similarly, when a pirate by the name of Andrew White terrorised English and Welsh shipping in the Irish Sea between 1563 and 1565, offloading his goods in Whithorn after each freebooting cruise, Sir John Maxwell of Terregles was commissioned to investigate. Terregles was instructed to find the buyers of the pirated goods in the locality; a daunting task, as these turned out to be local urban and landed elites.[37]

Terregles was entrusted with the same task a decade later, when he was ordered to investigate those individuals who had bought a stolen horde sold in Kirkcudbright by the pirate Leonard Robertson. In 1575, Robertson had robbed an English merchant of Chester, Anthony Hankey, in the Irish Sea.

[35] Murdoch, *Terror of the Seas?*, pp. 114–20.
[36] *Ibid.*, p. 135.
[37] TNA, HCA 1/38, High Court of Admiralty: Oyer and Terminer Records, 1565–70, fols 124–40; *RPCS*, vol. 1, pp. 503–4; vol. 2, pp. 636–8, 645–6; W. S. Borthwick, 'A Case of Piracy: 1565', *Transactions of the Dumfries and Galloway Natural History and Antiquarian Society, Third Series*, 23 (1946), 11–18.

Robertson's attack resulted in English diplomatic pressure being exerted on the Scottish regent, James Douglas, 4th earl of Morton. As had been the case in 1565, the privy council delegated the matter to Terregles, who had by now succeeded as 4th Lord Herries. Herries was to operate on behalf of the crown alongside his kinsman John Maxwell, 8th Lord Maxwell – the former and current wardens of the West March respectively, and both also privy councillors. Remarkably, the list eventually drawn up, which contained sixteen buyers of Robertson's stolen goods, also named Herries and Maxwell themselves; the noblemen responsible for tracking down pirated goods were themselves culpable in the purchase. This underlines one of the key challenges which central administrations faced in tackling piracy: that in the localities where pirates operated, the dominant figures were often themselves involved in the black market of pirated goods.[38]

The links between central and local authorities grew tenuous when it came to tackling piracy in the late sixteenth century. The difficulties caused by lack of naval resources and erratic, mostly reactive, government policies, alongside the frequent complicity of local grandees in pirate activities, were compounded in the south-west by the fact that burghs like Kirkcudbright and Whithorn generally saw very little legitimate trade, and therefore often depended on piracy and smuggling to boost their economies.[39] For towns like Ayr and Glasgow, which were more prosperous and regularly engaged in international commerce, there was a far greater need for protection against piracy. In order to do this, merchants and mariners could deploy their own measures to protect their ship and goods, or the burghs could enact measures to protect against piracy and hunt down pirates who had robbed any of their citizens. The most common local response to piracy in these areas was simply to outfit an expedition to chase down the perpetrators. In 1583, for example, a consortium of merchants of the burghs of Renfrew and Glasgow were spoiled by a band of Highlanders under the leadership of Angus MacDonald of Dunivaig. In response, a collective expeditionary force was assembled from some of the western burghs situated on the Clyde and the Ayrshire coast.[40] Similarly, in 1590, Ayr merchants were harassed by the 'Scots hielend men' lying behind the Ailsa Craig (a small island off the south Ayrshire coast), who were ambushing merchant shipping as it travelled south. One burgess, Gilbert McDuff, reported being shot by hagbuts during an attack.[41] On this

[38] *RPCS*, vol. 2, pp. 150, 601, 603–5, 612. This attack is also covered in R. C. Reid, 'Early Records of Kirkcudbright', *Transactions of the Dumfries and Galloway Natural History and Antiquarian Society, Third Series*, 23 (1942), 142–53.

[39] For studies which demonstrate how piracy boosted the economies of small peripheral communities, see K. Pluymers, 'Pirates and the Problem of Plantation in Seventeenth Century Ireland', in P. Mancall and C. Shammas (eds), *Governing the Sea in the Early Modern Era: Essays in Honor of Robert C. Ritchie* (San Marino, 2015), pp. 79–107; C. Kelleher, 'Pirate Ports and Harbours of West Cork in the Early Seventeenth Century', *Journal of Maritime Archaeology*, 8:2 (2013), 347–66.

[40] *Glasgow Rec.*, vol. 1, pp. 103–5.

[41] D. M. Lyon, *Ayr in Olden Times* (Ayr, 1928), pp. 6–7.

occasion, it was the burgh that covered the expense for a pirate-hunting expedition into the Western Isles.[42] Furthermore, in 1602, money was granted by Ayr's burgh council to Malcolm Hunter and William Thom of Ardgowan, men in the employ of 'the laird of Blackhall' (John Stewart of Ardgowan), who had been spoiled by 'the clan Donnald' near Pladda, a small island off the south coast of Arran.[43]

This was the most common and straightforward response to piracy. However, it was only deployed in cases where there was a chance of catching the perpetrators, and if there was no legal recourse to seek redress for loss of goods in a foreign court. If the circumstances were otherwise, alternative strategies might be deployed. In 1587, for instance, a consortium of merchants from Ayr was robbed of their goods by English pirates while trading in Wales, and responded by entering into a lengthy legal process in the English admiralty court.[44] Redress in foreign courts was rarely forthcoming, but nonetheless, it provided merchants with an extra avenue to recoup their losses. There was, however, a limit to the utility of this approach, since it was only available to those robbed by venture pirates or who were the victims of opportunistic merchant plunder. As we have seen, the maritime environment off the west coast of Scotland was markedly different from that of the east, since the threat of Gaelic piracy was far more pronounced, and these attacks were often associated with violence. There was little recourse for those affected by Gaelic piracy to seek redress in Scottish courts, as the punishment typically handed out – horning, meaning outlawry – was ineffective when applied to the those who were already disaffected and displaced.[45]

The prominent role of disaffected clansmen in the piracy of the North Channel and Irish Sea, as well as the absence of regular naval patrols, led some of the burghs to turn for protection to the Campbells of Argyll, who, as we have seen, were already involved in anti-pirate activities further north. The Campbells were happy to oblige, exploiting the burghs' vulnerability to expand their sphere of influence. As early as 1507, Archibald Campbell, 2nd earl of Argyll had entered into a league with the burghs of Ayr, Irvine, and Dumbarton, offering maritime protection in return for waiving customs duties, in effect allowing the Campbells to move goods in and out of the trading burghs for free. This league was renewed by the burgh of Irvine in 1572, this time with Archibald Campbell, 5th earl of Argyll, and in 1580 a similar agreement was concluded between the burgh of Renfrew and Colin Campbell, 6th earl of Argyll.[46] Evidently, Campbell protection was perceived

[42] G. S. Pryde (ed.), *Ayr Burgh Accounts 1534–1624* (Edinburgh, 1937), p. 163.
[43] *Ibid.*, p. 216.
[44] TNA, SP 52/42, State Papers Scotland, 1587–8, fol. 82, 'Spoils committed upon the Scots by the English since 1569, 2 December 1587'.
[45] K. M. Brown, *Bloodfeud in Scotland, 1573–1625: Violence, Justice and Politics in an Early Modern Society* (Edinburgh, 1986), pp. 47–8; J. Goodare, *The Government of Scotland, 1560–1625* (Oxford, 2004), pp. 178–80.
[46] M. Livingstone et al. (eds), *The Register of the Privy Seal of Scotland* (8 vols, Edinburgh, 1908–82), vol. 1, p. 205; J. Shedden-Dobbie (ed.), *Muniments of the Royal Burgh of Irvine*

as beneficial by these smaller burghs. However, there is no evidence that the larger towns of Ayr and Glasgow sought to forge such a relationship with the Campbells in the later sixteenth century.

In summary, then, the absence of both effective policy responses from central authorities and any coastal patrols meant that a range of local initiatives had to be employed to protect against pirates. It is frustratingly rare for the outcomes of these local efforts at chasing away pirates or protecting ports to be recorded in local source material, so their effectiveness is difficult to gauge with any certainty. However, the continuation of piratical attacks throughout the period is a reliable indicator that local responses were not always successful.

Ayr Mariners' Society

So far, this essay has explored the various methods employed by central and local authorities to combat piracy, or to recoup the losses incurred at the hands of pirates. Some of the most proactive measures came at the local level, not least because piracy was often viewed as a local problem or left to local officials to deal with. One important method of offsetting the damages incurred at sea was the local sailors' societies that emerged towards the end of the sixteenth century, a phenomenon which has not yet been covered by historians in any depth. These societies varied in their operations, but they were generally funded by local taxes or levies taken from ships entering or leaving a port, and they distributed money to victims of seaborne disasters.[47] Occasionally referred to as a 'seaman's box' or a 'sailor's box', they were developed from an earlier initiative created in the port of Leith during the reign of Robert II (r.1371–90), called the 'prime gilt' fund. By 1592, the prime gilt fund had evolved into a robust system of tax collecting in the port, overseen by the 'Skippers, Maisters and Mariners of the saide Town and their Kirkmasters present', suggesting that there was some oversight from the Kirk, given that the fund served a primarily charitable purpose.[48] Similar societies emerged elsewhere during the sixteenth century at Ayr (1581), Kirkcaldy (1591), and Aberdeen (1597). It is entirely possible that other burghs adopted similar systems, but records have not yet been discovered for the period under study.[49]

(2 vols, Edinburgh, 1890–1), vol. 1, pp. 59–60; J. D. Marwick, *The River Clyde and the Clyde Burghs: the City of Glasgow and its Old Relations with Rutherglen, Renfrew, Paisley, Dumbarton, Port-Glasgow, Greenock, Rothesay, and Irvine* (Glasgow, 1909), pp. 30–1.

[47] Carballo, 'Piracy and the Southwest Burghs of Scotland', pp. 164–8.

[48] AUL, Aberdeen Shipmaster Society Papers, Prime Gilt, Table of Prime Gilt for the Port and Haven of Leith (1590–2), MS 3070/13/1.

[49] L. MacBean, *The Kirkcaldy Burgh Records, with the Annals of Kirkcaldy, the Town's Charter, Extracts from Original Documents, and a Description of the Ancient Burgh* (Kirkcaldy, 1908), p. 127; NLS, MS 941, Minute-book of the Mariners' Society of Ayr, fol. 2; AUL,

Analysis of the charters of each of these local societies reveals that they had their own objectives and prerogatives. Essentially, though, they all worked towards a similar cause: providing compensation for those who incurred damages at sea, whether it was loss of goods, ship, life, or limb. They covered instances of shipwreck, sickness, loss of goods due to weather, and other maritime hazards. The Ayr Mariners' Society, which was the only known local initiative on the west coast at this time, differed from the others in one respect: it was the only initiative to include piracy in its constitution.[50] This document outlines its intended purpose of providing compensation, drawn from taxation, for those who suffered by:

> peussing [pushing] of thair guides [overboard], sum be pilleing [pillaging] and reifting of thair gudis be piraccie, sum be mutilatioun and greit hurt to thair boddie sustenit in defence of thair guidis and thair awnirs [owners] and merchands.[51]

As well as the loss of merchants' cargo to piracy, the remit of the Ayr Mariners Society additionally covered the physical damage to the maritime community incurred in such attacks. With that in mind, it is also noteworthy that the creation of the society came in 1581, after the clash between the convention of royal burghs and the wider maritime community discussed above, where mariners had been left unaccounted for in the convention's attempts to offset the damages caused by pirates.

Like the convention's proposed tax (on mariners), the Ayr Mariners' Society sought to offset the damages incurred at sea through a tax on goods entering and exiting the port, which would allow it to create a fund for injured or deceased mariners, and for merchants who lost their cargoes. While, like all the societies formed in the late sixteenth century, the Ayr Mariners' Society clearly took inspiration from Leith's 'prime gilt' fund, it developed distinctive features designed to meet the particular needs of its maritime communities. For example, Ayr's system was named the 'guidage' tax, presumably reflecting the fact that it was levied on specific goods, rather than, as in Leith's case, being based on cargoes' destination. Goods being taxed by Ayr were split into three distinct categories. Firstly, goods to and from France were subject to their own tax. Secondly, goods to and from England, Ireland, or the Isle of Man formed the middle category. And finally, goods being taken up the coast to the Isles formed the last category.[52] Individual goods were taxed moving to and from each destination – a last of herring exported from the burgh,

---

Table of Prime Gilt for the Port and Haven of Leith (1590–2), MS 3070/13/1; A. Clark, *A Short History of the Shipmaster Society or the Seamen's Box of Aberdeen* (Aberdeen, 1911), pp. 69–76.

[50] The records of this society are examined fully in Carballo, 'Piracy and the Southwest Burghs of Scotland', pp. 168–72.

[51] NLS, MS 941, fol. 2. Goods were often pushed overboard in rough weather to avoid a wreck.

[52] NLS, MS 941, fols 3–4.

for example, was taxed at two shillings and three pence Scots if it was sent to France, while the same quantity exported to England was taxed at three pence Sterling (one shilling and six pence Scots). Goods moving to and from the Scottish Isles, however, were taxed at 'Quhatsumevir can be gottin', indicating trade to the Isles was informal and that there was an element of bartering involved.[53] As well as demonstrating how a port town dealt with piracy and other dangers at sea, the records of Ayr Mariner's Society thus also give an insight into the trading activities of the west coast port.

But why did Ayr's charitable venture, alone among its Scottish counterparts, commit to covering damages from piracy as part of its constitution? The answer likely lies in the different maritime theatre in which its mariners operated. The society's tax system, set out alongside its constitution, included a tax on goods going to and from the Scottish Isles.[54] The dangers of Gaelic piracy, outlined above, which came with a higher risk of violence, may also explain why the society, uniquely, factored into its approach to compensation the 'mutilatioun and greit hurt to thair boddie sustenit in defence of thair guidis' that mariners might suffer.[55] For Ayr-based sailors, then, piracy was a fact of life, and a far more immediate threat than it was to their counterparts on the east coast, making it perhaps the single most important motivation for setting up the fund in the first place. None of this stopped piracy, of course, but it did ensure that some mechanisms existed for offsetting the damage it caused. At the same time, Ayr's innovation underlines the importance of highly localised responses in the battle against piracy, given how intermittent and often ineffective were central institutions' interventions.

Conclusion

Pirates were viewed by central and local authorities alike as deviant. Clearly, there were those in the south-west of Scotland who took part in this activity in the sixteenth century. Scots, like all others, were not averse to this type of behaviour when the allure of plunder was presented to them. Nonetheless, strategies for addressing the problem of piracy were varied at different levels of government. As central institutions attempted, with varying degrees of success, to chase pirates down by sending out expeditions, or by arming the maritime shires against pirates, it became clear that the lack of resources and effective proactive policies did not deter pirates from attacking Scots of the south-western burghs. The Scottish privy council and the convention of royal burghs both sought to limit the damage caused to Scottish merchant shipping by pirates. The former lacked strategy and effective means of patrolling the coastlines, while the latter was preoccupied with offsetting the financial

[53] *Ibid.*
[54] *Ibid.*
[55] *Ibid.*, fol. 2.

losses of the merchant community. Local solutions were also necessary in the west of Scotland. The use of regional nobles as agents of the crown in the shires could help recover some of the losses of goods taken by piracy, but these links were strained by complicity of these nobles in black markets of stolen goods. Burghs of the southwest often resorted to their own initiatives to ward off pirates or recoup damages. Historiography on Scottish piracy has yet to determine properly how far local initiatives offset the damages caused by pirates. This essay has also provided a fresh local perspective on deviance and marginality, through analysis of the records of the Ayr Mariners' Society. This charitable venture sought to limit the physical dangers to mariners of the town, as well as financial damages to the merchants. These records show how, in the absence of meaningful intervention from central institutions, the burgh of Ayr found its own innovative way of limiting the effects of piracy.

6

'Ane legall man quhairof we are glad':
Male Violence, Female Agency, and the Quest
for Legitimacy in the Story of Seumas an Tuim

Graham Watson

'Seumas an Tuim', or James Grant of Carron, was the son of a minor landholder in the eastern Highlands who, as the result of a violent feud, became one of the most infamous outlaws and brigands of the seventeenth century. Active from the 1620s to the mid-1640s, his tale is less well known today than it was to his contemporaries and to Victorian historians of the Highlands. This is despite the extraordinary level of detail we have about him. For example, we know that he was 'of little stature, bald headed, broad faced, fair coloured, brown bearded, weak eyed, bow hoghed [legged], fat bellied and about fifty years of age' when he escaped from Edinburgh Castle in October 1632.[1] The available detail allows for what might otherwise be just an interesting story to contribute to a number of current academic discussions. James VI and the Scottish state's attempts to control violence, particularly in the Highlands, have long been a focus of research.[2] But more recent is the recognition that the response to change in different parts of the Highlands varied depending on a number of geographical and social factors. This has allowed a more nuanced view of the response to external pressures and a greater understanding that evidence from the western Highlands cannot simply stand for the whole.[3] At the same time, and as the introduction to this volume shows, gender has been a significant area of increased awareness, not least through analysis of the witch-hunt as a mechanism of coercive control. This is the most recent

---

[1]   RPCS, 2nd Series, vol. 4, p. 544.

[2]   A. I. MacInnes, 'Crown, Clan and Fine: The "Civilizing" of Scottish Gaeldom, 1587–1638', Northern Scotland, 13 (1993), 31–55; A. MacCoinnich, '"His spirit was given only to warre": Conflict and Identity in the Scottish Gaidhealtachd, c.1580–c.1630', in S. Murdoch and A. Mackillop (eds), Fighting for Identity: Scottish Military Experience c.1550–1900 (Leiden, 2002), pp. 133–61; A. Cathcart, 'Crisis of Identity? Clan Chattan's Response to Government Policy', in ibid., pp. 163–84; A. MacCoinnich, 'The Maritime Dimension to Scotland's "Highland Problem", c1540–1630', Journal of the North Atlantic, 12:1 (2019), 44–72.

[3]   T. Brochard, 'Intellectual and Practical Education and its Patronage in the Northern Highlands in the Century after the Reformation (Part 2)', Northern Scotland, 13 (2022), 1–17; T. Brochard, The World of the Notary and Other Legal Personnel in Scotland's Northern Shires, 1500–1700 (Inverness, 2023).

Scottish example of the wider interest in the lives of women in the early seventeenth century.[4]

This chapter seeks to contribute to these discussions in a number of ways. It has a focus on the eastern Highlands, which had its own relationship to nearby low-lying Moray and Aberdeenshire. While it details some of the drivers that provoked a violent rather than a legal response to perceived wrongs from its main protagonist, it shows his desire to return to mainstream society, rather than adopting fully the persona of the excluded deviant. But more importantly, it provides insight into the response to male violence in the eastern Highlands. It shows an increased willingness to use legal options, and a society where legal respectability was becoming more important, matching trends normally credited to southern Scotland. At the same time, it highlights the role of women in this process. Female agency is further highlighted by the actions of Elspet Innes, wife of Seumas an Tuim, both in acting independently and in facing down male power in the form of the privy council through the bishop of Aberdeen. Through these elements, the chapter therefore places the eastern Highlands in the mainstream of developments in Scottish society and shows that there is yet more that can be added to our understanding of the role and place of women in early seventeenth century society.

Male Violence

As suggested above, there are a number of contemporary or near-contemporary sources for the story of Seumas an Tuim: Sir Robert Gordon wrote about him, having dealt with him directly on more than one occasion as sheriff of Inverness; John Spalding wrote about him in his history of the covenanting and royalist actions in the north-east of Scotland; and he also makes an appearance in James Gordon of Rothiemay's history of the Civil Wars.[5] There is also a considerable quantity of evidence in legal accounts, including the minutes of the privy council. These sources are all Scots and English and only name him through the land unit he was either 'in' or 'of', which also helps to determine his class and standing in society. We cannot therefore be sure that 'Seumas an Tuim' is not a later coinage. Its use here

---

[4] Including L. W. Ambrose, 'Moved by God: Mobility and Agency in Anna Trapnel's Report and Plea', *Renaissance Studies*, 33:4 (2019), 609–23; S. Dropuljic, 'The Role of Women in Pursuing Scottish Criminal Actions, 1580–1650', *Edinburgh Law Review*, 24:2, (2020), 232–50; L. Yeoman, 'A Godly Possession? Margaret Mitchelson and the Performance of Covenanting Identity', in C. R. Langley (ed.), *The National Covenant in Scotland, 1638–1689* (Woodbridge, 2020), pp. 105–23; R. K. Marshall (ed.), *Discovered Lives: Ladies of St Giles', Edinburgh, 1587–1672* (Edinburgh, 2019).

[5] Robert Gordon, *A Genealogical History of the Earldom of Sutherland, From Its Origin to the Year 1630: With a Continuation to the Year 1651* (Edinburgh, 1813); John Spalding, *Memorialls of the trubles in Scotland and in England, A.D. 1624–A.D. 1645*, ed. J. Stuart (2 vols, Aberdeen, 1850); James Gordon, *History of Scots Affairs from MDCXXXVII to MDCXLI* (Aberdeen, 1841).

helps differentiate 'Seumas' from the numerous other Grants involved in the story, and it also highlights the Gaelic-speaking society in which he lived.

According to these accounts, Seumas an Tuim was outlawed for actions that were part of a long-term feud between the Grants of Carron and their immediate neighbours on the Spey, the Grants of Ballindalloch. He was the younger son of a landowner, and his brother, Patrick Grant of Carron, was deputy sheriff of Inverness in 1620 and a justice of the peace in 1623. His story begins in 1618 with a fight at a fair in Elgin, itself part of an ongoing feud between the Grants of Ballindalloch and those of Carron. The Ballindallochs and their associates were chasing one of the Carrons, and when Seumas an Tuim intervened, it resulted in the death of Patrick Grant of Lettoch, one of the Ballindalloch family. Attempts were made to reconcile the parties, but Patrick Grant of Ballindalloch refused all overtures, including those from the laird of Grant, the chief of the clan. Seumas an Tuim was then accused of the murder of John Grant of Dalnabo, who the privy council were told was Ballindalloch's brother.[6]

The feuding continued, and in 1628 John Grant of Ballindalloch took matters into his own hands. When John Grant of Carron, Seumas an Tuim's nephew, took a party to Rothiemurchus to cut down trees, Ballindalloch attacked them, and John Grant of Carron and Thomas Grant of Dalvey, amongst others, were killed. All of this led the privy council to intervene, and in 1630 the earl of Moray was given a commission to capture Seumas an Tuim. This was done in late 1630 and by the spring Seumas an Tuim was in prison in Edinburgh Castle. However, being a resourceful man, he escaped in October 1632 and fled, possibly to Ireland. But instead of lying low and this being the end of the story, by 1634 he was back in Strathspey, where he kidnapped John Grant of Ballindalloch and held him for a number of days.

Efforts to recapture Seumas an Tuim continued. In 1636 he was ambushed, and although he escaped, some of his men were taken, including his illegitimate son.[7] These men were taken to Edinburgh and hanged. However, in 1639, at the advent of the Civil Wars, Seumas an Tuim's fortunes were reversed. The marquis of Huntly persuaded the king that men like Seumas might be useful to the royalist cause, if pardoned. When Huntly's son Lewis, Lord Aboyne landed in the north-east to lead a royalist campaign, Seumas an Tuim got a commission and took part in the fight at the Brig o' Dee, when the earl of Montrose led the covenanting side. By February 1640, Seumas an Tuim was described as 'James Grant of Carron' and 'ane legal man'.[8] Spalding states that James Grant was with Huntly when he raised 200 horse and 800 foot and took Aberdeen in March 1644, and Sir Robert Gordon confirms that

[6] RPCS, 2nd Series, vol. 3, p. 411. Sir William Fraser does not identify this information in his genealogy of the Ballindalloch family, although he does identify a John as a brother of Patrick Grant of Ballindalloch. W. Fraser, The Chiefs of Grant (3 vols, Edinburgh, 1883), vol. 1, p. 520.

[7] Spalding, Memorialls, vol. 1, p. 70.

[8] Fraser, Chiefs of Grant, vol. 1, p. 68.

James Grant of Carron was amongst Huntly's commanders who dispersed along with the rest of Huntly's troops soon after. We hear no more of Seumas an Tuim, who presumably died in his bed, his crimes remitted, an accepted member of society again.

The sympathetic slant of our narrative sources is laid bare by the alternative details of his activities outlined in the privy council and legal records. He had actually been declared a broken man and an outlaw as early as 1612, where he is called James Grant in Flotterlettir (Fodderletter, Stratha'an) and seems to have been part of a gang led by James Gordon in Auchdreignye.[9] In November that year he was named first in a group accused of an armed attack on the house of William Farquharson in Auchriachan.[10] In 1630, he was accused of forcibly entering the house of a Mr Robert Udnie (Udny of Straloche), abusing and threatening his family, and stealing 8,000 merks.[11] Udnie was later to claim the specific crime of stouthreif, meaning using violence against a householder defending himself during a housebreaking. In Scots law this was differentiated from hamesucken, which was a premeditated assault in someone's own dwelling, so there is no evidence that this was part of the feud, and it looks more like armed robbery.

One of the reasons that the privy council took such an interest in Seumas an Tuim was the possibility that he was involved in the infamous fire of Frendraught. There had been a dispute between the Crichtons and the Leslies which had included fighting and deaths on both sides. To resolve the dispute, James Crichton of Frendraught had turned to the marquis of Huntly and, following a meeting at Strathbogie, Huntly had sent his son, Lord Aboyne, and John Gordon of Rothiemay with others to accompany James Crichton back to Frendraught. That night there was a fire in the separate tower in which Aboyne and Rothiemay were sleeping, and both were killed. Multiple accusations were made, including that James Crichton and his wife had started the fire themselves. Given the status of the individuals, and the crown's attitude to feuding, this became a national scandal. According to Sir Robert Gordon, the rumour went about that it was the Leslies who had caused the fire, probably using Seumas an Tuim to do it.[12] Late additions to Gordon's *Genealogy* by Gilbert Gordon of Sallagh say that Sir Robert Gordon was convinced that this was the case, because in 1634, when he was sheriff of Inverness, two of Seumas an Tuim's men had confessed their part.[13] Eventually, the focus of the law fell on one John Meldrum, who was found guilty and hanged in 1633.[14] At his trial John Meldrum stated that Seumas an Tuim's involvement had first been suggested by James Crichton himself. Meldrum then said that he had met Seumas an Tuim by accident and tried to

[9] *RPCS, 1st Series*, vol. 9, p. 421.
[10] *Ibid.*, p. 595.
[11] *RPCS, 2nd Series*, vol. 4, p. 92.
[12] Gordon, *Genealogical History*, p. 420.
[13] *Ibid.*, p. 468.
[14] Spalding, *Memorialls*, vol. 1, pp. 382–411.

persuade him to make a show of force and visit his house as if making plans to frighten Frendraught into paying debts he owed Meldrum. The prosecution brought various witnesses, particularly Meldrum's servant Richard Mowatt, to the effect that Meldrum had planned to meet Seumas an Tuim and was told where he was. Seumas an Tuim's own testimony confirmed that Meldrum had tried to persuade him to do as he asked, but he had refused because he did not want to take on any more feuds until he had revenged the death of his nephew at the fight at Rothiemurchus. Seumas an Tuim's testimony was taken while he was a prisoner in Edinburgh Castle. The court decided that Meldrum was trying to use Seumas an Tuim as a front to take the blame after the fire, but not everyone accepted the verdict, and there were further trials and feuding, although not involving Seumas an Tuim.

There were other violent incidents. In 1635, Sir Robert Innes of Balvenie brought a complaint to the privy council that Thomas Grant, tutor of Carron, and his brother Patrick had sheltered Seumas an Tuim since his escape from Edinburgh Castle and employed him to attack Balvanie's lands.[15] Spalding tells us that Seumas an Tuim killed Thomas Grant, brother of Patrick Grant of Culquoich, because he believed that Thomas Grant had been paid by the earl of Moray for his capture.[16]

By the 1630s, Seumas an Tuim was gaining fame and notoriety. In January 1631, his name was used as a defence (unsuccessfully) against a charge of carrying illegal weapons.[17] Seumas' fame also stretched well beyond the north-east, for in 1635 James and George Clelland claimed to be him when they attacked the house of Mr Walter Whiteford in Monkland, near Glasgow, and threatening that they would 'commit ma(r)e insolenceis than fell out be him'.[18]

Both Spalding and Gordon are sympathetic sources. According to Sir Robert Gordon, Seumas an Tuim had little option but to 'turn rebel' following Ballindalloch's intransigence in refusing to come to a settlement for the original murder in Elgin in 1618. In these sources male revenge violence is presented as an understandable, if not a legal, activity, and in service of this narrative the other depredations noted above are ignored.

Female Agency

One of the first things to stand out in the difference between the narrative and legal sources is the former's silence about the role of women. Yet women played key roles in the story, with four being particularly prominent. Elspet Innes was married to Seumas an Tuim. Margaret Sinclair had been married to John Grant of Carron and, following his death at the hands of John Grant of

---

[15] *RPCS, 2nd Series*, vol. 4, p. 111.
[16] Spalding, *Memorialls*, vol. 1, p. 54.
[17] *RPCS, 2nd Series*, vol. 4, pp. 123–4.
[18] *RPCS, 2nd Series*, vol. 5, p. 507.

Ballindalloch, took a lead role in managing the estate of Carron. Janet Grant was the mother of Thomas Grant of Dalvey, who had been killed alongside John Grant of Carron by Ballindalloch and his men.

The first woman we can identify and who also took a personal role, however, was Jean Innes, the wife of Thomas Grant of Cardaillis (modern Kirdells). A complaint in her name (and by her husband Thomas 'for his interest') was brought to the privy council on 28 August 1616 to the effect that she had been physically attacked by a number of men under the instruction of Patrick Grant of Carron, Seumas an Tuim's father.[19] She was represented by Patrick Kynnaird of Middletoun. The accused did not turn up, so were declared outlawed. However, in October they complained to the privy council that they had come to Edinburgh on 7 August to appear, but the council had not sat because the lords were on their way to the assembly of the Church of Scotland in Aberdeen. They had not been informed that the hearing would instead be held on 28 August. This time the accusers failed to appear, so having agreed sums of caution to be paid if they failed to appear in future, the privy council suspended the process. A number of 'interactions' between the Grants of Carron, Cardaillis, and Ballindalloch can be followed through the privy council records, but it is sufficient here to note that the case against Carron was brought by Jean Innes as opposed to her husband or relations.

This is not, in itself, revelatory. After all, personal assault and the murder of a male relative were, according to Sir George Mackenzie's *Laws and Customs of Scotland in Matters Criminal* (1678), the only two types of prosecution a woman could technically bring. Stephanie Dropuljic has recently shown that women could, and did, take the legal initiative in raising criminal actions; 26 per cent of justiciary court cases between 1580 and 1650 had a woman named among the pursuers. Dropuljic notes that 'uncertainty remains as to whether women also had standing and involvement in the pursuit of crimes beyond the Justiciary Court'.[20] The Jean Innes complaint to the privy council, and the actions of John Grant of Carron about to be detailed, suggests that they did. Whilst nothing can be proved from one case, noting times where women had agency or were given positions of legal status is a corrective to many years of disempowerment.

The next example again requires wading through and differentiating between various Grant families. Following the fight in Elgin and the murder of John Grant of Dalnabo, both Spalding and Gordon highlight an event in the forest of Rothiemurchus as a major element of the story.[21] John Grant of Carron and a party of twenty-five men went to cut wood in Rothiemurchus.[22]

---

[19] *RPCS, 1st Series*, vol. 10, p. 616.
[20] S. Dropuljic, 'The Role of Women in Pursuing Scottish Criminal Actions, 1580–1650', *The Edinburgh Law Review*, 24 (2020), 232–50, at p. 233.
[21] Spalding, *Memorialls*, vol. 1, p. 11.
[22] We have all the names of both parties in various subsequent legal depositions to the Privy Council. *RPCS, 2nd Series*, vol. 4, p. 4.

They were ambushed by John Grant of Ballindalloch[23] and his group of thirty. In the ensuing fight, John Grant of Carron was killed, as was Thomas Grant of Dalvey and Lachlan McIntosh of Rockinoyr on the Ballindalloch side. Subsequently, John Grant of Ballindalloch was able to claim that he had been trying to capture outlawed men, particularly one Finlay MacGrinnon, one of Seumas an Tuim's men, so that his actions were legal.[24] What makes this case stand out is that the king got personally involved. On 4 December 1628, the privy council recorded a petition from the widow and children of the deceased John Grant of Carron. On the same day, they received a request from John Grant, fiar of Ballindalloch seeking the council's protection for his witnesses, who feared action against them because they had been put to the horn. What seems to have happened is that actions had been taken both locally and in Edinburgh by both sides seeking justice. So far this is fairly straightforward. The privy council had already written to Huntly and Lovat asking them to intervene because the two local leading representatives of the law, the earl of Moray and Lord Gordon, were both 'absent'. However, the king's direct involvement, as shown by his letters to the privy council of 19 November 1628, and his personal instruction that the council should hear both sides, suggests that he had been approached directly on the matter. It would seem that a copy of the correspondence survives in the family papers of Grants. These contain a 'humble peticioun of Margarret Sinclair, the relicte of John Graunt of Carron'.[25]

Having investigated the matter through hearing depositions from the parties concerned, the privy council wrote to the king who, on 2 March 1629, responded that he accepted the findings but with an unusual (for the time) addition.[26] In 1598, the 'Act anent deidlie feids' specifically militated against remission from the king and stated that the parties must go to law, particularly where only one side suffered death. The king's decision was that Ballindalloch be excused for the death of John Grant of Carron, but should pay recompense to the widow. The privy council ordered Ballindalloch to 'make offeris of assythment and satisfactoun', but also wrote to 'the relict and freindis of Carron' to instruct them to accept the offers. From the perspective of Edinburgh and the court, this may have seemed an elegant solution. However, it did not suit Margaret Sinclair. On 18 February 1630, Ballindalloch complained to the privy council that not only had agreement not been reached, but Seumas an Tuim and Finlay MacGrinnon were raiding his lands. The privy council summoned Margaret Sinclair and John Grant

---

[23]   John Grant was the son of Patrick Grant of Ballindalloch. He took over his father's estate before his father's death and is variously described as 'Ballindalloch', fiar of Ballindalloch, and 'the young laird'.

[24]   James McIntoshe of Downe (Doune) of Rothiemurchus, one of the Ballindalloch party, had been given a commission to apprehend Seumas an Tuim for the murder of Patrick Grant of Lettach. *RPCS, 2nd Series*, vol. 2, p. 274.

[25]   Fraser, *Chiefs of Grant*, vol. 1, p. 244.

[26]   *RPCS, 2nd Series*, vol. 3, pp. 113–14.

of Ballindalloch, and on 29 June 1630 both parties personally appeared in front of the lords to argue their cases. Ballindalloch's offer of recompense was adjudged to be legal, but still Margaret Sinclair held her ground. Her argument was that Ballindalloch was using the presence of Finlay MacGrinnon at the events at Rothiemurchus as the reason it took place – claiming, that is, that it was a legal attempt to capture an outlaw. However, both she and Finlay MacGrinnon claimed that he was not there, and therefore the death of John Grant of Carron was something Ballindalloch should face trial for. This was also the basis for the personal petition to the king that Margaret Sinclair made, mentioned above.

This is as far as we get in her story, and it provides a picture of female agency. Margaret Sinclair not only brought prosecution in her own name, but refused the state's attempts at reconciliation; petitioned the king himself about her situation; and stood up to pressure from the major lords of the country and refused their attempts at mediation to their faces. The last we hear of her is when she appeared personally again in front of the privy council to defend herself against accusations that she had failed, as a landlord, to bring her guilty tenants to justice. This does not detract from the picture we have of her.

Women on both sides of the dispute played a role. Janet Grant, the mother of Thomas Grant of Dalvey, also killed at Rothiemurchus but on the Ballindalloch side, brought a complaint to the privy council in August 1630 that Huntly had failed in his duty to apprehend Seumas an Tuim and 'William McGrumman' and others who were at the horn. The following year, she made a similar complaint about Grant of Freuchie.[27]

We do not hear anything of Elspet Innes, Seumas an Tuim's wife, until after his escape from Edinburgh Castle on 15 October 1632. Spalding states that it was his wife who brought Seumas the ropes with which he was able to climb down the wall of the castle.[28] Sir Robert Gordon says it was his son,[29] and this seems to be backed up by the evidence in the records of the privy council.[30] However, Elspet Innes was in Edinburgh at the time, as we shall see. On 27 October, the marquis of Huntly wrote to the privy council that she had come to the Bog of Gight 'and forced lodging to herself' (he did not know how), but he had taken her prisoner and asked what he should do next.[31] The council responded on 1 November that she should be sent to the bishop of Aberdeen, a member of the council, for questioning. The bishop was sent very clear instructions that he was to find out what she knew about her husband's escape, who helped him and where he was now. It is the bishop's response and the inclusion in it of her full deposition that

---

[27]   RPCS, 2nd Series, vol. 2, pp. 113–14.
[28]   Spalding, Memorialls, vol. 1, p. 21.
[29]   Gordon, A Genealogical History, p. 499.
[30]   RPCS, 2nd Series, vol. 4, p. 551.
[31]   Ibid., p. 562.

provides an insight into Elspet Innes and her place in society.[32] The speed of the process should be noted, as she was questioned, and released, on 12 November 1632.

She began her evidence by stating that when she had last visited her husband in Edinburgh Castle, on 13 October, two days before he escaped, she had warned the keeper that Seumas an Tuim might take a desperate course because of the recent death of his son. She had spent that night in Edinburgh with her servant, Margaret Scot, and in the morning travelled north. She gave a very full itinerary of her route and the names of everyone she stayed with. Her route was north via Dundee, Forfar, and Glenesk, to Aboyne and then to Kirkton of Glenbucket, where her son was buried. She stayed a few days with Robert Grant, her brother-in-law, at Rothes. She stopped at the Bog of Gight on her way to the Garioch 'for doing some of her business', and came to the house of Thomsoun beside the Bog where she was taken by Huntly's servants, held, and then sent to the bishop. She was sworn on her oath and stated that she knew nothing of her husband's escape until some days after, first hearing about it at Robert Farquharson's house in Fugzeane from a post passing north by the Mure alehouse. She had given her husband nothing to help his escape and had only left him to try to find out the manner of her son's death. She suggested that it might have been either his lawful (legitimate) son, who was now deceased, or his natural (illegitimate) son, who had remained in the castle with him, who helped him. Lastly, she did not know where he was except that she had heard him say that if he ever escaped, he would go to his daughter in Ireland. Finally, she subscribed to the deposition with her own hand in front of witnesses.

There is enough in this story for a small novel, but it is sufficient here to point out that the wife of a younger son of a landowner in a rural parish could persuade a bishop that she had legitimate business of her own to undertake; had a maidservant; could travel freely from Edinburgh to the north staying in various accommodation; and could sign her own deposition. She could also create and deliver a plausible story of innocence and deliver it to a senior cleric of the Church, and in front of lawyers and witnesses.

We hear again about Elspet Innes the following year, in 1633, this time in Spalding's *History*. She was heavily pregnant, and Seumas an Tuim took a house in Carron where he could visit regularly. It was on one of these visits that a group of MacGregors, paid by Grant of Ballindalloch, tried to capture him. However, their leader, Patrick Ger MacGregor, was shot and killed. Spalding goes on to tell the tale of Seumas an Tuim capturing John Grant of Ballindalloch. On 7 December 1634, Innes came at night to Ballindalloch's lodgings at Pitchaise and spoke to him privately, while he was at supper. Ballindalloch left the house with his sword and targe in his hand, forbidding anyone to follow him. But his wife insisted, and accompanied by Innes, they went to his own mill at Pitchaise 'where the tryst was set'. But Seumas an

---

[32] *RPCS, 2nd Series*, vol. 4, pp. 576–8.

Tuim was waiting with a dozen men lying in secret. Elspet Innes 'crie[d] the watch word' and Seumas an Tuim came out and shook Ballindalloch's hand and kissed Ballindalloch's wife greeting. But immediately following this, the twelve men rushed out and took both Ballindalloch and his wife. They went to Culquholly, three miles away, and there left Ballindalloch's wife. Ballindalloch's eventual escape was noted above. Ballindalloch only escaped by persuading one of his captors, one John Leslie, to help him. According to Spalding he did so by speaking to Leslie in Latin, which the other captors did not understand.[33]

Both accounts of Elspet Innes make remarkable stories, but from a historical perspective, even without this part in an adventure, Elspet Innes can be seen to demonstrate many abilities and significant personal agency. Some of this, for example the role of women in business in Scotland, has begun to be examined, but further research is required.[34]

Steps to Legitimacy

It was noted above that there was a level of sympathy for Seumas an Tuim, and an understanding of the role of male violence in settling personal disputes. However, from the start Seumas an Tuim appears to have been seeking a way back to acceptance in mainstream society. Sir Robert Gordon thought that Seumas only 'turned rebel' because his enemies' 'revengeful spite' meant that a resolution to the original death at the fight in Elgin was not possible. It would seem that Seumas an Tuim was prepared to take the normally expected steps to make amends, by offering financial compensation.[35]

According to Spalding, the kidnapping of Ballindalloch had been because there had been some understanding between the men that Ballindalloch would seek a remission for Seumas an Tuim. Instead, he hired MacGregors to try and have him killed.[36]

The final steps in Seumas an Tuim's story come with the start of the Covenanting Wars. As early as February 1639, Huntly had written to the duke of Hamilton saying that if the king would offer pardons to outlaws such as James Grant and the MacGregors, the troops they would bring to the cause would result in much discomfort to the other side.[37] In April 1639, when Huntly was in Aberdeen and about to be arrested and taken south, he was

---

[33] Spalding, *Memorialls*, vol. 1, p. 54.
[34] C. M. Macleod, 'Enterprising Widows: Family, Business, and the Succession Process', in J. Heinonen and K. Vainio-Korhonen (eds), *Women in Business Families: From Past to Present* (London 2018), pp. 199–217; C. Spence, *Women, Credit, and Debt in Early Modern Scotland* (Manchester 2016).
[35] Gordon, *A Genealogical History*, p. 475.
[36] Spalding, *Memorialls*, vol. 1, p. 66.
[37] B. Robertson, *Royalists at War in Scotland and Ireland, 1638–1650* (Abingdon, 2014), p. 39.

questioned by General Alexander Leslie, and asked about capturing Seumas an Tuim, John Dugar (John MacGregor alias John Dow Ger) and other criminals. But Huntly replied that he had no office or commission to that effect, and that James Grant/Seumas an Tuim had got the king's remission. This is confirmed by James Gordon's *History of Scots Affairs*.[38] Following the Trot of Turriff, when the royalists came to Aberdeen, Huntly's fourth son, Ludovick, came down Deeside with Highlanders from the Brae of Mar under Donald Farquharson, and others under Seumas an Tuim. James Gordon says that he had twenty men.[39] They took Durris, belonging to John Forbes of Leslie, and then Echt, Skene, Monymusk, and other houses belonging to the Forbes family. When Huntly's son, Lewis, Lord Aboyne, landed, he took service from Seumas an Tuim and John Dugar. But James Gordon confirms that they could not work together because of previous Carron/MacGregor antipathy, rooted in the fact that Seumas an Tuim had killed Patrick Ger MacGregor.[40] In June, Seumas an Tuim was with Lord Aboyne, Huntly's son, when he prepared for battle with Montrose at the Brig o' Dee.

The last point in the story came in March 1644 with a further royalist rising in the north-east. Huntly came to Aberdeen with 200 horse and 800 foot. Spalding says that there were few commanders, but one was Seumas an Tuim. Seumas was sent out on 9 April to plunder Sir Thomas Crombie's lands of Kemnay. His men were described as 'Highlanders' and various companies of Lowlanders. At Kemnay, he stole 6,000 merks and plundered the girnals and barns. They did the same to Pittodrie and 'Mwny' (perhaps Monymusk).[41] However, Huntly disbanded his troops with the arrival of the covenanting forces. James Gordon, without mentioning him in any other context of the war, states that Seumas an Tuim was among those of Huntly's commanders who dispersed in 1644.[42] This is the last we hear of Seumas.

As has been noted, Seumas an Tuim is consistently referred to as James Grant, his Gaelic by-name likely a later usage. Spalding refers to him as James Grant 'of Carron' and this is followed by a number of modern historians.[43] This would usually suggest that he was a heritable landowner. In the other sources, James Grant is first referred to as 'in Fotterlettir', and then 'in Daltulies'. However, following the death of his nephew at the hands of Ballindalloch, and the point where James Gordon says that he took to crime, he became James Grant 'the rebel', the 'arch-rebel', and then 'the traitor'. Soon his fame was such that he was simply 'James Grant'. It might be taken

---

[38] Gordon, *History of Scots Affairs*, vol. 1, p. 235.

[39] *Ibid.*

[40] However, James Gordon names the wrong Patrick MacGregor. He states that James Grant killed the brother of the then chief, but it was actually Patrick Ger, son of John Dow Ger, which would better explain the antipathy. See also A. Kennedy, 'The Bandit King', *History Scotland*, 22.6 (2022), 14–19.

[41] Spalding, *Memorialls*, vol. 2, p. 341.

[42] Gordon, *Genealogical History*, p. 519.

[43] See, for example, B. Robertson, *Lordship and Power in the North of Scotland* (Edinburgh, 2011), p. 73.

MALE VIOLENCE, FEMALE AGENCY, AND THE QUEST FOR LEGITIMACY

that calling him James Grant of Carron improved the story by raising his status, were it not for two letters. In February 1640, James Grant of Freuchie and Patrick Grant of Glenmoriston wrote to a number of people to the effect that now that James Grant 'of Carroun' was 'ane legall man quhairof we are glad', there was nothing to hinder his employment or undertakings.[44] This was followed by a letter dated the last day of February 1640 from James Grant of Carron himself to James Grant of Dalnabo, referring to Freuchie's letter and saying that as soon as his relaxing (from the horn) was proclaimed in the north he would 'sett cautione for the lairdis relief of the general band'.[45] He was effectively participating again in legitimate society, but this time taking on the responsibilities of a landholder, not a rentier. How he came to this position is not clear. John Grant of Carron, killed at Rothiemurchus in 1629, had children, and in 1635 Seumas an Tuim's older brother Thomas was their tutor. The 1641 rental role of the bishop of Moray has John Grant's widow responsible for the feu duty rental of the lands of Carron.[46]

One of the wider issues regarding legal legitimacy that comes to the fore is the position taken on the legal responsibilities of landowners and clan chiefs. The privy council instructed Sir John Grant of Freuchie to capture Seumas an Tuim and several times his response was to argue that he had no duty to hunt for him outwith the boundaries of his lands.[47] By 1635, the privy council was getting suspicious of Sir John Grant of Freuchie's motives or commitment. In response to yet another claim of no responsibility, it replied that Sir John Grant was 'answerable for his haill kin and clan of the surname of Grant', and that as 'cheiff and chiftane of the surname of Grant [he should] bring and exhibite the said James Grant, Robert Grant, his brother, and George Grant, his bastard son'.[48] By June, Freuchie felt it necessary to tell the privy council of the efforts that he had made.[49] The lords responded by giving him a set deadline to capture Seumas an Tuim, and also charged John Grant of Ballindalloch to inform the council of Freuchie's diligence in the matter. Despite both appearing together to reassure the privy council, Freuchie was censured in July.[50] All the evidence presented to the privy council from those in Strathspey spoke of the responsibility of landlords for their tenants. It was the Edinburgh-based privy council that stated that some of the duty arose from being a clan chief.

Freuchie's arguments with the privy council over the limits of his jurisdiction and responsibilities were mirrored by the marquis of Huntly's responses to questioning by the council about the fire of Frendraught. Here

---

[44] Fraser, *Chiefs of Grant*, vol. 1, p. 69.
[45] *Ibid.*, p. 70.
[46] C. Fraser-Mackintosh, *Antiquarian Notes: A Series of Papers Regarding Families and Places in the Highlands* (Stirling, 1913), p. 110.
[47] *RPCS, 2nd series*, vol. 3, p. 582; *RPCS, 1st Series*, vol. 4, p. 201.
[48] *RPCS, 2nd Series*, vol. 5, p. 503.
[49] *Ibid.*, vol. 6, p. 17.
[50] *Ibid.*, p. 44.

Huntly's defence was that not only was he not sheriff, so lacked authority, but because he was old and feeble, he could not control people 'descendit of ane stok be them selfis, who wes seking revenge of their blood, and wold nather be counsallit nor reullit be him'.[51] In 1634, in a connected case, Huntly argued that the Gordons of Strathdon were not his tenants, so he could not act against them.[52]

Sweeping generalisations or new historical models cannot and should not be developed from one series of events. However, all this does illustrate the danger of an over-simplistic view both of the Highlands and of Highland society. Mark Godfrey reminds us of the risk of over-emphasising a single characteristic of society into an unduly reductionist statement of its general character, particularly when we refer to 'feuding society'.[53] So we need to be careful with any suggestion that what happened here can be taken as a baseline 'norm' for the Highlands as a whole. However, Alison Cathcart has already noted that the period from 1451 to 1609 saw movement from the clan chief being dominant to 'governing with the consent of the clan'.[54] There are elements in the Seumas an Tuim evidence that suggest further movement in this direction. The Frasers provide further examples of agency within clans. To take just one example, when Simon, Lord Lovat sent two senior clan members, Culbokie and Belladrum, to negotiate the purchase of land from the laird of Mackintosh, according to James Fraser they 'betrayed his trust' and, spotting a bargain, bought the land for themselves.[55] It should also be noted that Seumas an Tuim went to the wars alongside Huntly, despite the initial attitudes of his 'chief', Freuchie, to the National Covenant, which were much more ambivalent, verging on the supportive. It was seen above that both Freuchie and Huntly were prepared to argue that their legal responsibilities were limited to controlling their tenants, while it was the privy council that argued they had wider responsibilities as leading nobles and chiefs. This might be a further pointer to the direction signalled by Alison Cathcart of a contraction of the role of the clan chief.

Yet it would be possible to tend too far in this direction. What was argued in court in order to avoid fines or worse, and how people acted locally, might be different things. And the attitudes of the Strathspey community might well be discerned by the fact that Lewis Gordon 'dressed as a Highlander' when recruiting in Stratha'an during the second of the Bishops' Wars.[56] The implication was that this was required in order to recruit the men that he did, and that the people of Stratha'an reacted better to a closer reflection of their

51   Spalding, *Memorialls*, vol. 1, p. 60.
52   Gordon, *Genealogical History*, p. 474.
53   A. M. Godfrey, *Civil Justice in Renaissance Scotland: The Origins of a Central Court* (Leiden, 2009), p. 403.
54   A. Cathcart, *Kinship and Clientage: Highland Clanship 1451–1609* (Leiden, 2006), p. 76.
55   James Fraser, *Chronicles of the Frasers*, ed. W. Mackay (Edinburgh, 1905), p. 253.
56   Patrick Gordon, *A Short Abridgement of Britane's Distemper: From the Yeare of God MDCXXXIX. to MDCXLIX*, ed. J. Dunn (Aberdeen, 1844), p. 40.

own sense of identity than when presented with an overtly Lowland one. David Allan points out that the early family genealogies were being written at this time to counteract the centrifugal effects of intermarriage and physical migration and that their comprehensiveness was to demonstrate the widest possible extension of familial association.[57] Likewise, the clan histories, such as Lachlan Mackintosh of Kinrara's 'Chronicle' of 1680, served a similar connecting purpose.[58] For every social and economic force pushing society apart, there was a local and kin connection moving in the opposite direction.

Allan Kennedy points out that we should not overlook the personal factors that might have led to outlawry, using as an example Calum Oig McGrigor. Kennedy discusses the role of banditry as a social element, although he follows the modern consensus in the academy that Eric Hobsbawm's theory of social banditry is too simplistic.[59] As well as usefully putting banditry into the wider historiographical context regarding the growth of the state, he sees its suppression as a partnership between ruler and ruled, and in Scotland one between central and local power. What this meant in practice was that the crown relied on local power-holders to implement justice, but also that local luminaries increasingly turned to the crown for legal approval to use violence to achieve their ends. If a general overview was to be taken, it is of a willingness by protagonists to use the method that best achieved the desired end, irrespective of its legality, presumably tempered by the likelihood of discovery, prosecution, and punishment. As such, were the Highlands that different from elsewhere?

Conclusion

A close reading of the evidence for the story of Seumas an Tuim reveals some important insights into the society of the eastern Highlands in the early seventeenth century. Male violence remained an unpleasant fact, and was often viewed sympathetically, even though its illegality was fully accepted. Likewise, a return to legal legitimacy seems to have been a powerful motivator for those of a certain class. The insight provided by the legal sources into the role of female agency is an important corrective to the male dominated narrative sources. Here we see women petitioning and representing their own positions at all levels of the legal system, including petitioning the ultimate authority, the king. We also see a society where women of middle standing

---

[57] D. Allan, 'What's in a Name? Pedigree and Propaganda in Seventeenth Century Scotland', in E. J. Cowan and R. J. Finlay (eds), *Scottish History: The Power of the Past* (Edinburgh, 2002), pp. 147–67, at p. 149.
[58] J. Munro (ed.), *A Chronicle of the Family of Mackintosh to the year 1680 by Lachlan Mackintosh of Kinrara* (Penicuik, 2009).
[59] A. Kennedy, 'State, Community and the Suppression of Banditry in Seventeenth Century Scotland', *IRSS*, 46 (2021), 1–26, at p. 3.

could travel, do business, and present themselves to power with a strong defensive stance.

Lastly we see the end of the two Scotlands of John Mair: the 'wild Scots' living in the mountainous area and 'householding Scots' who 'understand the nature of a civil polity'.[60] Jane Stevenson and Peter Davidson have suggested that many in the seventeenth century would have recognised a tripartite division of *Scoti, Scoti Boreali* and *Scoti Montani*, the last two differentiating between the Gordon lands of Moray and the Gaelic-speaking territories.[61] Our evidence suggests that, at the very least, some in Strathspey could choose which of these identities they wished to adopt in a given set of circumstances. The story we have followed points to a version of Highland history that sees a desire for legitimacy despite an acceptance of male violence; for women to have significant personal agency in some circumstances; and for clan society and landlord/tenant relations to be a complicated and individualistic affair. Overall, although there is still much to be done to discover the nuanced complications of Highland society, that society can provide evidence that matches the detail normally reserved for the Lowlands and urban Scotland in the early modern period.

---

[60] A. Constable (ed. and trans.), *A History of Greater Britain as well as England and Scotland, compiled from the Ancient Authorities by John Major* (Edinburgh, 1892), pp. 48–9.
[61] J. Stevenson and P. Davidson, 'Ficino in Aberdeen: The Continuing Problem of the Scottish Renaissance', *Journal of the Northern Renaissance*, 1 (2009), 1–10, at p. 1.

7

Covenanting Women in Scotland: Nonconformity, Marginality, and Community, c.1660–1690

Scott Eaton

In the seventeenth century, Scottish covenanters experienced zeniths and nadirs of power and influence.[1] The introduction of the Book of Common Prayer in 1637 convinced the Scottish nobility, ministers, and burgesses to take a unified stand against Charles I's perceived assault on true religion.[2] The following year, in the prayer book riots of 1638, women took a leading role, their actions representative of public opinion, yet their position in the wider movement uncertain; Walter Balcanquhall described the civil unrest as more than a 'needlesse noyse of simple women but [...] the absolute desire of all our hearts'. Women were not admitted to the signing of the subsequent National Covenant, but many swore the covenant instead, publicly or privately, investing women in its success.[3] As the covenanter movement phased into the Restoration period, women continued to be active members of local religious and spiritual life, in spite of the widespread persecution of conventiclers. The re-establishment of Presbyterianism within the Church of Scotland in 1690 seemed to vindicate the martyrs of the 'killing times', with only the most fervent of believers refusing to accept the new settlement as it neglected to ratify the covenants.[4]

---

[1] My thanks to the Royal Historical Society for providing funding which enabled me to conduct this research.

[2] D. Stevenson, *The Covenantors: The National Covenant and Scotland* (Edinburgh, 1988), pp. 17–22; R. Cust, *Charles I: A Political Life* (London, 2014), pp. 97–9; D. Wallace, Jr., 'Puritan Polemical Divinity and Doctrinal Controversy', in J. Coffey and P. Lim (eds), *The Cambridge Companion to Puritanism* (Cambridge, 2008), pp. 206–22, at pp. 206–17; S. Hardman-Moore, 'Reformed Theology and Puritanism', in P. Nimmo and D. Ferguson (eds), *The Cambridge Companion to Reformed Theology* (Cambridge, 2016), pp. 119–214.

[3] Walter Balcanquhall, *A Large Declaration Concerning the Late Tumults in Scotland* (London, 1639), p. 41; L. Stewart and J. Nugent, *Union and Revolution: Scotland and Beyond, 1625–1745* (Edinburgh, 2020), p. 162; L. Stewart, *Rethinking the Scottish Revolution: Covenanted Scotland, 1637–1651* (Oxford, 2016), pp. 56–62, 113–14; A. McSeveney, 'Non-Conforming Presbyterian Women in Restoration Scotland: 1660–1679' (Unpublished PhD thesis, University of Strathclyde, 2005).

[4] *RPS*, 1690/4/43.

Until recently, women's part in the covenanting movement has received little sustained attention, despite women's central role in the disturbances. Building on the pioneering work of Laura Stewart, Laura Doak, and Michelle Brock, this chapter will highlight and examine women's role as actors throughout the later covenanting movement, showing how and why they deliberately diverged from mainstream religion and society to pursue their nonconformity.[5] It will analyse the writings of three later seventeenth-century covenanting women to explore how they interacted with other members of society and how the latter responded to their zealotry and civil disobedience. It argues that women played a vital role in the covenanting movement, enduring social marginalisation and spiritual isolation to help further the Presbyterian cause.

Covenanters, Women, and Gender in Early Modern Scotland

To properly explore how these women diverged from society, a very brief sketch of early modern Scottish gender roles will follow. The construction of and adherence to gender roles in early modern Scotland was vital to maintaining structured society. Women formed part of a patriarchal society in which they were subordinate to men in all spheres; in practice, though, there were many exceptions to this rule.[6] In his popular conduct book *Domesticall duties* (1622), William Gouge devoted an entire chapter to discussing the place of women in early modern society. He argued that since God 'placed an eminencie in the male over the female', man's rule over the 'weaker vessel' was divinely sanctioned. Men were to fulfil this scriptural commandment by governing women through marriage and by ruling their households.[7] Gouge argued that husbands and wives were both responsible for their family's wealth but traditional gender roles still had to be maintained: wives were to manage the running of their households (domestic sphere) while remaining subordinate to their husbands, who dealt with public matters

---

[5]   L. A. M. Stewart, 'Contesting Reformation: Truth-Telling, the Female Voice, and the Gendering of Political Polemic in Early Modern Scotland', *Huntingdon Library Quarterly*, 84:4 (2021), 717–43; L. Doak, 'Rediscovering the Voices of "fanatick wives": The Cultural Authority of Covenanting Women in Restoration Scotland', *SHR*, 102:2 (2023), 254–72; M. Brock, '"She-zealots" and "Satanesses": Women, Patriarchy and the Covenanting Movement' in J. Nugent, C. Spence and M. Cowan (eds), *Gender in Scotland, 1200–1800: Place, Faith and Politics* (forthcoming). I am very grateful to Dr Brock for sharing this chapter before publication.

[6]   J. Eales, *Women in Early Modern England* (London, 1998), p. 4.

[7]   S. Eaton, *John Stearne's Confirmation and Discovery of Witchcraft: Text, Context and Afterlife* (London, 2020), pp. 114–15; William Gouge, *Of Domesticall Duties...of Wives* (London, 1622), pp. 270, 283. Also see Edmund Tilney, *A Briefe and Pleasant Discourse of Duties in Marriage* (London, 1571), sig. C5v.

(public sphere).[8] Disobedience or disarray in the family unit threatened to lead to widespread disorder.

Members of the godly stuck strictly to this social order, or, as Anne Hughes observes, they 'urged particularly zealous adherence to mostly conventional family duties with complex implications'.[9] Yet women's standing within marriages and households was not as bleak as it first appears. Since godliness demanded high moral standards from men and women, it typically 'tempered rather than reinforced patriarchy', promoting the creation of loving households, giving each other 'sanctified affection'.[10] Godly women had a degree of agency and spiritual initiative within this model. The household was not insular as it included guests, neighbours, servants, and children, while wealthy estates also operated as hubs of economic, political, and religious influence. Women oversaw the running of the household and caring for the family, but were left ample time for their practices of piety – bible reading, introspection, writing, prayers, and attending sermons. They were thus well placed to teach and catechise servants, neighbours, and children within their female networks.[11] Calvinism, especially among Scottish covenanters, helped create a contradiction in that women were subordinate to men but were equal in salvific terms ('ungendered Christian godliness'), and could challenge superiors – husbands, ministers, magistrates – if they believed they were opposing God, under the banner of true religion.[12] Michelle Brock has highlighted this complex patriarchy, commenting that covenanting women 'usually participated in protest in explicit support of some men – most often their ministers and husbands – while in overt defiance of others'; in doing so, their nonconformity negotiated and maintained a social, patriarchal equilibrium.[13] While the National Covenant justified religious resistance on legal grounds, ordinary women broke gendered stereotypes and engaged in civil disobedience out of a communally discerned duty to protect their Church and localities.[14]

In the 1640s, Scottish covenanters reached the peak of their power and influence. This was short lived. Their support of Charles II in 1649–51 caused lasting internal political strife, and military defeat shortly followed

[8] Gouge, *Of Domesticall Duties*, pp. 255–6.
[9] A. Hughes, 'Puritanism and Gender', in Coffey and Lim, *Cambridge Companion to Puritanism*, pp. 294–308, at p. 295.
[10] *Ibid.*, p. 296. See also D. Mullan, 'Women in Scottish Divinity, c.1590–c.1640', in E. Ewen and M. Meikle (eds), *Women in Scotland, c.1100–c.1750* (East Linton, 1999), pp. 29–41.
[11] Hughes, 'Puritanism and Gender', pp. 299–300; Mullan, 'Women in Scottish Divinity', pp. 31–7; L. Doak, 'Rediscovering the Voices of "fanatick wives": The Cultural Authority of Covenanting Women in Restoration Scotland', *SHR*, 102:2 (2023), 254–72, at pp. 265–6.
[12] Mullan, 'Women in Scottish Divinity', pp. 34–7; Doak, 'Rediscovering the Voices', pp. 255–9, 271–2.
[13] Brock, '"She-zealots" and "Satanesses"'.
[14] Doak, 'Rediscovering the Voices', at pp. 271–2; Stevenson, *The Covenantors*, pp. 35–44; Stewart, *Rethinking the Scottish Revolution*, p. 87, pp. 98–9.

– at this point, many had lost faith in the covenants, bringing nothing but disaster to Scotland. With the restoration of Charles II in 1660, persecution of the covenanters began. Charles passed the Rescissory Act, annulling legislation passed since 1633, reinstalled bishops in Scotland, and declared the covenants unlawful. This also meant that ministers who were 'irregularly' appointed during the wars had to go to bishops to have their positions regularised. Many ministers refused. Hundreds of clergy were ejected from the ministry, but they continued to teach their form of religion illegally. Despite the risk of persecution, their efforts were met with much support from fellow covenanters and previous congregants.[15] Many of these adherents were women who engaged in overt dissident activities, including rioting, petitioning, conventicling, and housing refugee ministers. Doak has argued that women of all social ranks engaged in nonconformity as they were committed to the 'Presbyterian process' and acted out of a sense of duty to participate in an ongoing 'work of reformation against tyranny and prelacy' in Church and state. Female covenanters, therefore, charged themselves with a shared cultural and communal duty to further the Presbyterian cause – they spoke and acted to defend their religion and expected to be heard.[16] Some covenanting women documented their experiences during this persecutory time through spiritual and life-writings.

In the seventeenth century, covenanting women were part of a literate Presbyterian culture in which they read the bible and sermons, took notes on scripture, wrote introspective accounts, or frequently penned personal covenants. As Mullan has noted, this evangelical culture helped shape women's narratives. Authors relied heavily on the bible to invent their 'literary selves', personalising the selection and content to best represent their narrative and articulate their experiences to readers. Women wrote as representatives of the covenanting community, writing to a particular audience to inform, inspire, and conform to its ideals. While covenanting women wrote 'to explore a defined sphere rather than transgress boundaries', that did not prevent them from boldly confronting a range of male figures and recording their encounters – Katherine Collace, on whom more below, being a good example.[17]

The case-studies in this chapter take the form of memoirs by three women from eastern Scotland. The authors selected shared commonalities regarding their religious beliefs and desire to further reform Scotland. But each differed in how they experienced their life on the margins of society, and how they chose to record and present their accounts. Their extant manuscripts are important. They demonstrate how women were central to the later covenanting movement and highlight both how and why some

---

[15] I. Cowan, *The Scottish Covenanters, 1660–88* (London, 1976), pp. 30–63.
[16] Doak, 'Rediscovering the Voices', p. 257.
[17] D. Mullan, *Women's Life Writing in Early Modern Scotland: Writing the Evangelical Self, c.1670–c.1730* (Aldershot, 2003), pp. 9–19.

women engaged extensively in dissident activities, and how members of society responded to their actions.

Katherine and Jean Collace

Katherine and Jean Collaces' writings effectively document their covenanting fervour and civil disobedience. Katherine, better known as Mistress Ross (c.1635–1697), was a memoirist, schoolmistress (who taught sewing), and devout Presbyterian who became heavily involved with the Scottish covenanter movement in the 1650s. Jean's life (b. c.1644) had a similar trajectory; she became a domestic servant at Elgin and a teacher in Fife. Little is known about the sisters outside of their writings. They were daughters of Marion Muirhead and Francis Collace, a Presbyterian minister in Earlston, and both experienced an 'effectual calling' under the minister Hew MacKail. While Katherine entered a disastrous marriage to John Ross in 1650 (her husband is almost entirely absent in her writings), Jean never married. Katherine's 'Memoirs' recount a life filled with suffering, including the tragic deaths of her children, chronic bouts of illness, poverty, and frequent quarrels with locals.[18] Although relatively moderate covenanters, their religious zealotry was abrasive to many, often leading to their marginalisation.

From the beginning of their memoirs, they are afflicted and marginalised, yet remain hopeful, endeavouring to follow God's will through intense introspection. Katherine experienced spiritual isolation, narrating how she 'lived almost four years in Tain like a hermit', a place she described as a 'vast howling wilderness, [with] neither ministers nor people knowing anything of God'.[19] But she confided in her sister and found fellow covenanters nearby in Moray and Auldearn – notably Thomas Hog – with whom she shared her religious experiences. She received permanent accommodation and work through the noble Lady Park, who was sympathetic to the covenanting cause. She invited Katherine to live in the vicinity of Nairn and Auldearn to teach her daughters needlework, but she most certainly offered spiritual guidance too, illustrating how Katherine had substantial yet informal status in the covenanting community from her early twenties. Joining this small group

---

[18] S. Eaton, 'Collace (Ross), Katherine (b.1635–d.1697)', in P. Pender and R. Smith (eds), *Palgrave Encyclopaedia of Early Modern Women's Writing in English: The Restoration* (Palgrave, 2021), https://doi.org/10.1007/978-3-030-01537-4_159-2; Mullan, *Women's Life Writing*, pp. 28, 39–98; Katherine Ross (Collace), *Memoirs or Spiritual Exercises of Mrs Ross* (Edinburgh, 1735), pp. 11–16; D. Laing (ed.), *The Diary of Alexander Brodie of Brodie...and his son, James Brodie* (Aberdeen, 1863), pp. 76, 320–4, 340–1, 349, 372, 374, 378, 385. Their sister, Elizabeth Collace, is passingly mentioned in their memoirs – she was also a committed covenanter who travelled with them; see Mullan, *Women's Life Writing*, pp. 116–17; NLS, Adv. MS 32.4.4. I will use Mullan's version as it is more accessible and contains useful explanatory footnotes for readers.

[19] Mullan, *Women's Life Writing*, pp. 45–6.

of covenanting resistance emboldened Katherine to defend her faith when necessary, fomenting opposition from locals.

In Auldearn, her perceived godliness resulted in a dispute with the local minister Harry Forbes and his wife. She claimed that 'I being noticed (though most undeservedly) by some fearing God, more than that person, that proved such an affliction to me that I was either necessitate to leave the place or suffer the way of God to be reproached'.[20] She moved to Forres thereafter. In her 'Memoirs', she included a reflective statement, accusing Forbes of taking 'a liberty in his conversation which I could never go with', and in the marginalia of the Wodrow manuscript the author commented that Forbes soon after committed adultery with his female servant. Emma Wilby has suggested that Forbes either sexually propositioned Collace or she was witness to some form of open relationship between Forbes and his servant. Regardless, it could explain why Forbes' wife forced Katherine to leave, for speaking of what she witnessed and endangering the family's reputation.[21] This event continued to trouble Katherine as they were both 'highly esteemed' Presbyterians; it radicalised her, instructing her that even ministers could falter and that not all divines could be trusted.

Following this revelation, Katherine lambasted all who swore the oaths to bishops and king. She believed that their 'foundation was laid in the overturning of this kingdom, they coming in by the Oath of Supremacy'. Indeed, both sisters had 'sworn to the extirpation of prelacy' and desired to rid Scotland 'from the Bondage of Prelacy'.[22] This led to an altercation between Katherine, Jean, and a gentleman in Innes House, Elgin – possibly Sir James Innes. Both Katherine and Jean were troubled by the success of bishops in their area and prayed for answers. Jean lamented of locals' 'woeful and sad sin of hearing the curate', while Katherine shows how they were feeling vulnerable and marginalised: 'the curate there was triumphing over us; we were also near the prelate, and both like to die. None were near that understood soul-work; we were far from friends and acquaintances'. But before leaving the area, Katherine confronted the gentleman at Innes in the belief that it would please God, forcefully reproaching him for accepting bishops and revoking the covenants. She removed Jean from the house and they both left the area, presumably because it had become dangerous.[23] This was not the end of their troubles as they continued to clash with their male social superiors. Over the next few years, they flitted across Scotland, connected with fellow covenanters, and successfully, if narrowly, evaded prosecution for nonconformity.

After the death of her husband John Ross around 1674, Katherine and Jean moved to Fife, where they continued their civil disobedience, again forming

[20] *Ibid.*, p. 49.
[21] *Ibid.*, pp. 49–52; E. Wilby, *The Visions of Isobel Gowdie: Magic, Witchcraft and Dark Shamanism in Seventeenth-Century Scotland* (Brighton, 2013), pp. 174–9.
[22] Mullan, *Women's Life Writing*, pp. 50–1.
[23] *Ibid.*, pp. 62–4, 96–7. Unfortunately, the details of this fallout are scant.

a small circle of covenanting resistance in a mostly conforming area. As before, they taught sewing to the daughters of sympathetic gentry, along with religious instruction, but knowledge of their teaching and nonconformity reached local government. Jean recounted how 'there was nothing but searching for ministers and private Christians and haling to prison such as the enemy found'.[24] In April 1675, a week after Katherine left for Auldearn, they were summoned to court. Louise Yeoman has commented that their public nonconformity 'no doubt contributed to their appearance before a local court where they were only saved from prosecution by the interposition of a local noblewoman (perhaps the Countess of Rothes [Margaret Leslie]). It would also account for the attempted kidnap of one of their scholars by her episcopal relatives'.[25] The Collace sisters operated on the edges of mainstream society and continued to follow their faith, regardless of any persecution or social hostility incurred.

In June 1675, Jean returned to Auldearn to regroup with Katherine. However, further litigation loomed. In this area, the Collaces took a central role with nonconformists, attending conventicles and travelling with the prominent preachers Thomas Hog, John Welwood, and James Urquhart. In response to their activity, the earl of Moray decided in March 1676 to fine those who attended conventicles, taking a firmer stance in November after Urquhart baptised his son in public.[26] The Collaces were in imminent danger. From early 1676, Jean was 'warned of God to flee', 'to prepare for death' and to 'prepare for a storm' from their enemies.[27] Indeed, Moray had the full weight of the law behind him, with parliament having passed a series of acts throughout the 1670s to encourage the suppression of field and house conventicles, and punishment of their attendees. The 'Act against Conventicles' (1670) stated 'that every person who shall be found to have been present at any such meetings shall be on every occasion fined according to their qualities in the respective sums following, and imprisoned until they pay their fines', while non-conforming ministers who 'without licence or authority foresaid, shall preach, expound scripture or pray at any of these meetings in the field, or in any house where there are more persons than the house contains [...] shall be punished with death and confiscation of

---

[24]   *Ibid.*, p. 108.
[25]   *Ibid.*, pp. 108–15; L. A. Yeoman, 'Ross [*née* Collace], Katherine', *ODNB*, https://doi.org/10.1093/ref:odnb/45821 [accessed 06/09/2023].
[26]   Mullan, *Women's Life Writing*, pp. 54, 102–3, 117–20; H. Scott, *Fasti Ecclesiae Scoticanae: The Succession of Ministers in the Church of Scotland from the Reformation* (7 vols, Edinburgh, 1915–28), vol. 7, pp. 351, 354; R. Keith, *An Historical Catalogue of the Scottish Bishops* (Edinburgh, 1824), pp. 152–3; J. Lewis and D. Pringle, *Spynie Palace and the Bishops of Moray* (Edinburgh, 2002), p. 9. See also Laing, *Diary of Alexander Brodie*, p. 350.
[27]   Mullan, *Women's Life Writing*, pp. 127, 132, 135. Jean Collace's account ends in July 1676.

their goods'.[28] The Collace sisters thus faced fines or imprisonment for their nonconformity. As before, this did not deter them.

The earl of Moray and Alexander Douglas of Spynie expressed much 'ill' and 'bitterness' towards Katherine, and considered arraigning her in late December 1676. Luckily for Katherine, a locally influential noble, Alexander Brodie, spoke to the earl on her behalf:

> I offerd shee should leav the countree once in March, soe he did let her alon. He did not promis, but he said he would not tak words for it; but he should consider it against the court which would be on the second Tuisday or Wedensday in Feb.[29]

After another close escape from the courts, Katherine moved to Edinburgh within a few months, where she remained until her death in 1697. There, she undoubtedly continued practising her faith, but became further marginalised: she had 'constant contentions' with those who swore any oaths or indulgences and distanced herself from a group of covenanters she had joined (likely United Societies) out of aversion to 'their Extremes of Separation'.[30] Throughout Jean and Katherine's life, they were abrasive characters to their neighbours, and they remained committed covenanters who zealously engaged in nonconformity and proselytising, regardless of whether this risked imprisonment or death. Their accounts demonstrate how they were socially marginalised for most of their lives; however, the Collaces circumvented this by finding and joining like-minded individuals wherever they went, creating pockets of resistance in which they strengthened each other's faith, preached, and enacted further civil disobedience in the form of conventicles.

Helen Alexander

Helen Alexander (c.1654–1729) was a radical covenanter who lived in Pentland, south-east of Edinburgh. Alexander's narrative is punctuated with tales of nonconformity and danger, but also shows her compassion for other covenanters, whom she helped financially and spiritually in times of need. Alexander was married twice, first to Charles Umpherston in 1672, then to James Currie in 1687. While Alexander received no official education, her narrative demonstrates that she was scripturally sound, well-connected in local covenanting circles, and politically aware.[31] Indeed, Doak has recently

---

[28] RPS, 1670/7/11. See also RPS, 1672/6/51, 1673/11/4, A1678/6/1.

[29] Brodie, Diary of Alexander Brodie, pp. 372–4, 378, 383, 385.

[30] H. Paton, Register of Interments in the Greyfriars Burying-Ground (Edinburgh, 1902), pp. 135, 560; Mullan, Women's Life Writing, pp. 78, 80–1.

[31] C. U. Aitchison (ed.), Passages in the Lives of Helen Alexander and James Currie of Pentland (Belfast, 1869), pp. 8–9, p. 13; 'Alexander, Helen', in E. Ewen, R. Pipes, J. Rendall and S. Reynolds (eds), The New Biographical Dictionary of Scottish Women (Edinburgh, 2018), p. 10.

discovered Alexander's commonplace book which contains extensive notes on texts, sermons, letters, and poems, evidencing Alexander's intellect. Throughout her nonconformity, she managed to evade the authorities and survive persecution, though she did come very close to execution. The writings of Alexander, and those of Currie, detail their life on the margins, their conflict with authorities, and their continued social deviance in the name of the covenanting tradition.[32]

Alexander married Umpherston in 1672 and moved to the parish of Pentland. He travelled with 'several godly persons who were going to hear the persecuted ministers about Edinburgh'. It was here that she first encountered covenanting ministers, including John Welsh, Donald Cargill, and David Williamson. After hearing a sermon by Williamson at Dalkeith and conversing with her sister, Alexander became convinced that the hearing of curates was evil.[33] This marked the start of Alexander's nonconformity, which was supported and galvanised by a small group of local covenanters. Alexander's radical views put her in stark opposition to the then-orthodox Church and state, isolating her from the mainstream of society. Her rejection of curates meant that she refused to attend the kirk, choosing instead to travel to conventicles. She also refused to pay fines or taxes, or to accept or participate in any type of government. Alexander's fear was that even oblique or tacit support of bishops was assenting to their office and was sinful. To avoid this trap, she became unshakeable in her beliefs. Her uncompromising stance can be highlighted by her exclamation that 'I was resolved to lay down my life rather than comply either with the prelatical curates, or any other course of compliance, or to own the authority of the tyrant who was then upon the throne [Charles II]'.[34] Alexander's civil disobedience brought her into conflict with locals on several occasions.

After the assassination of Archbishop James Sharp in 1679, the Stuart government pursued and punished non-conformists intensely. Helen Alexander experienced the effects of this in her locality, revealing both sympathisers and adversaries in response to her nonconformity. In the same year as her husband's death, 1681, she was arrested for attending a conventicle and fined £50. She did not deny that she attended the conventicle, nor did she appear in court. Fearing that her assets would be seized, she deposited all her belongings and wealth with her brother-in-law, Robert Umpherston. This left her destitute, but she was willing to suffer rather than hand her possessions to the government. Alexander's account states that she found a new lodging which she also used to harbour fleeing ministers, 'for I always

---

[32] Doak, 'Rediscovering the Voices', pp. 265–6; St Andrews University Library, MS38977/6/4/2/12, Collectione Booke of James Currie (currently uncatalogued); A. Muir, 'Alexander [Other Married Names, Umpherston, Currie], Helen (1653/4–1729)', *ODNB*, https://doi.org/10.1093/ref:odnb/330 [accessed 06/09/2023]. See also Aitchison, *Passages*.

[33] Mullan, *Women's Life Writing*, pp. 190–2; Aitchison, *Passages*, pp. 1–3.

[34] *Ibid.*, pp. 4, 9–10.

thought that to be my duty'. One of these refugees was Andrew Guillon, who was involved in the murder of Archbishop Sharp. A local informed the local laird of Gullon's presence, and Alexander was arrested and taken to Edinburgh's Canongate tolbooth, where she remained for eleven weeks. She continued to be resolute. After being advised to attend the kirk, she quipped that 'I would rather beg my bread with my children'.[35] As Muir commented on Alexander's discharge, 'the official account of her release reports a caution of 3,000 merks to appear before the council when called and her denial of any knowledge of Guillon's deed'. But this is contrary to the traditional account, which suggests she was released because of Sir Alexander Gibson's intervention, who forged her submission. Alexander maintained that she was released 'without the least compliance', and her reaction to the suggestion that she might be put to death was to send word to her home to have her grave clothes prepared.[36] Indeed, she continued her nonconformity and pursued her covenanting faith throughout her life, which was only bolstered by her like-minded husband, James Currie. In Alexander's last recorded encounter with the authorities, their house was searched 'for uncustomed goods', and twelve copies of James Renwick's *Vindication* (Edinburgh, 1687), which the couple had intended to distribute, were discovered. Renwick was arrested but Alexander and Currie were not arraigned – fearing that they might be, they had fled once more. Despite the restoration of Presbyterianism in 1689, Alexander's account closes with a radical stance, criticising the Toleration Act, oath of allegiance, and treaty of union for their political distance from the covenants.[37]

Alexander's account is one of constant struggles as she fervently followed her beliefs and attempted to evade the authorities. Her physical and ideological separation from mainstream society propelled her into a very close-knit group of like-minded individuals. Alexander's social interactions with local covenanting groups highlight different aspects of life at the margins of Scottish society. Alexander offered support and refuge for covenanters, and she put great effort into charity and ministering to those in prison, considering this as her religious duty. On multiple occasions, her narrative recounts how she gathered money, clothes, and food for those in need. For instance, when prisoners were transported from Bothwell to Edinburgh in 1679, she gathered personal money and shirts for the captives. Likewise, after Argyll's rebellion in 1685, over 100 covenanting prisoners were taken to Dunnottar Castle: Alexander recorded that 'I did gather some money and some shirts and gave to them who needed them, as I did many a time when they were in prison'.[38] Many women would have supported fellow covenanters and ministers in this way, but these small, yet important actions have left few historical records.[39]

[35]   *Ibid.*, pp. 5–9.
[36]   Muir, 'Alexander, Helen'.
[37]   Mullan, *Women's Life Writing*, pp. 200–3; Aitchison, *Passages*, pp. 11–13, 39.
[38]   *Ibid.*, pp. 4, 6, 11–12.
[39]   Brock, '"She-zealots" and "Satanesses"'.

In her later years, Alexander seems to have shifted from active philanthropy to a more pedagogical role in her community, focusing on the next generation of covenanters. Around 1683, she was instructing approximately ten children in Pentland in the covenanting tradition, one of whom was her daughter, Beatrix Umpherston. They signed and followed a new, short children's covenant, which reflected Alexander's faith and ardent anti-prelatical stance. Reflecting on this, Alexander recalled how 'the Lord helped me to be very useful among them, and I did encourage them, for which they had respect to me to my dying day'.[40] At first glance, Alexander's life was one of nonconformity, persecution, and destitution. But her faith, relationships with fellow covenanters, and involvement in furthering the Presbyterian cause gave meaning and purpose to her suffering. Alexander's account demonstrates how some individuals could forge their own successful, minority groups on the edges of society, and how women were central to this, supporting local non-conforming networks.

Marion Veitch

Marion Veitch (1639–1722) is our final example of a covenanting woman operating on the margins of society. More than the others discussed, Veitch was often very isolated, with her family taking asylum in another country. And yet she pursued the Presbyterian cause just as rigorously in the face of local persecution. Veitch survived and spiritually prospered by attending conventicles, reading Presbyterian literature, and joining local non-conformist groups.[41]

Marion Veitch, *née* Fairley, was born in Edinburgh in 1639, the daughter of James Fairley, a shoemaker, and Euphan Kincaid. Marion did not stay long in the city – a recurrent theme throughout her life. She was moved to Lanark when she was six to stay with family to escape Edinburgh's virulent plague outbreak.[42] Recounting her formative years in Lanark, Veitch remembered that she 'was born in a land where the gospel was at that time purely and powerfully preached; as also, that I was born of godly parents, and well educated'.[43] It was also where she met and married her husband William Veitch, a Presbyterian minister, in November 1664. Marion recorded that she had desired to marry a godly man to advance her faith, to be 'matched

---

[40] Mullan, *Women's Life Writing*, p. 201; Aitchison, *Passages*, pp. 12, 67–8.
[41] NLS, Adv. MS 34.6.22. For accessibility, I will use the printed reproduction found in J. Carstairs (ed.), *Memoirs of Mrs William Veitch, Mr Thomas Hog of Kiltearn, Mr Henry Erskine, and Mr John Carstairs* (Edinburgh, 1846), pp. 26–9, 35.
[42] 'Veitch, Marion', in Ewen et al., *Biographical Dictionary of Scottish Women*, pp. 439–40; K. Howard, *Marion Veitch* (Ossett, 1992), pp. 11–12, 18; A. Du Toit, 'Veitch [née Fairlie], Marion (1639–1722)', *ODNB*, https://doi.org/10.1093/ref:odnb/45831 [accessed 06/09/2023].
[43] Carstairs, *Memoirs of Mrs William Veitch*, p. 1.

in Him and for His glory'. Several of her friends tried to dissuade her from marrying a nonconforming minister, as it would relegate her to a life filled with peril. Marion, of course, did not listen. She seems to have had a successful, loving marriage with William, producing five children. But her friends were correct, as she quickly discovered: 'A little after I was married, the storm of persecution arose upon us, to the parting of my husband and me, and increased so, as I was necessitated to leave my native land'.[44]

The storm took the form of Sir James Turner, who was dispatched by the government to quash nonconformity. His success in this led to unrest and an outright covenanter uprising, which culminated in the battle of Rullion Green in November 1666. William Veitch was heavily involved in the insurrection and the battle. With the defeat of the covenanting army, he was captured, but miraculously managed to escape and went into hiding. Marion bore the brunt of this decision. On the evening after the battle, Marion harboured three covenanting officers who had escaped, and awaited word of her husband. Turner's local spies quickly located Veitch's home, and the following day the authorities searched her house in an attempt to seize William.[45] Marion was watched and harassed for weeks until her character, and provision of drink, made the troopers decide that 'it were a pity to disturb such a good gentlewoman'.[46] Regardless of her efforts, a proclamation for the rebels was issued mentioning William by name, so he hurriedly sought refuge in Margaret Muir's house in Edinburgh, and then fled to Northumberland where he stayed until 1671. He was captured and imprisoned on the Bass Rock in 1679. William was released the following year, but was forced to flee yet again, this time to the Netherlands in 1683. Similarly, Marion's life was filled with frequent moves, and she was out of Scotland for many years – much to her disappointment. As Alex Du Toit has shown, while in England, Marion 'lived at Hanham Hall, Northumberland (1672–7), Stanton Hall in the same county (1677–85), and Newcastle (1685–8), sometimes with and sometimes without her husband', but finally moved back to Scotland after the revolution, settling first at Peebles (1690–4), and then Dumfries (1694–1722).[47] For much of her life, Marion was an isolated, single mother maintaining her faith in the face of local adversity.

Veitch's memoirs are deeply introspective and spiritual. They show her doubts and fears for the safety of her family, often in response to national political events. Her awareness of national politics and detailing of local experiences provide a unique perspective on nonconformists as they transitioned from a time of persecution before the revolution to a time of

---

[44]   Howard, *Marion Veitch*, pp. 54–9; Carstairs, *Memoirs of Mrs William Veitch*, pp. 2–3.
[45]   Howard, *Marion Veitch*, pp. 70–88; T. M'Crie (ed.), *Memoirs of Mr William Veitch and George Brysson* (Edinburgh, 1825), pp. 23–50.
[46]   *Ibid.*, pp. 52–3.
[47]   Howard, *Marion Veitch*, pp. 385–592; Carstairs, *Memoirs of Mrs William Veitch*, pp. 7–8, 14, 30–1, 35; Mullan, *Women's Life Writing*, p. 6; Du Toit, 'Veitch'; McSeveney, 'Non-Conforming Presbyterian Women', p. 135.

toleration afterwards. Marion's memoirs chronicle clashes with government forces and internal conflicts within godly circles as they grappled with the practicalities of rebuilding Scottish Presbyterianism. In reading Marion's account, it is easy to negate her agency and consider her as merely a satellite of her husband. But she was involved in dissident activity in the 1660s and continued to engage with covenanting circles until the revolution. Certainly, there is evidence that Marion was active in conventicle attendance in her late twenties. In late 1665, she helped organise and hold a conventicle at her house in Dunsyre. The ministers John Welsh and John Blackadder were in attendance, along with some unnamed others. Blackadder records how he 'came to the parish of Dunsyre on Saturday night, to Mr Veitch's house at Hills, where he preached on the morrow, being Sabbath, but to a few persons, publick preaching not having been practised in these bounds before'.[48] Later in 1667, after William had fled, Marion attended house conventicles in Edinburgh hosted by James Guthrie's wife until they were discovered and disbanded. Despite her isolation, Veitch continued to engage with and move in important nonconformist circles, with prominent preachers such as Blackadder, Welsh, and Donald Cargill.[49] Marion's diary is largely silent about conventicles and does not mention her attendance, perhaps to ensure the safety of all involved. It is highly likely that she went to local house conventicles, particularly in Northumberland and Newcastle, where she had connections and where there was strong nonconformism.[50] To support this, immediately after the declaration of indulgence was issued in 1687, Veitch attended a sermon by Richard Gilpin at a nearby meeting house. And very shortly after, Marion's memoirs details two separate conversations about the pitfalls of religious toleration with a godly woman and another group of people.[51] It is reasonable to suggest that these were pre-existing nonconformist groups that Marion was already part of. Veitch would have used these networks to practise her faith, gather with like-minded people, and listen for news of her family. Although pushed to the edges of mainstream society, Marion found ways to combat her isolation and to support and strengthen her local covenanting groups.

Marion Veitch's memoir contains details of parochial reactions to nonconformist activity, but it also highlights religious conflict after the revolution, as they tried to implement their religious freedoms. Marion experienced this in Peebles, when her husband secured a preaching post. It should have been a new and exciting chapter, inaugurating their return to Scotland; however, for the Veitches, 'out of this rose sprang many a thorn, for

---

[48] Howard, *Marion Veitch*, pp. 63–5; M'Crie, *Memoirs of Mr William Veitch*, p. 23; A. Crichton (ed.), *Memoirs of the Rev. John Blackadder* (Edinburgh, 1826), p. 115.
[49] Howard, *Marion Veitch*, pp. 101, 120. See McSeveney, 'Non-Conforming Presbyterian Women', pp. 218–21, for a list of conventicles held by women discovered by the privy council.
[50] Howard, *Marion Veitch*, pp. 285–6, 639–75.
[51] Carstairs, *Memoirs of Mrs William Veitch*, pp. 23, 26–8.

both friends and foes reproached [them]'.[52] In Peebles, Presbyterianism was strong. And while the newly disenfranchised Episcopalians of the town were in the minority, they still enjoyed the patronage and protection of William Douglas, duke of Queensberry. Prior to the Veitches' arrival, Queensberry nominated a new minister, Robert Knox, to replace John Hay in November 1689. But shortly after the declaration of indulgence, the town's Presbyterians had sourced their own minister, James Feithie, who preached from a meeting house until his death in 1689. Peebles was denominationally divided between the two preachers.[53] In the summer of 1690, the Scottish government abolished patronage and episcopacy, removing Queensberry's legal mandate to appoint ministers. According to Marion, 'a friend of mine [...] wrote a letter desiring her to come and see her', and on the journey, William encountered the provost of Peebles, who invited him to be their minister. William entered this bitter dispute – and a lengthy litigation battle – in August 1690. Queensberry's camp fought his appointment and supported their nominees, Knox and Henry Hay, who continued to preach unabated. Even in their new community, religious conflict shadowed Marion. Queensberry's faction turned to print and, as Marion remarked, 'printed lies against the presbytery and my husband'.[54] The issue was elevated to the general assembly, but they failed to legally confirm William's position, possibly to avoid the anger of Queensberry. Against their wishes, the Veitches moved to Dumfries, as William fulfilled another ministerial appointment.[55]

Marion Veitch's short account of Peebles highlights the post-revolution settlement, and the troublesome practicalities of liberty of conscience and religious pluralism. Previously marginalised Presbyterians were granted religious freedoms and thrust into power at the expense of other groups, who took their place, and jostled for influence. Veitch's narrative discusses this brief transitory period as her covenanting hopes returned and Scotland's Presbyterian ascendency began.

Conclusion

Women played a vital role in the later covenanting movement. Brock has remarked that 'after the return of episcopacy to Scotland in 1662, women

[52] *Ibid.*, p. 38. Additionally, when a few young non-conformists smuggled in seditious books, they were hunted by magistrates, and tried to place the blame on Marion Veitch; Carstairs, *Memoirs of Mrs William Veitch*, pp. 18–20. For religious legislation post-Revolution, see R. Stevens, *Protestant Pluralism: The Reception of the Toleration Act, 1689–1720* (Woodbridge, 2018).

[53] . Howard, *Marion Veitch*, pp. 385–450.

[54] *Ibid.*, pp. 381–2, 387–8; Carstairs, *Memoirs of Mrs William Veitch*, pp. 38–9; M'Crie, *Memoirs of Mr William Veitch*, pp. 187–8; J. D. Ford, 'Douglas, William, First Duke of Queensberry (1637–1695)', *ODNB*, https://doi.org/10.1093/ref:odnb/7936 [accessed 06/09/2023].

[55] Carstairs, *Memoirs of Mrs William Veitch*, pp. 41–2, 49–50.

became central, visible figures of nonconformity, petitioning the privy council, attending and hosting conventicles and composing accounts of their own religious experiences in the face of persecution'.[56] The narratives of the Collaces, Helen Alexander, and Marion Veitch help demonstrate this. They recorded their experiences to chronicle their struggles and give future generations of covenanters spiritual guidance, circulating these accounts in manuscript and then print, while others assumed a more informal, pedagogical role to educate the budding youth. Doak has observed that women of all social ranks engaged in this nonconformity because they were committed to the 'Presbyterian process'.[57] Women who swore the covenants became heavily invested in this 'process' and acted out of and responded to a shared cultural and communal duty to further the Presbyterian cause. Importantly, they spoke and acted to defend their religion and expected to be heard – and were.

Covenanting women were often isolated and nomadic because they were fleeing persecution; some were zealous and abrasive, frequently clashing with male social superiors due to differing religious and political opinions. All this paints a picture of women on the margins who voluntarily relegated themselves to the peripheries of society to follow their faith. But in the cases discussed in this chapter, women offset this with piety and by connecting with strong networks of fellow covenanters to reinforce their beliefs and perpetuate the movement. Covenanting women survived persecution from the state and skirmishes with locals thanks to sheer luck, faith, and their networks of supporters. As Veitch explained, covenanters chose to suffer during their own lives to realise the covenants and Presbyterianism, and in the conviction of their reward thereafter – 'They that sow in tears, shall reap in joy'.

---

[56] Brock, '"She-zealots" and "Satanesses"'.
[57] Doak, 'Rediscovering the Voices', p. 257.

8

Life on the Margins of Law and Order: James Macpherson – The Scottish Robin Hood

Anne-Marie Kilday

How was crime perceived and managed by the Scottish authorities in the period before centralised justice? What type of crimes and criminals did the Scottish authorities target and for what reasons? Was crime regarded during the early modern period as something committed on the margins of society by individuals from specific social groups, or was it thought of as more mainstream than that? Which marginalised groups existed in early modern Scotland, and how were they regarded by the authorities and by society more widely? To answer these various questions, this chapter offers a case study of the infamous Gypsy freebooter James Macpherson, who was simultaneously a recidivist nuisance to the authorities and an idolised folk-hero to the masses, despite existing during a pre-industrial era where press sensationalism about criminals and their activities did not yet exist.[1] The chapter will expose his history, the competing attitudes and reactions to his behaviour, and the legacy that he left behind for the development of Scottish justice. It will also, at the same time, offer a specific exploration into the treatment of Gypsies like Macpherson, who have endured, and indeed continue to endure, enforced marginalisation and systemic abuse in the British Isles and beyond.

The Pervasive Marginalisation of the Gypsy

A significant proportion of the scholarship regarding European Gypsies is consumed by a seemingly unceasing debate about the origins of this specific ethnic group.[2] Whilst there is an evident lack of clarity on this issue, there

---

[1] For the purposes of this chapter, the term 'Gypsy' rather than 'Romani' will be used as Gypsy was the term utilised in all the primary sources relating to this case, as well as the pertinent legislation from this particular period. Additionally, Gypsies will be defined as a people who prefer an itinerant way of life to a more conventionally settled one. They are free-spirited in their lifestyle choices and do not recognise the sorts of rules that normally govern society

[2] See for instance F. Timbers, *'The Damned Fraternitie': Constructing Gypsy Identity in Early Modern England, 1500–1700* (London and New York, 2016), chapter 1; A. Fraser, *The Gypsies* (Oxford, 1995); D. Kenrick, *Gypsies: From the Ganges to the Thames* (Hatfield, 2004); W. Simson, *A History of the Gipsies: With Specimens of the Gipsy Language* (London,

is certainly no dispute about how Gypsies were regarded. Throughout history, wherever they came to be located, Gypsies attracted uniform hostility.[3] Some historians, such as Miriam Eliav-Feldon, have argued that the reason for this enduring enmity lies in the fact that Gypsies were regarded as a social problem: a financial burden on the state or parish. Whilst this might be true in part for certain locations, evidence suggests that the rancour perpetually directed towards Gypsies was less transactional and more sinister and prejudicial than that. Patently, Gypsies were perceived to be an active and visible threat to the social and moral stability of populations, and as such, they needed to be separated or 'othered' from mainstream society.[4]

The reasons Gypsies were believed to be problematic are multifarious, complex, and historically fluid. For example, at times they were associated with an infamously savage disposition, with lawlessness and boisterousness, with mystery, cunning, and falsehood, with ungodliness, and with certain ineffable primitive behaviours which were believed to be endemic among their 'kind'.[5] All these perceived characteristics and behaviours served to trigger efforts to ostracise the group from more conventional 'civilised' society. In addition, Gypsies' distinctive language, customs, dress, and interests also served to fuel their ghettoisation, within a prevailing and enduring context of racism.[6] In part, however, we should acknowledge that this ostracism was not only welcomed but was routinely perpetuated by Gypsy folk at various historical junctures, as they were rightly proud of their heritage, their customs, and what made them distinct.

In any event, the perceived association between Gypsies and social depravity is arguably evidence of an early 'moral panic' in pre-modern history. Despite the absence of a press media to fuel the prevailing concerns and any substantive evidence to validate them, the vast majority of the early modern populace still managed to turn Gypsies into social pariahs. Not only were Gypsies shunned by communities at every conceivable opportunity, but they were 'othered' and dehumanised in a variety of ways, such as through

---

1866); D. Epstein Nord, *Gypsies and the British Imagination, 1807–1930* (New York, 2006), p. 8; B. Vesey-Fitzgerald, *Gypsies of Britain: An Introduction to their History* (Newton Abbot, 1974), p. 20.

[3] See J.-P. Liégeois, *Gypsies: An Illustrated History* (London, 2005), pp. 87–141; J. Keet-Black *Gypsies of Britain* (Oxford, 2013), p. 5; D. Mayall, *Gypsy Identities 1500–2000: From Egipcyans to Moon-men to the Ethic Romany* (London, 2004); D. Cressy, *Gypsies: An English History* (Oxford, 2018).

[4] For evidence of this see Timbers, 'The Damned Fraternitie', p. 39 and chapters 5 and 6; Simson, *History of the Gipsies*, p. 28; Epstein Nord, *Gypsies and the British Imagination*, p. 3; M. Eliav-Feldon, 'Vagrants or Vermin? Attitudes towards Gypsies in Early Modern Europe', in M. Eliav-Feldon, B. Isaac and J. Ziegler (eds), *The Origins of Racism in the West* (Cambridge, 2009), pp. 276–91, at pp. 277–8, 283–6.

[5] Epstein Nord, *Gypsies*, p. 3, Simson, *History of the Gypsies*, p. 13; Eliav-Feldon, 'Vagrants or Vermin?', at pp. 278, 284, 288.

[6] Keet-Black *Gypsies*, p. 8; Timbers, 'The Damned Fraternitie', p. 39 and chapters 5 and 6; Eliav-Feldon, 'Vagrants or Vermin?', p. 285; J. Crabb, *The Gypsy's Advocate, etc* (London, 1831), p. 23.

the language used to describe them. Gypsies were variously designated as 'rogues', 'barbarians', 'land-pirates', 'moon-men' (lunatics), 'wolves', 'apes', and 'swine'. Then, over the course of the early modern period in particular, they were also increasingly characterised as 'rodents', 'locusts', 'grasshoppers', and 'lice', and depicted as hideous primordial hybrid creatures who were only human in part.[7] In effect, then, not only did Gypsies come to be associated with deviance, violence, and the criminal underworld, but they were also deemed to be social vermin capable of spreading harm across populations. Like any menacing contagion or parasite, they needed to be contained and, where possible, exterminated.

The main solution offered to this problem was provided by state authorities across Europe, who from the sixteenth century onwards repeatedly passed items of legislation (each one more austere than the last) aimed at eradicating, or to use modern parlance, 'ethnically cleansing' Gypsy men, women, and children from society.[8] We can see from this that not only does the Gypsy experience constitute one of the earliest examples of a 'moral panic', but it also, arguably, provides one of the earliest recorded instances of flagrant racism in early modern social history. As this bigoted sentiment undoubtedly persists today, it can be argued that the discrimination endured by Gypsies is more historically significant compared to that of many other ethnic minority groups in the British and European past, and moreover we have explicit written evidence of it dating back some six centuries.

One interesting exception to the persistent and consistent hostility experienced by Gypsies across Europe occurred in Scotland, where there was more of a pendulum of opinion that swung for and against this group at various points during the early modern period.[9] Certainly, Scottish attitudes to Gypsies seem to have been more nuanced than elsewhere at this time.[10] Initially, Gypsies were evidently distrusted and unwelcomed in the Scottish context, as one of the first records which mentions their existence is a piece of anti-Gypsy legislation passed in the mid-fifteenth century, which some scholars believe may be the very first reference to the presence of Gypsies in Europe. In 1449, parliament passed an act for the prosecution of 'sorners',

---

[7]   See for instance T. Dekker, *Villanies Discovered by Lanthorne and Candle-light, etc* (London, 1616), chapter 6; Timbers, 'The Damned Fraternitie', chapter 2; Eliav-Feldon, 'Vagrants or Vermin?', pp. 287–9.

[8]   Liégeois, *Gypsies*, pp. 87–141; Timbers, 'The Damned Fraternitie', chapter 2.

[9]   For general scholarship on the history of gypsies in Scotland see Simson, *History of the Gipsies*, chapters III–X and A. McCormick, *The Tinkler-Gypsies of Galloway* (Dumfries, 1906). It should be noted that scant reference is made to Gypsy activity further north than Stirling in these works. The Highland Gypsy remains something of an historiographical enigma, which this chapter will go some way to explicate.

[10]   There is as yet, no concrete evidence about the size and extent of the Gypsy population in Scotland during the early modern period. In 1866, it was estimated that there were more than 100,000 gypsies by one scholar, although another, just twenty years later, identified just 500 throughout Scotland – see respectively Simson, *History of the Gipsies*, p. 61 and W. Chambers, *Exploits and Anecdotes of the Scottish Gypsies, etc* (Edinburgh, 1886), p. 11.

'fancied fools', 'vagabonds', 'over-liers', 'masterful beggars', 'cairds', and 'such like runners'.[11] Whilst there were no individuals in this list specifically referred to as 'Gypsies' or 'Egyptians' (according to etymologists, the term Gypsy comes from this word as it was the place where Gypsies were once thought to originate), the characteristics of those described in this act mirrored those that were later to become associated with this particular ethnic group.[12]

The initial adverse opinion towards Gypsies soon changed, however, and it is clear that they became a source of fascination for many Scottish people, and they grew to be accepted as a group that was evidently different, but not one that was particularly menacing or which posed an obvious threat.[13] In 1505, for instance, the accounts of the lord high treasurer make mention of a payment of £7 to the 'Egyptians' by the king's command.[14] It is thought that James IV (r.1488–1513) may have offered this sum as a charitable donation, believing that the Gypsies in his kingdom were displaced pilgrims. Certainly, royal patronage and protection was enjoyed by the Gypsies during the remainder of his reign and into the early decades of that of his son.[15] By the 1530s, however, scepticism and concern over the characteristics that made Gypsies 'different' started to be voiced in parallel to the preferential treatment they were enjoying, and their supposed latent immorality and evident criminal exploits challenged those attitudes which had seen them gain favour amongst certain social elites and the royal family.[16]

According to legend, it was their treatment of one monarch in particular, James V (r.1513–42), which effectively pushed the pendulum of collective opinion strongly towards antagonism. Although James V was said to have

[11] Departmental Committee on Tinkers (Scotland) [hereafter DCT(S)], *Report of the Departmental Committee on Tinkers in Scotland* (Edinburgh, 1918), p. 6; D. MacRitchie, *Scottish Gypsies under the Stewarts* (Edinburgh, 1894), p. 17; R. Dawson, *Empty Lands: Aspects of Scottish Gypsy and Traveller Survival* (Alfreton, 2007), p. 15; Vesey-Fitzgerald, *Gypsies of Britain*, p. 20. There is some evidence to support the presence of Gypsies in Scotland prior to this in the reign of James II (r.1437–1460) – see Dawson, *Empty Lands*, pp. 12–14 – but this has not been substantiated elsewhere.

[12] 'Sorning', for instance, was a regular charge in Scottish indictments during the early modern period and a sorner was a menace who took advantage of the good will and hospitality of others. 'Cairds' were also known as tinkers who were famed for being mischievous itinerants.

[13] Palmistry and fortune-telling, as well as the folk medicine conducted by Gypsies, were seen by many in the early modern period to be enthralling and invaluable. See Vesey-Fitzgerald, *Gypsies of Britain*, pp. 125–37, 138–60, and MacRitchie, *Scottish Gypsies*, p. 2. For further evidence of early Gypsies being well-received into Scotland see DCT(S), *Report*, p. 6.

[14] See MacRitchie, *Scottish Gypsies*, pp. 29–30; Vesey-Fitzgerald, *Gypsies of Britain*, p. 21.

[15] Simson, *History of the Gipsies*, pp. 99–103; Chambers, *Exploits*, p. 8; MacRitchie, *Scottish Gypsies*, pp. 46, 48; Vesey-Fitzgerald, *Gypsies of Britain*, p. 28.

[16] For evidence of the seemingly recalcitrant bad behaviour amongst Scottish Gypsies during the early modern period, see Anonymous, 'Scottish Gypsies', *Blackwood's Edinburgh Magazine*, 1 (1817), p. 44, pp. 50–8, 154–61 and 615–20; DCT(S), *Report*, pp. 6–7; Crabb, *The Gypsy's Advocate*, p. 91; MacRitchie, *Scottish Gypsies*, pp. 17–18, 32, 34, 81; Simson, *History of the Gipsies*, pp. 124–7; Vesey-Fitzgerald, *Gypsies of Britain*, p. 21.

had good cause to favour the Gypsies, as he had been restored to health by their curative endeavours and because his wife preferred their womenfolk as handmaidens at court, this warmth dissipated when the monarch decided to dress up as a Gypsy and spend some time with a band of them near Pittenweem in Fife. James disguised himself a bit too well, it seems, and became embroiled in a fracas over a woman, in which he was roughly handled and gravely insulted.[17] Whether or not this story is true, it is certainly the case that developments in James' reign, such as legislation passed in 1533 and again in 1541 ordering their banishment forth of Scotland, essentially made Gypsies' position irrecoverable, given the prejudicial climate of opinion prevailing elsewhere in Europe at this time.[18]

Although the government of Mary I (r.1542–67) gave some respite to the Gypsies in 1553 by ordering various writs in their favour,[19] when James VI (r.1567–1625) took to the throne, the fate of the Gypsy in Scotland was effectively sealed, at least from an authoritative point of view. James' personal ambition, to unite the crowns of Scotland and England, meant that he had to regularly demonstrate influence and control over his kingdom and the various peoples within it. The stringent anti-Gypsy legislation passed during his reign, which culminated in the 1609 'Act regarding the Egyptians', making it legal to apprehend and execute individuals purely on the grounds of being 'callit, knawin, repute and haldin Egiptianis', as well as the various prosecutions flowing from it, were part of his wider effort to do just that.[20] In any case, the Scottish persecution or purge of Gypsies was certainly most evident during his rule.[21]

Despite the passage of laws to control and ultimately eradicate Gypsies in early modern Scotland, the actual provision of 'justice' was wholly problematic. This fact goes some way to explain why so many anti-Gypsy laws and policies were introduced from the 1530s and throughout the remainder of the sixteenth and seventeenth centuries.[22] In the absence of a fully centralised system of justice (which was not effectively put in place until 1747), the administration of law and order could be both inconsistent and, sometimes, ineffective.[23] Justice, moreover, tended to be bound up with

[17] See Simson, *History of the Gipsies*, pp. 104–5; Dawson, *Empty Lands*, p. 23.
[18] See Simson, *History of the Gipsies*, pp. 105–6; MacRitchie, *Scottish Gypsies*, p. 40.
[19] Dawson, *Empty Lands*, p. 23.
[20] *RPS*, 1609/4/32. For other anti-Gypsy statutes, see *RPS*, A1575/3/5, 1579/10/27, 1592/4/46, 1572/4/91, A1593/9/14, and 1597/11/46. See also DCT(S), *Report*, p. 7; MacRitchie, *Scottish Gypsies*, pp. 62–6, 79–80 and chapters X and XI; Simson, *History of the Gipsies*, pp. 107–12; Vesey-Fitzgerald, *Gypsies of Britain*, p. 28; T. Tyson, 'The Marginalisation of Gypsies in Scotland, 1573–c.1625', in A. Kennedy and S. Weston (eds), *Life at the Margins in Early Modern Scotland* (Woodbridge, 2024), 47–61.
[21] For further discussion, see H. Gentleman and S. Swift, *Scotland's Travelling People: Problems and Solutions* (Edinburgh, 1971), p. 10; S. McPhee 'The Persecution of Gypsy Travellers in Scotland – A Timeline', *Historic Environment Scotland Blog*, 23 June 2023, pp. 1–3; MacRitchie, *Scottish Gypsies*, p. 78, p. 85.
[22] See DCT(S), *Report*, p. 7; Vesey-Fitzgerald, *Gypsies of Britain*, p. 31.
[23] For further discussion see A.-M. Kilday, *Women and Violent Crime in Enlightenment*

wider questions of power and status. As a consequence, personal vendettas were rife, and at certain times and in certain places, the unpredictable application of judicial authority served to increase unrest and criminality rather than curb it.

Nevertheless, it came to be recognised over the course of the seventeenth century that keeping order within communities and between individuals was essential in order to foster economic stability and social development. Consequently, any individual or group with a suspect reputation or a perceived unruly nature came to be seen as problematic. For the Scottish authorities at least, Gypsies fell into this troublesome category and had to be tamed, or preferably removed from society altogether. For the rest of the populace, on the other hand, attitudes to Gypsies remained slightly more ambivalent. Many Gypsies were regarded as folk heroes who rebelled against the authorities and willed their independence and survival through their daredevil exploits.[24] Their actions and characters were romanticised, and hyperbole served to make them household names within the oral tradition that was so important to Scottish society in the pre-industrial period, and indeed beyond. This fact probably explains why, even by the eighteenth century, Gypsies were still regarded as a social nuisance by the Scottish authorities.[25] Gypsies, like James Macpherson, were only ever outlaws in part and to some, and that must have been infuriating for those trying to establish some sense of lawfulness and stability in what came to be referred to as the 'untamed North'.[26]

The Embodiment of Marginalised Justice: The Story of James Macpherson

James Macpherson was born in 1675. He was illegitimate, his father being one of the renowned and powerful Macphersons of Invereshie based in Inverness-shire, while his mother was a Gypsy woman said to have been forcibly carried off by Macpherson senior while she attended a wedding party.[27] Despite his bastardy, James Macpherson was recognised by his father and lived with him until the latter was killed at Badenoch while attempting to rescue stolen cattle. After this, James was brought up by his mother's side of the family

---

Scotland (Woodbridge, 2007), chapter 2.

[24] For further discussion see MacRitchie, *Scottish Gypsies*, p. 54, and Simson, *History of the Gipsies*, p. 131.

[25] See Anonymous, 'Scottish Gypsies', at pp. 50, 58, and Simson, *History of the Gipsies*, p. 164.

[26] For further discussion, see A.-M. Kilday, *Crime in Scotland 1660–1960: The Violent North* (London, 2019).

[27] Anonymous, 'A Parcel of Rogues: Jamie MacPherson etc.', *The National*, 23 April 2016, pp. 1–2. This incident is depicted in an etching see W. Dyce, *A Book Illustration: MacPherson of Invereshie*, Scottish National Gallery of Modern Art (Modern Two – Print Room), Undated. [Accession No. P 2875.7].

and embraced the unconventional lifestyle of a Scottish Gypsy.[28] Like many other Gypsies during the early modern period, and in the late seventeenth and early eighteenth centuries in particular, James Macpherson soon gained a formidable reputation as an outlaw and a freebooter (essentially a land-based pirate).[29] In addition, however, he was also famed with more cultured attributes, such as being an adept swordsman, a celebrated musician (fiddler), and a keen composer.[30] At any rate, Macpherson certainly had charisma and leadership qualities that saw him form a band of Gypsies and orchestrate numerous, repeated raids and other successful criminal ventures across Forres, Elgin, Banff, and various other Highland or Highland-fringe locations.[31] His Gypsy gang became so effective, in fact, that their 'reign of terror' became infamous, and evidence of their notoriety (and the brazenness that came with it) can be seen in the fact that, when they chose a new location to further their malevolent exploits, they marched into their proposed *locus operandi* led by a piper with all of their weapons on show, announcing their presence (and arguably their threat) to the entire community, entirely unafraid of the consequences of their actions.[32]

Despite these repeated acts of 'gallusness', James Macpherson and his gang were wanted men as far as the Scottish authorities were concerned. Indeed, they were captured twice during their aforementioned exploits, but managed to escape justice on both occasions. These acts of defiance only added to the gang's renown amongst the common people in Scotland, and this, coupled with tales of their audacious and intrepid criminal escapades, cemented their reputation as folk heroes to the masses.[33] In particular, Macpherson himself came to be widely regarded as something akin to a Scottish equivalent of the fabled Robin Hood. He was said to have given his ill-gotten gains out to Gypsy folk and among the Highland poor, and it was claimed that 'no act of cruelty, or robbery of the widow, the fatherless, or the distressed was ever perpetrated under his command'.[34] In other words, Macpherson and

---

[28] B. G., 'Anecdotes of J. Macpherson, The Ancient Freebooter and Musician', *The New Monthly Magazine and Literary Journal*, 1 (1821), 142–4, at p. 142; J. Imlach, *History of Banff and Familiar Account of its Inhabitants and Belongings, etc.* (Banff, 1808), p. 26.

[29] See for instance W. Cramond, *The Annals of Banff* (Aberdeen, 1891), p. 99, and James Macpherson's supposed confession prior to his execution, *The Last Words of James Mackpherson Murderer* (Edinburgh, 1700).

[30] See for instance R. Chambers, *Domestic Annals of Scotland from the Revolution to the Rebellion of 1745* (Edinburgh and London, 1840), p. 234; Imlach, *History of Banff*, p. 26; Dawson, *Empty Lands*, p. 23.

[31] For evidence, see Imlach, *History of Banff*, p. 25, and Chambers, *Domestic Annals*, pp. 233–4.

[32] See the description provided in Chambers, *Domestic Annals*, p. 234.

[33] See for instance Cramond, *Annals of Banff*, p. 109; B. G., 'Anecdotes', p. 143; *The New Statistical Account of Scotland, etc.* No. XI (August 1836), p. 22.

[34] See Anonymous, 'A Parcel of Rogues', p. 2 as well as Cramond, *Annals of Banff*, pp. 110–11; Simson *History of the Gypsies*, p. 131; *The New Statistical Account of Scotland*, vol. 13, p. 22.

his men only ever attacked the rich or those who deserved it. Exaggerated accounts of his activities and character, which contributed to his folk hero status, evidently blurred the lines between fact and fiction and between right and wrong, and he became a (anti)hero to many in the late seventeenth and early eighteenth centuries.[35]

While it is debatable whether we should consider him as a Scottish version of the 'real' Robin Hood as opposed to the legend from English folklore, Macpherson was certainly a hunted and a persecuted man, largely on account of his heritage, his reputation, and his persistent bad behaviour, all of which became starkly evident, of course, within a burgeoning judicial context where anti-Gypsy sentiment resiliently prevailed.[36] Strong evidence of the determined pursuit of Scottish Gypsies, and of James Macpherson in particular, came in September 1700 at St Rufus Fair in the Moray town of Keith. It was there that the 'stout hearted' laird of Braco, Alexander Duff, who had made previous attempts to capture Macpherson and members of his gang, hatched a further plan for the apprehension of these 'notorious breakers of the peace in all sorts of villainy'.[37] Bringing a dozen strong and able men with him, and with the aid of his brother-in-law, the laird of Lesmurdie, Braco watched in the market square till the Gypsy band were visible and then attacked them using the element of surprise. Macpherson and his men made 'a desperate resistance', and one of their number was stabbed to death in the affray that ensued.[38]

The Gypsy men were then carried off by their captors to a secure house in Keith and kept under armed guard, but they were released after just a short period of time, following a jurisdictional argument between Braco and the laird of Grant.[39] Grant, who had brought a posse of armed men with him, claimed that Braco had made an unlawful arrest, and had acted without due warrant. Undeterred, Braco quickly returned to the marketplace, grabbed two justices of the peace, held an impromptu court, and verified his territorial prerogative. He then assembled 'sixty able bold men' to retake his prisoners,

---

[35] See *Miscellany of the Spalding Club, Volume III* (Aberdeen, 1846), p. xiv. Macpherson was not alone in achieving a folk-hero status whilst being blatantly unlawful during the early modern period. Pirates such as Bartholomew 'Black Bart' Roberts (1682–1722) and several thieves and highway robbers including Jack Sheppard (1702–24) and Richard 'Dick' Turpin (1705–39) attained similar notoriety for their criminal endeavours. Evidently, the public had an endemic and enduring lurid fascination for certain crimes and certain criminals. For further discussion see the forthcoming monograph by A.-M. Kilday, entitled *The Invention of Infamy: Charting the Cult of the Criminal in Britain since 1500*.

[36] *Miscellany of the Spalding Club, Volume III*, p. xv.

[37] Anonymous, *Genealogical Memoirs of the Duffs* (Aberdeen, 1869), p. 53. See also Chambers, *Domestic Annals*, p. 235.

[38] Anonymous, *Genealogical Memoirs of the Duffs*, pp. 53–4.

[39] Most likely to be Ludovick Grant (1641–1716), 8th laird of Freuchie and 1st laird of Grant, who was nicknamed 'The Highland King' due to his various acts of rebellion and treachery against the crown over a prolonged period of time. He was a known harbourer of outlaws.

which he successfully achieved, after a further (albeit relatively minor) skirmish, during which Macpherson was somewhat comedically caught after he tripped over a gravestone in a churchyard while trying to flee.[40] Despite this calamity, the amount of manpower deemed necessary to ensure the eventual arrest of Macpherson and his crew is compelling testimony to the perceived threat that they were believed to pose.

James Macpherson and three of his fellow Gypsies (Peter Broun, Donald Broun, and James Gordon) were brought before Nicholas Dunbar, sheriff of Banff on 7 November 1700.[41] They were charged under a modified version of the 1609 statute with 'being habit and repute Egyptians and vagabonds and keeping the markets in their ordinary manner of thieving and purse-cutting' and 'being guilty also of masterful bangstrie [violent bullying] and oppression'.[42] A defence procurator appeared for the two Brouns on behalf of the laird of Grant, offering a pledge (culreach) for them and arguing (just as he had done previously with Lord Braco) that they should be tried within the court of his regality, as that was where they were domiciled. However, given the association between Gypsies and a peripatetic lifestyle, it was hard to demonstrate that the men had a permanent residence anywhere, and so this request was quickly rejected.[43]

Macpherson and Gordon, for their part, also tried to have the indictment against them thrown out of court. They claimed that they were being prosecuted under obsolete legislation and that they had not displayed any of the typical traits associated with Gypsies and described within the statute provision (for example, there was no evidence of them participating in idle begging, fortune-telling, cheating using superstition, or charming through the use of magic).[44] They also tried to argue that the proceedings were redundant because too much time had lapsed between the alleged offences being committed and them being brought to justice, and because the indictment served against them was administratively invalid since it contained numerous blank sections (relating to the personal details of the supposed victims).[45] These arguments were also rebuffed by the judiciary after negligible deliberation and the trial was ordered to proceed.

The testimony of some twenty-one witnesses brought before the court gives us the first detailed glimpse of the exploits of James Macpherson and his band of Gypsies. It was recounted that they had stolen livestock (such

---

[40] Cramond, *Annals of Banff*, p. 100; *New Statistical Account*, vol. 13, p. 22.

[41] *Ibid.*, p. 112. The record of the trial from 1700 was reprinted from the original in its entirety in the *Miscellany of the Spalding Club* in 1846, which previous and subsequent references in this essay refer to. It should be noted that the surnames of the four accused are spelled in a variety of ways in the original record.

[42] Imlach, *History of Banff*, p. 25 – my addition in parenthesis. For more on the legislative provision for this indictment see D. Hume, *Commentaries on the Law of Scotland Respecting the Description and Punishment of Crimes – Volume II* (Edinburgh, 1797), pp. 339–45.

[43] *Miscellany of The Spalding Club, Volume III*, pp. 175–8.

[44] *Ibid.*, p. 179.

[45] *Ibid.*, p. 180.

as sheep, oxen, and horses), had broken into houses to take away property without permission, and were in regular receipt of stolen goods.[46] According to witnesses such as John Scot, a local minister, they had also robbed men of their purses, committed various acts of bullying and extortion, and had 'tyrannically oppressed' many poor people across the Highlands in a persistent fashion for many years.[47] Another man testified that not only had the Gypsy crew stolen the entirety of his flock of sheep, but they had also butchered all of his valuable lambs and carried off their carcasses, save for the entrails.[48] The 'othering' of the Gypsies was evidenced too, when individuals such as John Cruikshank and John Shand described how the group were in the habit of speaking 'a peculiar language' and were given to regularly spending whole nights 'in dancing and debauchery'.[49]

The interesting thing about all this evidence is that most of it does not refer to James Macpherson directly, nor suggest his active involvement in the nefarious activities described. Several testimonies, in fact, name Peter Broun – not James Macpherson – as the 'captain' or leader of the Gypsy band.[50] Macpherson is instead referred to as more of an onlooker, rather than an active participant in what was recounted before the court. Two pieces of testimony provide exceptions to this general retelling of prosecution evidence. The first describes how Macpherson came to see William Robertson, an inhabitant of Keith, and finding him not home, he 'stobbed [stabbed] the bed' of the victim repeatedly to make sure of Robertson's absence, and then set the ale-barrel running, before leaving the increasingly flooded scene.[51] Robertson was so traumatised upon hearing what had happened at his house that he fled to another village for refuge, and bought some protection from men who were willing to try to apprehend Macpherson for his misdeeds.[52]

The second piece of testimony to mention James Macpherson and charge him with something actively nefarious came from a man called Peter Duncan. Duncan had apparently paid a lot of money for a white plaid (a piece of twilled woollen cloth typically used as an outer garment). Two of Macpherson's men must have come to know about this purchase, as they came to Duncan's house in Pitlurg, south of Keith, broke open his pantry door, and made off with the fabric without paying for it. James Macpherson soon thereafter arrived on the scene, saying that his possession of the plaid had been necessary because Peter Duncan had some of his goods and had neither returned them to Macpherson, nor paid for them. Duncan, for his

---

[46] For the testimony, see *ibid.*, p. 183 (John Scott), p. 184 (Lachlan McPherson), pp. 185–6 (Archibald Grant), p. 187 (Alexander Young), p. 188 (Thomas Milne), and p. 189 (Peter Brouster).

[47] For various testimonies which reinforce this view, see *ibid.*, pp. 183, 187–9.

[48] See the testimony of John Fraser, *ibid.*, p. 185.

[49] *Ibid.*, pp. 182, 184.

[50] See for instance the testimony of Peter Baird, *ibid.*, pp. 183–4, Peter Reid, *ibid.*, p. 185, and Thomas Umphray, *ibid.*, p. 189.

[51] *Ibid.*, p. 186.

[52] *Ibid.*

part, threatened to take Macpherson to the Scottish authorities on account of the theft committed upon him, whereupon Macpherson picked him up 'roughly' and carried him many miles, threatening all the while to throw his charge into a large pit in the town of Elgin and to leave him there to rot unaided. Peter Duncan feared for his life and truly believed that Macpherson would make good on his savage threat. However, he was eventually set free.[53]

Despite the largely circumstantial evidence of direct criminality presented to the court by the prosecution, all four men were convicted of the charges against them on 9 November 1700. This was because the key element of the legal provision under which they were prosecuted was whether they were 'known and reput to be Egyptians, soroners, and vagabonds'.[54] As every single witness testified to this being the case, based on their knowledge and experience of the accused individuals, the Gypsy men's fate was sealed, in effect, by a judicial 'othering' process.[55] Sentencing against Peter and Donald Broun was deferred, whilst the following pronouncement was made against James Gordon and James Macpherson:

> Forsameikle as you, James McPhersone and James Gordon, pannals [accused] are found guilty, by ane verdict of ane assyse, to be knoun, holden, and repute, to be Egiptians and vagabonds, and oppressors of his Majesties free lieges, in ane bangstrie manner, and going up and doune the country armed, and keeping mercats in ane hostile manner, and that you are thieves, and recepters of thieves, and that you are of *pessima famae* [bad reputation]: Therefor the Shirreff-deput of Banff, and I, in his name, adjudges, and decernes you, the said James McPhersone and James Gordon to be taken to the Cross of Banff, from the tolbuith thereof, where you now lye, and ther upon ane gibbet to be erected, to be hanged by the neck to the death by the hand of the common execution, upon Friday nixt, being the sixteenth of November instant, being a publick weeklie mercat day, betwixt the hours of two and three in the afternoon, and in the meantime, declairs their heall moveable goods and gear to be escheat [forfeited], and inbrought to the Fiscall, for his majesties interest, and recommends this sentence to be seen put in executione by the magistrats of Banff.[56]

Endgame, Reflections, and Conclusions

The unpredictable nature of early modern Scottish justice was reinforced in the aftermath of this trial, since, of the four men convicted, only James Macpherson was in fact executed. It is widely believed that James Gordon was pardoned, and it is known that the laird of Grant successfully rescued

---

[53] *Ibid.*, p. 187.
[54] *Ibid.*, p. 178.
[55] See all the testimony presented in *ibid*, pp. 182–9.
[56] *Ibid.*, p. 190. My additions in parenthesis.

the Brouns, at the third attempt, from their impending fate by essentially buying their freedom from the authorities.[57] So why was Macpherson put to death at the relatively young age of twenty-five, when there was arguably more compelling evidence of criminality and proscribed behaviour against the other three men accused, and especially James Gordon? One reason might be that Macpherson was regarded as the ringleader and the authorities reasoned that, if they removed him, the Gypsy band he was involved in would disperse and diminish. Another reason could be related to some sort of personal vendetta between Macpherson and his nemesis Lord Braco, which the Scottish authorities were only too keen to resolve in favour of the latter. A further reason could be because Highland Gypsies, from the start of the eighteenth century onwards, were regarded as endemically troublesome, unashamedly violent, and increasingly unbridled, meaning that one of their number needed to be made an example of in order to quell their behaviour in a general sense and to evidence or showcase authoritative control in that area.[58] As James Macpherson already had the beginnings of a cultish following in his characterisation as heroic outlaw, his very public demise would surely offer the perfect antidote to growing concerns of lawlessness on the margins of society and nationhood.

The use of Macpherson as a sacrificial lamb by the Scottish authorities, for whatever reason, did not really work as planned, however. Indeed, arguably, his execution ended up affording him more celebrity, renown, and indeed admiration than if he had been left unfettered. Macpherson remained defiant to the last and seemingly played his fiddle on the gallows, offering it to his audience when he had finished his somewhat macabre serenade. When no-one offered to take it from him, he dramatically smashed it over his knee and threw the broken parts into the crowd, just as the noose was placed around his neck.[59] Although, unsurprisingly, official sources, including the printed, 'authorised' version of his 'dying speech',[60] make no mention of this incident, it was widely recounted amongst more popular literary sources,

---

[57] See *New Statistical Account*, vol. 13, p. 26; Cramond, *Annals of Banff*, pp. 110, 112–13; Imlach, *History of Banff*, p. 27.

[58] For evidence of this view see for instance the discussion in Anonymous, 'Scottish Gypsies', p. 58.

[59] See D. K. Wilgus, 'Fiddler's Farewell: The Legend of the Hanged Fiddler', *Studia Musicologica Academiae Scientiarum Hungaricae*, 7 (1965), 196–209, at pp. 195–6, 198; Cramond, *Annals of Banff*, in the notes at pp. 101–2; Chambers, *Domestic Annals*, p. 236; Dawson, *Empty Lands*, p. 24.

[60] *Last Words of James Mackpherson Murderer*. It is interesting that this official document, relating to the supposed confession of James Macpherson ahead of his execution, refers to him as a murderer when there was no charge of that nature laid against him and no evidence whatsoever submitted to the court during his trial to suggest that he had participated in such a crime. Clearly the authorities saw this publication as an opportunity to vilify Macpherson and his name in the aftermath of his death. That they saw the need to do so, is of course telling in itself in terms of Macpherson's reputation amongst the Scottish populace.

probably most famously when Robert Burns wrote a song called 'Macpherson's Rant' (sometimes referred to as 'Macpherson's Lament') in 1788, recounting his protagonist's bravery and impudence more than eight decades after the execution.[61] The first verse and chorus of the song runs:

> Farewell, ye dungeons dark and strong,
> The wretch's destinie!
> McPherson's time will not be long
> On yonder gallows-tree
> Sae rantingly, sae wantonly,
> Sae dauntingly gaed he;
> He play'd a spring, and danc'd it round
> Below the gallows-tree.[62]

The hype surrounding Macpherson, before and after his death, soon rendered him a martyr, not only for the Gypsy cause, but also for marginalised individuals and groups more broadly.[63] This was intensified even further when it was rumoured that the town clock in Banff, where Macpherson was executed, had been moved forward fifteen minutes by the authorities to ensure that his hanging would not be prevented by the arrival of the laird of Grant, who was travelling to the town at speed on horseback with a reprieve for him.[64] The magistrates of Banff were evidently punished for this duplicity, and the populace determined in their own minds that, at best, Macpherson had at best been unfairly treated, and at worst had been unlawfully slain by the Scottish authorities. So strong was this sentiment, in fact, that towns near to Banff (such as Doune) built parish clock-towers with only three faces, ensuring that the missing face pointed towards Banff to symbolise their disgust at the behaviour of their neighbours and to offer an ongoing reminder to them of their reprehensible actions.[65]

In the aftermath of Macpherson's death, justice grew more centralised and more consistently applied as the court system in Scotland became more firmly established. Personal and political scores were no longer settled through the application of justice, and prejudice had less of a part to play in law and order than it had done in previous centuries.[66] In the Scottish

---

[61] For further discussion of this work, see Cramond, *Annals of Banff*, pp. 103–9.

[62] R. Chambers (ed.) *The Life and Works of Robert Burns* [revised by William Wallace] (New York, 1896), p. 286.

[63] *Miscellany of The Spalding Club, Volume III*, p. xv.

[64] See for instance Cramond, *Annals of Banff*, p. 109.

[65] See Anonymous, 'Parcel of Rogues', pp. 3–4.

[66] For further discussion see A. Kennedy, 'Crime and Punishment in Early-Modern Scotland: The Secular Courts of Restoration Argyllshire, 1660–1688', *IRSS*, 41 (2016), 1–36; J. Findlay, *All Manner of People: The History of Justices of the Peace in Scotland* (Edinburgh, 2000); S. J. Davies, 'The Courts and the Scottish Legal System, 1600–1747: The Case of Stirlingshire', in V. A. C. Gatrell, B. Lenman and G. Parker (eds), *Crime and the Law: The Social History of Crime in Western Europe since 1500* (London, 1980), pp. 120–54; Kilday, *Women and Violent Crime*, chapter 2.

context at least, after 1750, there were fewer folk hero criminals for the populace to champion and mourn in equal measure.[67] Nevertheless, the marginalisation of the Gypsy continued in Scotland during the pre-industrial period and into the more modern era too. Arguably this was done more covertly and less blatantly than in Macpherson's time, but the 'othering' of Gypsies, and the racism directed towards those who chose a more nomadic or unconventional existence, persisted nonetheless.[68] The history of the persecution of the Gypsy in Scotland has been largely excluded from scholarship, and this historiographical ignorance has in itself perpetuated further marginalisation.[69] It is only through exploring the treatment of individuals like James Macpherson, and the many other men and women like him, that we will be able to both confront the past and remedy the future for those who dare to be different.

[67] For further discussion see Kilday, *Crime in Scotland 1660–1960*.

[68] See the discussion in Gentleman and Swift, *Scotland's Travelling People*, p. 1 and *passim*; McPhee 'The Persecution of Gypsy Travellers in Scotland', pp. 1–10; and particularly DCT(S), *Report*, *passim*, for evidence of the continued repression of, and prejudice against, Gypsies in twentieth-century Scotland.

[69] See for instance Eliav-Feldon, 'Vagrants or Vermin?', p. 277; J. Matthews, *Connected Communities: Romanies/Gypsies, Roma & Irish and Scottish Travellers – Histories, Perceptions and Representations* (AHRC, 2012), found at https://eprints.hud.ac.uk/id/eprint/16390/1/Discussion_Paper.pdf.

PART III

TESTING THE BOUNDARIES

9

The Common Musician and Deviance in Early Modern Scotland

Aaron McGregor

Scottish ecclesiastical, burgh, and criminal records contain a plethora of proceedings against musicians and attempts to ban musical activities. In 1560, Edinburgh burgh council decreed that 'vagaboundis fydlaris, and otheris without maisteris' lacking a house in the city should depart on pain of branding on the cheek.[1] The Scottish parliament introduced anti-vagrancy laws in 1575–9, declaring that all musicians not in the service of lords of parliament, barons, or burghs were to be 'punished as strong beggars and vagabonds'. In 1595, the Church of Scotland drew up a report on the progress of the Reformation, lumping in 'pypers', 'fidlers', and 'songsters' with other 'idle persons having no lawfull callings'.[2]

What all of these actions demonstrate is that, while playing music was not considered a deviant activity *per se*, the 'common' musician (that is, those without privileged permanent employment) was a marginalised figure in early modern Scotland. Musicians were focal points for transgressive behaviour and activities, notably 'promiscuous dancing' between men and women (and accompanying sexual misconduct), drunkenness, and festivities associated with Catholicism or pagan ritual, including feast day celebrations, weddings, and lykewakes (vigils, often raucous, over the body of newly-deceased persons). Motivations behind the suppression of musicians were diverse, and changed over time, from the desire after the Reformation to create a godly state, to issues around vagrancy in the 1600s, and association with political causes such as Jacobitism in the 18th century. Underlying much of the distrust by the authorities was a keen awareness of music's power in voicing dissatisfaction with the political and religious hegemons.

It is easy to paint a bleak picture of the lives of common musicians in this period, but there were mitigating factors. The authorities offered charity and employment opportunities to musicians, though patronage could also be a means of controlling unwanted behaviours. Despite what might seem to be an unfavourable environment, musicians and musical culture

---

[1] *Edinburgh Rec.*, vol. 3, p. 69; vol. 4, pp. 507–8.
[2] *RPS*, A1575/3/5, 1579/10/27; A. Peterkin and T. Thomson (eds), *The Booke of the Universall Kirk: Acts and Proceedings of the General Assemblies of the Kirk of Scotland 1560–1618* (3 vols, Edinburgh, 1839), vol. 3, p. 874.

were flourishing in Scotland by the eighteenth century, and a vernacular revival brought about a gradual shift in the popular negative and deviant associations of the common musician.

Music as Deviant Behaviour

The urban soundscape has become a growing area of historical enquiry. Sounds connected people across space; they were used to mark the passing of time and even to set the boundaries of communities, for example in the use of church bells and town drummers. Sounds can act as markers of social and political identity, and various authorities have used the regulation of noise to control social order and mitigate differences with marginalised groups.[3]

Musical sounds might have positive connotations of enjoyment, sociability, and creativity, but when unwanted or out of place, they can become perceived as noise. For example, *charivari* or 'rough music' was a form of mock parade in which participants made as much noise as possible with musical instruments as well as pots and pans, often as a form of protest or ritual humiliation towards those who had taken part in deviant behaviour.[4] Bells, trumpets, bagpipes, and drums were among the loudest sounds to be heard in early modern Scotland, and were used to assert the social, political, and religious hierarchy. These musical sounds could also become a nuisance when misappropriated. In December 1577, one Jhon Fyvie confessed before Perth kirk session that he had ridden through the town on a horse at night and struck the drum belonging to the town. In 1623, James Wilson was also called before Perth kirk session for playing the bagpipes under silence of night, 'to the offence of God and terrifying the neighbours, as tho' either fire or sword had been within the town'.[5] Such offences were not only disruptive, but represented a threat to social order by interfering with the regulated urban soundscape.[6]

---

[3]   For example, see D. Hendy, *Noise: A Human History of Sound and Listening* (London, 2013); D. Garrioch, 'Sounds of the City: The Soundscape of Early Modern European Towns', *Urban History*, 30:1 (2003), 5–25. For a specifically Scottish perspective, see E. Foyster, 'Sensory Experiences: Smells, Sounds and Touch', in C. A. Whatley and E. Foyster (eds), *A History of Everyday Life in Scotland, 1600 to 1800* (Edinburgh, 2010), pp. 217–33.

[4]   For a Scottish example of the practice, see J. J. McGavin, 'Robert III's "Rough Music": Charivari and Diplomacy in a Medieval Scottish Court', *SHR*, 74:2 (1995), 144–58.

[5]   M. Todd (ed.), *The Perth Kirk Session Books, 1577–1590* (Woodbridge, 2012), pp. 83–4. J. Maidment (ed.), *The Chronicle of Perth* (Edinburgh, 1831), p. 93.

[6]   Even the softer sounds of fiddle, viol, or voice could become disruptive within the relatively quiet soundscape of early modern Scotland. As Bruce Smith points out, with ambient sounds under 70 dB, even outdoor conversations could become a major factor in the sonic environment. B. R. Smith, *The Acoustic World of Early Modern England: Attending to the O-Factor* (Chicago, Il., 1999), p. 58.

Just as important as the qualities of sounds were the associations of certain types of music-making, and of the musicians themselves. Like other depictions of the poor, the common musician's low social status and poverty went together with assumptions of laziness, immorality, and excess.[7] In England, John Earle's 'A poore fidler' (1629) describes an individual subsisting on charity, playing at fairs, alehouses, and country weddings. 'Just so many strings above a beggar', he was often drunk and delighted in bawdy songs, hating the Puritan 'as an enemy to his mirth'.[8] Such popular caricatures in seventeenth-century England commonly singled out fiddlers and pipers, though occasionally they took aim at other musicians such as trumpeters, drummers, and even cathedral singers.[9]

In their persecution of musicians, church and burgh authorities in Scotland were likely influenced by similar negative associations of musicians as immoral, idle, drunk, or simply a nuisance. In 1540, David Lyndsay's *Ane Satyre of the Thrie Estaitis* includes a description of 'idill men' as 'strang beggers / Fidlers, pypers, and pardoners [scoundrels] / Thir jugglars, jestars, and idill cuitchours [gamblers]'. One of David Fergusson's *Scottish Proverbs* of 1641 reads 'Fidlers, dogs and flies come to feasts uncalled', and a sonnet by William Drummond of Hawthornden describes the corruption of the times, ending with the lines:

Where flatterers, fooles, baudes, fidlers are rewarded
Whilst Vertue sterves [starves] unpittied, unregarded.[10]

These literary stereotypes were not entirely without real-world basis. Since common musicians' work was often based around playing for people enjoying themselves, alcoholism and excessive behaviour were occupational hazards. The convention of paying musicians 'drink money' in addition to wages did not help matters.[11] In 1641, Robert Kerr, earl of Lothian wrote that he could not 'out of our armie furnish' a single 'sober fidler'. Despite one individual playing 'exceading well', he was 'untolerably given to drink'.[12]

Numerous others were accused of drunkenness, adultery, and other misdemeanours. Elgin's church and burgh records contain a litany of charges

---

[7] On early modern depictions of the poor, see T. R. Nichols, *Others and Outcasts in Early Modern Europe: Picturing the Social Margins* (Aldershot, 2007); R. Jütte, *Poverty and Deviance in Early Modern Europe*, New Approaches to European History (Cambridge, 1994).
[8] John Earle, *Micro-Cosmographie* (London, 1629).
[9] C. Marsh, *Music and Society in Early Modern England* (Cambridge, 2013), pp. 80–3.
[10] David Lindsay, *Ane Satyre Of The Thrie Estaitis*, ed. R. Lyall (Edinburgh, 2012), p. 95; E. Beveridge (ed.), *Fergusson's Scottish Proverbs from the Original Print of 1641* (Edinburgh, 1924), pp. 34, 58; William Drummond, *Poetical Works of William Drummond of Hawthornden*, ed. L. E. Kastner (2 vols, Edinburgh, 1913), vol. 2, p. 230.
[11] For example, in 1647, Francis, earl of Buccleuch paid £375 14s to 'fiddlers, pipers, and others' at his wedding, including 'drink money because there was too little thereof'. E. Fraser (ed.), *The Scotts of Buccleuch* (2 vols, Edinburgh, 1878), vol. 1, p. 284.
[12] D. Laing (ed.), *Correspondence of Sir Robert Kerr, First Earl of Ancrum and his son, William, Third Earl of Lothian* (2 vols, Edinburgh, 1875), vol. 1, p. 108.

against the fiddler/violer Alexander Glass. In 1647, he was fined £40 for playing and gambling at night. Two years later, he was reprimanded for drinking and playing on the viol to debauched men at night. He was ordered not to play at penny weddings and to leave the area or face a £20 fine.[13] In 1652–61, Inveraray fiddler Angus McMarquess was cautioned on numerous occasions, and eventually excommunicated by the presbytery of Argyll, for cases of adultery, drunkenness, fighting, and 'lewd carriage'.[14] Several musicians were charged with more serious crimes. In two cases of musician-on-musician violence in Edinburgh, fiddler Robert Dugude was in 1565 jailed for nineteen years for murdering the 'sangstare' Johne Murdo, and in 1594, a fiddler named Ogilby was executed for murdering a harper by the name of Caldell. Edinburgh violer James Johnstone, hanged in 1672, had murdered his wife, Agnes Strachan, in token of which his hand was ordained to be cut off and placed on public display after death.[15]

The distrust of musicians was also sometimes down to xenophobic and religious bigotry, given the high numbers of Catholics and foreigners in their ranks. In 1700, the general assembly demanded that parliament prohibit Protestants from employing Catholics to teach their children music, dancing, or the French language. In 1703, a list of Catholics drawn up by the Edinburgh presbytery included French viol player Peter Saint Colme [Saint Colombe] and dancing master Peter La-Hersie.[16] The Jacobite rebellions of 1715 and 1745 exacerbated this atmosphere of suspicion: in 1714, an anti-Papist tract published in Edinburgh accused La-Hersie of being a Jacobite spy, and after 1745, newspapers singled out fiddlers and dancing masters in xenophobic articles against French residents.[17] In 1751, a letter to the *Caledonian Mercury* complained of an 'inundation' of French and other foreigners, including 'Ten or Twelve Thousand French Valets, Barbers, Fidlers, and Dancing Masters'. The complainant drew on the familiar cry of stealing food and opportunities from the 'native' population, while sailors and tradesmen were forced to seek their fortunes elsewhere, but there was also a clear attempt to associate the immigrant French population with Jacobitism.[18]

---

[13] *Elgin Rec.*, vol. 1, pp. 181, 286; vol. 2, p. 266.

[14] D. MacTavish, (ed.), *Minutes of the Synod of Argyll 1652–1661* (2 vols, Edinburgh, 1944), vol. 2, pp. 53, 59–60, 77–8, 81, 91–2, 150, 163, 195, 202, 219.

[15] M. Livingstone et al. (eds), *Registrum Secreti Sigilli Regum Scotorum* (8 vols, Edinburgh, 1908–82), vol. 5, p. 666; vol. 3, p. 51; George Mackenzie, *The Laws and Customes of Scotland in Matters Criminal* (Edinburgh, 1699), p. 185; John Lauder, *Historical Notices of Scotish Affairs*, ed. W. Scott (2 vols, Edinburgh, 1842), vol. 1, p. 85.

[16] *RPS*, A1700/10/3. 'Popish Parents and their Children, 1701–5', in *Miscellany of the Maitland Club, Volume 3* (Edinburgh, 1843), pp. 299, 432–3.

[17] *Popery and slavery reviving: or, an account of the growth of popery, and the insolence of papists and Jacobites in Scotland* (Edinburgh and London, 1714), p. 10; *Aberdeen Press and Journal*, 19 March 1751, p. 3; *Caledonian Mercury*, 14 October 1755, p. 1; *ibid.*, 5 November 1759, p. 1.

[18] *Caledonian Mercury*, 26 March 1751, pp. 1–2.

THE COMMON MUSICIAN AND DEVIANCE

The ability of musicians to spread sedition was a commonly held notion. Musical performance could offer a visible (and audible) form of dissent, and political elites were not blind to this: in 1724, the *Caledonian Mercury* described a justice of the peace in Edinburgh who had 'a strong aversion to Fidlers'. He wanted them 'burned by the Hands of the common Hangman, and an Act of Parliament against the Importation of Cat Gut, because of a certain tune which keeps up the Disaffection in the People'.[19] Jacobitism, in particular, often exploited the subversive potential of music. On 21 August 1714, John Erskine, earl of Mar wrote to Whitehall noting that 'ill disposed' men had proclaimed the Jacobite pretender in Aberdeen, processing through the streets with violers playing the Jacobite anthem, 'The King Shall Enjoy His Own Again'.[20] Another incident occurred at the Edinburgh Canongate Theatre in 1749: on the anniversary of the battle of Culloden, a group of military officers requested the orchestra to play the tune 'Culloden', but they instead played the Jacobite tune 'You're Welcome Charlie Stuart'. The officers attacked the orchestra, shouting 'damn'd the fidlers'.[21] Popular music, therefore, was associated with a wide range of deviant behaviours, and so too were the people who made it.

Vagrancy

A more concrete reason for targeting musicians was regulation against vagrancy. Between 1500 and 1630, Scotland's population more than doubled, and periods of inflation and famine resulted in the rural poor taking to the roads in large numbers, often ending up in urban areas. Anti-vagrancy measures targeted 'strong beggars' deemed able but unwilling to work, viewed as a threat to social order and a drain on local economies.[22]

The inclusion of musicians in such measures was in part a by-product of their itinerant lifestyles, with many of them relying on 'portfolio' careers, involving a variety of roles across a wide geographical area. The measures aimed to restrict beggars or criminals masquerading as musicians, such as the 'Egyptian [Gypsy] and vagabond' Peter Broun, a leader of James Macpherson's band of outlaws in the north-east (for more on Macpherson, see chapter 8). At Broun's trial in 1700, it was noted that he 'got money sometymes for playing on the wiol'. In 1744, the *Caledonian Mercury* described the imprisonment at

---

[19] *Ibid.*, 10 September 1724, p. 2.
[20] J. Allardyce, (ed.), *Historical Papers Related to the Jacobite Period, 1699–1750* (2 vols, Aberdeen, 1895), vol. 1, pp. 28–9.
[21] *Caledonian Mercury*, 20 April 1749, p. 2.
[22] I. D. Whyte, 'Population Mobility in Early Modern Scotland', in R. A. Houston and I. D. Whyte (eds), *Scottish Society, 1500–1800* (Cambridge, 2005), pp. 37–58; K. Cullen, *Famine in Scotland: The 'Ill Years' of the 1690s* (Edinburgh, 2010), pp. 157–8.

145

Jedburgh of Shadrach and Henry Greg, 'notorious vagrants' who had 'been in use about the Country as Tinkers and Fiddlers'.[23]

Anti-vagrancy measures must also have limited the activities of some genuine occupational performers, who officially required an upper-class patron or permission from each burgh to operate. Officials sometimes used vagrancy laws as licence to act violently towards musicians. On 9 June 1685, Edward Aitcheson, servant to John Graham, captain of the Edinburgh city guard, killed the violer John Watson because he was 'serenading in the night-time with his fidle, in the street, contrair to ane act discharging it, and giving him bad words'. Aitcheson was executed, but only after opposition from the magistrates, including bringing the case before the high commissioner and chancellor.[24] In 1704, John Robertsone, another captain of the Edinburgh city guard, beat a boy for playing bass viol in the street, breaking the boy's instrument. The council ordered Robertsone to pay £4 sterling for a new viol, but ended up paying the sum themselves, with no punishment given for the beating.[25] These cases suggest it was standard practice to 'move on' street musicians, sometimes using violence; it was only the crimes of murder and destruction of property that brought the cases before the authorities.

Specific instances of musicians being banished from Scottish towns are, nonetheless, relatively hard to find, and those that are recorded commonly involved more than simply playing music. In 1587, Bartelmo Bell was ordered to leave Edinburgh for being a 'vicious and sclanderous' person and singing bawdy songs. In Glasgow in 1612, Matthew Thomson, 'Hieland man, fidler', was accused of rape; the council found a lack of evidence but banished him as an 'idill vagabound', threatening execution should he return. Genuine musicians were sometimes treated sympathetically, even when being asked to leave. In 1540, Elgin burgh council offered the minstrel John Kyntor the payment of a crown for past service, provided he departed the burgh.[26] In 1580, rather than banishing the fiddler John MacGregor, Dundee burgh council ordered him to take up another trade. It is possible that he decided piping and a change of location were more suitable; a piper of the same name died in Edinburgh in 1585.[27]

While the treatment of itinerant musicians in Scotland could be harsh, it is worth noting that anti-vagrancy measures were if anything more

[23] J. Stuart, (ed.), 'Process: Procurator Phiscall against the Egyptians', in *Miscellany of the Spalding Club, Volume III* (Aberdeen, 1846), pp. 175–94, at p. 184; *Caledonian Mercury*, 5 July 1744, p. 3.

[24] *Edinburgh Rec.*, vol. 11, p. 145; vol. 13, pp. 84–5; W. Scott (ed.), *Chronological Notes of Scottish Affairs, from 1680 Till 1701: Being Chiefly Taken from the Diary of Lord Fountainhall* (Edinburgh, 1822), pp. 132–3.

[25] *Edinburgh Rec.*, vol. 13, pp. 84–5.

[26] *Ibid.*, vol. 4, p. 509; *Glasgow Rec.*, vol. 1, p. 330; *Elgin Rec.*, vol. 1, p. 46.

[27] J. McGavin, 'Secular Music in the Burgh of Haddington 1530–1640', in F. Kisby (ed.), *Music and Musicians in Renaissance Cities and Towns* (Cambridge, 2001), pp. 45–56, at p. 49; NRS, Edinburgh Commissary Court, CC8/8/25, Testament Dative of Johnne McGregoure, 1585.

draconian in England. In 1572, an 'acte for the punishment of vacabondes' required minstrels to be retained by aristocrats of at least baronial status, or to be licensed by two justices of the peace in each shire they visited. Unlicensed musicians faced a three-tiered punishment system culminating in execution, and Christopher Marsh has shown that hundreds of individuals were persecuted under these regulations between 1570 and 1660.[28] Scottish musicians might have been vulnerable in the case of anti-vagrancy laws, therefore, but their situation was not uniquely precarious.

The Scottish Church and 'Profane Pastimes'

Music and musicians were affected by a fundamental shift in the sensory experience of worship after the Reformation. The medieval Scottish Church had been marked by a sensuality of expression, the church a site of 'image, sound, and smell', and the mundanity of daily life broken up by festivals, and rituals marking birth, marriage, and death. After the Reformation, worship became a more intellectual experience, concentrating on the word of God, through sermon, bible, and prayer.[29] After 1560, music in worship retained an important but much more restricted role, limited to congregational singing of unaccompanied psalms. Music became a focal point for attacks against Catholicism, as well as a means of enforcing the new regime, including through the burning of choir books and removal and destruction of organs.[30]

This shift in musical style was part of a wider attempt to regulate the soundscape of the Reformed Church and beyond. The focus in worship shifted from a variety of sensory experiences to the sermon and the voice of the minister. The rhetorical style of some Scottish Presbyterian ministers became well known. The English writer and traveller Edward Burt described an unpopular minister in the 1720s whose characteristic *sough* (the whine or drawl of his sermon) was imitated on the fiddle by a local musician.[31]

The Church authorities made efforts to maintain silence in and around the church, from banning children from sermons to preventing talking and other disruptive behaviour. Some of the sanctions against musicians were due to revelry actually taking place outside the church at times of sermon. In 1592, the piper James Roy was punished by Elgin kirk session for playing on his 'gryt pipe at efternoon in tyme of preaching in Contempt of God

---

[28] Marsh, *Music and Society*, pp. 73–7.

[29] M. Todd, *The Culture of Protestantism in Early Modern Scotland* (New Haven and London, 2002), pp. 1–23, pp. 183–226.

[30] J. Porter, '"Blessed spirits, sing with me!": Psalm-singing in Context and Practice', in J. Porter (ed.), *Defining Strains: The Musical Life of Scots in the Seventeenth Century* (Bern, 2007), pp. 299–322; G. Munro, 'Scottish Church Music and Musicians, 1500–1700' (Unpublished PhD thesis, University of Glasgow, 1999), p. 71, p. 287.

[31] [Edward Burt], *Letters from a Gentleman in the North of Scotland* (2 vols, London, 1754), vol. 1, p. 180.

His word and Kirk', as well as playing pipes through the town at night, without being licensed by the town or magistrates. Roy was called for public penitence, wearing sackcloth as a sign of repentance.[32] More important were the prominent roles of musicians in activities banned by the Church. After the Reformation, the Scottish Church tried to suppress all 'profane pastimes' – activities deemed immoral, Papist, or a distraction from worship and Protestant identity. In 1561–96, a series of measures by both the general assembly and parliament banned pre-Reformation days of celebration such as Yule, Easter, May Days, and Saints' Days, as well as gambling, singing profane or bawdy songs, sabbath-breaking, drunkenness, and theatrical activities such as guising. Of particular importance to musicians were attempts to ban dancing. The activity was named a common corruption of the nation in the *Second Book of Discipline* (1578), and by the general assembly in 1587, 1596, and 1638. Eventually, in 1649, the assembly introduced an 'Act discharging Promiscuous dancing' (dancing between men and women).[33]

Fiddlers, pipers, and other musicians were frequently included in local measures against banned pastimes. The profusion of dancers and musicians who fell afoul of Elgin kirk session included twenty-two men and women charged with dancing on communion day in 1603, and one Alexander Andersone, who collected the piper's payment.[34] The fiddler William Stewart and town piper James Mylne were punished by the Aberdeen elders in 1609 for 'playing and singing' on sabbath days.[35] In April 1650, a host of young men were brought before the Culross kirk session for debauched behaviour at the house of Thomas Eizat, including drunkenness, having 'a fiddler with them', and 'singing and dancing every night till three or four houres in the morning'.[36]

The most frequent occasions for 'profane' offending were weddings and funerals, targeted by the Church for facilitating excessive feasting, drinking, promiscuous dancing, and superstitious ritual. The Scottish 'penny wedding' was described by Burt in the 1720s. The custom was popular among commoners 'all over the Lowlands', and involved a small contribution from each guest in lieu of a dowry, which paid for the 'expense of the Feast and Fiddlers'. After dinner, there was music and dancing, and the bride would 'go about the Room and kiss every Man in the Company' before receiving their financial contribution. One reason for the penny wedding's continued popularity was

---

[32] W. M. Cramond (ed.), *Records of the Kirk-Session of Elgin, 1584–1779* (Elgin, 1897), p. 15. For further examples, see Todd, *Culture of Protestantism*, pp. 37–8, 113–14, 164–5, 224.

[33] *The Books of Discipline and of Common Order* (Edinburgh, 1836), p. 112; Peterkin and Thomson, *Acts and Proceedings of the General Assemblies*, vol. 2, p. 724; vol. 3, pp. 866, 874; *Acts of the General Assembly of the Church of Scotland, 1638–1842* (Edinburgh, 1843), pp. 24, 201; RPS, 1592/4/26.

[34] *Elgin Rec.*, pp. 102–6.

[35] Todd, *Culture of Protestantism*, p. 195.

[36] D. Beveridge and J. J. Dalgleish, *Culross and Tulliallan: Or Perthshire on Forth* (2 vols, Edinburgh and London, 1885), vol. 1, pp. 196, 236.

THE COMMON MUSICIAN AND DEVIANCE

its important social role; it brought together individuals across class divides, with the bride's 'Master or Mistress' attending alongside friends and family of the married couple. The landed classes could show their benevolence and generosity in their larger financial contributions.[37] The authorities had long sought to suppress such celebrations. As early as 1562, the general assembly ordered that all marriages and burials should be solemnised according to the *Book of Common Order*, which banned Popish ritual and excessive celebration. Similar local measures were recorded across the country in the following century, and the general assembly issued an 'Act against Abuses at Likewakes, Penny-Bridals, and Promiscuous Dancing' in 1701.[38]

Frequent attempts to discourage musicians from performing at weddings are testament to their continued important social roles, particularly in leading dancing and bridal processions. In December 1583, Stirling presbytery banned processions led by fiddlers and pipers, fining the minister Robert Mentayth for attending bridals on the sabbath and permitting pipers to accompany wedding parties to the church. In 1648, Edinburgh burgh council banned pipers, fiddlers, and 'any uther mercenarie musicianes' from being employed at weddings altogether, and restricted the number of guests and money each person could contribute.[39] Musicians were similarly targeted for their roles in 'lykewakes'.[40] Burt's description from the 1720s notes the importance of dance at such events, functioning as a physical manifestation of grief:

> Friends and Acquaintance of the Deceased assemble to keep the near Relations Company the first Night: and they dance, as if it were a Wedding, 'till the next Morning, tho' all the Time the Corps lies before them in the same Room.[41]

A biographical sketch of fiddler John Cameron written by the son of his friend and fellow fiddler, poet Alexander Ross (1699–1784), notes Cameron's similar reminiscences in Aberdeenshire in the early 1700s:

> when any member of a family died, a musician was immediately sent for [...] the whole family, excepting children, were desirous to vent their sorrow by a kind of dancing. The musician accordingly played on the violin or bagpipe slow plaintive music, the nearest of friends of the deceased appeared first on the floor, took the first dance, and expressed their grief by their motion as well as by their tears.[42]

---

[37] Burt, *Letters*, vol. 1, pp. 261–3.
[38] *Acts of the General Assembly*, pp. 128, 311. Similar measures were recorded in Glasgow (1574) Aberdeen (1633), Edinburgh (1645), and Inverness (1673). *Glasgow Rec.*, vol. 1, p. 106; *Aberdeen Rec.*, pp. 54–5; *Edinburgh Rec.*, vol. 11, pp. 65–6; W. MacKay (ed.), *Records of the Presbyteries of Inverness and Dingwall, 1643–1688* (Edinburgh, 1896), p. 41.
[39] J. Kirk, (ed.), *Stirling Presbytery Records 1581–1587* (Edinburgh, 1981), pp. 190–2; *Edinburgh Rec.*, vol. 8, p. 141. Also see Todd, *Culture of Protestantism*, p. 274.
[40] Described in more detail in *ibid.*, pp. 212–13.
[41] Burt, *Letters*, vol. 2, pp. 209–10.
[42] A. Thomson, 'Life of the Author', in A. Ross, *Helenore or the Fortunate Shepherdess, a*

Despite the general assembly's outright ban of lykewakes in 1645, the Church was forced to act against fiddlers at such events into the late seventeenth century. In 1675, Mr Rorie, the minister of the village of Moy (near Inverness) received a warning from the presbytery of Inverness for failing to ban piping, violing, and dancing at lykewakes. The minister at the nearby village of Dores was less indulgent: when questioned in 1675, the elders of his congregation noted his zeal in punishing sabbath-breaking and 'pyping violeing and danceing at Lykwaks'.[43] Both music and musicians, then, attracted consistent suspicion because of their strong association with the sort of ill-disciplined and 'profane' customs or activities that the Reformation had officially rendered anathema.

Success of the Campaign

It is difficult to ascertain the full effect of the restrictions on musicians. The measures must have placed strain on fiddlers like Alexander Glass and John Cameron, who made their livings playing for the banned activities. Nevertheless, the traditions of musicians at dances, weddings, funerals, and processions were resilient, surviving into the eighteenth century and beyond.[44] Those further down the social hierarchy were not passive victims but sometimes fought back against Church suppression. Musical performance could even be a subversive act. Numerous Scottish music manuscripts contain tunes with anti-clerical titles such as 'The Kirk Wad Let Me Be'; such tunes were well known, and their performance in public was sometimes viewed as an open attack against Church censure. In 1683, one individual was punished by the circuit court of Stirling for having 'reviled the Minister' by asking a piper to play the tune 'The Deill stick the Minister'. The court had 'sundry fiddlers' to present as witnesses and declare that it was the tune so named.[45]

The authorities were not monolithic in their approach to the regulation of musicians, however, and some individuals in the political and religious elite held attitudes at odds with official policy. Even ministers sometimes organised penny weddings. John Martiall, the minister of Dundurcas (Rothes) was rebuked by the presbytery of Inverness in 1675 for not only holding a penny wedding on the sabbath, but allowing a minstrel to lead the procession to the church for the marriage ceremony.[46] Patrick Hume, earl

---

Pastoral Tale (Dundee, 1812), pp. xix–xx.

[43] MacKay, *Presbyteries of Inverness and Dingwall,* pp. 52–5.

[44] K. Campbell, *The Fiddle in Scottish Culture: Aspects of the Tradition* (Edinburgh, 2007), pp. 44–101; P. Cooke, *The Fiddle Tradition of the Shetland Isles* (Cambridge, 1986).

[45] Lauder, *Historical Notices,* vol. 1, p. 442.

[46] Mackay, *Presbyteries of Inverness and Dingwall,* p. 121. Robert Houston has noted several other examples of ministers organizing penny weddings. R. A. Houston, *Bride Ales and Penny Weddings: Recreations, Reciprocity, and Regions in Britain from the Sixteenth to the Nineteenth Centuries* (Oxford, 2014), p. 72.

of Marchmont and chancellor of Scotland in 1696–1702, was a celebrated covenanter, having earlier fled the country for his strict Presbyterian beliefs, and yet his appreciation for dance is well documented. During his exile, Hume instructed his wife that their grandchildren should not 'pass a week day without dancing'. Hume's granddaughter remembered his opinion that dancing was 'the best medicine he knew, for at the same time that it gave exercise to the body, it cheered the mind'. The account books of both his wife and daughter accordingly include numerous outlays on fiddlers, balls, and dancing lessons.[47]

The other side to anti-musician measures was that the authorities recognised their duty in caring for the poor. Charity was offered to musicians in the form of money and the purchase of instruments. In 1582, Edinburgh burgh council supported the 'blindman' John Mowatt by buying him a 'symphioun' [hurdy-gurdy]. In November 1677, Dumbarton burgh council received a supplication from violer William Houston that he was destitute and infirm; the burgh agreed to buy him a new viol and gave him £8. In April 1720, Dumfries kirk session noted that the violer Robert Hunter was in a 'dying condition' and granted him money for a physician, a one-off gift of 10s, and a weekly allowance of 8d. At times, charity was necessary even to support more well-to-do musicians. In 1732–3, the well-known music master and compiler of music manuscripts Andrew Adam was twice granted payments of £3 from Glasgow burgh council as he was 'very poor'.[48] Clearly music was a precarious vocation, and it is not altogether surprising that musicians called upon charitable support from Church and burgh. However, it is striking that the authorities suppressed musical activities at the same time as providing aid to the poorest musicians, and even viewing music as a suitable occupation for those not otherwise able to support themselves.

Burgh authorities were also responsible for much regular employment of musicians. Between the sixteenth and eighteenth centuries, most Scottish towns and cities employed one or more musicians, most often a piper and one or more drummers, as recorded in Stirling, Glasgow, and Aberdeen. Edinburgh was alone in Scottish burghs in following the English practice of employing a group of town waits: a larger ensemble of woodwind players who played for civic events, and often doubled on other instruments.[49] Town musicians combined musical and non-musical responsibilities. They

---

[47] G. Baillie Murray, *Memoirs of the Lives and Characters of the Right Honourable George Baillie of Jerviswood, and of Lady Grissell Baillie* (Edinburgh, 1822), pp. 77, 131. R. Scott-Moncrieff (ed.), *The Household Book of Lady Grisell Baillie 1692–1733* (Edinburgh, 1911), pp. 9–35, 42–55, 60. H. Kelsall and R. Kelsall, *Scottish Lifestyle 300 Years Ago* (Edinburgh, 1993), pp. 127–8, 209.

[48] *Edinburgh Rec.*, vol. 4, pp. 563–4; *Dumbarton Burgh Records, 1627–1746* (Dumbarton, 1860), p. 88; Dumfries Historical Indexes: https://info.dumgal.gov.uk/HistoricalIndexes [accessed 17 April 2024]; *Glasgow Rec.*, vol. 5, pp. 379 and 404.

[49] *Stirling Rec.*, vol. 1, p. 136, pp. 183–4; vol. 2, pp. 12–13, 52, 332. *Glasgow Rec.*, vol. 1, pp. 203, 207–8, 347. *Aberdeen Rec.*, vol. 1, pp. 2, 40, 115; vol. 2 pp. 209–10. *Edinburgh Rec.*, vol. 6, p. 43, vol. 10, pp. 240–7, 404; vol. 11, p. 262; vol. 12, pp. 29, 162.

processed through the town in the early morning and evening for curfew, performed for *wappenshaws* (military displays), and sometimes doubled as the town watch, again highlighting how sound and music helped to set the official boundaries and standards of a town.[50]

Outside regular salaried roles, musicians were employed on an *ad hoc* basis, or given licence to operate within a town. It is notable that such individuals often took part in the very activities the Church was attempting to ban. Edinburgh burgh employed string players for royal events in 1561, 1579, and 1617, and Aberdeen town council paid 12s to violers to play for a dinner in celebration of William Forbes upon his appointment as minister of St Giles, Edinburgh in 1621.[51] In 1686, Glasgow paid £12 to a group of fiddlers and drummers who played for the king's birthday.[52] The convener's book for the Incorporated Trades of Dundee includes payments of £2 3s 6d 'to the violers at Denner' [dinner] in 1696, and £2 to 'the violens' at another meeting in 1697. Stirling similarly paid a group of violers to play for a celebration marking the coronation of George I in 1714, as well a group of violers and pipers for the convener's dinner in September 1717.[53] From the 1660s onwards, successive high commissioners and chancellors regularly employed instrumentalists to play for dancing and lavish banquets, often in celebration of military events or coronations.[54]

From the late seventeenth century onwards, string players began to receive longer-term civic patronage, often being given a monopoly on activities in a particular area. A town violer or piper was offered a house rent free by the town council of Burntisland in the second half of the seventeenth century, additionally receiving an annual salary of 10 merks and the 'sole right to teach music or provide it at marriages, dances, etc'. In 1714, Stirling burgh council awarded £14 3s for livery to the 'violner' Hector McLean, with the proviso that they would not award the same to any future individual 'upon pretence of being touns violner [*sic*]', without a special act of council.[55] In 1718, Dundee town council awarded a monopoly to violers Alexander Nielson and George Morison, giving them the 'sole privelege of playing at

---

[50]   R. Rastall, 'The origin of the Town Waits, and the myth of the watchman-turned-musician', *Town Waits* website, https://townwaits.org.uk/wp-content/uploads/2022/02/waits-origin-1.pdf [accessed 27 October 2023]; E. Williamson and J. McGavin, 'Crossing the Border: The Provincial Records of South-East Scotland', in A. Douglas and S. Maclean (eds), *REED in Review: Essays in Celebration of the First Twenty-Five Years* (Toronto, 2006), 157–77.

[51]   R. Adam (ed.), *Edinburgh Records: The Burgh Accounts* (2 vols, Edinburgh., 1899), vol. 1, p. 343; *Edinburgh Rec.*, vol. 4, p. 124; *Aberdeen Rec.*, vol. 2, pp. 96–7, 103–4.

[52]   *Glasgow Rec.*, vol. 3, p. 610.

[53]   'Convener's Book, 1695–1833', *The Nine Incorporated Trades of Dundee*, https://archive.ninetradesofdundee.co.uk/city-history [accessed 27 Oct. 2023; expired link]; *Stirling Rec.*, vol. 2, p. 351.

[54]   John Nicoll, *A Diary of Public Transactions and Other Occurrences, Chiefly in Scotland, from January 1650 to June 1667* (Edinburgh, 1836), pp. 283, 289, 332–5, 368, 374–5, 391, 399, 436, 448.

[55]   *Stirling Recs*, vol. 2, p. 134.

THE COMMON MUSICIAN AND DEVIANCE

all weddings within the Burgh', and banning inhabitants from allowing other musicians to play at such events.[56]

The motivation behind such patronage was in part to control the activities and numbers of musicians. Burgesses were given access to musicians for social and civic occasions, but the licences restricted the numbers of musicians within a burgh, and the musicians themselves had reason to discourage visiting performers. Individuals held posts at the discretion of the burgh council and had extra reason for obeying its regulations. In February 1600, Glasgow burgh threatened to dismiss town drummer Robert Spens for numerous misdemeanours, including travelling to other burghs, playing at weddings, excessive drinking, and neglecting his duties.[57]

There are signs that more positive methods yielded results. After many threats and punishments against the Elgin fiddler Alexander Glass, the town council in 1659 offered him a rent-free plot of land on the town common, providing he followed their rules of not brewing beer or associating with vagabonds.[58] The change in tactics seems to have worked: Glass disappears from Elgin Church and burgh records after this date. Evidently the movement between persecution and patronage was elastic and ever-changing.

Developments in Musical Culture and the Vernacular Revival

After over a century of the Church's campaign against profane pastimes, there was a huge shift in musical culture in Scotland in the eighteenth century, together with vastly improved prospects for musicians. The emergence of polite society and a growing middle class brought demand for public entertainments. By the late seventeenth century, public concerts, dancing assemblies, and theatres had begun to operate in Edinburgh, though they often attracted protest on religious grounds. The following decades saw similar activities in Aberdeen, Glasgow, and other Scottish towns.[59]

The fact that such activities could flourish by the eighteenth century was down to multiple factors, including societal changes and the more moderate approach of the Church. The occupation of musicians had also been undergoing a gradual professionalisation over the seventeenth century, including a steady increase in musicians made burgesses or guild

---

[56] W. Hay (ed.), *Charters, Writs and Public Documents of the Royal Burgh of Dundee* (Dundee, 1880), p. 161.

[57] Later that year, the council clearly set out the duties and rules for their town drummer and piper. *Glasgow Recs*, vol. 1, pp. 203, 207–8.

[58] *Edinburgh Rec.*, vol. 4, pp. 563–4; *Dumbarton Burgh Records*, p. 88; *Elgin Rec.*, vol. 1, p. 310.

[59] D. Johnson, *Music and Society in Lowland Scotland in the Eighteenth Century* (Edinburgh, 2003), pp. 32–50; P. Holman, 'An Early Edinburgh Concert', *Early Music Performer*, 13 (2004), 9–17; I. Brown, 'Public and Private Performance: 1650–1800', in I. Brown (ed.), *Edinburgh Companion to Scottish Drama* (Edinburgh, 2011), pp. 22–40; G. S. Emmerson, *A Social History of Scottish Dance: Ane Celestial Recreatioun* (Montreal, 1972).

brothers of Aberdeen, Edinburgh, and Glasgow.[60] For musicians, these were honorary roles, but they offered implicit permission to operate within a burgh, as well as acceptance into fraternal networks and the more official system of trade guilds.

A similar move towards legitimacy is reflected in evidence for musical apprenticeships. By way of example, a draft apprenticeship contract was finalised in 1705 between Alexander Chisholm, 'violer and servitor to Fraserdale' (Alexander Mackenzie of Fraserdale, c.1683–1755), and his prospective apprentice Lauchlin Cameron from Glenmoriston. For the five-year apprenticeship, Chisholm agreed 'to instruct, learn and teach the said Lauchlin his prentice, in the hail art and practice of his said trade of playing on the viol'. Lauchlin agreed to be a 'leall, dilligent, servisible, and obedient servant', and to refrain from frequenting ale houses, gambling, or fornicating.[61] Such measures projected an image of sobriety and proper behaviour, counteracting the popular association of musicians with deviance.

The amelioration of the image of the common musician was also linked to a growing interest in, and respect for, traditional musical culture in eighteenth-century Scotland. The vernacular revival of the early 1700s had its roots in the collecting of traditional melodies and songs in the seventeenth century, recorded in music manuscripts written for lute, keyboard, viol, and violin, and often written by or for the use of upper-class amateur musicians.[62] A revival of vernacular literature in the early eighteenth century gained huge momentum after the union of 1707, when writers such as Allan Ramsay pursued a form of cultural nationalism after the loss of political independence. In his collection *The Tea-Table Miscellany* (1724), Ramsay forged a new style of Scots song, combining traditional and newly-written material, and Scots dialect with fashionable London verse, as well as bowdlerising lyrics to make them fit for polite society. With Ramsay's encouragement, Edinburgh-based musicians such as James Oswald, William McGibbon, and Francesco Barsanti similarly created a drawing-room style Scots music, combining traditional melodies and fiddle variations with Italianate concert music. The second half of the eighteenth century saw a gradual shift in the presentation of published Scottish music towards a more authentic representation of the style of ordinary musicians, including music directly published by dance musicians

---

[60] H. Armet (ed.), *Register of the Burgesses of the Burgh of the Canongate 1622–1733* (Edinburgh, 1951); C. B. Watson (ed.), *Roll of Edinburgh Burgesses and Guild Brethren 1406–1700* (Edinburgh, 1929); J. R. Anderson (ed.), *The Burgesses and Guild Brethren of Glasgow 1573–1750* (Edinburgh, 1925); A. M. Munro (ed.), 'Register of Burgesses of Burgh of Aberdeen, 1399–1631', in *Miscellany of the New Spalding Club, Volume I* (Aberdeen, 1890), 1–162. Also see J. K. McMillan, 'A Study of the Edinburgh Burgess Community and its Economic Activities, 1600–1680' (Unpublished PhD thesis, University of Edinburgh, 1984).

[61] NRS, Warrand of Bught Papers, Draft apprenticeship contract between Lauchlin Camron [Cameron] and Alexander Chisholm, violer and servitor to Fraserdale, 1705, GD23/4/69.

[62] W. Edwards, 'The Musical Sources', in Porter, *Defining Strains*, pp. 47–72.

THE COMMON MUSICIAN AND DEVIANCE

whose background was not far removed from the common musicians of the previous centuries.[63]

The fiddler-composer Niel Gow (1727–1807) is perhaps the clearest example of this improvement in both the prospects of performers and the wider associations of musicians in Scotland. Gow was born in the village of Inver, near Dunkeld, and initially trained as a weaver. In a biography published in the *Scots Magazine* shortly after his death, Gow is described as having been self-taught in music apart from some lessons as a teenager from the fiddler John Cameron. Gow achieved early recognition by winning a fiddling competition, in which a blind judge claimed 'he could distinguish the stroke of Neil's [*sic*] Bow amongst a hundred players'. After finding patrons among the aristocracy, most notably the duke and duchess of Atholl, Gow became a national figure after his first publication, *A Collection of Strathspey Reels* (1784).[64]

Gow was so well known that he became a popular attraction on tourist routes across Scotland, as described by Alexander Campbell, Thomas Garnett, James McNayr, and perhaps most famously, Robert Burns. These descriptions share several characteristics: they describe Gow's lack of formal education, and his entirely vernacular repertoire, consisting of strathspeys, reels, airs, and laments, rather than Italianate concert music. Writers not only emphasise Gow's talent, but show an interest in the aesthetic qualities of his performance, from the expressive pathos in laments, to the rhythmic vibrancy of reels, and the unique 'driven' style of his bowing in strathspeys.[65]

Descriptions of Gow also emphasise the positive aspects of his character. Burns described Gow as a 'short, stout built, honest highland figure with his grayish hair shed on his honest social brow [and] an interesting face marking strong sense, kind openheartedness mixed with unmistrusting simplicity'. The *Scots Magazine* biography draws attention to Gow's moral and religious principles, the integrity, prudence, and propriety of his conduct, and his respected position amongst his social equals and superiors alike.

---

[63] M. Gelbart, 'Allan Ramsay, the Idea of "Scottish Music" and the Beginnings of "National Music", in Europe', *Eighteenth-Century Music*, 9:1 (2012): 81–108; A. A. Greenwood, 'Song and Improvement in the Scottish Enlightenment', *Journal of Musicological Research*, 39:1 (2020), 42–68; Johnson, *Music and Society*, pp. 130–63; D. Johnson, *Scottish Fiddle Music in the 18th Century: A Music Collection and Historical Study* (Edinburgh, 2005).

[64] 'A Brief Biographical Account of Neil Gow', *The Scots Magazine and Edinburgh Literary Miscellany*, January 1809, pp. 3–5. Also see M. A. Alburger, *Scottish Fiddlers and Their Music* (Edinburgh, 1996).

[65] A. Campbell, *A Journey from Edinburgh Through Parts of North Britain* (2 vols, London, 1802), vol. 2, p. 275; T. Garnett, *Observations on a Tour Through the Highlands and Part of the Western Isles of Scotland* (2 vols, London, 1800), vol. 2, pp. 73–4; J. McNayr, *A Guide from Glasgow, to Some of the Most Remarkable Scenes in the Highlands of Scotland and to the Falls of the Clyde* (Glasgow, 1797), p. 101; R. Burns, *The Oxford Edition of the Works of Robert Burns Volume 1: Commonplace Books, Tour Journals, and Miscellaneous Prose*, ed. N. Leask (Oxford, 2014), p. 147.

Such descriptions were a product of their time and were likely influenced by Enlightenment ideas around the 'noble savage' and romantic depictions of Highland culture. Nevertheless, there is a stark contrast between the literary trope of the common musician and the descriptions of Gow and his contemporaries. Gow's background and repertoire were likely not far removed from common musicians in previous centuries, and yet the ability to perform music now went together with the strength of his character, rather than being necessarily linked with loose morals and deviant behaviour.

Conclusion

Musicians had a complex and shifting relationship with Church and burgh authorities in early modern Scotland. Despite their important social functions, musicians suffered from being stereotyped as lascivious and immoral. They were targeted by burgh councils in measures to control social order, including regulating the urban soundscape, tackling vagrancy, and curbing criminal and seditious behaviour. For the Church, musicians were focal points for a litany of proscribed activities, notably promiscuous dancing, weddings, lykewakes, and activities viewed as Catholic or pagan.

There were mitigating factors, notably charity and employment opportunities offered to musicians, though patronage often went together with attempts to control social activities and the movement of people. Nevertheless, musicians had agency; they pushed back against overly repressive regulation and brought about an increased professionalisation of their occupation through a system of apprenticeships and networks. In the eighteenth century, societal changes, the emergence of public entertainments, and a vernacular revival led to better prospects for musicians and a more positive image of the common musician. No doubt music remained a precarious living for many, but Scottish music, musicians, and their associated traditions had proved remarkably resilient through centuries of repression.

10

Marginally Speaking:
Insults and Concepts of Marginality in
Sixteenth-Century Scottish Towns[1]

Elizabeth Ewan

On 2 July 1575, two women appeared before Inverness burgh court, each pursuing the other for insulting her. Jonet Dempster complained that on the previous Friday night on the High Street, without any provocation made by her, Christian NykQuhene had called her 'glangoir myssaell lypper carles geit' (syphilitic, leprous leper, peasant's bastard) and said that her father was so leprous he was forced to steal though the town at night. NykQuhene brought a counter-complaint against Dempster, stating that she had abused NykQuhene's daughter and called her 'outland stredling and cruikit carles geit scho was that nane of ws aucht to dwell within this towne' (country dweller/outsider of little account and crooked peasant's bastard she was, that none of us ought to dwell within this town). Then, claimed NykQuhene, Dempster came to her booth and called her 'commond theiff that all my kyn and freindis war hangit for pikere and thift' (common thief, that all my kin and friends were hanged for petty theft and theft).[2]

In hurling these insults, both women equated their victims and their kin with marginalised groups in contemporary urban society: people from outside the town (outsider, peasant, those who ought not to dwell within the town, one who dared not be seen on the streets during daytime); those suffering from disease or disfigurement (syphilitic, leprous, leper, crooked); people of low social status (peasant, person of little account, bastard); and those who had marginalised themselves through their criminal actions (hanged for theft and petty theft). By denigrating the status of her victim, by implying her marginalisation or even exclusion from the community, each woman was attempting to consolidate or even enhance her own position in society; she was making an implicit statement about her own superior status relative to her opponent. Indeed, it has been argued that such insults say more about the offender's anxieties about his or her own status than about the actual status of

---

[1] I would like to thank Allan Kennedy and the anonymous reviewer for very helpful comments. I also thank the Social Sciences and Humanities Research Council of Canada for financial support for the research.
[2] HAC, BI/1/1/2, Inverness Burgh Court Books, fol. 319v. The insult to Jonet Dempster is printed in *Inverness Rec.*, vol. 2, p. 242.

the victim.[3] In a hierarchical society where individuals were deeply sensitive to their place in the social hierarchy and where honour and identity rested on being an accepted and respectable member of the urban community, it was highly effective to accuse someone of being an outsider or being marginalised through their social status or deviant behaviour.

This case was but one of thousands of verbal conflicts that came before the burgh courts and, after the Reformation of 1559–60, the kirk sessions of sixteenth-century Scottish towns. They provide a glimpse into interpersonal relationships, enmities and friendships, the jostling for and acceptance of status, family and social networks, and much else about the townsfolk of early modern Scotland. Unfortunately for later historians, in most cases the specific insults are not recorded, the scribe merely describing them as 'injurious words' or other forms of verbal abuse; however, enough records survive where at least some words were noted that we can glimpse the insulting language used between opponents. As the Dempster-NykQuhene case demonstrates, this can shed light on attitudes towards and perceptions of marginals and outsiders, those who did not fit comfortably within the social parameters of the established urban community.

Communities are defined as much by who they exclude as who they include.[4] Although these interpersonal conflicts temporarily disturbed the peace of the community, the use of such 'marginal insults' actually functioned in the long run to maintain the social hierarchy by reinforcing concepts of marginality. The words used provide insight into how that hierarchy was constructed in the minds of contemporaries. They help demonstrate what constituted secure status and acceptance in urban societies and what marginalised or excluded individuals from membership of the urban community.

Early modern Scots were inventive in their choice of vitriolic language. Insults included accusations of inappropriate behaviour and corruption, loathsome appearance and disease, lying and cheating, sexual promiscuity, and many other unacceptable characteristics. This chapter focuses on insults that attempted to marginalise the position of the targets, by identifying them as people who should be excluded from the community completely and/or by identifying them with those who existed precariously on the margins of urban

---

[3]   S. Lipscomb, *The Voices of Nimes: Women, Sex and Marriage in Reformation Languedoc* (Oxford, 2022), pp. 157, 165; L. Gowing, *Domestic Dangers: Women, Words, and Sex in Early Modern London* (Oxford, 1998), p. 87.

[4]   S. Hindle, 'A Sense of Place? Becoming and Belonging in the Rural Parish, 1550–1650', in A. Shepard and P. Withington (eds), *Communities in Early Modern England* (Manchester, 2000), pp. 98–114, at p. 97; E. P. Dennison, 'Power to the People? The Myth of the Medieval Burgh Community', in S. Foster, A. Macinnes and R. MacInnes (eds), *Scottish Power Centres from the Early Middle Ages to the Twentieth Century* (Glasgow, 1998), pp. 100–31, at p. 112. See also A. Allen, 'Working on the Margins: Freemen, Unfreemen and Stallangers in Early Modern Scotland', in A. Kennedy and S. Weston (eds), *Life at the Margins in Early Modern Scotland* (Woodbridge, 2024), pp. 97–113.

society. It also examines how attempts were made to extend the concept of marginalisation from individuals to entire families.

This discussion focuses on *perceptions* of marginalisation rather than the lived reality of life at the margins. Most recorded conflicts were between opponents who had at least some claim to be included in the community, rather than between those who were marginalised (as defined elsewhere in this and the companion volume, *Life at the Margins in Early Modern Scotland*), as the latter are much more difficult to find. Both Christian NykQuhene and Jonet Dempster were married women who lived and worked in Inverness. Court cases rarely involved those whose social and economic status really was marginal in the town. This may be partly because those of truly marginal status lacked the standing to bring such cases before courts staffed by the townspeople above them in the hierarchy, or, if they did manage to do so, they would have had a hard time winning cases against higher-status defendants. Moreover, it was harder to argue that their own status, which was marginal at best, was made any worse by such insults – if one was a vagabond, there was little use in complaining to the authorities about being called one. The majority of court cases (or at least those where relative status can be determined), were between townspeople of roughly similar status and who normally would have been considered as settled members of the urban community.[5]

Since the focus of this volume is on marginality, transgression, and deviance, and for reasons of space, this chapter will engage in its own form of exclusion and omit certain types of insult which could be argued to be marginalising. The most common insults hurled at men and women were 'thief' and 'whore', with the latter being reserved for women, but as has been argued for both Scotland and elsewhere, these were used so widely as to have largely become divorced from their literal meaning and instead acted as a type of shorthand for accusations of bad character, not necessarily actual theft or prostitution.[6] Insults about disease such as syphilis or leprosy often performed several functions – as well as drawing attention to the victim's displeasing appearance, they carried connotations of sexual sin. Lepers, and those affected by syphilis (commonly called grandgore) or plague, were often moved to separate hospitals or places outside the urban boundaries, being physically excluded from the town. These types of insults will be discussed elsewhere. The discussion here will concentrate on insults that questioned the opponent's right to be considered part of the community either by settled residence in the town, lawful conduct, or as a member of an established urban

---

[5] The exception to conflicts between those of relatively similar status was insults against the authorities, but these occupied a special place in local laws and will be considered elsewhere.

[6] E. Ewan, '"Many Injurious Words": Defamation and Gender in Late Medieval Scotland', in R. Andrew McDonald (ed.), *History, Literature and Music in Scotland, 700–1560* (Toronto, 2002), pp. 163–86, at pp. 167–70. On 'whore' in England, see Gowing, *Domestic Dangers*, p. 66.

family. Both men and women hurled and were the targets of these insults; there was no evident gendered pattern to their use, at least as far as the surviving evidence can reveal, although some, such as those implying lack of control over the members of one's household, may have affected their male and female targets in different ways (see below).

There are limitations in using the court records when considering examples of common speech. As mentioned, most clerks transcribed only a few, if any, of the insults that were thrown, and those words recorded reflect their deliberate choice. Litigants were also selective, presenting the insults that would seem most egregious to the court and most favourable to their case, telling the audience what they thought it wanted to hear.[7] Historians cannot get at the 'truth' of what actually happened in a conflict, but the words presented had to be convincing and appeal to common ideas of what was acceptable and unacceptable behaviour, as well as to reflect or at least approximate actual speech.[8] The existing evidence is partial, but it can be used to provide a glimpse of widely held attitudes towards those who were marginalised in the community.

Why did the targets of such insults bring their opponents before the local courts? In a society where most transactions were conducted on credit, a reputation for honesty was critical to functioning in everyday life.[9] A person's word had to be trusted, otherwise there were practical implications. Patrick Broun of St Andrews complained that the tailor William Burne and his wife Christian Small had done everything they could to 'put him out of guid name and fame, and rendering him in evill opinion of sindry honest personis'; this had put Broun 'to his grit hindrance and disadvantaige in sindry his honest intromissionis.'[10] Moreover, this was a society where one's honour was critical to one's identity. To be characterised as being excluded from the community, either as an outsider or as belonging to a marginalised group, struck at the heart of one's self-perception as a fully integrated member of the town. When John Ross of Inverness brought a complaint against a burgess and his wife who had accused him of being 'ane manteiner of thift', he said that if it was true he 'wer nocht worthie to be ane nychtbour of this towne nor yit to be on lywe' (was not worthy to be a neighbour of this town or even to be alive).[11]

---

[7]   E. Horodowich, 'The Gossiping Tongue: Oral Networks, Public Life and Political Culture in Early Modern Venice', *Renaissance Studies*, 19.1 (2005), 22–45, at p. 30.

[8]   A. L. Capern, 'Rumour and Reputation in the Early Modern English Family', in C. Walker and H. Kerr (eds), *'Fama' and Her Sisters: Gossip and Rumour in Early Modern Europe* (Turnhout, 2015), pp. 85–113, at p. 88; E. Cohen, 'She Said, He Said: Situated Oralities in Judicial Courts in Early Modern Rome', *Journal of Early Modern History*, 16 (2012), 403–30, at pp. 417–18.

[9]   C. Muldrew, *The Economy of Obligation: The Culture of Credit and Social Relations in Early Modern England* (Basingstoke, 1998); C. Spence, *Women, Credit and Debt in Early Modern Towns* (Manchester, 2016), pp. 1–3; M. Todd, *The Culture of Protestantism in Early Modern Scotland* (New Haven, 2002), p. 247.

[10]   SUL, B65/8/1, St Andrews Burgh Court, 1588–92, no pagination [17 April 1590].

[11]   HAC, BI/1/1/2, fol. 35r–v.

The concern for maintaining one's reputation was shared by both litigants and the burgh authorities. The insults examined here were treated as cases of injurious words, rather than as evidence of actual wrongdoing by the target. The concise nature of the surviving record means that the context in which words were hurled is only rarely revealed. However, that context would have been familiar to the court and the community and taken into account when assessing the veracity of such charges; moreover, the role of provocation and hot temper in producing injudicious speech and spurious claims was recognised. Many insults, including those about low social status or the misdeeds of one's relatives, were not criminal accusations against their targets. Where they did include such charges, they were usually fairly generic (common thief), they were combined with other insults (drunk witch and beggar), or they brought up vague crimes committed in the past or outside the town. Accusations intended to lead to trials for wrongdoing were generally much more specific in describing the victim's actions, for example the stealing of particular items in cases of theft. In the cases discussed here, the real issue at play, for both the litigants and burgh authorities, was their acceptance as integral and trusted members of the local community.

Outsiders, Beggars, and Vagabonds

One of Christian NykQuhene's claims against Jonet Dempster was that she had said that NykQuhene's family was not worthy to be in the town. Her complaint spoke to townspeople's deeply held fears about being considered outsiders to the urban community. She also complained that Jonet Dempster had called her daughter an 'outland stredling' – an outsider of little account.[12] There had long been suspicion of outsiders and strangers in Scottish towns, as in urban communities throughout Europe. From at least the thirteenth century, law codes used by the Scottish burghs imposed restrictions on inhabitants offering accommodation to strangers.[13] Such people, unless there for lawful business such as selling produce on market days, or as foreign merchants visiting from abroad, were seen as potential threats to the peace of the community.[14] Some towns allowed certain people to pay for burgess status and enjoy its attendant privileges in the town without being resident, but they were known as 'outland burgesses' and distinguished from those who did make their home in the town itself.[15]

---

[12] The *Dictionary of Scots Language* also gives as a definition for 'striddler' someone who does agricultural work, https://dsl.ac.uk/entry/snd/striddle [accessed 15 Aug 2023].

[13] E. Ewan, *Townlife in Fourteenth-Century Scotland* (Edinburgh, 1990), p. 13. For Europe, see M. Rubin, *Cities of Strangers: Making Lives in Medieval Europe* (Cambridge, 2020), pp. 15–16, 36–7.

[14] A. Kennedy, 'Migrants, Itinerants and the Marginality of Mobility in Seventeenth-Century Scotland', in Kennedy and Weston, *Life at the Margins*, pp. 163–78.

[15] Allen, 'Working on the Margins', p. 104.

One type of outsider, the peasant, combined both exclusion from the town and low status. 'Carl', meaning peasant, was therefore a particularly useful insult, especially when it was aimed at people who considered themselves part of the urban community. It was often combined with other terms of disapprobation. For example, in 1542 in Elgin John Innes called Nicoll Moresone 'swenger carle' (idler/disreputable peasant) and 'birsyn carle' (ruptured peasant), while Margaret Sellar insulted Andrew Gibson as 'smake carell' (contemptible peasant).[16] In the same year and place, Megot Stuart called Ellen and Margaret Ternway, 'shabbit, glangorit carlis birdis' (scabby syphilitic peasants' offspring).[17] In 1592, William Turnbull of St Andrews called his opponent, the merchant John Paterson, among other things, a 'pultrun carll' (spiritless coward peasant).[18]

The status of beggars was somewhat more ambiguous and partly dependent on whether or not they had been born in the town. Margaret Leslie of Aberdeen called John Arthur 'a carle and a beggaris geit' in 1511, implying that he was a peasant outsider, both a beggar and illegitimate.[19] In 1551, Isobel Douglas, involved in a brawl with another woman, insulted the bailie of Elgin who had intervened, calling him 'puyr harlot, beggar carlis geit' (poor rascal, beggar peasant's bastard) and said that she did not know where he came from or where he went. In other words, she questioned his worthiness to be in the town as someone who was wandering and rootless; at the same time, she underlined her own inclusion in the community by her ability to define those who were acceptable as members.[20]

There was some sympathy for townspeople who had been reduced to poverty through a reversal of their fortunes, and in the sixteenth century, following earlier parliamentary legislation, many towns made provision for those who had been locally born and were considered respectable by providing them with licences or tokens allowing them to beg, distinguishing them from 'unacceptable' beggars, those of suspect behaviour or who had come from outside the town.[21] Recent research has mitigated an earlier picture of unrelenting severity to beggars in the late sixteenth century by highlighting the role of the Reformation Church and local authorities in providing for at least some of the less fortunate members of the community.[22]

However, it appears that at least some popular attitudes to beggars increasingly moved from seeing them as fit subjects of Christian charity and

---

[16] *Elgin Rec.*, vol. 1, pp. 61, 68.

[17] *Ibid.*, p. 72.

[18] SUL, B65/8/1 [10 March 1592].

[19] ACA, CA1, Aberdeen Burgh Council Minutes, 1398-present, vol. 9, p. 22.

[20] Moray Council Local Heritage Centre, 1/1/1, Elgin Burgh Court Book 1540–51, pp. 306–7. This record is partially printed in *Elgin Rec.*, vol. 1, pp. 107–8.

[21] J. McCallum, *Poor Relief and the Church in Scotland 1560–1650* (Edinburgh, 2018), pp. 111–12, 194–6; R. Kerr and J. R. Lockie, 'Scottish Beggars Badges', *Proceedings of the Society of Antiquaries of Scotland*, 95 (1964), 291–9.

[22] McCallum, *Poor Relief*; C. R. Langley, *Cultures of Care: Domestic Welfare, Discipline and the Church of Scotland c.1600 to 1689* (Leiden, 2020).

almsgiving to characters who were regarded with suspicion and contempt. This is reflected in the ways in which the word was used as an insult. Even 'respectable' beggars occupied a marginal position, and to call someone a beggar carried the implication that he or she deserved to be of low or marginal status, certainly lower than that of the person using the insult. When the term 'beggar', like 'carl', was used it was often deployed alongside other words which implied a disreputable, suspicious, or criminal character. In 1591, Margaret Gadderar of Elgin complained that John Straquhan had called her 'ane drunkin skemlar karling witsche and beggar' (a drunk scrounger old woman witch and beggar),[23] while the terms beggar and beggar's 'bird' (offspring with implications of illegitimacy) were thrown in along with thief and whore in three exchanges of insults among Glasgow women in 1592.[24] The Aberdeen merchant Gilbert Mar was so incensed after John Davidson, a tailor, called him a beggar's brat in front of some visiting merchants from Danzig in 1536 that he struck him.[25] Some offenders expressed the wish to see their opponent reduced to beggary; Christian MacKane of Elgin was convicted in 1582 for saying to the burgess Thomas Richardson when he questioned the quality and price of her ale, 'Reisky carll scho wald leiff to sie his barnis beg yr meit' (moorland peasant, she would live/be glad to see his children beg their meat).[26]

Beggars from outside the town met with little sympathy; as the legislation regarding tokens shows, there was an increasingly strict demarcation between those from within the burgh, and therefore deserving of charity, and those rootless strangers from outside who were associated with violence and criminality; the latter were regarded as professional beggars, vagabonds, and criminals. 'Outland beggars' also unfairly decreased the alms available for the town's own poor inhabitants. In 1559, the Edinburgh authorities ordered that all beggars from elsewhere be kept out of or expelled from the town, and that alms only be given to those who were 'faillit burgessis merchands and craftismen or sic vtheris as has spendit thair youth in honest manner within this burgh.'[27] A distinction was thus made between 'honest' native poor and disreputable outsider beggars. Both religious and secular authorities took measures against such marginalised people. In Stirling in 1600, the kirk session ordered a public proclamation from the pulpit that 'all uncuth puir and idill beggaris' should remove themselves from this congregation and pass to where they were born by 29 September; any who remained would receive no alms.[28] In 1587, Edinburgh issued a

---

[23] NRS, CH2/145/1, Elgin St Giles Kirk Session, fol. 22v.
[24] GCA, CH2/550/1, Glasgow Kirk Session, 1583–93, fols 178r, 183r.
[25] ACA, CA1, vol. 9, p. 22; ACA, CA1, vol. 15, pp. 228–9.
[26] *Records of Elgin*, 167–8. 'Reisky' can also mean untilled land or moor – *Dictionary of Scots Language*, https://dsl.ac.uk/entry/snd/reesk [accessed 15 August 2023].
[27] M. Wood et al. (eds), *Extracts from the Records of the Burgh of Edinburgh* (9 vols, Edinburgh, 1927–67), vol. 3, p. 42.
[28] SCA, CH2/1026/1, Stirling Holy Rude Kirk Session, 1597–1614, p. 66.

proclamation excluding all vagabonds and masterless persons who had no service or honest industry to live by.[29] Vagabonds and 'masterless persons' were those who did not fit into the traditional household or family and were regarded with suspicion as a result.

A major concern was that such rootless persons were associated with criminal or morally suspect behaviour.[30] Insults about vagabonds picked up on this suspicion of such persons and their connection with crime. Jonet Philps of Aberdeen called Christian Cults a common thief, a wine stealer, and a vagabond in June 1583.[31] In Glasgow in 1585, one man claimed another was both a vagabond and a resetter (harbourer) of thieves, while in 1576 Muriel Gray of Inverness called Bessie Dundas both a land lowper (vagabond) and a common thief.[32] These insults, along with the others discussed above in this section, emphasised the victim's status as someone physically from outwith the community. They demonstrated the deeply held suspicions of townspeople about all outsiders, especially those of low social status. Such people were of unknown background and reputation, and it was feared that they would bring the moral contagion of the world beyond the town into its streets and homes.

Crime and Punishment

Insulting someone as a vagabond carried with it implications of criminal or immoral behaviour, but one of the most effective ways in which to marginalise opponents was to label them as an actual criminal. Committing a crime, a deliberate action on the part of the individual, was the most egregious way of setting oneself outside the community, and in serious cases could lead to the ultimate exclusion – execution. Other effective insults were ones that implied that the target had managed to escape the appropriate punishment, or had been punished but had then brought a polluting presence to a new community.

In 1565, Christian Aikman openly insulted John Williamson on a Stirling street, calling him 'theif, loun, scheep steillar, thou come furth of utheris pairtis for steilling of scheip' (For good measure she also called his wife a thief and a whore). The publicity of the insult, and Williamson's own standing in the burgh, was underlined by his being able to produce five witnesses willing to support his claim against her, and implicitly the wrongfulness of her charge.[33] Aikman tried to undermine Williamson's reputation by ascribing

---

[29] *Edinburgh Rec.*, vol. 4, pp. 507–8.

[30] Kennedy, 'Migrants, Itinerants, and the Marginality of Mobility'. For Europe, Rubin, *Cities of Strangers*, pp. 96–7.

[31] J. R. D. Falconer, *Crime and Community in Reformation Scotland: Negotiating Power in a Burgh Society* (London, 2014), p. 107.

[32] GCA, CH2/550/1, p. 49; HAC, BI/1/1/2, fol. 370v.

[33] *Stirling Rec.*, vol. 1, p. 83.

to him criminal activity carried out elsewhere, and also implying that he had either fled or been sentenced to leave his former abode for his actions. Such claims might be hard to disprove. John Morison, taking a dislike to the new Protestant minister of Inverness in June 1561, called him a 'common pulpet flitter and herlot' (pulpit scolder and rascal) who had 'stressed', probably sexually, other men's wives in Caithness and Orkney.[34]

Christian Aikman implied that John Williamson had been banished for theft, although she did not say from where he had come. Jonet Kembak, a mariner's wife in St Andrews, was more specific, claiming her opponent, a cordiner (shoemaker), had been punished for theft not only in Leith but also in Edinburgh.[35] Accusing someone of having been punished for criminal activities elsewhere was an effective strategy, as it fed into suspicions of those from outside the community. In March 1574, Mawsie Acheson in Canongate insulted Andrew Fergusson by saying that she had seen him thrice whipped through Edinburgh, the common punishment for theft[36] – since many Edinburgh criminals banished from the town simply moved down the High Street and across the boundary where Canongate began, this was a plausible claim. Such insults weakened the victim's connection with his or her present dwelling place as they implied the target was an incomer from elsewhere.

Criminals could be found within the burgh community as well as from outwith it. Insults identified such unsavoury elements by characterising these people as criminals who had not yet been punished, but deserved to be so. A few months after the quarrel of Jonet Dempster and Christian NykQuhene, Dempster's daughter Mage Grant was called a 'common resetter', that is a receiver of stolen goods.[37] Sometimes such insults helpfully specified the punishment that the victim should receive for the crime. Elspet Harrot of Inverness insulted James Gollan in 1559 by saying that she should cause his hands to be bound behind his back for theft that he had committed (implying either whipping or hanging).[38] James Vink and William Byrneth were found guilty of mutual insults in Elgin in 1542. Vink called Byrneth a 'loune false smaik' (lowly false rogue) and said that if he got him outside of the tolbooth he should have amends of him. Byrneth retaliated by saying that Vink was a common thief and that he should have been hanged four years ago. Both men were punished, but Byrneth's punishment was more severe, perhaps because insults like these implicitly criticised the authorities as well for failing to do justice.[39]

When Mawsie Acheson of Canongate insulted Andrew Fergussone by saying she saw him thrice scourged in Edinburgh, she also said that she had seen him burnt on the shoulder (one wonders how much time she spent

---

[34] *Inverness Rec.*, vol. 1, pp. 58–9.
[35] SUL, B65/8/1 [26 September 1589].
[36] ECA, SL150/1/1, Canongate Court Book, 1569–74, pp. 507–8.
[37] HAC, BI/1/1/2, fol. 331v.
[38] HAC, BI/1/1/1 fol. 102v.
[39] *Elgin Rec.*, vol. 1, pp. 69–70.

in Edinburgh to see all these punishments visited on one man). Corporal punishment for crimes such as theft included branding on the shoulder or cheek, and cutting of an ear, as well as whipping, although such punishments were more often threatened for repeat offenders than actually carried out.[40] Branding inscribed a person's criminal history on his or her body. Of the recorded insults collected for this study, only one makes reference to this type of punishment. This may have been either because such marks would speak for themselves if they existed on the opponent's body, or, if they did not, the absence of them would make such an insult instantly disprovable and therefore less effective.

One punishment that did provide useful fodder for insults was banishment, the ultimate form of marginalisation and exclusion, where the offender was cast out of the community altogether. Katty Paterson of Inverness called Andro Sutherland a common thief and thief's bastard and said that he would have to leave the town for theft, that is that he should be banished.[41] Banishment was usually imposed for theft, vagrancy, and, also in the later sixteenth century, in some towns for moral offences such as adultery and prostitution.[42] In 1592, Glasgow kirk session punished Jeane Herbertson for calling Jonet Campbell 'begger and beggeris burde theve and huir and that for huirdom scho left the cuntrey' (beggar and beggar's offspring, thief, and whore and that for whoredom she left the country).[43]

However, in comparison to many European towns of the period, most Scottish towns used banishment infrequently. It was far more common to threaten an offender with banishment if an offence was repeated in the future, than to actually impose the punishment.[44] Perhaps it was this relatively rare use of banishment that made the insult 'banished' particularly odious. For those from elsewhere, there was the suspicion that their banishment from their original place of residence was permanent and therefore reflected a particularly egregious case of wrongdoing. Andrew Hatmaker had been in trouble several times in Aberdeen when in 1504 John Kintor claimed that he had been banished out of two other burghs.[45] According to Bessie Dundas of Inverness, Muriel Gray not only called her a banished vagabond and thief but said that she had been banished from sundry burghs.[46]

---

[40] E. Ewan, 'Crossing Borders and Boundaries: The Use of Banishment in Sixteenth-Century Scottish Towns', in S. M. Butler and K. J. Kesselring (eds), *Crossing Borders: Boundaries and Margins in Medieval and Early Modern Britain. Essays in Honour of Cynthia J. Neville* (Leiden, 2018), pp. 237–57, at pp. 237, 240.

[41] HAC, BI/1/1/1 fol. 332v.

[42] Ewan, 'Crossing Borders and Boundaries' examines banishment in Elgin, Inverness, Canongate, and Dundee.

[43] GCA, CH2/550/1, p. 365. The word 'country' here probably means the local district rather than Scotland as a whole.

[44] Ewan, 'Crossing Borders', p. 254; Falconer, *Crime and Community*, p. 11.

[45] ACA, CA1, vol. 8, p. 360.

[46] HAC, BI/1/1/2, fol. 370v.

Banishment was a somewhat permeable boundary as the sentence was often imposed for a specified time (typically a year) rather than being permanent; many banished people were able to return to their community and, in theory, reintegrate. But memories of people's banishment continued, and it seems likely that reminders of their former banishment would be unwelcome. Ellen Thomson of Elgin, in a trading dispute with Thomas Lafrise in 1557, claimed that he had insulted her by saying that she had been banished from Inverness and had engaged in suspicious activity since then.[47] There was also the suspicion that people who had been banished from the community were back illegally and needed to sneak around the town at night, like Jonet Dempster's father whom Christian NykQuhene had accused of leprosy. Some men drinking in Christian Dict's Inverness alehouse in 1573 protested when faced with the bill, calling Christian and her sister 'common theiffs and houris, banneist ribaldis that war banneist of this towne all nycht and durst nocht be seyne pass of the towne in day lycht (common thieves and whores, banished loose women, that were banished of this town all night and dared not be seen to pass in the town in daylight).[48] The dangers of returning unlawfully included renewed banishment. In Stirling in 1601, Jonet Lin slandered Jonet Ednam by calling her 'harlet, beggar, quyne'. This proved a risky action for Lin as when Edman took her before the kirk session for it, the session found that Lin herself had been banished from the town before for many reasons and had returned without licence. They asked the bailies to banish her again.[49]

Banishment, even when it was used, was not necessarily very effective; many of those sentenced to banishment were back within the town fairly soon afterwards. This was reflected in legislation against harbouring which attempted to prevent kin and friends of those who had been banished from giving them housing. In Dundee in 1572, for example, when Agnes Sym was banished, neighbours were warned that there would be a 40s fine for those who harboured her and if they were found guilty a second time, they would lose their trading privileges in the town.[50]

Suspicion of outsiders was expressed in legislation against harbouring vagabonds and criminals, both those from outside the town and those who had been expelled from the community. This drew on the long-standing prohibition against providing hospitality for strangers from outside the burgh without informing the burgh authorities. A thirteenth-century burgh law stipulated that no-one living in the town ought to harbour any stranger (*advenam*) more than one night in his or her house unless he became pledge

---

[47] *Inverness Rec.*, vol. 1, p. 11.

[48] *Inverness Rec.*, vol. 1, p. 224.

[49] NRS, CH2/1066/1, p. 78. For banished Canongate people returning several times in the 1620s, see A. Glaze, 'Women and Kirk Discipline: Prosecution, Negotiation and the Limits of Control', *Journal of Scottish Historical Studies*, 36:2 (2016), 125–42, at pp. 139–40.

[50] DCA, Burgh and Head Court Book, 1572–4, no pagination [12 December 1572].

for the person's good behaviour.[51] However, harbouring laws were also about townspeople providing refuge for those that the authorities had deemed unworthy to remain within the burgh.

Apart from the practical consideration that harbouring undercut the punishment meted out by the authorities, it was felt that the harbourers themselves could be infected by the moral contagion of such unsavoury characters. In practice, judging by the number of local statutes against the practice of 'harbouring' vagabonds and other suspect persons, many town dwellers did offer succour to such people, perhaps especially to those who were their kin or friends.[52] Despite this, the practice of harbouring suspicious persons was regarded with disapproval by other townspeople who might become victims of the bad behaviour of these people, and the term 'resetter' (usually used for those who received stolen goods) was occasionally used to insult people as harbourers of people as well as goods. In 1584, Elizabeth Steile of Canongate called James Gilgor 'ane commoun theif and resettar of theves'.[53]

Insults that used accusations of criminal behaviour were particularly effective in demonising one's opponent. They could be used both against those who were already marginalised as newcomers to the town, drawing on the suspicion of outsiders, and also against those whose social position and long residence should have guaranteed their acceptance and standing within the community. Moreover, by also branding others as enablers of criminal activity, these insults underlined the ways in which crime not only hurt the economic and physical well-being of the townspeople, but also had the potential to corrupt the morals of the inhabitants themselves.

Family and Kin

Harbouring involved other members of the town in the misdeeds of criminals. It seems likely that such harbourers were often kin to the person harboured. The concept that one's kin were also affected, or indeed infected, by criminal or deviant behaviour was a powerful tool in the repertoire of insult. Christian NykQuhene attacked Jonet Dempster, it will be remembered, by insulting her father as a leper who had to creep through the town at night, while Dempster was alleged to have said of NykQuhene that none of her family were worthy to remain in the town and that all of her kin and friends were thieves. The latter insult was made at NykQuhene's booth, the site of her work and her home and therefore probably in the presence of her family. Such insults were

---

[51] *Leges Quatuor Burgorum*, in C. Innes and R. Renwick (eds), *Ancient Laws and Customs of the Burghs of Scotland* (2 vols, Edinburgh, 1868–1920), vol. 1, p. 41.

[52] A. Glaze, 'Sanctioned and Illicit Support Networks at the Margins of a Scottish Town in the Early Seventeenth Century', *Social History*, 45.1 (2020), 26–51. See also Kennedy, 'Migrants, Itinerants, and the Marginality of Mobility'.

[53] ECA, SL150/1/5, Canongate Court Book 1584–6, p. 95.

particularly wounding as they were aimed at families who had probably had a settled status in the town for more than one generation; they were not the rootless strangers or low-status people who were actually marginalised within urban society. The household and family were the basic building blocks of society, so if their reputation, character, or position were called into question, it further marginalised the target as a member of that group and destroyed his or her established roots in the community.

Insults thrown at a target's family were not necessarily entirely wide of the mark. A study of Aberdeen in the later sixteenth century has found that about one sixth of the cases of crime or misbehaviour involved multiple members of households.[54] Studies elsewhere have also highlighted how the actions of individuals needed to be considered in the wider context of disputes between households.[55] Insults involving the target's kin therefore appealed to widely accepted ideas about the place of the individual within the larger context of household and family.

Insults could be aimed both at specific members of the family or at the family as a whole. In 1592, Marion Struthers of Glasgow said that she hoped James Fleming would be hanged as he should have been twenty years earlier, that his children were evil-gotten brats, and that his wife Jonet Fergus was a thief and a whore.[56] Parents were a favourite target, as such insults carried the implication that the target had inherited the stain of deviant or criminal behaviour. Gilbert Menzies, a former provost of Aberdeen, took action against a woman who said that his mother had been a common witch to her end day; as he stated, this seriously degraded *his* honour, fame, and dignity.[57] Sometimes the connection was made more deliberate, as when Elspeth Barnat of Inverness raged against her former employer in 1563, saying, among other things, that she wished he would drown himself as his sister did.[58]

Targeting the spouse of the intended victim was also effective, particularly if the victim was a man. It was the responsibility, both moral and legal, of household heads to uphold the good reputations of their households,[59] and for men, this included the sexual behaviour of their wives. Calling a man's wife a whore or accusing her of other deviant behaviour implied that the

---

[54] J. R. D. Falconer, 'A Family Affair: Households, Misbehaving and the Community in Sixteenth-Century Aberdeen', in E. Ewan and J. Nugent (eds), *Finding the Family in Medieval and Early Modern Scotland* (Aldershot, 2008), pp. 139–50, at p. 139.

[55] G. Walker, *Crime, Gender and Social Order in Early Modern England* (Cambridge, 2003), pp. 9–13.

[56] GCA, CH2/550/1, pp. 351–2.

[57] ACA, CA1, vol. 17, pp. 470, 478. See discussion in Falconer, 'A Family Affair', p. 147. Menzies was father of the current provost at the time so the attack on him may also have been aimed at his son.

[58] *Inverness Rec.*, vol. 1, p. 98.

[59] Glaze, 'Sanctioned and Illicit Support Networks', p. 39; Janay Nugent, '"None must meddle betueene man and wife": Assessing Family and the Fluidity of Public and Private in Early Modern Scotland', *Journal of Family History*, 35.3 (2010), 219–31, at p. 222; Falconer, 'A Family Affair', p. 149.

man was unable to control his wife's actions and was a serious slur on his masculinity and patriarchal power.[60] John Schiphird of Aberdeen, angry at a tax imposed on him by the baxters in 1538, attacked them by saying that all the baxters' wives were whores, although his conflict was with the baxters rather than their wives.[61] Similarly, household heads were responsible for the well-being of the whole family, so wishing that someone's bairns or family would be reduced to beggary, as Christian MacKane did when she hoped that she would see Thomas Richardson's bairns beg their meat, cut to the heart of the household head's responsibility and identity.[62]

Insults involving families also drew on ideas of lineage and inherited characteristics, as well as ideas about the honour of the individual and its connection to the honour of the family. In a case of an unhappy marriage in January 1559, Alison Calland complained to the kirk session of St Andrews that within a few months of her wedding, her new husband daily abused and reproached her and also all her 'lynag and offspring', saying that he had entered among thieves, brothel keepers, and beggars. A divorce was granted in May 1561.[63] A common insult was to call someone the offspring (legitimate or, even better, illegitimate) of someone of marginal status or deviant character. Both Jonet Dempster and Christian NykQuhene, as we have seen, used this strategy: NykQuhene called Dempster a leprous peasant's brat and Dempster called NykQuhene's daughter a crooked/lame peasant's brat. An Elgin couple insulted the parson of Mortlik by calling him, among other things, a crooked peasant's brat and 'cumm of carlis'.[64] A person's illegitimacy was a stain not only on their own character but also a reminder of the disreputable character of the family from which they came.

In a kin-based society, insults about one's family cut deeply. The honour of both an individual and the family were inextricably bound up with each other. An insult against an individual damaged the reputation of that person's family, while insults about relatives of the victim damaged the target by associating him or her with family members' immorality or criminality. Such insults also undercut one of the hallmarks of respectability and integration within the community, belonging to a long-established and respectable urban family.

[60] Ewan, '"Many Injurious Words"', p. 167.

[61] ACA, CA1, vol. 15, p. 618.

[62] See note 26.

[63] *Register of the Minister, Elders and Deacons of the Christian Congregation of St Andrews* (Edinburgh, 1889), pp. 63–4, 70–2.

[64] *Elgin Rec.*, vol. 1, pp. 74–5. 'Cumm' also means grime so there may have been a double-entendre here. See Todd, *Culture of Protestantism*, pp. 237–8, for other examples of insults about lineage. This trope was also used in literary flyting contests such as that between William Dunbar and Walter Kennedy c.1508, Ewan, '"Many Injurious Words"', p. 170.

Conclusion

The insults discussed in this chapter reflected and incorporated perceptions of marginality and deviant behaviour that were subject to laws and punishments by the local and central authorities. As such they drew on images of exclusion or peripheral status within the urban community, of crime and punishment, and of deviant kin and family. The insults that were recorded in the courts were mainly those used between people of settled status in the burgh. Perhaps such litigants were even more sensitive to slights to their social status because of the lack of huge status differences between them and their opponents. In this way, rather than undercutting the social hierarchy, the language of marginalising insult rather functioned to remind people of the permeable lines between acceptable and unacceptable conduct, and the ease with which one could find oneself on the wrong side of that all-important boundary.

11

Ejected Academics: Marginalised Scottish University Professors between Reformation and Revolution[1]

Salvatore Cipriano

On 20 April 1641, the general assembly expelled John Forbes of Corse, the leading Aberdeen Doctor, from his divinity professorship at King's College, Aberdeen for his refusal to subscribe to the National Covenant. Forbes is perhaps best known for his formidable opposition to the covenanting movement. But before then, he was a learned academic and theologian, educated at King's and then at Heidelberg and Sedan, where he studied under the exiled Andrew Melville, the firebrand Presbyterian reformer and former master of Glasgow University and St Mary's College, St Andrews. From 1620, Forbes occupied the divinity chair at King's, where his theological work influenced his students and defined north-east Scotland's religious ethos.[2] By spring 1641, however, the covenanters were ascendant, and the holding of university posts was contingent on subscription to the Covenants. The 1640 general assembly had already barred Forbes from teaching, and he now faced a stark choice: defile his conscience and subscribe to the Covenant in order to maintain his professorship, or refuse subscription and lose his position.[3] After months of agonising reflection, he chose the latter.[4] According to the account of John Spalding – hardly a sympathetic commentator – Forbes was deposed from his office 'to the gryte greif of the youth and young studentis of theologie, who were weill instructit and teachit by this lerned doctor'.[5]

With his expulsion, Forbes joined a long list of Scottish academics who were ejected from their posts for deviating too far from the day's ascendant confessional standard (all known ejections are listed in the appendix at the

---

[1]   I am grateful to Alasdair Raffe for providing comments on an earlier draft of this chapter.

[2]   D. G. Mullan, 'Forbes, John, of Corse (1593–1648)', *ODNB*.

[3]   A. C. Denlinger, 'Swimming with the Reformed Tide: John Forbes of Corse (1593–1648) on Double Predestination and Particular Redemption', *Journal of Ecclesiastical History*, 66:1 (2015), 67–89, at pp. 67–9; R. Newton, 'United Opposition? The Aberdeen Doctors and the National Covenant', in C. R. Langley (ed.), *The National Covenant in Scotland, 1638–1689* (Woodbridge, 2020), pp. 53–70, at pp. 65–6.

[4]   AUL, Papers of John Forbes of Corse, Professor of Divinity, MS 635, pp. 391–4.

[5]   John Spalding, *Memorialls of the Trubles in Scotland and in England, A.D. 1624–A.D. 1645*, ed. J. Stuart (2 vols, Aberdeen, 1850–1), vol. 2, p. 57.

end of this chapter). These 'intellectual casualties' and 'political victims' spanned the sixteenth and seventeenth centuries.[6] This chapter explores this phenomenon of academic marginalisation in Scotland between the Reformation and revolution, a period of pronounced political, social, and religious upheaval. It highlights the nature of ejections and the conditions that spurred removals. In doing so, it also assesses the ways in which authorities employed languages that emphasised the dangers of professorial insufficiency, broadly defined, to marginalise ejected academics' antithetical ideas and influence. While early modern universities, like modern institutions, employed a range of staff with varying degrees of responsibility and interaction with students, this chapter focuses on staff with didactic responsibilities: the principals, regents, and specialised professors who distilled religious and political ideas and shaped the outlooks of their students.[7] It shows how, as moulders of future governing elites, professors were especially vulnerable to the impulses of the reformers, monarchs, and revolutionaries who sought to control the universities to serve their agendas.[8]

The university as an institution was not a marginalised space in early modern Europe. In Scotland, it was a place where the well-educated, rarely impoverished, and mostly able-bodied sons – sons only – of noblemen, gentry, ministers, merchants, and magistrates continued their elite formation by receiving grounding in the classical languages and ancient, Christian knowledge and philosophy that were thought to be crucial to preserve in order for society to function properly.[9] Thomas Hobbes contended that the universities were 'fountains of civil and moral doctrine' and thus required protection from 'deceiving spirits'.[10] There was, therefore, widespread concern with student behaviour, over which professors exercised strict control, while authorities were at pains to ensure that students did not interact with social deviants and prohibited masters and students from frequenting inns and taverns.[11] The university was to be an archetype, a beacon that

---

[6] S. J. Reid, 'Reformed Scholasticism, Proto-Empiricism and the Intellectual "Long Reformation", in Scotland: The Philosophy of the "Aberdeen Doctors", c.1619–c.1641', in J. McCallum (ed.), *Scotland's Long Reformation: New Perspectives on Scottish Religion, c.1500–c.1660* (Leiden, 2016), pp. 149–78, at p. 178.

[7] See especially K. Schultz, 'Protestant Intellectual Culture and Political Ideas in the Scottish Universities, ca. 1600–50', *Journal of the History of Ideas*, 83:1 (2022), 41–62.

[8] R. L. Emerson, *Academic Patronage in the Scottish Enlightenment: Glasgow, Edinburgh, and St Andrews Universities* (Edinburgh, 2008), pp. 26–7.

[9] G. F. Lytle, 'Universities as Religious Authorities in the Later Middle Ages and Reformation', in G. F. Lytle and U-R. Blumenthal (eds), *Reform and Authority in the Medieval and Reformation Church* (Washington, 1981), pp. 69–97; R. Kirwan, 'Introduction: Scholarly Self-Fashioning and the Cultural History of Universities', in R. Kirwan (ed.), *Scholarly Self-Fashioning and Community in the Early Modern University* (Farnham, 2013), pp. 1–20, at pp. 2–3.

[10] Thomas Hobbes, *Leviathan*, ed. R. Tuck (Cambridge, 1996), pp. 225–6. See also A. Pollnitz, *Princely Education in Early Modern Britain* (Cambridge, 2015), pp. 314–15.

[11] See for example A. Morgan and R. K. Hannay (eds), *University of Edinburgh Charters, Statutes, and Acts of the Town Council and Senatus 1583–1853* (Edinburgh, 1937), pp.

sustained extramural society through the production of governing elites.[12] The teacher, therefore, played a key role in a mature, orderly society: a 'model of morality' who possessed the education, credentials, and, most importantly, conformability to political, religious, and social mores. In many ways, the professor was the antithesis of the 'dishonourable' trades stigmatised in early modern Europe – executioners, gravediggers, and skinners, all closely associated with pollution – for they guarded and promoted intellectual purity, from which order and sobriety flowed.[13] Hobbes, writing in the aftermath of the Civil Wars, a calamity that he partly attributed to the failings of universities, argued that 'the Instruction of the people, [is] dependent wholly, on the right teaching of Youth in the Universities'.[14]

But what happened when professors transgressed – when they deviated from authorised confessional norms, disobeyed officials, espoused heterodox ideas (or worse), or taught in an unacceptable manner? Such misbehaviour rankled authorities of all confessions.[15] When issuing punishments, Scottish authorities wielded a language of marginality that drew upon established narratives concerning clerical (in)sufficiency, as well as wider rhetorical traditions that amplified the virtues of orthodoxy and sobriety while employing draconian public language that denigrated deviants.[16] Academic transgression could thus 'poison' or 'pollute' the impressionable minds of students (who were mostly young teenagers), infect wider society, and breed disorder.[17] From the monarchy to the clerical establishment, authorities in

---

117–25; R. A. Müller, 'Student Education, Student Life', in H. de Ridder-Symoens (ed.), *A History of the University in Europe, Volume II: Universities in Early Modern Europe (1500–1800)* (Cambridge, 1996), pp. 326–54; J. Davis, 'The Ideal Student: Manuals of Student Behaviours in Early Modern Italy', in Kirwan, *Scholarly Self-Fashioning*, pp. 21–37; H. Skoda, 'Collective Violence in Fourteenth- and Fifteenth-Century Oxford', in P. Dhondt and E. Boran (eds), *Student Revolt, City, and Society in Europe: From the Middle Ages to the Present* (London, 2018), pp. 222–34.

[12] K. Sharpe, 'Archbishop Laud and the University of Oxford', in H. Lloyd-Jones, V. Pearl, and B. Worden (eds), *History and Imagination: Essays in Honour of H. R. Trevor-Roper* (London, 1981), pp. 146–64, at pp. 160–2.

[13] P. A. Vandermeersch, 'Teachers', in de Ridder-Symoens, *History of the University*, pp. 210–55, at pp. 214–18, 224–5; K. E. Hollewand, *The Banishment of Beverland: Sex, Sin, and Scholarship in the Seventeenth-Century Dutch Republic* (Leiden, 2019), pp. 113–14; K. Stuart, *Defiled Trades and Social Outcasts: Honor and Ritual Pollution in Early Modern Germany* (Cambridge, 1999), pp. 3–17.

[14] Hobbes, *Leviathan*, p. 237.

[15] Hollewand, *Banishment*, pp. 241–5; S. Kivistö, *The Vices of Learning: Morality and Knowledge at Early Modern Universities* (Leiden, 2014); A. Ryrie, *Unbelievers: An Emotional History of Doubt* (Cambridge, MA, 2019), esp. chapter 2.

[16] C. R. Langley, '"Diligence in His Ministrie": Languages of Clerical Sufficiency in Mid-Seventeenth-Century Scotland', *Archiv für Reformationsgeschichte*, 104:1 (2013), 272–96; Stuart, *Defiled Trades*, p. 143; R. G. Newhauser, 'The Seven Devils: The Capital Vices on the Way to Modernity', in R. G. Newhauser and S. J. Ridyard (eds), *Sin in Medieval and Early Modern Culture: The Tradition of the Seven Deadly Sins* (York, 2013), pp. 157–88.

[17] M. Douglas, *Purity and Danger: An Analysis of Concepts of Pollution and Taboo* (London, 2002).

early modern Scotland insisted on religious uniformity and political unity, though, as this chapter highlights, how these ideals were defined changed regularly. Therefore, universities had to be staffed by men who agreed with the orthodoxies of the day. During this era, running afoul of those who held power was the most common way that professors in Scotland found themselves marginalised, removed from their positions, and replaced by more politically acceptable masters.

Enforcing Political Conformity

Early modern Scotland was a small kingdom with limited resources that nevertheless possessed five university centres.[18] Three 'ancient' universities that predated the Reformation – St Andrews (1411/13), with its constituent colleges of St Leonard's, St Salvator's, and St Mary's; Glasgow (1451); and King's College, Aberdeen (1495) – were later joined by Edinburgh (1583) and Marischal College, Aberdeen (1593). A university was also established at Fraserburgh in 1595, but it operated for only a decade. At the universities, regents (instructors who shepherded classes through the entirety of the four-year arts course) were largely made up of capable recent graduates making a living prior to ordination.[19] Principals and professors of divinity, medicine, and law were often, though not always, ministers plucked from parishes or other universities, domestic or foreign. As a product of Andrew Melville's educational reforms, the universities did experiment with 'fixed' specialised professorships in place of regenting.[20] However, these reforms were either scuttled or lapsed by the 1640s. Generally, each university had a principal (or provost at St Salvator's) who managed each institution's affairs and often taught divinity, in addition to up to four teaching regents.[21] During this era, the universities also added, or maintained, additional professors of divinity, medicine, mathematics, or law, who offered specialised instruction beyond the arts course.[22]

The Church of Scotland – in both its episcopal and Presbyterian variations – was often the ultimate arbiter in university affairs in the 150 years between

[18] W. Frijhoff, 'Patterns', in de Ridder-Symoens, *History of the University*, pp. 43–110, at p. 78; R. G. Cant, *The University of St Andrews: A Short History*, 2nd edn (Edinburgh, 1970), p. 40.
[19] R. G. Cant, 'The Scottish Universities in the Seventeenth Century', *Aberdeen University Review*, 43:143 (1970), 223–33, at pp. 227–30.
[20] A. Raffe, 'Academic Specialisation in the Early Modern Scottish Universities', in Bo Lindberg (ed.), *Early Modern Academic Culture*, pp. 177–88, at pp. 179–81.
[21] C. M. Shepherd, 'Philosophy and Science in the Arts Curriculum of the Scottish Universities in the 17th Century' (Unpublished PhD thesis, University of Edinburgh, 1974), pp. 365–97.
[22] D. Stevenson, *King's College, Aberdeen, 1560–1641: From Protestant Reformation to Covenanting Revolution* (Aberdeen, 1990), pp. 61–93.

the Reformation and the revolution. Extra-ecclesiastical authorities, through either parliamentary or royal mandate, also regularly removed transgressive teachers. The mechanisms of marginalisation included sentences of 'deposition' or 'deprivation'– the removal of one's office and benefice – in addition to forced 'demissions', or resignations.[23] Among ejected academics in the period examined, we see professors who were deposed or deprived, compelled to demit, resign, or retire, or otherwise forcibly removed through imprisonment or exile.

Most removals were clustered around the major upheavals of the sixteenth and seventeenth centuries. Successive transformations in Scotland's political and religious status quo defined, and redefined, the parameters for the quality and orthodoxy for university staff, thus girding power structures with strictures with which to gauge the conformity of professors. At the Reformation, the *First Book of Discipline* (1560) stated that it was 'needfull that there be chosen of the bodie of the University to every Colledge, a principall man of learning, discretion and diligence', while parliament adopted a Protestant confession of faith to which all university masters had to subscribe.[24] Concern with professorial ability was also inscribed in the *Second Book of Discipline* (1578), which expounded upon the office of the doctor, whose role it was to 'oppine up be simple teaching the mystereis of the fayth, to the pasture the gift of wisdome to apply the same be exhortatioun to the maneris of the flok as occasioun cravit'.[25] Requirements that Scottish professors possess the ability and learning to instruct students were coupled with specific religious and political criteria. In this way, successive authorities defined the bounds of professorial ability and introduced the mechanisms, and language, of marginalisation that empowered authorities to remove members of the professoriate deemed unfit. This was first evident at King's College, where Catholic academics remained beyond the Reformation of 1560, shielded by the political might of the earl of Huntly. Following Huntly's submission during the Marian Civil War, in June 1569 both the Kirk and privy council proceeded against the King's recusants: Principal Alexander Anderson, Sub-Principal Alexander Galloway, and the regents Andrew Anderson, Thomas Owsten, and Duncan Norie.[26] The Kirk deprived the staff for refusing to

---

[23] D. Stevenson, 'Deposition of Ministers in the Church of Scotland under the Covenanters, 1638–1651', *Church History*, 44:3 (1975), 321–35, at p. 322.

[24] *RPS*, A1560/8/3; J. K. Cameron (ed.), *The First Book of Discipline: With Introduction and Commentary* (Edinburgh, 1972), p. 144. On the *First Book of Discipline* and the Reformation, see S. J. Reid, *Humanism and Calvinism: Andrew Melville and the Universities of Scotland, 1560–1625* (Aldershot, 2011), pp. 24–7; J. C. Whytock, '*An Educated Clergy*': *Scottish Theological Education and Training in the Kirk and Secession, 1560–1850* (Eugene, Or., 2008), chapter 2.

[25] J. Kirk (ed.), *The Second Book of Discipline: With Introduction and Commentary* (Edinburgh, 1980), pp. 187–8.

[26] C. Innes (ed.), *Fasti Aberdonenses: Selections from the Records of the University and King's College of Aberdeen* (Aberdeen, 1854), pp. xxv–xxviii; P. J. Anderson (ed.), *Officers and Graduates of University and King's College Aberdeen, MVD-MDCCCLX* (Aberdeen, 1893), p. 25.

subscribe to the Scots Confession, while contemporary opponents lambasted the recusants.[27] The deprivation records highlighted a rhetoric that linked religious conformity to political loyalty, a recurring theme in subsequent removals. Protestant authorities argued that Anderson and his staff were dangerous, 'unmeet to have the cure of instruction of the youth, for the perril of inconveniences both to body and soul', and later commentators labelled the instructors as corrupters of youths who 'disseminated disaffection to the government'.[28] The sentence of deprivation barred the Catholics from 'all instruction of youth within this realme' and underlined the determination that subsequent professors be 'qualified persons, of sound doctrine and sufficient literature'.[29]

The linkage between nonconformity and disloyalty and the dangers they posed to students were at the heart of many expulsions. The removal of university staff, however, did not always stem from direct transgressions within the academy. For example, Andrew Melville, then principal of St Mary's, was imprisoned in 1607 not necessarily for his work at the college – though his reforms won him few supporters at Glasgow, King's College, and St Andrews – but instead for having defended the 1605 general assembly at Aberdeen, which had been held without royal consent, and for having disparaged the English Church as papist.[30] Similarly, Charles Ferme, a zealous Presbyterian who in 1600 had been appointed principal of the abortive college at Fraserburgh, was also imprisoned for having attended the 1605 assembly.[31] But, in Melville's case at least, the removal marked the culmination of an effort that began in 1597 to marginalise Presbyterian academics, and Melville especially, in Scotland's oldest university. Melville's ouster, while not directly caused by academic transgressions, nevertheless provided royal authorities with the opportunity to plant an amenable principal, Robert Howie, who was more willing to accept episcopacy's ascendancy in the Kirk.[32]

There existed a tension between conformity and ability, illustrated most clearly in the era prior to 1638 by the case of Robert Boyd of Trochrig. Boyd was the son of the archbishop of Glasgow and was educated at Edinburgh before teaching at the Huguenot academies; he held the chair of divinity at Saumur before James VI called him to the Glasgow principalship in 1614.[33] Such were his abilities that in August 1618 John Young, the Scottish dean of

---

[27] David Calderwood, *The History of the Kirk of Scotland*, ed. D. Laing and T. Thomson (8 vols, Edinburgh, 1842–8), vol. 2, p. 48; John Knox, *History of the Reformation in Scotland*, ed. W. Croft Dickinson (2 vols, London, 1949), vol. 1, p. 352.

[28] *BUK*, vol. 1, pp. 142–3; *RPCS, First Series*, vol. 1, p. 675; Robert Wodrow, *Collections upon the Lives of the Reformers and Most Eminent Ministers of the Church of Scotland*, ed. W. J. Duncan (2 vols, Glasgow, 1834–45), vol. 1, p. 25.

[29] *BUK*, vol. 1, p. 143.

[30] Reid, *Humanism and Calvinism*, pp. 234–5.

[31] *BUK*, vol. 3, p. 958; *RPCS, First Series*, vol. 7, pp. 109, 260–1, 372.

[32] Reid, *Humanism and Calvinism*, pp. 160–72, 236–7.

[33] H. M. B. Reid, *The Divinity Principals in the University of Glasgow 1545–1654* (Glasgow, 1917), chapter 4.

Winchester, wished that Boyd's 'precious talent may be imployed in a more fruitful ground, where more profit might be made', namely by moving from Glasgow to St Andrews.[34] But despite his academic acumen, he resigned this post in 1621 after refusing to conform to the Five Articles of Perth. Boyd's refusal to conform, however, did not immediately end his university career. In October 1622, the Edinburgh town council invited him to take the vacant principalship at the university.[35] John Spottiswoode, archbishop of St Andrews, supported this move, but urged Boyd to conform. In a letter to Boyd, Spottiswoode wrote that:

> the sight of your conformity with those worthy men that are pastors there may be a great occasion of setling the people in their doubts, and draw our Bretheren to that consent which is meet to be in our Church; and in the respect, I must be earnest with you not to shew yourself difficil where you may be the occasion of so great a good, both to the Church in general, and to that City in particular. Neither will I at this time labour to move you by any persuasions that I can give, seeing your own mind does tell you what an ill it is to impropriate those gifts wherewith God hath blessed you to yourself, being conferred for the use of others.[36]

Indeed, it is intriguing that the archbishop of St Andrews would entertain employing the services of an academic who had disavowed the Perth Articles. It is telling that Spottiswoode wrote that the 'sight' of Boyd's conformity would benefit his cause. This suggests that the archbishop may have been urging Boyd to adhere to a superficial type of outward conformity in order securely to install his man (on the issue of partial conformity, see chapter 12). Nevertheless, Spottiswoode emphasised that Boyd's hypothetical conformity and his academic abilities were crucially beneficial to both Kirk and burgh, thus underlining the influence he exercised as a principal. His focus on Boyd's abilities is especially revealing, for Edinburgh's previous principal, the layman Patrick Sands, demitted his place because he had 'given small satisfaction in the government of the Colledge', exemplified by his inability to preach at Greyfriars.[37] The king, however, would have none of it. In a rebuke to Edinburgh's magistrates, James wrote that, 'we thinke [Boyd's] byding there will doe much evill; and therefore, as ye will answeir to us in your obedience, we command you to putt him not onlie from his office, but out of your toun, at the sight heirof,

---

[34] B. Botfield (ed.), *Original Letters Relating to the Ecclesiastical Affairs of Scotland, 1603–1625* (2 vols, Edinburgh, 1851), vol. 2, pp. 578–9.

[35] M. Wood et al. (eds), *Extracts from the Records of the Burgh of Edinburgh* (9 vols, Edinburgh, 1927–67), vol. 2, p. 238.

[36] Botfield, *Original Letters*, vol. 2, pp. 697–8.

[37] T. Craufurd, *History of the University of Edinburgh, from 1580 to 1646* (Edinburgh, 1808), p. 94; A. Grant, *The Story of the University of Edinburgh during Its First Three Hundred Years* (2 vols, London, 1884), vol. 2, p. 243.

unlesse he conforme totallie'.[38] Both the king and archbishop recognised the influence a principal wielded. Spottiswoode's vision of a conforming, capable academic that reaped benefits for wider society clashed with James' vision of a nonconforming university head who, irrespective of his abilities, would only cause evil because of his deviance. Boyd did not conform and was forced to demit in January 1623.[39] He was thus marginalised from Scottish academe for a second time in three years.

The covenanting revolution that began in 1638 likewise tied Scottish academics' political and religious conformity to the health of the nation. Under the covenanters, Scotland's professors were obliged to subscribe to the National Covenant.[40] Beginning in 1638, the general assembly passed a series of acts that redefined academic orthodoxy and sufficiency and empowered visitation committees to examine instructors for the 'the soundnesse of their judgment in matters of Religion, their abilitie for discharge of their calling, and the honesty of their conversation', and to remove any who were found insufficient.[41] Thus, most expulsions resulted from refusals to subscribe to the Covenant. This was largely the case in respect to the Aberdeen Doctors, though religious and theological transgressions were also highlighted.[42] James Sibbald, King's dean of divinity and an Aberdeen Doctor, was cited for harbouring both Arminian and irenic sympathies.[43] William Blackhall, a Marischal regent, was deposed in 1642 for refusing the Covenant, but was also discovered to be a Catholic.[44] Yet, like the earlier case of Boyd of Trochrig, conformity ultimately mattered more than ability. John Forbes of Corse's expulsion was, at its core, a political manoeuvre pushed by a ruling regime that had reached the limits of its willingness to accommodate nonconformity. Forbes noted that general assembly commissioners could find no fault in his theology or pedagogy – no errors rooted in popery or

---

[38] Calderwood, *History*, vol. 7, pp. 569–70.
[39] Wood, *Edinburgh*, vol. 2, p. 240.
[40] A. Peterkin (ed.), *Records of the Kirk of Scotland, Containing the Acts and Proceedings of the General Assemblies from the Year 1638 Downwards* (Edinburgh, 1843), p. 40. See also L. A. M. Stewart, *Rethinking the Scottish Revolution: Covenanted Scotland, 1637–1651* (Oxford, 2016), p. 145.
[41] SUL, Records of St Leonard's College, UYSL 156, p. 288; Peterkin, *Records of the Kirk*, pp. 34, 154, 208; Robert Baillie, *The Letters and Journals of Robert Baillie*, ed. D. Laing (3 vols, Edinburgh, 1841), vol. 1, pp. 491–2.
[42] On covenanting expulsions, see S. Cipriano, 'Seminaries of Identity: The Universities of Scotland and Ireland in the Age of British Revolution' (Unpublished PhD thesis, Fordham University, 2018), pp. 130–42.
[43] AUL, King's College Minutes, MSK 36, p. 53; NLS, Wodrow Quartos XXVI, fols 85r–88v.
[44] P. J. Anderson and J. F. K. Johnstone (eds), *Fasti Academiae Mariscallanae Aberdonensis: Selections from the Records of Marischal College and University, MDXCIII-MDCCCLX* (3 vols, Aberdeen, 1889), vol. 2, p. 34; John Spalding, *Memorialls of the Trubles in Scotland and in England, A.D.1624–A.D.1645*, ed. J. Stuart (2 vols, Aberdeen, 1850), vol. 2, pp. 102–3; James Gordon, *History of Scots Affairs, from 1637 to 1641*, ed. J. Robertson and G. Grub (Aberdeen, 1841), pp. 129–30.

Arminianism – 'notwithstanding my scruples concerning the Covenant'.[45] The refusal of King's divinity students to subscribe the Covenant at the 1640 assembly underscored Forbes' influence and the high-stakes nature of his ejection, for building conformity to a revolutionary regime required fidelity in the universities.[46]

Yet the specific nature of conformity to the Covenant, as it was defined in the early 1640s, was fleeting, for the prolonged nature of the Civil Wars sparked regime change that in turn heralded new waves of expulsions. The Engagement crisis of 1647 saw a hardline covenanting faction seize control of the Scottish Church and state and swiftly bar 'engagers' from the universities. The anti-engagers in power, including ministers within the powerful commission of the Kirk, drew upon a rhetoric that labelled as 'malignant' any minister, magistrate, and professor who supported the Engagement, thereby betraying the Covenant.[47] The anti-engagers – who viewed themselves as the true upholders of the Covenant – required all staff to oppose the Engagement and expelled any found 'unqualiefied or corrupt'.[48] This saw the expulsion of staff who had several years earlier replaced academics who refused the Covenant.[49] William Guild, whom the covenanters had planted as principal of King's, was deposed for his 'malignancy'. But Guild's removal was inconsequential, as the somewhat aimless nature of the anti-engager purges was exemplified by the fact that commissioners were unable to find a suitable replacement.[50] Nevertheless, anti-engager ejections linked the danger of nonconformity to the health of the university and thus the education of students. In deposing the St Leonard's regent David Nevay, an anti-engager visitation commission labelled the transgressor as 'dangerous and prejudiciall to the flourisching of the university' and unfit to 'continew ane professoure and teacher of youth'.[51] Between the Restoration of 1660 and the revolution of 1690, Scottish academics' refusals of oaths and tests, and thus their explicit refusal to submit to ascendant political and confessional paradigms, impelled most removals. Under Charles II (r.1660–85), professorial ability was realigned with the royal supremacy in the Church.[52] At the Restoration, royal authorities required university staff to be 'sober, learned, well-qualified and loyal persons' who were required to swear oaths to the monarchy and

---

45   AUL, MS 635, pp. 381–3; Baillie, *Letters and Journals*, vol. 1, p. 248.
46   NLS, Wodrow Quartos XXVI, fols 101, 102v–103r; Stevenson, *King's College*, p. 119.
47   Stewart, *Scottish Revolution*, pp. 219–20.
48   SUL, Non-Collegiate Records of the University of St Andrews, UYUY 812, p. 80; Peterkin, *Records of the Kirk*, pp. 510, 517. See also S. Cipriano, 'The Engagement, the Universities and the Fracturing of the Covenanter Movement, 1647–51', in Langley, *National Covenant in Scotland*, pp. 145–60.
49   *Ibid.*, at pp. 145–52.
50   Anderson, *Officers and Graduates*, p. 26; A. F. Mitchell and J. Christie (eds), *The Records of the Commissions of the General Assemblies of the Church of Scotland* (3 vols, Edinburgh, 1892–1909), vol. 2, p. 327.
51   SUL, UYUY 812, fols 94–5; Cipriano, 'Engagement', at p. 149.
52   F. D. Dow, *Cromwellian Scotland 1651–1660* (Edinburgh, 1979), pp. 262–4.

submit to 'the government of the church by archbishops and bishops'.[53] In 1681, the Test Act ordered 'all masters and doctors in universities, colleges and schools' to take a new oath in support of Protestant religion – in its Episcopalian hue – and the royal supremacy.[54] During the Restoration, some covenanting professors, like Edinburgh divinity professor David Dickson, were deprived of their places for refusing the oath of allegiance.[55] But others were not afforded the opportunity to refuse, and rather fell victim to post-Restoration reprisals. Samuel Rutherford, principal of St Mary's College, was deprived of his living and university post, while the committee of estates issued a declaration against his controversial treatise, *Lex, Rex*, labelling anyone who maintained a copy an enemy of the monarchy. So heated was the campaign against Rutherford that there were fears parliament would order his execution, a possibility only avoided by his death from illness in March 1661.[56]

Royal authorities also deprived Cromwellian collaborators, with Glasgow principal Patrick Gillespie among the most notable.[57] Following the conquest, the Cromwellian regime had instituted similar requirements concerning the conformity and ability of professors, empowering commissioners to expel professors who were 'found scandalous in their lives and conversations, or that shall oppose the Authority of the Common-wealth of England, exercised in Scotland'.[58] In truth, there was little purging, and the regime instead planted amenable men in vacant posts. Gillespie, initially charged with treason, feigned ignorance to save his life, pleading that 'English judges' did not appoint him to the Glasgow principalship in 1653.[59] Gillespie was nevertheless replaced in the principalship by Glasgow divinity professor Robert Baillie, ever Gillespie's opponent. Some academics, like Marischal principal John Menzies, survived the early Restoration only to later be removed for refusing the Test, which explicitly repudiated the covenants.[60] Such oaths were meant to be public rituals – refusals by both teachers and students, especially at laureations, made public to the extramural community disorder within the academy.[61]

---

[53] AUL, MSK, 266; *RPS*, 1661/1/79, 1662/5/21; C. Innes (ed.), *Munimenta Alme Universitatis Glasguensis: Records of the University of Glasgow, from Its Foundation till 1727* (4 vols, Glasgow, 1854), vol. 2, pp. 332–3.

[54] *RPS*, 1681/7/29. On the Test Act, see A. Raffe, *The Culture of Controversy: Religious Arguments in Scotland, 1660–1714* (Woodbridge, 2012), pp. 73–4.

[55] H. Scott, *Fasti Ecclesiae Scoticanae: The Succession of Ministers in the Church of Scotland from the Reformation* (7 vols, Edinburgh, 1915–28), vol. 7, p. 383.

[56] Baillie, *Letters and Journals*, vol. 3, p. 447.

[57] Scott, *Fasti*, vol. 7, pp. 357–8, 366, 395, 418–19; Baillie, *Letters and Journals*, vol. 3, pp. 417–18, 422–3, 454–5; Innes, *Munimenta*, vol. 2, pp. 329–32.

[58] C. H. Firth (ed.), *Scotland and the Commonwealth: Letters and Papers Relating to the Military Government of Scotland, from August 1651 to December 1653* (Edinburgh, 1895), pp. 44–5.

[59] GUL, Papers Relating to Patrick Gillespie, 1577–1689, MS Gen 1769/1/17.

[60] Scott, *Fasti*, vol. 7, p. 362.

[61] GUL, MS Gen 1769/1/49; A. Raffe, 'Scottish State Oaths and the Revolution of

The extent to which the monarchy had succeeded in marginalising academics who adhered to the covenants is perhaps best exemplified by widespread purging at the revolution, when William II (r.1689–1702) reaffirmed the ascendancy of Presbyterianism.[62] The revolution of 1690 revoked the strictures of the Restoration as parliament introduced new rules that required all university staff 'be of a pious, loyal and peaceable conversation, and of good and sufficient literature and abilities for their respective employments, and submitting to the government of the church now settled by law'.[63] Parliament issued instructions to visitors for each university to investigate all masters for erroneous doctrine, immorality, negligence, and conformity to the new monarchy and confession.[64] The period thus witnessed the privy council and parliament deprive nearly the entire staffs of Glasgow, Edinburgh, and St Andrews, who all refused to take oaths of allegiance to the new monarchs and the Presbyterian Kirk.[65] Indeed, a visitation commission of 1690 deprived nearly every professor at St Andrews after a lengthy visitation that evaluated their conformity, discipline, and teaching. While faults were found with divinity teaching, the commission charged St Andrews' staff with refusing the oath and provoking students to violent acts of disobedience at the burgh's public proclamations of William and Mary, thus rendering 'themselfes incapable to officiat in the said universitie'.[66]

Pedagogical and Philosophical Expulsion

While political and religious nonconformity prompted most removals, Scottish academics also faced ejection for employing divergent pedagogies or philosophies, for espousing heterodoxy, or, simply, for lacking ability. Andrew Aidie, Marischal principal from 1616 to 1619, voluntarily demitted his place after emerging second best to William Forbes in a disputation on the lawfulness of prayers for the dead. Forbes, who argued for their legality, would replace Aidie as principal and go on to assume the bishopric of Edinburgh newly created under Charles I (r.1625–49).[67] The Edinburgh regent James

---

1688–1690', in S. Adams and J. Goodare (eds), *Scotland in the Age of Two Revolutions* (Woodbridge, 2014), pp. 173–92, at pp. 182–3.

[62] See for example Emerson, *Academic Patronage*, pp. 27, 213–26.

[63] *RPS*, 1690/4/80; R. K. Hannay, 'The Visitation of St Andrews University in 1690', *SHR*, 13 (1915), 1–15, at pp. 1–2; J. D. Mackie, *The University of Glasgow 1541–1951: A Short History* (Glasgow, 1954), pp. 132–4.

[64] Alexander Monro, *Presbyterian Inquisition; As It Was Lately Practised against the Professors of the Colledge of Edinburgh. August and September. 1690.* (London, 1691), pp. 24–5.

[65] Scott, *Fasti*, vol. 7, pp. 362, 381, 383, 386, 396, 413; Innes, *Munimenta*, vol. 2, p. 501.

[66] Hannay, 'Visitation of St Andrews', at pp. 9–15.

[67] G. Grub, *An Ecclesiastical History of Scotland from the Introduction of Christianity to the Present Time* (4 vols, Edinburgh, 1861), vol. 2, p. 331.

Reid, a proponent of Copernican theories, lost his post in 1626 after running afoul of minister William Struthers, who belittled natural philosophy as the 'dish-clout to divinity'.[68] In 1653, Robert Baillie, then divinity professor at Glasgow, led a charge to oust the regent Richard Robertson, who 'had putt in his Dictats exceeding many open errors, heresies, and blasphemies', including denying the trinity. Because Robertson had the backing of Principal Gillespie, he was permitted to demit his place with a pension and without censure, much to Baillie's disgust, who lamented that harsher actions were not taken 'against the most grievous errors'.[69] And, in November 1665, the Marischal regent Patrick Strachan demitted his place after clashing with Principal William Leslie, with the college's rector condemning Strachan's 'heterodox and profane theses [...] which became no Christiane nor civill mane to maintaine, they altogether reflecting upon the fame of the Universitie, and being an open floodget to murder, drunkenness and idolatrie'.[70] In the rectorial court's summation, Strachan's transgressions would lead to rampant disorder, a trifecta of death, insobriety, and idolatry.

Authorities often amplified philosophical, pedagogical, or moral deviance when political transgressions also occurred – when there existed political momentum from ruling regimes to cement their confessional agendas. The expulsion of St Mary's divinity professor Patrick Panter is a case in point. The general assembly deposed Panter in 1639 for refusing the Covenant, but his opponents also highlighted their grievances with his theology and teaching methods. Glasgow minister James Ferguson wrote that Panter 'did maintaine justificatioune by works and sundrie other gross papisticall errours which he publictlie taught in this his theological annotations'.[71] Baillie likewise faulted Panter for promoting the 'English method of studie to our youth', teaching 'the Popish schoolmen and Fathers' and the 'Protestant neotericks'. This pedagogy, rooted in the Church Fathers and scholasticism, all subjects that had experienced a resurgence at Oxford under William Laud's chancellorship, was out of step with a covenanting regime that sought to cement Reformed pedagogy in the universities; divergent methods, especially those that buttressed a sacramental, hierarchical Church, were dangerous.[72] In 1690, amidst the widespread purges at the revolution, one Edinburgh regent, Thomas Burnet, was found to be at fault for theses that he had issued four years earlier as a regent at Marischal, when he argued that the Reformation was a 'villainous rebellion' and asserted the doctrine of royal

---

[68] J. Ridder-Patrick, 'The Marginalization of Astrology in Seventeenth-Century Scotland', *Early Science and Medicine*, 22:5/6 (2017), 464–86, at pp. 476–7.

[69] Baillie, *Letters and Journals*, vol. 3, pp. 223–4, 239–40.

[70] AUL, MSM 387/11/3/7; Anderson and Johnstone, *Fasti*, vol. 2, pp. 36–7.

[71] EUL, Laing Manuscripts, MS Laing, III.207, p. 91.

[72] N. Tyacke, 'Religious Controversy', in N. Tyacke (ed.), *The History of the University of Oxford, Vol. IV Seventeenth-Century Oxford* (Oxford, 1997), pp. 569–619, at pp. 581–2; S. J. Reid, '"Ane Uniformitie in Doctrine and Good Order": The Scottish Universities in the Age of the Covenant, 1638–1649', *History of Universities*, 29:2 (2016), 13–41.

absolutism.[73] Such ideas were welcome during James VII's reign but were out of step as the political climate changed during the revolution. Beyond his refusal to take the oath of allegiance to William and Mary, the visitation commission levelled charges against Burnet and Principal Alexander Monro that they conspired to pack Burnet's classes with scholars in order expose them to his absolutist and 'popish' ideas. Both were deprived of their places.[74]

The evidence suggests that punishment for an academic's deviations in philosophy, theology, or pedagogy was largely subordinate to political and confessional transgressions. While Andrew Melville clashed with his colleagues at St Andrews over his pedagogical reforms, for example, it was his strict adherence to Presbyterianism and regular sparring with the king, amidst the monarchy's drive to rehabilitate episcopacy and the royal supremacy, which spurred his imprisonment and exile.[75] Likewise, the Aberdeen Doctors espoused a theology that was tinged with irenicism, one that embraced Protestant concord and was thus less concerned with Church government and ceremony.[76] The Doctors' ejections between 1638 and 1640, however, ultimately resulted from their refusal to subscribe to the Covenant. Additionally, as historians have demonstrated, during the latter half of the seventeenth century, Scottish academics engaged with a range of intellectual currents that emanated from the continent, from Copernican theories to Cartesian philosophy.[77] Nevertheless, Cartesianism, which found favour during the Episcopalian ascendancy of the Restoration era, did not supplant established curricula. The structure of curricula did not necessarily change in this period, though it did fuel a 'growing eclecticism of academic philosophy teaching' in the universities, as regents might mix Aristotelian and Cartesian elements.[78] At the revolution of 1688–9, newly-dominant Presbyterians sought to root out Cartesianism because of the threat it posed to Reformed orthodoxy. But while parliamentary and Church authorities were successful in expunging academics who refused allegiance to William and Mary, preventing regents from engaging with Cartesian tenets proved more difficult, as academics continued to incorporate these

[73] Anderson and Johnstone, *Fasti*, vol. 2, p. 39.

[74] Monro, *Presbyterian Inquisition*, pp. 30–1, 52–8.

[75] Reid, *Humanism and Calvinism*, chapter 6.

[76] S. Cipriano, 'The Scottish Universities and Opposition to the National Covenant, 1638', *SHR*, 97:1 (2018), 12–37; A. C. Denlinger, '"Men of Gallio's Naughty Faith?": The Aberdeen Doctors on Reformed and Lutheran Concord', *Church History and Religious Culture*, 92:1 (2012), 57–83, at pp. 63–79.

[77] See for example G. Gellera, 'The Reception of Descartes in the Seventeenth-Century Scottish Universities: Metaphysics and Natural Philosophy (1650–1680)', *Journal of Scottish Philosophy*, 13:3 (2015), 179–201; G. Gallera, 'The Scottish Faculties of Arts and Cartesianism (1650–1700)', *History of Universities*, 29:2 (2016), 166–87; D. McOmish, 'The Scientific Revolution in Scotland Revisited: New Sciences in Edinburgh', *History of Universities*, 31:2 (2018), 153–72.

[78] A. Raffe, 'Intellectual Change before the Enlightenment: Scotland, the Netherlands and the Reception of Cartesian Thought, 1650–1700', *SHR*, 94:1 (2015), 24–47, at p. 27.

ideas post-1690.[79] Secular and religious authorities often drew from a recurring list of concerns – including Arminianism, Socinianism, popery, fanaticism, and innovation – to amplify cases and marginalise academics when political transgressions occurred. Despite widespread purging in the sixteenth and seventeenth centuries, it was rare that academics were deposed for intellectual deviance alone.

What happened to Scotland's ejected academics after their removals? Many who were in advanced age or failing health died shortly after their removals, as was the case for John Strang, David Dickson, and Samuel Rutherford. There is some evidence of marginalised academics continuing in ministerial charges, whether in Scotland or elsewhere, sometimes in more amenable religious environs. This included Patrick Panter, who became rector of Holgate in Shropshire, and James Sibbald, who took a charge in Dublin where he was authorised to preach. Likewise, Alexander Monro ministered to Episcopalians in Edinburgh before moving to London, while Edinburgh divinity professor Laurence Charteris became minister of Dirleton in East Lothian after demitting his place for refusing the Test in 1681.[80]

Forced removal from an academic post, however, did not mean the cessation of intellectual activity. The Scottish experience was part of a wider early modern phenomenon that saw the proliferation of religious migrants, which included scholars and students who migrated to and from educational centres in various confessional spheres.[81] Marginalised Scottish academics had potential recourse to welcoming settings abroad. Scholarship has highlighted the peripatetic nature of Scottish academics and the movement of staff and students between Scotland and Europe. Interpersonal, religious, and economic links facilitated much of this movement.[82] Peter Burke argues that the experience of exile, even if temporary, endowed exiles and expatriates with new experiences that energised and catalysed intellectual

---

[79] *Ibid.*, pp. 41–5; Ridder-Patrick, 'Marginalization of Astrology', pp. 478–9; Shepherd, 'Philosophy and Science', pp. 143–56.

[80] Scott, *Fasti*, vol. 7, pp. 381, 383, 428; Gordon, *Scots Affairs*, vol. 3, pp. 228–30.

[81] See for example K. Wolf, 'Censorship and Exile in Medieval and Early Modern Universities', in J. Hartmann and H. Zapf (eds), *Censorship and Exile* (Göttingen, 2015), pp. 113–19; N. Terpstra, *Religious Refugees in the Early Modern World: An Alternative History of the Reformation* (Cambridge, 2015), pp. 165–8. On academic migration, see for example H. de Ridder-Symoens, 'Mobility', in de Ridder-Symoens, *History of the University*, pp. 416–48.

[82] See for example W. Caird Taylor, 'Scottish Students in Heidelberg, 1386–1662', *SHR*, 5 (1907), 67–75; J. K. Cameron, 'Some Scottish Students and Teachers at the University of Leiden in the Late Sixteenth and Early Seventeenth Centuries', in G. Simpson (ed.), *Scotland and the Low Countries, 1124–1994* (East Linton, 1996), pp. 122–36; E. Mijers, 'Scottish Students in the Netherlands 1680–1730', in A. Grosjean and A. Murdoch (eds), *Scottish Communities Abroad in the Early Modern Period* (Leiden, 2005), pp. 301–31; E. Mijers, *'News from the Republick of Letters': Scottish Students, Charles Mackie and the United Provinces, 1650–1750* (Leiden, 2012); M.-C. Tucker, 'Scottish Masters in Huguenot Academies', *History of Universities*, 29:2 (2016), 42–68.

activity.[83] Thus Scottish recusants removed to the continent during the sixteenth and seventeenth centuries: the King's regents Andrew Youngson and John Strachan, for instance, became Jesuits and taught at the Scots colleges of Madrid and Rome, respectively.[84] After his brief and unhappy experience as principal of Glasgow, in 1622 John Cameron returned to France at Montauban, while, most famously, Andrew Melville, banned from returning to Scotland, took up a post as professor of biblical theology at Sedan in 1611, where he would teach a young John Forbes of Corse.[85] In 1643, Forbes, deprived of his position at King's, absconded to Amsterdam where he completed and published his great treatise, *Instructiones historico theologicae de doctrina Christiana*, while also preaching to Scottish and English congregations in the Netherlands.[86] In the rarest of cases, some academics continued their intellectual endeavours at a Scottish university. Ejected in 1666 from Glasgow for refusing the oath of allegiance to Charles II, former regent George Sinclair soon found himself giving public 'professions' on scientific topics at Edinburgh. Records suggest that by 1672 he was once again teaching students, without having sworn the oath of allegiance. It is unclear how Sinclair might have managed this, but it does point to the existence of varying degrees of conformity to the Restoration's authorised confessional norms among academics and clerics.[87] Nevertheless, when compared to the experiences of academics like Robert Boyd of Trochrig and John Forbes of Corse earlier in the century, Sinclair's continued teaching of 'usefull sciences' might be one of the rare cases in which ability eclipsed conformity.[88]

Conclusion

The post-ejection experience of Scottish academics remains a research subject of much potential. When we assess forced removals of academic staff between the Reformation and revolution, key themes emerge, especially the primacy of political and confessional conformity over intellectual ability

[83] Peter Burke, *Exiles and Expatriates in the History of Knowledge, 1500–2000* (Waltham, 2017), pp. 16–17.
[84] See for example Anderson, *Officers and Graduates*, pp. 56–7; Anderson and Johnstone, *Fasti*, vol. 2, pp. 34–5; Thomas McCrie, *Life of Andrew Melville, Containing Illustrations of the Ecclesiastical and Literary History of Scotland* (Edinburgh, 1856), p. 12. See also Reid, *Humanism and Calvinism*, p. 45; J. K. Cameron, 'St Mary's College 1547–1574 – The Second Foundation: The Principalship of John Douglas', in D. W. D. Shaw (ed.), *In Divers Manners: A St Mary's Miscellany* (St Andrews, 1990), pp. 43–57; B. M. Halloran, 'John Strachan, SJ, Rector of the Scots College, Rome, 1670–1671', *Innes Review*, 48:1 (1997), pp. 85–7.
[85] McCrie, *Life of Andrew Melville*, pp. 315–23; Tucker, 'Scottish Masters', at pp. 58–62.
[86] AUL, MS 635, pp. 483–92; Mullan, 'Forbes, John'.
[87] See especially Raffe, *Culture of Controversy*, chapter 7.
[88] A. D. D. Craik and D. Spittle, 'The Hydrostatical Works of George Sinclair (c.1630–1696): An Addendum', *Notes and Records: The Royal Society Journal of the History of Science*, 73:1 (2019), 125–30.

and the employment, and endurance, of potentially novel philosophical and pedagogical ideas, so long as professors did not run afoul of authorities. An examination of academics post-ejection may also uncover new insights about the influence and impact of Scottish intellectual cultures. How did the experience of ejection, and in some cases exile, inform scholars' intellectual outlooks? What was the impact of scholars who took teaching positions at universities beyond Scotland? What type of impact did their ideas continue to have, if at all, in their native Scotland? As we continue to engage with these questions, what is already evident from the Scottish experience is that professors, as moulders of future governing elites, were susceptible to the forces of marginalisation emanating from secular and religious power structures that regularly defined, and redefined, notions of conformity and deviance amidst the upheavals of the sixteenth and seventeenth centuries.

Appendix: Scotland's Ejected Academics, c.1559–1697

Name	Position	University	Tenure	Departure	Reason
John Black	Master	St Mary's	- c.1559	Removed/Fled	Reformation
Richard Marshall	Master	St Mary's	- c.1559	Removed/Fled	Reformation
William Cranston	Provost	St Salvator's	- c.1559	Removed	Reformation
Simon Simson	Regent	St Salvator's	- c.1559	Demitted(?)	Reformation
Edmund Hay	Regent	St Salvator's	- c.1560	Fled	Reformation
Robert Cunningham	Regent	Glasgow	1555–c.1560	Fled	Reformation
John Houston	Principal/Regent	Glasgow	c.1556–1560	Fled	Reformation
Andrew Anderson	Regent	King's	1543–1569	Deposed	Reformation
Alexander Anderson	Principal	King's	1557–1569	Deposed	Reformation
Thomas Owsten	Regent	King's	1559–1569	Deposed	Reformation
Duncan Norie	Regent	King's	1559–1569	Deposed	Reformation
Alexander Galloway	Sub-Principal	King's	1568–1569	Deposed	Reformation
Archibald Hamilton	Regent	St Mary's	c.1552–1576	Absconded	Recusancy
Robert Hamilton	Principal	St Mary's	1574–1579	Deprived	Financial Mismanagement
William Wellwood	Law	St Salvator's	1587–1597	Deprived	Religion; Dereliction of duties
Charles Ferme	Principal	Fraserburgh	c.1600–1605	Imprisoned	Presbyterianism; clashes with James VI
Andrew Melville	Principal	St Mary's	1580–1607	Exiled	Presbyterianism; clashes with James VI
David Monipenny	Second Master	St Salvator's	1585–1617	Deprived	Unknown
Andrew Aidie	Principal	Marischal	1616–1619	Demitted	Insufficiency
Patrick Sands	Principal	Edinburgh	1620–1622	Demitted	Insufficiency
Robert Boyd of Trochrig	Principal	Edinburgh	1622–1623	Removed	Perth Articles
John Cameron	Principal	Glasgow	1622–c.1625	Removed	Politics/Religion
James Reid	Regent	Edinburgh	1607–c.1626	Deprived	Teaching; clashes with local ministers
William Wishart	Regent	St Mary's	???–1638	Deposed	National Covenant
Robert Ranken	Regent	Edinburgh	1625–1638	Deposed	National Covenant
John Broun	Regent	Edinburgh	1628–1638	Deposed	National Covenant

Name	Position	University	Tenure	Departure	Reason
Robert Baron	Divinity	Marischal	1625–1639	Died	National Covenant
Patrick Panter	Divinity	St Mary's	1627–1639	Deposed	National Covenant
Alexander Scroggie	Regent	King's	1638–c.1639	Deposed	National Covenant
William Leslie	Principal	King's	1632–1640	Deposed	National Covenant
James Sibbald	Dean	King's	c.1639–1640	Deposed	National Covenant
John Forbes of Corse	Divinity	King's	1635–1641	Deprived	National Covenant
William Blackhall	Regent	Marischal	c.1635–1642	Deposed	National Covenant; Recusancy
Andrew Youngson	Regent	King's	1644–c.1646	Removed(?)	Recusancy
David Nevay	Regent	St Leonard's	1640–1649	Deposed	Engagement
Thomas Gleg	Third Master	St Salvator's	c.1645–1649	Demitted	Engagement
John Barron	Provost	St Salvator's	1646–1649	Demitted	Engagement
John Strang	Principal	Glasgow	1626–1650	Demitted	Engagement
William Guild	Principal	King's	1640–1649/51	Deposed	Engagement; Cromwellian Conquest
William Colville	Principal	Edinburgh	1652–1652	Blocked	Cromwellian Conquest
Richard Robertson	Regent	Glasgow	1649–1653	Demitted	Heresy
John Strachan	Regent	King's	1651–c.1655	Removed	Recusancy
Patrick Gillespie	Principal	Glasgow	1653–1660	Deprived	Restoration
Alexander Jameson	Dean	Glasgow	1659–1660	Deprived	Restoration
Samuel Rutherford	Principal	St Mary's	1647–c.1661	Deprived	Restoration
William Moir	Principal	Marischal	1649–1661	Resigned	Restoration
John Row	Principal	King's	1652–1661	Resigned	Restoration
David Dickson	Divinity	Edinburgh	1650–1662	Deprived	Restoration
Patrick Strachan	Regent	Marischal	c.1663–1665	Demitted	Heresy; Teaching
George Sinclair	Regent	Glasgow	1654–1666	Resigned	Restoration
Robert Hamilton	Regent	St Salvator's	1666–1668	Deposed	Assault
Alexander Dickson	Hebrew	Edinburgh	1656–1679	Deprived	Refused Oath of Allegiance
Laurence Charteris	Divinity	Edinburgh	1675–1681	Demitted	Test Act

Name	Position	University	Tenure	Departure	Reason
John Menzies	Divinity	Marischal	1649–1678/84	Resigned	Test Act
James Wemyss	Principal	St Leonard's	1662–1689	Deprived	Revolution
James Martin	Regent	St Salvator's	1677–1689	Deprived	Revolution
John Menzies	Regent	St Salvator's	c.1680–1690	Deprived	Revolution
John Strachan	Divinity	Edinburgh	1683–1690	Deprived	Revolution
James Fall	Principal	Glasgow	1683–1690	Deprived	Revolution
William Comrie	Regent	St Leonard's	1684–1690	Deprived	Revolution
Alexander Monro	Principal	Edinburgh	1685–c.1690	Deprived	Revolution
Thomas Burnet	Regent	Edinburgh	1686–1690	Deprived	Revolution; anti-Presbyterian
Andrew Skene	Regent/Provost	St Salvator's	1686–1690	Deprived	Revolution
George Waddell	Regent	St Leonard's	c.1686–1690	Deprived	Revolution
James Wemyss	Divinity	Glasgow	1687–c.1690	Deprived	Revolution
Alexander Ross	Regent	St Leonard's	1688–1690	Deprived	Revolution
James Fenton	Mathematics	St Leonard's	1688–1690	Deprived	Revolution
Patrick Gordon	Divinity	St Mary's	1688–1690	Deprived	Revolution
David MacGill	Regent	St Salvator's	1688–1690	Deprived	Revolution
James Gregory	Regent	St Salvator's	1688–1690	Deprived	Revolution
John Drummond	Regent	Edinburgh	1689–1690	Deprived	Revolution
Patrick Sibbald	Divinity	Marischal	1684–c.1691	Deprived	Revolution
Alexander Douglas	Hebrew	Edinburgh	1681–1692	Deprived	Revolution
Thomas Gordon	Regent	Glasgow	1682–c.1689	Demitted	Revolution
David Gregorie	Mathematics	Edinburgh	1683–1690	Deprived	Revolution
Alexander Cunningham	Regent	Edinburgh	1689–1692	Demitted	Revolution
James Garden	Divinity	King's	1680–1697	Deprived	Revolution

12

Partial Conformity in Restoration Scotland, 1662–1669

Jamie McDougall

According to much of the historiography of Restoration Scotland, those who opposed Charles II's political and religious settlement displayed their dissent by separating from the established Church, organising and attending conventicles, rioting, petitioning, and rising against the government in 1666 and 1679.[1] Nonconformists acted in this way because of the raft of legislation in 1661 and 1662 which reintroduced episcopacy, overturned the covenants, and placed the monarch as supreme head of Church and state. The implication of this line of argument is that the majority of clergy and countless lay people who conformed to the Restoration settlement accepted the regime entirely and abandoned their former covenanted oaths. This chapter explores an under-examined middle grouping in Restoration Scotland: partial conformists. These were people who conformed but refused to take part in certain aspects of worship or displayed acts of mild dissent. In doing so, it challenges the dichotomous way in which the Restoration period has often been presented and sheds new light on marginality and deviance in early modern Scotland.

The existence of partial conformity has long been acknowledged by historians of Restoration England, but Alasdair Raffe was the first historian of Scotland to broach the topic. He argues that there was a fluid spectrum of conformity and that partial conformity was essentially a moderate wing of nonconformity, or a stepping stone to full nonconformity.[2] More recently,

[1] I. Cowan, *The Scottish Covenanters, 1660–1688* (London, 1976); V. G. Kiernan, 'A Banner with a Strange Device: The Later Covenanters', in T. Brotherstone (ed.), *Covenant, Charter, and Party: Traditions of Revolt and Protest in Modern Scottish History* (Aberdeen, 1989), pp. 25–49; E. H. Hyman, 'A Church Militant: Scotland, 1661–1690', *The Sixteenth Century Journal*, 26:1 (1995), 49–74; C. Erskine, 'The Political Thought of the Restoration Covenanters', in S. Adams and J. Goodare (eds), *Scotland in the Age of Two Revolutions* (Woodbridge, 2014), pp. 155–72.

[2] A. Raffe, *The Culture of Controversy: Religious Arguments in Scotland, 1660–1714* (Woodbridge, 2012), pp. 180–8; M. Knights, 'Occasional Conformity and the Representation of Dissent: Hypocrisy, Sincerity, Moderation and Zeal?', in S. Taylor and D. Wykes (eds), *Parliament and Dissent* (Edinburgh, 2005), pp. 41–57; C. Hill, 'Occasional Conformity', in R. B. Knox (ed.), *Restoration Conformity and Dissent: Essays in Honour of Geoffrey Nuttall* (London, 1977), pp. 199–220; J. Flaningham, 'The Occasional Conformity Controversy: Ideology and Party Politics, 1697–1711', *Journal of British Studies*, 17:1 (1977), 38–62.

Raffe has called for historians to 'pay more attention to the porous boundary between nonconformity and conformity after the Restoration'.[3] At the same time, other scholars have noted that the Restoration Church was, in some way, surprisingly broad, giving significant latitude for this kind of activity.[4] Using the wealth of extant kirk session and presbytery records, this chapter builds on Raffe's observations to explore key features of partial conformity, and to reflect on why people expressed this form of deviance.

Partial conformity is defined here as a refusal to fully conform to the Restoration settlement without separating entirely from the established Church. Among the clergy, this involved refusal to take oaths that abrogated the covenants and not making outward signs of loyalty towards the Restoration regime. Lay men and women partially conformed to the regime by regularly attending church but refusing to observe aspects of worship that went against their conscience and avoiding communion and baptism by a fully conformist minister. The timescale under discussion is from the Restoration settlement of 1662 to the introduction of the first indulgence of 1669. Although partial conformity continued after the indulgences, it operated in the face of repressive government measures which require more space to be explored than is available in this chapter.[5]

The Restoration Settlement

Contemporaries agreed that Charles II's return in 1660 was met in Scotland with widespread enthusiasm.[6] It was not until the Erastian, Episcopalian Church settlement of 1661–2 that dissent became noticeable; altogether only around half of the ministry fully conformed with new requirements of presentation by a lay patron and collation by a bishop.[7] Those who refused to conform in 1662 did so because they could not countenance adhering to a regime that explicitly denounced the covenants and altered the government

---

[3]   A. Raffe, 'Who Were the "Later Covenanters"?', in C. Langley (ed.), *The National Covenant in Scotland 1638–1689* (Woodbridge, 2020), pp. 197–214.

[4]   C. Jackson, *Restoration Scotland, 1660–1690: Royalist Politics, Religion and Ideas* (Woodbridge, 2003); C. Kidd, 'Religious Realignment between the Restoration and the Union', in J. Robertson (ed.), *A Union for Empire: Political Thought and the British Union of 1707* (Cambridge, 1995), pp. 145–68; A. Carter, 'The Episcopal Church of Scotland, 1660–1685' (Unpublished PhD thesis, University of St. Andrews, 2019).

[5]   For post-1669 partial conformity, see J. McDougall, 'Covenants and Covenanters in Scotland 1638–1672' (Unpublished PhD thesis, University of Glasgow, 2018), chapter 5.

[6]   For example, see A. Chrichton (ed.), *Memoirs of the Rev. John Blackadder*, 2nd edn (Edinburgh, 1826), 51; T. M'Crie (ed.), *The Life of Mr Robert Blair, Minister of St Andrews* (Edinburgh, 1848), p. 354; James Kirkton, *The Secret and True History of the Church of Scotland from the Restoration to the year 1678* (Edinburgh, 1817), p. 58.

[7]   195 ministers, roughly 20 per cent, had entered their charge before 1649 and therefore did not need to be presented and collated. Based on information gathered from H. Scott, *Fasti Ecclesiae Scoticanae: The Succession of Ministers in the Church of Scotland from the Reformation* (7 vols, Edinburgh, 1915–28).

of the Church to include bishops.[8] The full nonconformity displayed by such people involved separating from the established Church entirely due to a total ideological opposition to the Restoration settlement.

Conformist positions, on the other hand, were sufficiently broad to allow for significant shades of opinion. The bedrock for conformity to the Restoration settlement was the belief that covenanting and episcopacy were not incompatible. This argument stems from the contentious addition of the Glasgow Declaration to the National Covenant in December 1638. The Glasgow Declaration added an explicitly anti-episcopal statement to the National Covenant, several months after the subscription campaign in the spring of 1638.[9] Andrew Honyman, minister of Ferryport-on-Craig and later of St Andrews and then bishop of Orkney from 1664, was a signatory of the covenants and a leading polemicist for the conformists throughout the Restoration period. In 1662, he argued that the Glasgow Declaration merely represented the opinion of that assembly and was therefore not a covenanted obligation: 'So then, whatever was done at Glasgow after the Covenant was taken by the body of the Land, could not oblige all takers of it to own their declaration of the sense of the Covenant'.[10] This argument was echoed by Robert Leighton, professor of divinity at Edinburgh's Toun College, signatory of the covenants, bishop of Dunblane from 1661, and archbishop of Glasgow from 1671 to 1674.[11] In his *A Modest Defence of Moderate Episcopacy*, he focused on the Solemn League and Covenant (1643), arguing that the word 'prelacy' in the Covenant referred to English prelacy and not moderate Scottish episcopacy.[12] The arguments presented by these two conformists show that there was ideological space to adhere to the Restoration regime while maintaining some level of commitment to the covenants.

The scope for ideological fluidity on the ground was made more realistic by the lack of rigour and uniformity deployed by those responsible for implementing the ecclesiastical settlement. Synods, headed by their respective bishops, met in autumn 1662 before authorising presbyteries and sessions to meet.[13] Some small but significant changes to worship were introduced thereafter. All synods produced instructions for the governance

---

[8] See, for example, the position of James Guthrie, as laid out in Robert Wodrow, *The History of the Sufferings of the Church of Scotland, from the Restoration to the Revolution* (4 vols, Edinburgh, 1721–2), vol. 1, appendix, p. 46.

[9] For further analysis, see J. McDougall 'Episcopacy and the National Covenant', *Records of the Scottish Church History Society*, 47:1 (2018), 3–30.

[10] Andrew Honyman, *The Seasonable Case of Submission to the Church-government as now re-established by law, briefly stated and determined* (Edinburgh, 1662), p. 36.

[11] For a robust analysis of Robert Leighton, see A. J. Hamilton, 'In Mitiorem Partem: Robert Leighton's Journey towards Episcopacy' (Unpublished PhD thesis, University of Glasgow, 2013).

[12] Robert Leighton, 'A Modest Defence of Moderate Episcopacy, As Established in Scotland at the Restoration of King Charles II', in G. Jerment (ed.), *The Works of Robert Leighton* (5 vols, London, 1808), vol. 5, p. 79.

[13] *RPCS, Third Series*, vol. 1, pp. 130–1.

of the Kirk; these were virtually identical, with some minor but revealing variations. The 1645 *Westminster Directory for Public Worship* was banned, as were weekday lectures in church. Readers were reintroduced; ministers were ordered to enforce standing or kneeling during prayer; affirmations of faith were to be made by parents at baptism; the creed was to be recited at baptism; the doxology was ordered to be sung, standing rather than seated; and sermons were to be concluded with the lord's prayer.[14] There was now no official liturgy for the Kirk, and most ministers either continued to use the *Directory* illegally, or used Knox's *Book of Common Order* or the English *Book of Common Prayer*.[15] Much like the state settlement, the ecclesiastical settlement was an attempt at undoing the covenanting period by returning the Church to its early seventeenth century form, with the exception of the use of the English *Book of Common Prayer*, which was an innovation. Although not formally adopted by Episcopalians in Scotland until after the reinstatement of Presbyterianism in 1690, the use of the English prayer book at this stage can be understood as the beginning of what Raffe has identified as the development of Episcopalian confessional culture in Scotland.[16]

In theory, by 1662 the shape of the civil and ecclesiastical settlement was quite clear: the king was supreme head of Church and state, bishops were to manage the church courts, forms of worship used under the covenanters were no longer allowed, and those who refused to acknowledge the authority of the bishops and supremacy of the king were to be deprived. Although this effort was co-ordinated across the nation, there was significant variation on the ground. Ministers who had entered their charges before 1649 were often required to give some form of statement of loyalty to the king and established form of Church government. It was not until 1681 that the ministry was required to denounce the covenants under the Test Act.[17] However, presbyteries were often already extracting oaths from their ministers, chaplains, schoolmasters, and readers from as early as 1662. In the synod of Aberdeen, all ministers were ordered to swear an oath in which they promised 'due canonicall obedience' to the bishop and 'to them to whome the government and charge is committed over me, following with a glad mynd and will ther godlie admonitiones'.[18] In Linlithgow presbytery, the bishop gave the moderator permission to 'administer the othe of allegance to schoolmasters and Readers etc'.[19] The privy council pursued several ministers

---

[14] W. R. Foster, *Bishop and Presbytery: The Church of Scotland, 1661–1688* (London, 1958), pp. 125–31; J. Stuart (ed.), *Selections from the Records of the Kirk Session, Presbytery, and Synod of Aberdeen* (Aberdeen, 1846), p. 267; *Selections from the Minutes of the Synod of Fife, MDCXI-MDCLXXXVII* (Edinburgh, 1838), p. 184; NRS, CH2/271/2, Synod of Moray, p. 374; NRS, CH2/724/2, Synod of Dunblane, p. 2; NRS, CH2/165/1, Synod of Galloway, p. 4.

[15] Foster, *Bishop and Presbytery*, pp. 128–33.

[16] Raffe, *Culture of Controversy*, pp. 51–61.

[17] *Ibid.*, p. 69.

[18] Stuart, *Synod of Aberdeen*, p. 265.

[19] NRS, CH2/242/5, Linlithgow Presbytery, p. 315.

throughout 1662 and 1663 for refusal to subscribe the oath of allegiance, but the records of Linlithgow and Dunbar presbyteries are the only ones that survive which mention the oath. However, there are signed copies of the oath of allegiance in both Linlithgow and Kirkwall presbytery records, and neither contain the final part of the oath of allegiance which asked the subscribers to acknowledge the king's prerogative and denounce the covenants.[20] Practices clearly varied, as seen by the further deviation of Dunfermline presbytery, which ordered their chaplains, readers, and schoolmasters to declare their 'heartie satisfaction & contentment with the government of the kirk and ther loyaltie to the kings majestie'.[21] Moreover, the new form of prayer for Charles II seems only to have been observed in the bounds of three synods: Aberdeen, Perth and Stirling, and Lothian and Tweeddale.

A range of different attitudes to the king and worship was also shown by the bishops themselves in 1662. The only bishop who imposed both the oath of allegiance and the new prayer for Charles II was George Wishart. Unsurprisingly, Archbishop James Sharp (St Andrews) recommended the prayer in the bounds of his diocese, and the two well-known Episcopalians, Thomas Sydserf (Orkney) and David Mitchell (Aberdeen), took strict approaches. Records survive for five out of the remaining ten dioceses, and the evidence shows that their bishops took a more moderate approach by not enforcing oaths or the prayer for Charles. Indeed, David Strachan (Brechin), former resolutioner and close friend of John Middleton, did not instigate any changes, and the functioning of the Church his diocese cannot have changed much after the Restoration.[22] The degree to which local governance reflected national imperatives varied between regions. However, whether or not a bishop pressed a strict Episcopalian and royalist settlement in his diocese does not seem to have had an impact on the prevalence of partial conformity. Indeed, clerical and lay partial conformity is evidenced in all the areas for which records survive. What the levels of compromise uncovered here demonstrate is that middle ground opinion and practice existed at the highest clerical level. But, as the rest of this chapter will show, similar thinking was prevalent at the grassroots level as well.

Partial Conformity among Local Clergy and Elders

Disobeying acts made by parliament, privy council, and synods was one way in which ministers and kirk session elders could express a degree of dissent and deviate from the directives of the Restoration regime. In 1661, parliament instructed that 29 May, the date of Charles II's birth

[20] *Ibid.*, p. 535.
[21] NRS, CH2/105/1/1, Dunfermline Presbytery, p. 379.
[22] NRS CH2/1082/3, Kirkwall Presbytery, p. 5; NRS CH2/299/43/9, Perth Presbytery, pp. 5–7, 9; NRS CH2/40/1, Brechin Presbytery; Stuart, *Synod of Aberdeen*, p. 265.

and restoration, should be celebrated as a day of national thanksgiving.[23] Sermons were to be held on that day, rather than on the nearest sabbath. When kirk sessions formally reconvened in 1663, a point at which the full implications of the changes to the Kirk were clear, thirty-one of them (46 per cent of those for which records survive) did not observe the thanksgiving. Although Charles' restoration was met with widespread enthusiasm, some, such as John Brown of Wamphray, viewed the imposition of a holy day as an encroachment on the power of ecclesiastical authority.[24] Moreover, the act itself intimated that this day was to be observed as a remembrance of God's mercy, he who delivered the nation from twenty years of 'slaverie and bondage [...] violently caried on against sacred authority'.[25] Thus, celebrating the anniversary of Charles' birth and restoration also involved celebrating both the demise of the Commonwealth and of the covenanting regime. Brown argued that anyone who observed this day 'condemn[ed] all which had been done for twenty three yeers space, in carrying on of the work of Reformation'.[26] Refusal to observe the 29 May thanksgiving can therefore be used as an indication of discontent with the nature of the 1662 settlement. Although Brown separated from the Kirk, there is an abundance of evidence of ministers and lay people refusing to acknowledge this day without withdrawing from parish worship the rest of the year.

Ministers and lay men and women who did not observe the thanksgiving on conscientious grounds could afford to do so as it was not rigorously enforced. This was one of the reasons why partial conformity was a viable option locally. The only instances of punishments being imposed for non-observance were when it was combined with more serious evidence of nonconformity. For example, the privy council deposed Donald Cargill, minister of Barony church, Glasgow, and Thomas Wylie, minister of Kirkcudbright, for refusing to observe the thanksgiving *and* not obtaining presentation and collation for their charges.[27] Similarly, Dunbar presbytery heard evidence from the heritors of Innerwick against their minister, John Bairdie, for 'seditious preaching and What he hath spoken against the goverments, his carriage upon the anniversarie day 1661 and his nether intimating nor keeping the samin'.[28] Unsurprisingly, Bairdie, too, was deprived.[29] There is no evidence of punishments being meted out to any ministers or members of the laity purely for refusing to observe this day of thanksgiving. The southern parish of Stow did not observe the thanksgiving between 1662 and 1665. There was no sermon held on 19 May 1663; 'No preaching by reasone of the ministers

23 RPS, 1661/1/255.
24 See, for example, Brown, *Apologeticall Relation*, pp. 88–9.
25 RPS, 1661/1/255.
26 Brown, *Apologeticall Relation*, pp. 88–9.
27 RPCS, *Third Series*, vol. 1, pp. 270–1.
28 NRS, CH2/99/2, Dunbar Presbytery, p. 80.
29 Scott, *Fasti*, vol. 3, p. 165.

siknes' on 27 May 1663; nothing recorded in the session minutes on 29 May 1663; and 'no preaching in respect of the ministers absence' at the same time the following year.[30] The minister was former protester John Cleland, who died in August 1665, and it therefore may be that he was genuinely ill.[31] However, there are no other reports of his absence at other times in the year, so this is unlikely. Cleland had entered his charge in 1640 and therefore did not need to be collated by a bishop after the settlement. The presbytery records for Earlston (which included Stow) do not exist for this period so it is not known whether Cleland was required to make an oath of loyalty to keep his charge. Regardless, John Cleland is an example of a covenanter who ministered in the Restoration Church while avoiding taking part in an aspect of the new regime which likely offended his covenanting sensibilities.

There are examples of dissent among the laity which also went unpunished. Dunfermline presbytery recorded that 'severall persons and families did not attend seramone' on 29 May. This was reported to the archbishop but never mentioned again.[32] Stirling kirk session pursued a woman for not attending the thanksgiving sermon. After she confessed that she did not attend due to the fact that 'she having ane child with hir which did not rest weell', she was reproved but issued with no punishment.[33] The evidence from Dunfermline and Stirling is symptomatic of the lenient way the Church observed the thanksgiving. This is further exemplified by the manner in which Haddington presbytery investigated observance simply by asking the ministers present if they kept the thanksgiving. Those present said they did and 'for ought they knew the brethren absent kept it in like manner'.[34] The failure of the Restoration Church to enforce observance of this thanksgiving allowed partial conformity to arise as those who did not observe the thanksgiving went unpunished.

In some cases, the clergy could avoid taking the oaths pressed upon them by the synods and presbyteries. Alexander Brodie recorded in his diary in autumn 1662 that there was much anxiety among the clergy in Moray over subscribing a declaration 'anent the disclaiming of the couenant'.[35] Although the synod of Moray records do not mention the imposition of oaths, the evidence in Brodie's diary suggest that the bishop, Murdoch MacKenzie, required his clergy to swear an oath to him in person rather than going through the Church judicatories. MacKenzie allowed Harry Forbes, minister of Wick to acknowledge the authority of the bishops 'but not ouned the government'.[36] The bishop also offered James Urquhart, minister of

[30] NRS CH2/338/2, Stow Kirk Session, p. 265, p. 267.
[31] Scott, *Fasti*, vol. 2, p. 163.
[32] NRS, CH2/105/1/1, p. 383.
[33] NRS, CH2/1026/2, Stirling Kirk Session, pp. 251–5.
[34] NRS, CH2/185/7, Haddington Presbytery, p. 3.
[35] D. Laing (ed.), *The Diary of Alexander Brodie of Brodie, 1652–1680* (Aberdeen, 1863), pp. 273–5.
[36] *Ibid.*, p. 278.

Kinloss, the chance to 'concur in common duties, and meit with him', but he 'inclind rather to quit his charg'.[37] Clearly, there was a spectrum of opinion between those who dissented entirely and those who were willing to work with the authorities as far as their consciences allowed.

Local case studies show that there was much unwillingness from clergy and schoolmasters in the bounds of Dunfermline, Dunbar, Forfar, and Linlithgow presbyteries to submit fully to the authority of the established government. Many schoolmasters had a university education, as did some readers. Both groups could use this role as a step towards ordination and service as a parish minister.[38] Teachers and readers were paid by the kirk session. Like ministers, they were expected to demonstrate their conformity to the new regime, and they were pursued with equal, if not greater, vigour. This reflects an acknowledgement that those in local positions of power – including ministers, schoolmasters, and readers – could both serve as examples and influence the degree to which ordinary people conformed. Dunbar presbytery read a declaration from the synod of Edinburgh and Lothian in January 1663 which observed that there were 'manie Readers Schoolmasters Chapplannes and pedagogues in the diocese who decline the oath of aleaggance and supremacie or any Submission to or owning of the present government of the Church', and ordered presbyteries to be more diligent.[39] As mentioned above, Dunfermline presbytery reported a high level of absence among the laity during the 29 May thanksgiving. They also had issues with a number of ministers, chaplains, schoolmasters, and 'expectants' (ministerial candidates) who refused to declare loyalty to the established Church. On 28 October 1662, three expectants, two schoolmasters, and a reader appeared before the presbytery to declare their 'heartie satisfaction and contentment with the government of the kirk and ther loyaltie to the kings majestie'.[40] As late as 1667, Dunfermline presbytery was referring schoolmasters and chaplains to the archbishop for refusal to give this declaration.[41] Similarly, in the presbytery of Forfar, the schoolmasters were asked to come before the presbytery to give a testimony of loyalty to the current form of Church government. After hearing them, the presbytery was 'satisfied with thar judgement anent the present establishment', and the testimonies and names were sent to the archbishop.[42] The testimonies in Forfar are not recorded, but it is likely that they were similar to the declaration given by the ministers in Dunfermline, since in Forfar, too, the oath of allegiance was not mentioned explicitly.

The Dunfermline declaration made no mention of either the covenants or bishops and was thus significantly more moderate than both the oath

---

[37] Ibid., p. 279.
[38] M. Todd, *The Culture of Protestantism in Early Modern Scotland* (New Haven, 2002), pp. 60–6.
[39] NRS, CH2/99/2, p. 89.
[40] NRS, CH2/105/1/1, p. 379.
[41] Ibid, p. 425.
[42] NRS, CH2/159/1, Forfar Presbytery, pp. 5–6.

of allegiance and the oath of canonical obedience, which suggests an acknowledgement by the presbytery that covenanting loyalties were still prevalent. Some ministers and others nonetheless refused to state their loyalty to the regime and remained nonconformist. However, most of the schoolmasters, chaplains, and expectants gave their statements of loyalty to Church and king. Five ministers were called before Dunfermline presbytery on 3 December 1662 for refusing to declare loyalty, a case which was twice referred to the archbishop. Remarkably, by the end of 1664 only one of the five ministers (George Belfrage, minister of Carnock) had been deposed.[43] As the cases were referred to the archbishop, it is possible that he was able to gain some form of submission from the other four. It is also possible, however, that these ministers slipped through the net and remained in their charges without declaring loyalty to the king and established Church. Moreover, neither those who declared loyalty to Church and king nor those who refused had explicitly disowned the covenants. It was entirely possible for ministers in the bounds of Dunfermline presbytery to remain in their charges while holding covenanting loyalties, making the scope for partial conformity particularly wide in this region.[44]

Some ministers conformed in 1662 but subsequently did not carry out any of the policies of the Church and were thus also partial conformists. The synod of Galloway ordered their ministers to be more diligent in punishing those who did not attend church in 1664 'under the paine of the highest censure', as they believed 'severall ministers have been somewhat too sparing hitherto to admonish such obstinate delinquents'.[45] It reiterated that the practices instigated in 1662, such as the singing of the doxology and reciting of the apostles' creed at marriage and baptism, must be used as 'some of the brethren within the Diocesse have not been carefull to put in practise these duties'.[46] The presbyteries were ordered to ensure that they were enforced. The synod also recorded that it was experiencing problems in gaining submission from schoolmasters, readers, and chaplains, a resistance which is almost ubiquitous in the surviving records.[47] Linlithgow presbytery found that the doxology was in 'disuse' in the parish of Midcalder in November 1667 and ordered the minister and reader to sing it.[48] Similarly, in 1665 and 1668 the synods of Fife and Dunblane reasserted the necessity for ministers to use the apostles' creed at baptisms, the lord's prayer and the doxology.[49] Recent research has shown that the *Directory* was widely adopted in the 1640s without any major objections and was understood as an obligation under the Solemn League

---

[43] NRS, CH2/105/1/1, pp. 380, 387–8, 391.
[44] Linlithgow Presbytery experienced similar issues. See NRS CH2/242/5, pp. 317–21; McDougall, 'Covenants and Covenanters', pp. 161–2.
[45] NRS, CH2/165/1, p. 3.
[46] *Ibid.*, p. 4.
[47] *Ibid.*, p. 6.
[48] NRS, CH2/242/5, p. 385.
[49] *Synod of Fife*, p. 184; NRS, CH2/724/2, p. 62.

and Covenant.[50] It is therefore unsurprising that there was widespread and sustained opposition to the changes after 1662. This suggests that many people held on to covenanting commitments or simply a preference for 1640s-style worship. There is no evidence of a minister being deposed for refusing to sing the doxology or recite the apostles' creed, which indicates an acceptance by the Church that complete uniformity of worship could not realistically be achieved. This paved the way for partial conformity, as ministers could retain their positions while ignoring orders to observe forms of worship for reasons of conscience.

Refusal to adhere to forms of worship revived at the Restoration is an area which has gone unexamined, but one which shows that there was a middle ground of opinion in the ranks of the ministry during the 1660s. While Raffe has discussed divergent Presbyterian and Episcopalian forms of worship, his analysis focuses primarily on the period after 1690 when differences became more marked after policies changed and the *Directory* was reinstated.[51] In the 1660s, differences in forms of worship were small but those who remained in the established Church and refused to use the creed and doxology were displaying a degree of dissent. Synods and presbyteries in the east, west, and central belt noted this form of dissent, but did not impose any punishments. This indicates that refusal to observe changes to worship instigated in 1662 was a form of mild dissent and offered an opportunity for ministers to continue working in the Restoration Church while holding reservations, without drawing too much attention to themselves. They continued working in the Church, and therefore conformed, but not wholeheartedly.

Lay Partial Conformity

Hearing a conformist minister preach, attending readers' services, and taking communion presented dilemmas for lay men and women who often found ways of testing the boundaries of the law. While lay partial conformists sometimes avoided hearing conformist ministers preach, the difference to nonconformity is that partial conformists appeared in church after being rebuked by the kirk session. There is also evidence to suggest that people made a distinction between hearing a conformist minister and attending readers' services, the latter being a departure from the form of worship practised in the 1640s and 1650s. Having a child baptised or a marriage solemnised by a minister in a different parish offered another avenue for partial conformity. The contentious issue of receiving the sacraments from a conformist minister blurs the line between partial conformity and nonconformity. In general, the people who took part in these forms of dissent did not separate from

[50] McDougall, 'Covenants and Covenanters', at pp. 74–8; C. Langley, *Worship, Civil War and Community, 1638–1660* (Abingdon, 2016), p. 69.
[51] Raffe, *Culture of Controversy*.

the Church but instead found alternatives between outright conformity and nonconformity.

After the 1663 parliament, absenting oneself from 'ordinary meitings of divine worship' could result in fines. If convicted, noblemen, gentlemen, and heritors would pay 'a fourt parte of ilk yeers rent' and commons would pay 'such a proportion of their frie moveables as his majesties councill shall think fit'.[52] Those who were the subject of Church censure often returned to church, making their dissent evidence of partial conformity. Between April 1665 and 1668, several people were brought before the kirk session of Alves for 'habituall absence from Church'.[53] Rather than being fined, the absentees were punished by putting their 'hand to the pen to keep the Church better in tyme coming under the paine of standing in the jogges'.[54] Anxiety about the humiliating and painful experience of being placed in the jougs (an iron collar fixed to a wall) was perhaps a more effective deterrent than fining, as the absentees in Alves did not continue their dissent. The minister was Alexander Stewart, a man presented by the earl of Moray and ordained in October 1661.[55] Ministers ordained during this period had a reputation for being very hardline royalist Episcopalians.[56] Although this is usually discussed with reference to those placed in south-western parishes, it is likely that Stewart was of similar stock. Moreover, the previous minister was William Campbell, who had entered his charge after the abolition of patronage in 1649.[57] He conformed but was moved to the Caithness parishes of Olrig in 1661 and Watten in 1668. He was also a member of the commission of the general assembly in 1644 and 1646: two years when the enacting of the Solemn League and Covenant and the Westminster Assembly were being worked out.[58] It is therefore likely that Campbell was, at the very least, less dedicated to the new regime than his successor in Alves, and the regular absence of members of the congregation under Stewart provides further evidence of ways in which the laity could express dissent with the established Church. Had the offenders had any other excuse for not attending church, it would have been recorded in the session minutes, as seen in the case of one of the Alves absenters who was excused because he was 'ane aged and diseased man'.[59] As their dissent did not continue after receiving ecclesiastical censure, partial conformity is a more appropriate label than nonconformity.

Lay men and women could also express dissent by not attending readers' services. The reading of scripture before a sermon had been a standard feature

[52] *RPS*, 1663/6/19.

[53] NRS CH2/11/1, Alves Kirk Session, pp. 203, 212, 223–4.

[54] *Ibid.*, p. 224.

[55] Scott, *Fasti*, vol. 6, p. 375.

[56] Cowan, *Scottish Covenanters*, pp. 56–7; W. L. Mathieson, *Politics and Religion: A Study in Scottish History from the Reformation to the Revolution* (2 vols, Glasgow, 1902), vol. 2, pp. 192–3.

[57] Scott, *Fasti*, vol. 6, p. 375.

[58] *Ibid.*, vol. 7, p. 138.

[59] NRS, CH2/11/1, p. 224.

of the Church before the covenants, but was dispensed with by the *Directory* and replaced by lectures explaining the scriptures.[60] Lectures were viewed by the new regime with suspicion as potentially fostering sedition. This is evidenced by the case of John Campbell, minister of Tealing (Angus), who continued lecturing in church until his deposition in November 1663 for 'wicked practises, still labouring to keip the hearts of the people from the present government of the Church and State by their pernicious doctrin'.[61] Reading of scripture was intended to provide the laity with exposure to the bible without the potential political interpretations presented in lectures. The records of Dunblane synod emphasised this point in 1666, stating that reading of scripture was crucial as 'manie of our commons cannot read, and so cannot use the Scriptures in private, and too manie that can, yet doe neglect it'.[62]

The reintroduction of readers' services was unacceptable for many people. In April 1664, in the Fife parish of Aberdour, the elders announced that 'severalls abides out in the church yeard in tyme of reading the scriptures', and ordered the minister to censure these people if they did not stop.[63] Dunblane synod similarly ordered ministers to be more diligent in enforcing attendance at readers' services in April 1665, and in October 1666 the moderator stated that 'none [were] permitted to stand about the dores, or ly in the kirk-yard during the tyme of reading'.[64] When ordering the repression of absence from readers' services in March 1664, the parish of Stirling made a distinction between people who roamed the streets on a Sunday and those who 'walketh in the church yeard or in the outer church in tyme of reading of the holy scriptures'.[65] Readers' services usually took place immediately before the Sunday sermon, and these instances indicate that people were often willing to attend church on a Sunday but waited outside or at the door during the readers' service, thus expressing a degree of dissent against the imposition of this practice. Evidence suggests that avoiding readers' services was viewed as less serious than avoiding sermons. While individual people were cited and punished for avoiding sermons, there is no evidence of anyone being brought before the session for refusal to attend readers' services, even though the kirk sessions noted it. Avoiding readers' services is thus an example of partial conformity: a practice which involved mild dissent without invoking a separation from the established Church.

Taking a child to be baptised in another parish caused further issues for the authorities. This point is highlighted by Semple, who observed that 'Many that went the length of hearing would not baptise with them [conformist

---

[60] Foster, *Bishop and Presbytery*, p. 128.
[61] Scott, *Fasti*, vol. 5, p. 370; NRS, CH2/352/2, Tealing Kirk Session, pp. 102–4, 113, 117–18.
[62] NRS, CH2/724/2, p. 33.
[63] NRS, CH2/3/1, Aberdour Kirk Session, p. 95.
[64] NRS, CH2/724/2, pp. 23–4, 32.
[65] NRS, CH2/1026/4, Stirling Kirk Session, pp. 272–3.

ministers], and several that did thro fear, it was observed some sudden accident befell these children; quich made others hold off them'.[66] Similarly, in 1664 the synod of Galloway recorded that many parishioners 'did refuse to bring their children to the church to be baptized by them, but either keepd them unbaptized or took them to outed ministers of their owne principles to be baptized privatly by them'.[67] At the baptism of a child, the parents were required to answer questions from the minister and recite the apostles' creed, a Calvinist catechism contained in Knox's *Book of Common Order* but dispensed with by the *Directory*.[68] The parish of Aberdour recorded two instances of parents taking their children to Auchtermuchty to be baptised in 1664 and 1666. The minister of Auchtermuchty was James Martin, who had entered his charge in 1641, and therefore did not need to receive collation from a bishop, and who may have been a partial conformist. He was suspended in 1649 for failing to observe communion two years in a row and poor record-keeping.[69] Given this evidence, it is possible that Martin was less diligent in observing the parental requirements at baptism than the minister at Aberdour, Robert Bruce. Bruce had been a covenanter and resolutioner leader, but also had long-standing episcopal and royalist sympathies.[70] Many people were clearly unwilling to baptise their children with a conformist minister and instead turned to outed, or less overtly conformist, clergy; another form of dissent that falls clearly under the umbrella of partial conformity.

Raffe argues that partial conformists tended to appear in church only for special occasions.[71] However, the evidence above shows that there were also those who went to church regularly but refused to observe certain forms of worship. Raffe also acknowledges that some people may have attended weekly services in the kirk but would not receive the sacraments from conformist clergy.[72] Annual observance of the sacrament of communion was unchanged by the Restoration settlement: the kirk sessions handed out communion tickets to those who had been examined (catechised) by the minister or a church representative in the days preceding the celebration; fasting and sermons usually took place on a Saturday; then the bread and wine were taken by all adult parishioners and the minster while seated at tables on Sunday.[73] The 1661 Rescissory Act nullified the act of the general assembly of 1638 which outlawed the Five Articles of Perth, and thus kneeling at communion was permitted, but not required, in the Restoration

---

[66] G. Semple, 'Life', in *Protestant Piety in Early-Modern Scotland: Letters, Lives, and Covenants, 1650–1712*, ed. D. G. Mullan (Edinburgh, 2008), pp. 140–66.

[67] NRS, CH2/165/2, p. 2.

[68] Foster, *Bishop and Presbytery*, pp. 130, 148; G. D. Henderson, *Religious Life in Seventeenth-Century Scotland* (Cambridge, 1937), pp. 47, 152, 156.

[69] Scott, *Fasti*, vol. 5, p. 126.

[70] Ibid., p. 2

[71] Raffe, *Culture of Controversy*, pp. 184–5.

[72] Ibid.

[73] L. E. Schmidt, *Holy Fairs: Scottish Communions and American Revivals in the Early Modern Period* (Princeton, 1989), pp. 32–3; Todd, *Culture of Protestantism*, chapter 2.

Kirk. There are no instances in the session records of ministers imposing kneeling while observing communion in the 1660s, which suggests that the widely unpopular practice was not used. However, very few session records describe what actually happened on the communion day, with the exception of Edinburgh Canongate, where the records mention that tables were used.[74] It is known that Alexander Brodie did not take communion in 1663 as he heard that the bishop of Moray 'had drawn al the people to kneel at the communion'.[75] As with the implementation of changes to worship, oaths, and prayers for the king, it is likely that practices varied throughout the kingdom.

McIntyre and McDougall have demonstrated that covenanting and communion became intrinsically linked in the language of the hardline regime under the Solemn Acknowledgement and Engagement in 1648.[76] Perhaps as a result, many people refused to take communion in the Restoration Church. In the Aberdeenshire parish of Kemnay, twenty-four people did not take communion in 1665. Five people were refused entry for 'continueing ignorant efter offered instructiones'; five did not attend and were listed as not being permitted entry as they had 'wilfullie absentit themselfes from dyetis of catechizeing'; and the remaining fourteen were incomers to the parish who had not presented testimonials to the session.[77] As with marriage, observing communion with a conformist minister meant accepting the legality of the Restoration settlement and the overturning of the covenants. The 1669 pamphlet of the Episcopalian polemicist Gilbert Burnet, A Modest and Free Conference betwixt a Conformist and Non-conformist, was framed in a question-and-answer format between a fictional conformist and nonconformist. With regard to communion, the conformist asked why 'some of you joyn with us in the ordinary worship, but will not communicat [i.e. take communion] with us?' To this the nonconformist responded that taking communion meant 'acknowledg[ing] them our Pastors, who are intruders, and are in the places of our faithful shepherds'.[78] Raffe has demonstrated that the theme of clerical intrusion was common in nonconformist ideology as it highlighted the corrupt nature of a regime which had disregarded its covenanted commitments.[79] Avoidance of communion is an area where the distinction between partial conformity and nonconformity is blurred. Certainly, nonconformists did not take communion in church, instead taking the sacrament in house or field with a minister who had withdrawn from the Church. Gilbert Burnet, when discussing nonconformity, actually highlighted a crucial aspect of

[74] NRS, CH2/122/4, Edinburgh Canongate Kirk Session, pp. 420–1.

[75] Laing, Diary of Alexander Brodie, pp. 294–5.

[76] N. McIntyre and J. McDougall, 'Reframing the Covenant: A Solemn Acknowledgement (1648) and the Resubscription of the Solemn League and Covenant', The Seventeenth Century, 37:5 (2022), 733–56.

[77] NRS, CH2/542/1, Kemnay Kirk Session, p. 58.

[78] Gilbert Burnet, A Modest and Free Conference betwixt a Conformist and a Non-conformist, about the present distempers of Scotland (Edinburgh, 1669), pp. 53–4.

[79] Raffe, Culture of Controversy, pp. 182–3.

PARTIAL CONFORMITY IN RESTORATION SCOTLAND

partial conformity: those who attended ordinary services but refused to take communion as it meant acknowledging the legality of the 1662 ecclesiastical settlement. Nonconformists, such as Semple, argued that even hearing a conformist preach was a breach of the covenants.[80] However, there were others, such as Alexander Brodie and all the people cited by Kemnay kirk session, who regularly attended worship but refused to take communion and can therefore be classified as partial conformists rather than nonconformists.

The place of women in nonconformity has long been acknowledged, albeit with significant room for further research (see chapter 7). Raffe has broached the topic, arguing that nonconformist women were of pivotal importance in the organisation of, and attendance at, conventicles.[81] Women were also key partial conformists. Of all the people listed by kirk sessions and presbyteries for forms of mild dissent, women account for at least half. Of the twenty-four people cited by Kemnay kirk session in 1665, for example, fifteen were female. In this case, the male householder may have attended communion while his wife or daughter did not, in the hope that attendance of the head of the household would suffice. Evidently, this was not acceptable in Kemnay as many women were listed individually, not just as the wife of a dissenting male; the names included a woman and her daughter.[82] This pattern appears to have been particularly prevalent in the 1660s, for it was not until the 1670 Conventicle Act that the head of household was fined for dissenting activity of their wives and children.[83] Keirnan argues that, as a result of the Civil Wars, there were many widows, spinsters, and unmarried women in Scotland whose closest relationship was with the Church of the covenants, and this goes some way to explaining the high levels of female dissent during the Restoration period.[84] It is also worth considering the impact swearing the covenants had had on women, who, according to DesBrisay, were victims of a biased Church and state which regularly doled out comparatively harsher punishments to women than men.[85] Regarding partial conformity, it must be noted that women were active participants in this form of dissent.

Conclusion

The lack of rigour with which the authorities enforced the 1662 ecclesiastical settlement allowed for a body of people, both clerical and lay, to test the

---

[80] Semple, 'Life', pp. 153–4.

[81] A. Raffe, 'Female Authority and Lay Activism in Scottish Presbyterianism, 1660–1740', in S. Apetrei and H. Smith (eds), *Religion and Women in Britain, c.1660–1760* (Abingdon, 2014), pp. 59–74.

[82] NRS CH2/542/1, p. 58.

[83] *Ibid.*, p. 61.

[84] Kiernan, 'Banner with a Strange Device', p. 35.

[85] G. DesBrisay, 'Twisted by Definition: Women under Godly Discipline in Seventeenth-Century Scottish Towns', in Y. G. Brown and R. Ferguson (eds), *Twisted Sisters: Women, Crime and Deviance in Scotland Since 1400* (East Linton, 2002), pp. 137–55.

boundaries and avoid conforming fully. In the ranks of the ministry who retained their positions, there were two clearly identifiable opinion groups: conformists and partial conformists. Partial conformists were those who found ways of exploiting the non-rigorous way in which conformity was sought by refusing to acknowledge the changes in worship and avoiding taking an oath of loyalty to the Church or taking an oath with limitations. Refusal to observe the 29 May thanksgiving involved both clerical and lay dissenters who often went unpunished. Although conformity was not expected of the laity through public oath-taking, ordinary men and women found numerous ways of expressing dissent without separating from the established Church. Often, people opposed practices that deviated from the 1645 *Directory for Public Worship*, which suggests a preference for 1640s-style worship and perhaps an ongoing commitment to the Solemn League and Covenant. There was a difference between separating from the Church entirely and remaining a minister or lay member of the corporate body of the Church while holding reservations. Partial conformity was a realistic and prevalent phenomenon as it offered a way for people to express dissent without facing the severe consequences of separating from the Church entirely.

Afterword

Deviance and marginality are, in many ways, two manifestations of the same basic dynamic common to all social systems. A coherent, cohesive society requires some sense of shape and definition, as part of which a distinction between in-group and out-group – between 'mainstream' and 'margins' – is needed. But this structure necessarily invites deviance, either because those consigned to the social wilderness are forced to rely on unacceptable behaviours in order to survive, or because their very identities and ways of life end up being conceptualised as inherently aberrant. Deviance, moreover, often functions as a tool for deciding who belongs in which grouping. Unpicking the relationship between these two concepts, therefore, offers historians a powerful mechanism for uncovering the control mechanisms and ordering assumptions of past societies.

In exploring the intersection between deviance and marginality in the context of early modern Scotland, the essays in this volume have highlighted a number of recurring themes which, between them, tell us a great deal about Scottish society. Firstly, the distinction between 'mainstream' and 'marginal' was sharply defined. We see this, for example, in Kennedy's delineation of acceptable as against unacceptable sexual behaviour, Dye's exploration of 'disorderly' speech, Kilday's analysis of entrenched suspicion against the Romani, and both Cipriano's and McDougall's discussion of political dissidence. Secondly, and connected to this, enforcement of expected norms was consistently robust, albeit the tools and approaches used could vary greatly, from ecclesiastical discipline (Kennedy) to criminal prosecution (Cudney, Dye, Kilday) to collective resistance (Carballo, Watson) to more amorphous social pressure (Cipriano, Ewan). This was a society that had a very clear idea of where the border lay between welcome and unwelcome, and was not afraid to police it.

A third key theme to emerge from this collection is the extent to which deviance and marginality could become mutually reinforcing. We see this most obviously in Kilday's study, which demonstrates how the marginalisation of the Romani could force them into crime, in turn leading them, individually and collectively, ever further to the social fringes. Similar dynamics emerge from Carballo's work on piracy, McGregor's on 'common musicians', and Eaton's on covenanting women. Cudney's study of gendered assault, wherein criminal violence against women is understood as a mechanism for enforcing their preexisting subordination, highlights a rather different form of feedback loop. Different still is the dynamic explored by Ewan: in weaponising the concept of marginality when deploying verbal violence, Scots used deviant behaviour to reinforce not the actual experience of marginality, but its power as an organising and 'othering' paradigm.

The pervasive influence of gender is the fourth perspective requiring comment. Several of the essays in this volume, but most notably those of Cudney, Kennedy, and Dye, demonstrate that gender expectations played a pivotal role in defining what counted as 'deviant', usually with the result of narrowing the range of 'acceptable' behaviours for women in particular. In turn, punishment of 'deviant' behaviour had the effect of reinforcing gender norms. But there was another dynamic, too: since a reputation for not properly embodying gendered expectations could itself be a marginalising force, deviance could function as a means of self-protection. This is a dynamic observed particularly by Cudney, who sees it as an important driver of petty assault, particularly for men anxious to prove or defend their masculinity from (real or perceived) challenge. Just as significant as all this, however, is the revelation that deviance could, in some ways, represent a mechanism for questioning or negotiating gender, especially for women. Cudney and Dye, through the prisms of assault and witchcraft respectively, both observe this, and it is also part of the landscape of verbal violence as mapped by Ewan. Similarly, both Watson's contribution on banditry and Eaton's work on nonconformity demonstrate that part of the effect of these deviant activities was their potential for facilitating feminine agency. In a rich variety of ways, therefore, gender conditioned the way marginality and deviance interacted for early modern Scots.

One final theme inherent in this collection, and offering a partial counterpoint to all of the above, is that the relationship between deviance and marginality was not always straightforward. Falconer usefully reminds us that not all deviant activity sprang from social alienation; some of it, instead, represented an attempt to negotiate position from within the mainstream – a concept also implicit in Ewan's exploration of insulting language. Perhaps even more strikingly, it is apparent that the self-reinforcing loop between deviance and marginality could be challenged, or at least mitigated. This is clear, for example, from Watson's assessment of Seamas an Tuim, who developed a range of strategies for returning to the mainstream, or in McGregor's analysis of common musicians, whose valuable skills allowed them to keep one foot permanently on the side of acceptability. Different forms of mitigation emerge from study of Presbyterian dissidents: Eaton shows us that marginality could be offset by the construction of new, bespoke support networks among the godly, while McDougall demonstrates that careful modulation of behaviour could allow some people to flirt with deviance yet not suffer significant marginalising

AFTERWORD

consequences. There were, then, grey areas, and this provided some scope for weakening the link between deviance and marginality, or for escaping their consequences.

***

This book has done much to expand our understanding of the connection between deviant behaviour and social marginality in early modern Scotland. Nonetheless, it is not intended to be the last word on the topic; instead, the authors fervently hope that it will inspire further work. Perhaps the most fitting way to bring the volume to a close, therefore, would be to sketch out some of the potential new directions and approaches any such research might take. The most obvious place to start is with the sources. The essays in this volume have demonstrated the value of mining a range of primary materials, including central judicial records, self-writing, government and administrative papers, and the minutes of ecclesiastical courts. What is less prominent in this mix – while also being grossly under-utilised in the wider research environment – is local judicial material, and in particular the records of sheriff and justice of the peace courts. Such materials tend to suffer from inconsistent survival rates, limited cataloguing, and, in the case of sheriff courts in particular, dizzying eclecticism, all of which means historians have tended to avoid them in favour of easier, more readily accessible sources. Future work, therefore, taking its cue from the Kilday's exploratory reflections within these pages on the James Macpherson trial, might tackle documents like these head-on, an approach that would not only open up new angles on both deviance and marginality, but would also expand the currently rather threadbare baseload of detailed local perspectives, providing scholars with a more robust basis for nationwide synthesis and generalisation.

If there would be value in plugging gaps in the source-base, it would likewise be advantageous to address chronological lacunae. The study of criminal deviance, for example, is at present heavily skewed in favour of the post-1700 period, and further work in that mould dealing with earlier eras – as in this book's contributions from Cudney, Falconer, Carballo, and Watson – would greatly expand our understanding. In a similar vein, religious nonconformity is relatively well explored for the Restoration (thanks not least to the essays of Eaton and McDougall within this volume), and some work also exists for the 1650s and the decades immediately following the Reformation. Outside of these bright spots, however, deviant religiosity is much more poorly served and understood. More generally, the value of ecclesiastical records as a window into both deviant behaviour and social marginalisation has been extensively unpacked for the period up to around 1690, but far less has been done on the post-revolution period or the eighteenth century. There are, therefore, a range of chronological gaps in the existing scholarship, and filling them in would not only expand our understanding of these topics, but also give us a better sense of continuity and discontinuity across the early modern period.

Alongside exploiting new sources and filling in chronological black holes, future research might fruitfully address some particular issues. Perhaps the most obvious is the forms taken by the deviant activity of marginalised people. Some aspects of this are reasonably clear: we have a pretty solid understanding about the rhythms, imagery, and vocabulary of women's 'disorderly' speech, for instance, as reflected by the work of Dye and Ewan earlier in these pages. But many other forms of deviance – including sexual misconduct, unlicensed itineracy, culturally distinctive behaviours, and most forms of criminality, all of which are referenced at various points in this book – are understood primarily in terms of the responses they provoked, often leaving us with only a sketchy understanding of what they looked like in and of themselves. Of course, much of the explanation for this lies in the nature of our sources, which are almost exclusively external to the sorts of marginalised individuals discussed in this book. Yet careful handling of these materials could yield some insights, and such a shift in focus towards strategies of deviance instead of anti-deviance would add a fresh dimension to existing knowledge.

A redoubled focus on the lived reality of marginalised deviance would be of particular value if it focused on certain groups that are, at present, especially poorly understood. As has already been noted, the survival strategies of itinerants – whether in the form of mobility itself or supplementary activities like petty theft or poaching – are not clearly understood, which reflects a more general dearth of research into the migrant experience in early modern Scotland. Much the same point might be made about cultural minorities such as the Romani or Black people, albeit some recent work, for example into the phenomenon of 'freedom seeking' by enslaved people, has begun to shed a little light. There would also be value in further exploring the deviance of what might be called 'marginalised elites', perhaps most obviously in the form of religiously nonconforming, politically dissident, or criminally inclined members of the landholding or aristocratic classes. Essays in this volume, including those of Eaton, Watson, and Cipriano, have touched on this theme, but more expansive research would be welcome, and would have the benefit of reinforcing Falconer's observation that neither social marginality nor deviant behaviour were the exclusive preserve of the poor and dispossessed.

On the other side of the equation, more investigation is needed into how both deviance and marginality could be mitigated or challenged. As we have already seen, the essays in this volume pay some attention to this issue, but there is more to do in terms of understanding how far, and in what ways, early modern society was willing to forgive or overlook deviant behaviour, whether it be sexual, criminal, ideological, or anything else. What mechanisms were available for rehabilitating the deviant? To what extent could the model posited by McDougall of turning a blind eye to partial religious nonconformity be extended to other forms of deviance? Could culturally-rooted deviants like the Romani ever be accommodated? To what extent was deviant behaviour regarded as forgivable if it sprang from social or economic want, and did authorities make any attempt to eradicate the former by means of policy responses to the latter? Questions like these merit a lot of further reflection, and answering them would provide us with a much better understanding of the social and attitudinal context within which both deviance and marginalisation played out.

Yet perhaps the most glaringly underexplored point of intersection between marginality and deviance is queerness. Aside from some often rather tentative work on James VI, historians of Scotland have had virtually nothing to say about queer identities or sexualities in general, or about homosexual experiences in particular. Yet we know from research focused on other countries, particularly England, as well as from more modern evidence, that queerness could have a powerful marginalising effect, while also being one of the most stringently stigmatised behavioural patterns of the age. There are, of course, significant practical difficulties in exploring this topic, since most types of source tend to be silent on it, forcing historians to rely mostly on extrapolation from literary material – an approach that remains embryonic in a Scottish context. Nonetheless, as a near-perfect embodiment of the linked concepts underpinning this book, queerness not only represents a vital new intellectual frontier waiting to be explored, but could also emerge as one of the most powerful tools available to historians for unpacking the complex, self-reinforcing, and highly revealing relationship between 'deviance' and 'marginality' in early modern Scotland.

Index

Aberdeen, 47, 51, 53, 66, 69, 70, 71, 72, 90, 95, 96, 99, 103, 104, 145, 148, 151, 152, 153–4, 162, 163, 164, 166, 169, 170, 172, 175, 177
synod of, 194, 195
See also Universities
Aberdeen Doctors, 172, 179, 184
Aberdeenshire, 95, 149, 204
Aberdour, 202, 203
Aboyne, 102
Academics, 11, 172–90
Acheson, Mawsie, 165
Acheson, Robert, 51
Act anent Egyptians (1609), 128
Act of Toleration (1712), 118
Act Rescissory (1661), 112, 203
Act, Conventicles (1670), 115, 205
Act, Test (1681), 181, 185, 189, 190, 194
Adam, 20
Adam, Andrew, 151
Adultery, 15, 18–19, 21, 22, 23, 24, 26, 27, 114, 143, 144, 166
Africans, 8
Aidie, Andrew, 182, 188
Aikman, Christian, 164–5
Ailsa Craig, 88
Aitcheson, Edward, 146
Alcohol, drinking, 32–3, 44, 48, 57, 75, 120, 143–4, 148, 153, 167
Alehouses, 32, 33, 102, 143, 167
Alexander, Helen, 116–9, 123
Allan, Besse, 71
Allan, David, 107
Alves, 201

Amsterdam, 186
Anderson, Alexander, 176–7, 188
Anderson, Andrew, 176, 188
Anderson, James, 72
Anderson, Jonet, 48
Andersone, Alexander, 148
Angus, 202
Anomie, 1
Appleby, John, 81
Archbishops, 177, 181, 197, 198, 199. *See also* Leighton, Robert; Sharp, James; Spottiswoode, John
Argyll, 87
presbytery, 144
synod, 26
Argyll's rising (1685), 118
Arran, 89
Arson *see* Fire-raising
Arthur, John, 162
Assault, 19, 25, 30–44, 54, 61–2, 64, 66, 68–9, 70, 71, 73, 74, 97, 99, 146, 163, 189, 207–8
Assizes (juries), 66, 68
Auchriachan, 97
Auchtermuchty, 203
Auldearn, 113, 114, 115
Ayr, 81, 88–9, 90, 91, 92
Ayr Mariners Society, 90–2
Ayrshire, 45, 81, 88

Badenoch, 130
Bailies, 51, 66, 67, 69, 70, 71, 73, 162, 167
Baillie, Robert, 181, 183
Bairdie, John, 196

INDEX

Balcanquhall, Walter, 109
Ballads, 20
Balzart, Isobel, 73
Bandits, banditry, 10, 94–108, 208
Banff, 10, 130, 132, 134, 136
Banishment, 16, 26, 50, 54, 65, 128,
   146, 165, 166–7
Bannatyne, Hector, of Kames, 40
Baptism, 16, 24, 27, 58, 115, 192, 194,
   199, 200, 202–3
Baptists, 7
Barnat, Elspeth, 169
Baron, Robert, 189
Barony, 196
Barron, John, 189
Barsanti, Francesco, 154
Basilikon Doron, 18
Bass Rock, 120
Begging, beggars, 6, 45, 50, 127, 132,
   141, 142, 143, 145, 161, 162–3,
   166, 167, 170
Belfrage, George, 199
Bell, Bartelmo, 146
Beowis, Christine, 52
Bestiality, 3, 15, 18, 22, 23, 25
Bible, scriptures, 20, 22, 110, 111,
   112, 115, 116, 147, 201, 202
Binning, Hugh, 17
Bishops, 95, 101, 102, 105, 112, 114,
   117, 181, 182, 192, 193, 194, 195,
   197, 198, 203, 204
Bishops' Wars, 106
Bissett, Thomas, 72
Black, John, 188
Black people, 210
Blackadder, John, 121
Blackhall, William, 179, 189
Blackwood, Adam, 47
Blasphemy, 45, 49, 50, 53, 56, 60, 183
Bog of Gight, 101, 102
Bolly, John, 66–7
Bond, Robert, 61
Borders, 84, 87, 88
Bothwell, 118
Boussie, Jonet, 25

Boyd, Robert, of Trochrig, 177–9,
   186, 188
Brae of Mar, 104
Branding, 141, 166
Branks, 52
Brechin, 58
   bishopric, 195
Brewer, Richard, 73
Brig o' Dee, 96, 104
Britain, British Isles, 80, 81, 124, 126
Brittany, 84
Brock, Michelle, 110, 122
Brodie, Alexander, 116, 197, 204, 205
Broken men, 72, 84, 97, 164
Broun, Donald, 132, 134, 135
Broun, John, 188
Broun, Patrick, 160
Broun, Peter, 132, 133, 134, 135, 145
Broune, Johne, 23
Brown, James, 33
Brown, John, of Wamphray, 196
Bruce, Janet, 19
Bruce, Robert, 203
Buchanan, Janet, 57
Burghs, towns, 10, 11, 40, 136
   insults in, 157–71
   of south-west, and piracy, 79–93
   music and soundscape in, 151–3
   space within, 61–76
   See also individual burghs
Burke, Peter, 185
Burne, William, 160
Burnet, Gilbert, 15, 16, 204
Burnet, Thomas, 183–4, 190
Burns, Robert, 136, 155
Burt, Edward, 147, 148, 149
Bute, 9, 30–44
Byrneth, William, 165

Cairletoun, Agnes, 27
Caithness, 165, 201
   presbytery, 26
Caldell, 144
Calland, Alison, 170
Calvinism, 111, 203
Cameron, John, 149, 150, 155

213

INDEX

Cameron, John, 186, 188
Cameron, Lauchlin, 154
Campbell, Alexander, 155
Campbell, Archibald, 2nd earl of Argyll, 89
Campbell, Archibald, 5th earl of Argyll, 89
Campbell, Colin, earl of Argyll, 89
Campbell, John, 202
Campbell, Jonet, 166
Campbell, William, 201
Campbells of Argyll, 87, 89–90
Canongate, 26, 61, 66, 67, 68, 69, 74, 75, 118, 145, 165, 168, 204
Capron, Thomas, 81
Cargill, Donald, 117, 121, 196
Carmichael, William, 68
Carnock, 199
Carron, 102
Cartesianism, 184
Cassie, Helen, 56
Cassy, Walter, 73
Cathcart, Alison, 106
Catholicism, Catholics, 7, 17, 141, 144, 147, 156, 176, 177, 179
Chalmer, Anabell, 71
Chalmer, James, 58
Charity, 7, 90, 92, 93, 118, 119, 127, 141, 143, 151, 156, 162–3
Charles I, 109, 182
Charles II, 111, 112, 117, 180, 186, 191, 192, 195–6
Charming, 45, 46, 48–9, 56, 132
Charteris, Laurence, 185, 189
Chester, 87
Childbirth, 41, 147
Children, 17–8, 24, 25, 27, 41, 100, 105, 111, 113, 118, 119, 120, 126, 144, 147, 149, 163, 169, 197, 200, 202–3, 205
Chirnesyde, Sir Patrick, 19
Chisholm, Alexander, 154
Church of Scotland, 7, 27, 28, 42, 47, 49, 51, 90, 99, 102, 109, 111, 112,

117, 141, 147–8, 150–1, 152, 153, 156, 162
    and Universities, 175–8, 180, 182, 183, 184
    Restoration, 191–206. *See also* Discipline; Kirk sessions; Presbyteries; Synods
Civil Wars, 58, 95, 96, 174, 180, 205
Clan Donald South, 81
Clanship, 80, 81–2, 89, 96, 105, 106, 107, 108
Class, 9, 30, 35, 86, 95, 107, 146, 149, 153, 154, 210
Clelland, George, 98
Clelland, James, 98
Clergy *see* Ministers
Clyde, Firth of, 79, 84, 88
Cock, William, 54
Collace, Francis, 113
Collace, Jean, 113–6, 123
Collace, Katherine, 112, 113–6, 123
Colleges *see* Universities
Colville, William, 189
Comrie, William, 190
Conventicles, 109, 112, 115, 116, 117, 119, 121, 123, 191, 205
Convention of royal burghs, 84–7, 91, 92
Copernicanism, 183, 184
Corstorphine, 58
Couper, Janet, 58
Courts, 19, 30–1, 35, 37, 46, 49, 55, 57, 89, 98, 106, 115, 116, 117, 136, 209
    admiralty, 83, 86
    bailie, 72
    burgh, 31, 30–44, 49, 54, 61–76, 157–61, 171
    ecclesiastical, 3, 4, 30–44, 194, 209
    justiciary, 4, 99
Covenanters, covenanting, 10, 28, 38, 95, 96, 103, 104, 109–23, 151, 172, 179–81, 182, 183, 191–206, 207. *See also* National Covenant; Solemn League and Covenant

214

INDEX

Cranston, William, 188
Crawford, Eizabeth, 61–2
Crawfurd, Marion, 26
Crichton, James, of Frendraught, 97
Crombie, Sir Thomas, 104
Cruikshank, John, 133
Cryst, Margaret, 61–2, 67, 68, 76
Cullen, William, 66
Culloden, battle of, 145
Culquholly, 103
Culross, 148
Cults, Christian, 164
Cunningham, Alexander, 190
Cunningham, Robert, 188
Cupar, 21
Currie, James, 116–7, 118

Dalkeith, 117
Danzig, 163
Davidson, John, 163
Davidson, Margaret, 57
Davidson, Peter, 108
Deeside, 104
Dempster, Jasper, 52
Dempster, Jonet, 157–8, 159, 161, 165, 167, 168, 170
DesBrisay, Gordon, 205
Deviance
    and marginality, 1–9, 207–11
    See also Assault; Murder, homicide; Nonconformity; Piracy; Sexual deviance; Theft, thieves; Violence; Witchcraft
Devil, 28–9, 49, 55, 56, 57, 58, 59
Dick, Alison, 54
Dick, Andro, 52–3
Dickson, Alexander, 189
Dickson, David, 181, 185, 189
Dict, Christian, 167
Dingwall, 24
Dingwall, Helen, 4
Dirleton, 185
Discipline, ecclesiastical, 15, 18, 26, 29, 30, 34, 36, 38, 40, 44, 49

Disease, illness, 22, 48, 54, 57, 58, 62, 91, 113, 157, 158, 159, 167, 170, 181, 197, 201
Doak, Laura, 110, 112, 116, 123
Dores, 150
Douglas, Alexander, 190
Douglas, Alexander, of Spynie, 116
Douglas, Isobel, 162
Douglas, James, earl of Morton, 88
Douglas, William, duke of Queensberry, 122
Doune, 136
Downe, John, 70
Dropuljic, Stephanie, 99
Drummond, John, 190
Drummond, William, of Hawthornden, 143
Drunkenness, 23, 30, 32–3, 72, 141, 143, 144, 148, 161, 163, 183. *See also* Alcohol
Du Toit, Alex, 120
Dublin, 80–1, 185
Duff, Alexander, of Braco, 131
Duff, Isobel, 28–9
Dugar, John, 104
Dugude, Robert, 144
Dumbarton, 89, 151
Dumfries, 120, 122, 151
Dun, John, 57
Dunbar, presbytery, 195, 196, 198
Dunbar, Nicholas, 132
Dunblane, synod, 199, 202
Duncan, Peter, 133–4
Dundas, Bessie, 164, 166
Dundee, 62, 69, 102, 146, 152, 167
Dundonald, 45–6
Dundurcas, 150
Dunfermline, presbytery, 195, 197, 198, 199
Dunkeld, 155
Dunnottar Castle, 118
Dunsyre, 121
Durie, Janet, 47
Durkheim, Émile, 1
Durrant, Thomas, 71

INDEX

Durris, 104
Dutch Republic, 85, 120, 186

Earle, John, 143
Earlston, 113
   presbytery, 197
East Lothian, 25, 185
Echt, 104
Edinburgh, 4, 20, 23, 25, 26, 27, 72,
   84, 96, 99, 100, 101, 102, 105,
   116, 117, 118, 119, 120, 121, 144,
   145, 146, 151, 152, 153, 154, 163,
   165, 166, 178, 185, 204
   burgh council, 24, 141, 149, 151, 178
   and Tweeddale, synod, 198
   bishopric, 182
   castle, 94, 96, 98, 101, 102
   See also Universities
Edmestoun, John, 24
Ednam, Jonet, 167
Egyptions *see* Romani
Eizat, Thomas, 148
Ekirch, Roger, 73
Elders, 34, 35, 36, 37, 38, 40, 43, 50,
   51, 58, 148, 150, 195–200, 202
Elgin, 50, 52, 96, 98, 99, 103, 113,
   114, 130, 134, 143, 146, 147, 148,
   153, 162, 163, 165, 167, 170
Eliav-Feldon, Miriam, 125
Eliot, John, 24
Elizabeth I, 79–80, 82, 85
Engagement, 180, 189, 204
England, 3, 15, 27, 79, 81, 82, 85, 87,
   91, 92, 120, 128, 142, 147, 181,
   191, 211
Enlightenment, 156
Enslavement, 8, 210
Episcopalianism, Episcopalians, 11,
   115, 122, 175, 177, 181, 184, 185,
   191, 192–5, 200, 201, 203
Erskine, John, earl of Mar, 145
Ethnic minorities, 1, 3, 8, 35, 124,
   126, 127. *See also* Black people;
   Romani
Eve, 20

Ewan, Elizabeth, 11, 31, 49–50, 70
Ewyn, James, 71

Fairley, James, 119
Falkirk, 57
Falkland, 21
Fall, James, 190
Family, 18, 26, 28, 33, 37–8, 43, 55,
   61, 66, 107, 110, 111, 149, 158,
   164, 168–71
Farquharson, Donald, 104
Farquharson, Robert, 102
Farquharson, William, 97
Feithie, James, 122
Femininity *see* Gender
Fenton, James, 190
Fergus, Jonet, 169
Ferguson, Alexander, 70
Ferguson, Elizabeth, 68–9
Ferguson, Isobell, 55
Ferguson, James, 183
Fergusson, Andrew, 165
Fergusson, David, 143
Ferme, Charles, 177, 188
Ferryport-on-Craig, 193
Feuding, 94–8, 106
Fiddes, James, 23
Fife, 23, 113, 114, 128, 202
   synod, 199
Fire-raising, 19, 97–8
First Book of Discipline, 176
Fishing, fisheries, 82, 85
Flather, Amanda, 67
Fleming, James, 169
Flyting *see* Violence, verbal
Fodderletter, 97
Folk heroes, 124, 129, 130–1, 137
Forbes, Harry, 114, 197
Forbes, John, of Corse, 172, 179, 186,
   189
Forbes, John, of Leslie, 104
Forbes, William, 152, 182
Forest, William, 71
Forfar, 102
   presbytery, 198

216

INDEX

Forfarshire *see* Angus
Forgery, 24, 154
Forgushill, Margaret, 45, 46, 55
Fornication, 15, 17, 18, 19, 21, 22, 23, 24, 25, 26, 27, 28, 36, 40, 154
Forres, 114, 130
France, 80, 84, 91–2, 186
Fraser, James, 106
Fraser, Janet, 24
Fraser, John, 27
Fraser, Margaret, 26–7
Fraser, Simon, Lord Lovat, 106
Fraserburgh, 175, 177, 188
Frenche, Adam, of Thornydykis, 19
Frendraught, 97, 105
Frissel, James, 35, 43
Frissell, Elspeth, 31, 37–8, 43
Fugzeane, 102
Fyvie, Jhon, 142

Gadderar, Margaret, 163
Gaelic, 96, 104, 108
Gaels *see* Highlanders
Galie, John, 38–9
Galloway, synod, 199, 203
Galloway, Alexander, 176, 188
Garden, James, 190
Gardner, Violet, 51
Garioch, 102
Garlaw, Duncan, 61
Garnett, Thomas, 155
Gender, 5–6, 9, 10, 19–20, 94, 160, 170, 207–8
  and covenanting, 110–1
  and space, 64, 67
  and violence, 30–44
General assembly, 16, 25, 27, 28, 99, 122, 144, 148, 149–50, 172, 177, 179, 180, 183, 193, 201, 203
George I, 152
Gib, Helen, 56
Gibson, Andrew, 162
Gibson, Sir Alexander, 118
Gilgor, James, 168
Gillespie, Patrick, 181, 183, 189

Gilpin, Richard, 121
Glasgow, 28, 31, 81, 88, 90, 98, 146, 151, 152, 153, 154, 163, 164, 166, 169, 183, 193, 196. *See also* Universities
Glass, Alexander, 144, 150, 153
Glass, William, 34
Gleg, Thomas, 189
Glenesk, 102
Glenmoriston, 154
Glorious revolution *see* Revolution of 1688–9
Godfrey, Mark, 106
Godliness, 3, 10, 17, 28, 47, 49, 53, 59–60, 73, 111, 114, 117, 119, 121, 141, 208
Gollan, James, 165
'Good victim', 34–6, 38
Goodare, Julian, 9
Gordon, George, 1st marquis of Huntly, 100
Gordon, George, 2nd marquis of Huntly, 96–7
Gordon, Gilbert, of Sallagh, 97
Gordon, James, 97
Gordon, James, 132, 134, 135
Gordon, James, of Rothiemay, 95, 104
Gordon, John, of Rothiemay, 97
Gordon, Lewis, Lord Aboyne, 96, 87, 104, 106
Gordon, Patrick, 190
Gordon, Sir John, 104
Gordon, Sir Robert, 95, 96–7, 98, 99, 101, 103
Gordon, Thomas, 190
Gordons, 106, 108
Gouge, William, 110
Govan, 17
Gow, Neil, 155–6
Graham, James, marquis of Montrose, 96, 104
Graham, John, 146
Graham, Michael, 42
Grant, George, 105

217

INDEX

Grant, James, of Carron ('Seamas an Tuim'), 10, 94–108, 208
Grant, James, of Freuchie, 105, 106
Grant, Janet, 101
Grant, John, 100
Grant, John, of Ballindalloch, 96, 98–9, 100, 101, 102, 105
Grant, John, of Carron, 96, 99, 100
Grant, John, of Dalnabo, 96, 99, 105
Grant, John, of Freuchie, 96, 101, 105
Grant, Ludovick, of Freuchie and Grant, 131, 132, 135, 136
Grant, Mage, 165
Grant, Patrick, of Ballindalloch, 96
Grant, Patrick, of Carron, 96, 99
Grant, Patrick, of Culquoich, 98
Grant, Patrick, of Glenmoriston, 105
Grant, Patrick, of Lettoch, 96
Grant, Robert, 102, 105
Grant, Thomas, 98
Grant, Thomas, of Cardaillis, 99
Grant, Thomas, of Dalvey, 96, 99, 100, 101
Grant, Thomas, tutor of Carron, 98
Gray, Andrew, 72
Gray, Isobell, 24
Gray, Muriel, 164, 166
Gray, Peter, 39
Greg, Henry, 146
Greg, Shadrach, 146
Gregorie, David, 190
Gregory, James, 190
Greig, Walter, 21
Greyfriars, 178
Guild, William, 180, 189
Guilds, 70, 153–4
Guillon, Andrew, 117
Guthrie, Helen, 27
Guthrie, James, 19, 121
Gylour, Alexander, 25
Gypsies *see* Romani

Haldane, Isabell, 48
Hamilton, Archibald, 188

Hamilton, James, duke of Hamilton, 103
Hamilton, Jonet, 23
Hamilton, Robert, 188, 189
Hamilton, William, 23
Hamiltoune, Margaret, 26
Hankey, Anthony, 87
Harrison, John, 52
Harrot, Elspet, 165
Hatmaker, Andrew, 166
Hay, Andrew, 72
Hay, Edmund, 188
Hay, Henry, 122
Hay, John, 62
Hay, John, 122
Hebrides *see* Western Isles
Heidelberg, 172
Henderson, Gilbert, 51
Hendrie, Katte, 51
Henry VIII, 79
Henryson, Margaret, 68
Herberton, Jeane, 166
Highlanders, Gaels, 8, 79, 80, 81–2, 88, 89, 92, 94–108
Highlands, 80, 81–2, 85, 94–108, 130, 133, 135, 155
Hitchcock, David, 3
Hobbes, Thomas, 173, 174
Hobsbawm, Eric, 107
Hog, Thomas, 113
Honyman, Andrew, 193
Households, 31, 61, 62, 68, 69, 97, 110, 111, 160, 164, 169–70, 205. *See also* Family
Houston, John, 188
Houston, William, 151
Howie, Robert, 177
Hughes, Anne, 111
Huguenot, 177
Hume, Patrick, earl of Marchmont, 150–1
Humphries, Cathy, 42
Hunter, James, 31, 37–8
Hunter, Malcolm, 89
Hunter, Robert, 151

Illness *see* Disease
Immigrants *see* Migrants, migration
Incest, 15, 18, 21, 22, 27–8, 29
Infanticide, 5, 6, 24, 41
Inglis, Marion, 53
Ingram, Martin, 38
Innerwick, 196
Innes, Elspet, 95, 98–9, 101–3
Innes, Jean, 99
Innes, John, 162
Innes, Meddie, 50
Innes, Sir James, 114
Innes, Sir Robert, of Balvenie, 98
Insults *see* Violence, verbal
Inver, 155
Inveraray, 144
Inverness, 26, 27, 28–9, 51, 95, 96,
    97, 129, 149, 157, 160, 164, 165,
    166, 167, 169
  presbytery, 149, 150, 159
Inverness-shire, 85, 87
Ireland, 79, 80–1, 82, 91, 96, 102
Irish Sea, 79, 81, 82, 87, 89
Irvine, 84, 89
Irwing, Jaffray, 27
Itinerants *see* Migrants

Jacobitism, 141, 144–5
Jak, Robert, 65
James IV, 127
James V, 21, 84, 127–8
James VI, 18, 21, 80, 83, 85, 94, 177,
    179, 188, 211
James VII, 38, 184
Jameson, Alexander, 189
Jameson, Elizabeth, 73
Jameson, Robert, 81
Jamieson, Janet, 37
Jamiesoun, Alexander, 34
Jedburgh, 146
Jethseman, Jonet, 21
Johnson, Alexander, 70
Johnstone, James, 144
Jougs, 35, 38, 50, 201

Justices of the peace, 96, 132, 145,
    147, 209

Kanyeaucht, Katherine, 53
Kelburne, Adam, 34
Kembak, Jonet, 165
Kemnay, 104, 204–5
Kennedy, Allan, 107
Kerr, Adam, 38
Kerr, John, 38–9
Kerr, Patrick, 38–9
Kerr, Robert, earl of Lothian, 143
Kiernan, Victor, 205
Kidnap, 96, 103, 115
Kilday, Anne-Marie, 2
Killing Times, 109
Kincaid, Euphan, 119
Kincaid, Jon, 55
Kingarth, 34, 35, 36, 37, 43
Kinkaid, Isobel, 68–9, 76
Kinloss, 109–7
Kintor, John, 166
Kintyre, 25, 81
Kirk sessions 18, 30, 31, 34, 41, 42,
    44, 46, 47, 49, 51, 53, 56, 57, 59,
    158, 192, 193, 195, 196, 198,
    200, 202, 203, 204, 205. *See also*
    individual kirk sessions
Kirkcaldy, 47, 54, 90
Kirkcudbright, 87, 88, 196
Kirkton of Glenbucket, 102
Kirkwall, presbytery, 195
Kirkwood, John, 66
Knox, John, 194, 203
Knox, Robert, 122
Kodie, James, 47–8
Kynnaird, Patrick, of Middletoun, 99
Kyntor, John, 146
Kyntor, Marion, 71

Lafrise, Thomas, 167
La-Hersie, Peter, 144
Lanark, 119
Lands, Jean, 24
Lands, Margaret, 24
Largizean, 40

INDEX

Larner, Christina, 8–9
Last speeches, 135–6
Laud, William, 183
Law, Robert, 23
Leggat, Alison, 61–2, 67
Leggat, Margaret, 61–2
Leighton, Robert, 193
Leith, 26, 73, 90, 91, 165
Lennox, Barbara, 22
Leprosy *see* Disease
Leslie, Alexander, earl of Leven, 104
Leslie, John, 103
Leslie, Margaret, 162
Leslie, Margaret, countess of
    Rothes, 115
Leslie, Patrick, 70
Leslie, Robert, 22
Leslie, William, 189, 183
Lesmahagow, 23
Linlithgow, presbytery, 194–5, 198, 199
London, 27, 154, 185
Lothian and Tweeddale, synod,
    195, 198
Lothian, Andrew, 21
Love, Andro, 25
Low, Andrew, 68
Low, David, 71
Lowlands, 31, 79, 81, 82, 85, 104,
    107, 108, 148
Lykewakes, 141, 149–50, 156
Lyndsay, David, 143
Lyon, Agnes, 45, 46, 55

MacCoinnish, Aonghas, 82
MacDonald, Angus, of Dunivaig, 88
MacDowell, Elizabeth, 35
MacGill, David, 190
MacGregor, John (John Dow Geir), 104
MacGregor, John, 146
MacGregor, Patrick Ger, 102, 104
MacGrinnon, Finlay, 100–1
Macinnes, John, 26
MacKail, Hew, 113
MacKane, Christian, 163, 170
Mackenzie, Alexander, of Fraserdale, 154

Mackenzie, George, of Rosehaugh,
    18, 99
MacKenzie, Murdoch, 197
Mackintosh, Lachlan, of Kinrara, 107
Mackourtney, William, 71
Macpherson, James, 10, 124–37,
    145, 209
Madrid, 186
Magic, 46, 47, 49, 52, 53, 58, 132
Magistrates, 36, 62, 65, 66, 69, 71, 71,
    72, 73, 74–5, 86, 111, 134, 136,
    146, 148, 173, 178, 180
Mair, John, 108
Makluire, John, 17
Malleis, Robert, 52
M'Allester, Duncan, 32
Man, Isle of, 79, 82, 91
Mar, Gilbert, 163
Marginality, *passim*
    and deviance, 1–9, 207–11
    and gendered violence, 30–44
    and insults, 157–71
    and musicians, 141–56
    and sexual transgression, 15–29
    and universities, 172–90
    mitigation of, 103–7, 109–23,
        191–206
    Romani and, 124–37
Marian Civil War, 84, 176
Marriage, 18, 19, 25, 26, 27, 28, 29,
    38, 43, 107, 110, 111, 113, 120,
    147, 149, 150, 152, 170, 199,
    200, 204
Marsh, Christopher, 147
Marshall, Richard, 188
Martiall, John, 150
Martin, James, 190
Martin, James, 203
Mary I, 83, 128
Mary II, 182, 184
Masculinity *see* Gender
Masterless men *see* Broken men
Maxwell, John, Lord Maxwell, 88
Maxwell, John, of Terregles, 87
Maxwell, Marion, 24

INDEX

McDuff, Gilbert, 88
McGibbon, William, 154
McGrigor, Calum Oig, 107
McGrumman, William, 101
McIntosh, Lachland, of Rockinoyr, 100
McIntyre, Neil, 204
McKaw, John Bane, 36
McLean, Hector, 152
McMarquess, Angus, 144
McMath, James, 17
McNayr, James, 155
McShane, Angela, 32
McTeir, Katharine, 45–6
Medicine, 17, 151, 175
Meldrum, John, 97–8
Melville, Andrew, 172, 175, 177, 184, 186, 188
Melville, Elizabeth, 21
Memoirs *see* Writing
Mentayth, Robert, 149
Menzies, Gilbert, 169
Menzies, John, 181, 190
Menzies, Patrick, 66
Mercat crosses, 52, 70–1, 134
M'Gilcheren, Robert, 39
Midcalder, 199
Middleton, John, earl of Middleton, 195
Midwives, midwifery, 17, 41
Migrants, migration, 1, 3, 107, 144, 185, 210. *See also* Strangers
M'Ilhuy, Angus, 34
Mitchell, David, 195
Mitchison, Rosalind, 6
M'Lashen, 34
Moir, William, 189
Monipenny, David, 188
Monkland, 98
Monro, Alexander, 184, 185, 190
Monro, George, 17
Montauban, 186
Montgomery, Adam, of Braidstone, 81
Monymusk, 104
Moray, 95, 108, 113, 131, 197
    synod, 197
Moresone, Nicoll, 162

Morison, George, 152
Morison, John, 165
Morrison, John, 67
Mortlik, 170
Mowatt, John, 151
Mowatt, Richard, 98
Moy, 150
M'Pherson, Patrick, 36, 43
Muir, Alexander, 118
Muir, John, 31–2
Muir, Margaret, 120
Muir, Matthew, 32
Muirhead, Marion, 113
Mullan, David, 112
Mungwall, Patrick, 48
Murder, homicide, 6, 19, 24, 32, 37, 96, 97, 98, 99, 100, 101, 102, 104, 118, 144, 146, 183
Murdo, Johne, 144
Murdoch, Steve, 87
Murray, John, 25
Murray, John, 73, 75
Murray, Margaret, 48
Murray, Sir Mungo, 25
Murray, William, 25
Music, musicians, 10–1, 130, 135, 207, 208
    and deviance, 141–53
    vernacular revival, 142, 153–6
Mutilation, 33, 73, 91, 92, 144, 166
M'Vrarthie, Thomas, 33
Mylne, James, 148

Nairn, 113
Napier, John, 17
National Covenant, 28, 38, 106, 109, 111, 172, 179–80, 183, 184, 188, 189, 193
Navies, 82, 85, 87, 88, 89
N'Conochie, Marion, 32
Nether Mylne, 56
Netherlands *see* Dutch Republic
Nevay, David, 180, 189
Newbattle, 55
Newcastle, 120, 121

221

INDEX

Newspapers, 144
Nicolson, Daniel, 24
Nielson, Alexander, 152
Night, nighttime, 48 54, 58, 71–5, 97,
    102, 121, 133, 142, 144, 146, 148,
    149, 157, 167, 168
N'Ilrevie, More, 24
Nixon, Jennifer, 42
N'Nicoll, Margaret, 33
Nonconformity, 1, 7, 8, 11, 208,
    209, 210
  partial, 191–206
  women and, 109–23,
  universities, and, 175–82
Norie, Duncan, 176, 188
Northumberland, 120, 121
North Channel, 81, 89
NykQuhene, Christian, 157–8, 159,
    161, 165, 167, 168, 170

Oaths, 40, 54–5, 102, 194, 197, 199, 206
  of allegiance, 118, 181, 182, 184,
    186, 189, 195, 197, 198–9,
  of supremacy, 114
  Test, 181
Officers, 32, 38, 40, 57, 65, 66, 67
  military, 120, 145
Ogilby, 144
Olrig, 201
Orkney, 22, 165
Oswald, James, 154
Outlaws, outlawry, 10, 89, 94, 96, 97,
    99, 100, 101, 103, 105, 107, 129,
    130, 135, 145
Outsiders *see* Strangers
Owsten, Thomas, 176, 188
Oxford, 183

Panter, Patrick, 183, 185, 189
Parliament, 19, 21, 27, 83, 85, 86, 87,
    115, 126, 141, 144, 145, 148, 162,
    176, 181, 182, 184, 195, 201
Partial conformity *see* Nonconformity
Paterson, John, 162
Paterson, Katty, 166
Paterson, Robert, 74–5

Paterson, William, 74–5
Peebles, 120, 121–2
Penny weddings, 144, 148–9, 150
Penstoun, 25
Pentland, 116, 117
Pentland rising (1666), 120
'Perceivable perpetrator', 35–6
Perth, 51, 56, 142
  synod, 195
Perth, Five Articles of, 178, 188, 203
Philanthropy *see* Charity
Philps, Jonet, 164
Piracy, 10, 79–93, 207
Pitchaise, 102
Pitlurg, 133
Pittoddrie, 104
Pladda, 89
Poor relief, poor law, 4–6
Popes, 17
Porteous, Jonet, 61, 62
Poverty, poor, 1, 2, 4, 6–7, 8, 39–40,
    42–3, 44, 51, 56, 113, 130, 133,
    143, 145, 151, 162, 163, 173, 203,
    210. *See also* Vagrants, vagrancy
Pratt, Isobel, 66, 67
Prayer Book, 109, 194
Pregnancy, 19, 24, 36, 41, 102
Presbyterianism, Presbyterians, 4,
    109–23, 147, 151, 172, 175, 177,
    182, 184, 188, 190, 194, 200, 208
Presbyteries, 47, 48–9, 192, 193,
    194, 197, 198, 199, 205. *See also*
    individual presbyteries
Privy council, 21, 123, 176, 182, 194,
    195, 196,
  and piracy, 83–87, 88, 92
  and 'Seamas and Tuim', 95, 96, 97,
    98, 99, 100–1, 105, 106
Protestants, Protestantism, 3, 7, 144,
    148, 165, 176, 177, 181, 183, 184

Quakers, 7
Queerness, 4, 19, 211

Race *see* Ethnic minorities
Rae, Katherene, 25

INDEX

Raffe, Alasdair, 191–2, 194, 200, 203, 204, 205
Ramsay, Allan, 154
Ranken, Robert, 188
Rape, 19, 21, 23, 25, 27, 36, 146
Reformation, 7, 50, 51, 59, 109, 112, 141, 147, 148, 150, 158, 162, 173, 175–6, 183, 188, 196
Regents *see* Academics
Reid, James, 182–3, 188
Reid, Margaret, 26
Renfrew, 88, 89
Renfrewshire, 24
Renwick, James, 118
Repentance, 15, 34, 35, 36, 42, 46, 48, 50, 51, 52, 57, 65, 70, 148
Reputation, 2, 6, 35, 36, 44, 81, 114, 129, 130, 131, 134, 201, 208
    petty crime and, 68, 69, 71, 74, 75
    verbal violence and, 160, 161, 164, 169, 170
    witchcraft and, 46, 47, 50, 51, 53, 56, 57, 58, 59
Restoration, 11, 18, 109, 112, 180–2, 184, 186, 189, 209
    partial conformity during, 191–206
Revolution of 1688–9, 120–1, 122, 173, 176, 180, 182, 183, 184, 186, 190, 209
Richardson, Thomas, 163, 170
Riots, rioting, 109, 112, 191
Rob, Cathrine nein, 26
Robbery *see* Theft, thieves
Robert II, 90
Robertson, Leonard, 87–8
Robertson, Richard, 183, 189
Robertson, William, 133
Robertsone, John, 146
Robin Hood, 130–1
Robinson, Margaret, 53
Rolland, Alexander, 66
Rolland, Thomas, 66
Roman Catholicism, 7, 17, 141, 144, 147, 156, 176, 177, 179, 185
Romani, 10, 124–37, 145

marginalisation of, 124–9
Rome, 186
Ross, Alexander, 149, 190
Ross, John, 113, 114
Ross, John, 160
Rothes, 102, 150
Rothesay, 30, 32, 33, 38, 40, 42
Row, John, 189
Row, William, 21
Roy, James, 147–8
Rullion Green, battle of, 120
Russell, Margaret, 50
Rutherford, Samuel, 181, 185, 189

Sabbath, 34, 35, 36, 38, 50, 75, 121, 148, 149,150, 196, 202, 203
Sackcloth, 15, 52, 57, 148
Saint Colombe, Peter, 144
Sanders, John, 69
Sandilands, James, 1st Lord Abercrombie, 25
Sandness, 53
Sands, Patrick, 178, 188
Satan *see* Devil
Saumur, 177
Schiphird, John, 170
Scot, Margaret, 102
Scots Confession, 177
Scott, Robert, 59
Scourging, 54, 165, 166
Scripture *see* Bible
Scroggie, Alexander, 189
Seamas an Tuim *see* Grant, James, of Carron
Second Book of Discipline, 148, 176
Sedan, 172
Self–writing *see* Writing
Sellar, Margaret, 162
Selwood, Jacob, 3
Semple, George, 202, 205
Sex workers, 16, 26, 159, 166
Sex, sexuality, 3, 6, 9, 207, 211
Sexual deviance, 3–4, 5, 9, 36, 50, 52, 114, 141, 158, 159, 165, 169, 210
    conceptualisation of, 15–29

INDEX

Shame, shaming punishments, 3, 16, 21, 24, 28. *See also* Discipline
Shand, John, 133
Sharp, James, archbishop of St Andrews, 117, 118, 195
Shaw, Elspet, 21
Sherar, Marion, 73
Shetland, 52, 53
Shropshire, 185
Sibbald, James, 179, 185, 189
Sibbald, Patrick, 190
Simson, Simon, 188
Sinclair, George, 23
Sinclair, George, 186, 189
Sinclair, James, 19
Sinclair, Margaret, 98, 100–1
Skene, 104
Skene, Andrew, 190
Slander *see* Violence, verbal
Small, Christian, 160
Smout, T. C., 3
Sodomy, 15, 18, 19
Solemn League and Covenant, 193, 199–200, 201, 206
Solway, 79, 87
Soundscape *see* Music
Southampton, 33
Space, urban, 61–76
Spain, 80, 83
Spalding, John, 95, 96, 98, 99, 101, 102, 103, 104, 172
Spanky, David, 69
Speech, 9, 10, 207, 210
 insults, 157–71
 and witchcraft, 45–60
 See also Violence, verbal
Spens, Robert, 153
Spey, Strathspey, 96, 105, 106, 108
Spicer, Andrew, 70
Spottiswoode, John, 178–9
Squeyar, Thomas, 26
St Andrews, 106, 162, 165, 170, 193. *See also* Universities

State, 94, 101, 107, 112, 117, 123, 125, 126, 180, 191, 194, 202, 205
 and piracy, 80, 83–7
Steile, Elizabeth, 168
Stevenson, Jane, 108
Stewart, Alexander, 201
Stewart, Alexander, earl of Moray, 115–6, 201
Stewart, Geillis, 36
Stewart, James, 39
Stewart, James, 40
Stewart, James, earl of Moray, 96, 98, 100
Stewart, John, of Ardgowan, 89
Stewart, Laura, 109
Stewart, Sir James, of Goodtrees, 24
Stewart, William, 148
Stirling, 48, 52, 150, 151, 152, 163, 164, 167, 197, 202
 presbytery, 149
Stocks, 71, 84
Stones, Robert, 68
Stow, 196–7
Strachan, David, 195
Strachan, John, 186, 189, 190
Strachan, Patrick, 183, 189
Strachen, Agnes, 144
Strand, Jhone, 53
Strang, John, 185, 189
Strange, Walter, 72
Strangers, 157–8, 160, 161–4, 167, 168, 169
Straquhan, John, 163
Straquhen, Thomas, 62
Stratha'an, 97, 106
Strathbogie, 52, 55, 97
Strauchein, Isobel, 47
Strublance, 50
Struther, William, 28
Struthers, William, 183
Struthers, Marion, 169
Stuart, Megot, 162
Superstition, 45, 46, 55, 132, 148
Sutherland, Andro, 166

INDEX

Sydserf, Thomas, 195
Sym, Agnes, 167
Symmer, William, 74, 75–6
Symsoun, Thomas, 51
Synods, 193–4, 195, 197, 200. *See also* individual synods

Tain, 113
Taverns *see* Alehouses
Taxation, taxes, 4, 86, 90–2, 117, 170
Tealing, 202
Ternway, Ellen, 162
Theft, thieves, 6, 19, 36, 41, 61, 64, 65, 69, 87, 88, 89, 97, 130, 132, 133, 134, 157, 159, 161, 164, 165, 166, 167, 168, 170, 210
Thom, William, of Ardgowan, 89
Thomesone, Margaret, 24
Thomson, Ellen, 167
Thomson, Matthew, 146
Thomsone, Gilbert, 52
Todd, Margo, 3
Tolbooths, 32, 69, 71, 118, 165
Towns *see* Burghs
Trot of Turriff, 104
Troup, George, 70
Turnbull, William, 162
Turner, Sir James, 120

Udnie, Robert, 97
Umpherston, Beatrix, 119
Umpherston, Charles, 116–7
Umpherston, Robert, 117
United Societies, 116
Universities, 11, 25, 172–90, 193, 198
Urquhart, James, 115, 197

Vagrants, vagrancy, 2, 127, 132, 134, 141, 145–7, 153, 156, 159, 163–4, 166, 167, 168. *See also* Begging, beggars
Veitch, Marion, 119–22, 123
Veitch, William, 119–22
Vink, James, 165

Violence, 5, 10, 19, 30–44, 50, 59, 61–76, 82, 83, 89, 92, 94, 95–8, 103, 107, 126, 132, 135, 144, 146, 163, 182, 196, 207–8
verbal, 11, 34, 35, 37, 45–60, 157–71, 208
Vlissingen (Flushing), 85

Waddell, George, 190
Wales, 79, 81, 82, 89
Walker, James, 72
Wasser, Michael, 41
Watson, Alison, 73
Watson, Beatrix, 58
Watson, Christine, 57–8
Watson, Helen, 56
Watson, John, 56
Watson, John, 146
Watson, Margaret, 53
Watson, Margaret, 68
Watson, Robert, 56
Watsone, Magdalene, 48
Watten, 201
Weapons, weaponry, 30, 31–2, 39, 61, 66, 67, 72, 73, 98, 102, 130
Weir, Thomas, 22
Wellwood, William, 188
Welwood, John, 115
Wemyss, James, 190
Western Isles, 81, 82, 89
Westminster Assembly, 201
Whipping *see* Scourging
White, Andrew, 87
White, Janet, 51
Whiteford, Walter, 98
Whitehall, 145
Whithorn, 87, 88
Whyte, Jonet, 54
Whyte, Robert, 54
Wick, 22, 197
Wilby, Emma, 114
William I, prince of Orange, 85
William II, 182, 184
Williamsdochter, Maidlaine, 52

INDEX

Williamson, David, 117
Williamson, John, 164–5
Wilson, James, 142
Wiltshire, 38
Winchester, 178
Wishart, George, 195
Wishart, William, 188
Wisheart, Thomas, 23
Witches, witch-hunting
Wode, Alexander, 40
Women
  agency of, 98–103
  and gendered violence, 30–44
  and insults, 159–60
  and nonconformity, 109–23, 205

and sexual behaviour, 19–20, 24, 25–6
scholarship of deviance and marginality, 5–6
speech of, 45–60
Wood, John Carter, 67
Writing
  self, 209
  spiritual, 10, 109–23
Wylie, Thomas, 196

Yell, 24
Yeoman, Louise, 41, 115
Young, John, 177–8
Youngson, Andrew, 186, 189

St Andrews Studies in Scottish History
Previously published

I

Elite Women and Polite Society in Eighteenth-Century Scotland
Katharine Glover

II

Regency in Sixteenth-Century Scotland
Amy Blakeway

III

Scotland, England and France after the Loss of Normandy, 1204–1296
'Auld Amitie'
M.A. Pollock

IV

Children and Youth in Premodern Scotland
Edited by Janay Nugent and Elizabeth Ewan

V

Medieval St Andrews
Church, Cult, City
Edited by Michael Brown and Katie Stevenson

VI

The Life and Works of Robert Baillie (1602–1662)
Politics, Religion and Record-Keeping in the British Civil Wars
Alexander D. Campbell

VII

The Parish and the Chapel in Medieval Britain and Norway
Sarah E. Thomas

VIII

A Protestant Lord in James VI's Scotland
George Keith, Fifth Earl Marischal (1554–1623)
Miles Kerr-Peterson

IX

The Clergy in Early Modern Scotland
Edited by Chris R. Langley, Catherine E. McMillan and Russell Newton

X

Kingship, Lordship and Sanctity in Medieval Britain
Essays in Honour of Alexander Grant
Edited by Steve Boardman and David Ditchburn

XI

Rethinking the Renaissance and Reformation in Scotland

Essays in Honour of Roger A. Mason
Edited by Steven J. Reid

XII

Life at the Margins in Early Modern Scotland
Edited by Allan Kennedy and Susanne Weston

XIII

Death and the Royal Succession in Scotland, c.1214–c.1543
Ritual, Ceremony and Power
Lucinda H.S. Dean

XIV

The Life, Poems, and Letters of Peter Goldman (1587/8–1627)
A Dundee Physician in the Republic of Letters
William Poole

XV

The Advancement of Learning in Stuart Scotland, 1679–89
Hugh Ouston

XVI

Elite Hunting Culture and Mary Queen of Scots
John M. Gilbert